Strategic Entrepreneurship

Strategic Entrepreneurship

A decision-making approach to new venture creation and management

Philip A. Wickham

PITMAN
PUBLISHING

London · Hong Kong · Johannesburg · Melbourne · Singapore · Washington DC

To Louise

PITMAN PUBLISHING
128 Long Acre, London WC2E 9AN
Tel: +44(0)171 447 2000
Fax: +44(0)171 240 5771

A Division of Pearson Professional Limited

Visit the Pitman Publishing Website at
http://www.pitman.co.uk

First published in Great Britain in 1998

© Philip Wickham, 1998

The right of Philip Wickham to be identified as Author
of this Work has been asserted by him in accordance
with the Copyright, Designs and Patents Act 1988.

ISBN 0 273 62713 9

British Library Cataloguing in Publication Data
A CIP catalogue record for this book can be obtained from the British Library

10 9 8 7 6 5 4 3 2 1

Typeset by 🗡 Tek-Art, Croydon, Surrey
Printed and bound in Great Britain by Clays Ltd, St Ives plc

The Publishers' policy is to use paper manufactured from sustainable forests.

Contents

Preface

Learning outcomes

This book is about entrepreneurship as a *style* of management. It aims to provide an insight into entrepreneurship and entrepreneurial management from a *strategic* perspective. It is suitable for undergraduates, postgraduates and post-experience students on full-time, part-time or distance learning based courses in entrepreneurship, small business management and strategic management. It provides a useful supplementary source of information about entrepreneurship for specialist courses in areas such as organisational behaviour and organisational change management.

The book also aims to give practising managers, whatever the size, type and sector of their organisation or their position within it, an opportunity to explore the potential for approaching their managerial tasks in a more entrepreneurial style and of undertaking entrepreneurial projects more successfully.

These are challenging aims and obviously no book can 'make' somebody into an entrepreneur on its own. It may inform them; it may highlight the issues that are involved in entrepreneurial success; it may inspire them and give them a sense of direction; but at the end of the day, only the individual can turn themselves into an entrepreneur.

However, we must not lose sight of the fact that learning to be entrepreneurial is like learning to do anything else. It is, as we shall see, just a form of *behaviour*, and behaviour is learnt. Being entrepreneurial is certainly a complex and demanding form of behaviour requiring knowledge and skill. Proficiency cannot be acquired overnight, but then few valuable skills can be learnt that quickly.

Learning to be entrepreneurial means learning to *manage* in an *entrepreneurial* way. This means recognising the potential of a situation: the *opportunities* it presents, how *changes* may be made for the better and how *new value* can be created from it. This means being able to spot new possibilities, to recognise the decisions which need to be made and knowing how to follow them through. This book aims to give students and managers who want to understand entrepreneurial possibilities access to those decisions in order to understand how those decisions present themselves and the shape they take. To make this learning effective, this book takes an *active learning* approach.

An active learning strategy

This book, like any management text, can be only a part of the process of discovering and exploring the entrepreneurial option, but it aspires to be a valuable tool in that discovery. It aims to do this in four ways:

1 By being about decisions, not just knowledge

Every entrepreneur has his or her personal store of knowledge. This knowledge is a critical aspect of business venturing. Successful entrepreneurship demands a good knowledge of a particular business, the people who make it up, the industry it is in, the customers it serves and its competitors.

Having knowledge is a *necessary*, but not a *sufficient* condition for entrepreneurial success. What matters is what is *done* with that knowledge, that is how it is used to inform and aid decision making. While every entrepreneur will call upon a different repertoire of knowledge and use it in a wide variety of business situations, all use it to address a remarkably similar set of decisions.

The key learning outcome of the book is an understanding of entrepreneurship not as an abstract subject, but as the pattern of decisions that the entrepreneurial manager must identify, analyse, resolve and follow through. By clarifying these decisions, individual entrepreneurs become aware of the knowledge they have, the knowledge they need and the learning they must undertake, in a way which is specific to the venture they are managing.

2 By presenting frameworks for thinking, not just theories

A framework for thinking is just that: a guide to help us think. It is a conceptual device which highlights certain issues, suggests which factors might be important, draws attention to the way in which they are connected and links together things that might influence one another. A framework for thinking provides a scheme for clarifying the issues that are important in a business situation, helps to indicate the decisions that might be relevant to it and identifies the information needed before a good decision can be made.

A framework for thinking is not intended to reveal fundamental truths. It is intended as an *aide-memoire* to help decision making, that is as a reminder of what needs to be understood and addressed. This book will develop a number of frameworks for thinking which can be used to aid entrepreneurial decision making. Usually, the best way of presenting a framework for thinking is in a *visual* rather than written format. This makes the elements in the framework explicit and is efficient at depicting their interrelationships. So, whenever possible, this book will use visual representations.

'Theory' is often met with a great deal of suspicion, especially in the world of business. Some draw a hard line between 'theory' and 'practice'. Surely, it is often suggested, what matters is *practice*: being able to do the job rather than being able to speculate about it. To say that someone 'takes a theoretical view' is a double-edged compliment. It can be downright pejorative and suggest an inability to put ideas into action.

This is unfortunate and arises from a misunderstanding about what theory is and how it works. In fact, we all use theories all the time. A theory is just an expectation that a certain set of circumstances will lead to a particular outcome. For example, we all subscribe to the 'theory' that if we step off a cliff we will fall; and if we fall we will injure ourselves. This influences our behaviour: we do not step off cliffs. We constantly make theories about the world and test them. If they are useful, that is if their predictions are good, then we will hold on to them. If their predictions turn out to be false, then we will reject them and look for a better theory. We still do this even in situations where our theories must constantly adapt and evolve to make sense of a changing world. This is what the process of learning is all about. In this sense *experience*, including experience in business, is, in part, a matter of having access to a lot of 'good' theories.

3 By taking a strategic, rather than a tactical approach

This book considers that the decisions faced by an entrepreneur must be recognised as *strategic decisions*. The idea of strategy is a very important one in business. In essence, strategy relates to the *actions* that a business takes in order to achieve its *goals*. The idea of something being strategic touches on several things:

- it refers to issues which affect the *whole* organisation, not just some small part of it;
- it concerns the way in which the organisation interacts with its *environment*, not just its internal affairs;
- it concerns not merely what the company does – the business it is 'in' – but also how it *competes*;
- it involves consideration of how the business is performing not only in absolute terms but in *relation* to its competitors.

Tactical issues are still important though. To be successful, an entrepreneurial venture must be effective in its marketing, it must manage its finances competently and it must be proficient in its operations. What a strategic approach means is that entrepreneurs must think of all of these things not as isolated functions but as different facets of the venture as a *whole*. They must be seen to function in unison enabling the venture to deliver value to its customers, to attract investors' money and to grow in the face of competition.

4 By inviting active, not passive, learning

We all learn continually. Formal learning, when we sit down and deliberately acquire new knowledge, is only one, albeit a special, way in which we learn about the world. We learn quite naturally, often without realising we are doing it, particularly when we are motivated and interested in something. (Think about your hobby and consider how much knowledge and skill you bring to it. How much of that was 'deliberately' learnt?)

Effective learning occurs when we are called upon not only to retain knowledge but also to *use* it, and then to challenge and *revise* it in the light of experience.

This forms the basis of the *active learning* cycle. The first stage is to set up a framework for thinking, like the ones that will be developed in this book. Once this is in place, the next stage is to use it to *analyse* some situation facing us. The framework for thinking helps make sense of that situation, indicates the factors involved, highlights the important factors and suggests a direction to move forward.

In the third stage we apply the analysis by responding to the situation and taking *action*. A decision is made and followed through. In the fourth stage we examine the *consequences* of that action. We see if the outcomes are the ones we wanted. Did the decision produce the results we wanted? If not, how did they differ from what we wanted? What went right? What went wrong? As a result, we reflect on the framework for thinking that we used, and the actions we took based on it. This leads to a consideration of how useful it was.

We can then revise the framework in the light of our experience, or adjust the actions it suggests to us. This gives us a new framework for thinking which we can use to make new actions. And so we go round the cycle again. Eventually, we will get a framework for thinking that works for us, in our given situation. Then we begin to forget about it! We quickly learn to make decisions without constant reference to this process. At this point we have become experienced. Our knowledge is manifest as an 'unconscious' skill.

Performing as a business decision maker, and putting the resulting decisions into practice through initiative and leadership is a matter of learning. But that learning must be *active – see* Fig. A. Active learning of entrepreneurship involves setting up *frameworks* to aid decision making, using them to *guide action* and *revising* them in the light of *experience*.

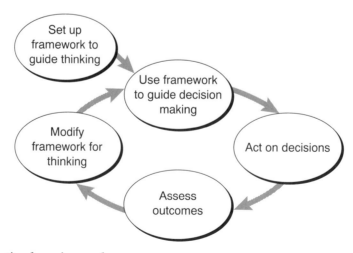

Fig. A The active learning cycle

Layout of the text

The material in this book is arranged so that ideas are presented in a logical order and accessible format. The book is organised into four parts.

Part 1 develops some introductory concepts that will be of use later in the book. The aim of this section is twofold. First, it provides a 'tool-kit' of ideas which will facilitate discussion about the entrepreneur. Second, it aims to put entrepreneurs into their proper *context*. It explores the nature of the entrepreneur and the process by which entrepreneurs create new value. This section is at pains to dispel some common myths about the entrepreneur, in particular, that an entrepreneur is born to be an entrepreneur or that to be a successful entrepreneur one must have a particular type of personality. The emphasis is on the fact that the entrepreneur is just a *manager*, albeit a very effective one.

Part 2 deals with the decisions the entrepreneur faces in giving the venture a direction, that is, deciding what the business will 'be about' and the *strategy* it will adopt. Also considered at this stage is the driving force behind the venture, that is, the *entrepreneurial vision*; what it is, how it might be developed, and how it might be used to give the venture direction and provide a foundation for leadership behaviour.

Part 3 is concerned with the initiation of the venture. This addresses how the entrepreneur can develop a detailed understanding of the opportunity that has presented itself to the business and the ways in which the venture can begin to exploit it. It also deals with the issues of attracting the financial and human investment that is needed to actually start up the business.

Part 4 addresses the issues and decisions that the entrepreneur must consider in successfully managing the growth of the venture and its eventual consolidation. Options for growing the business are explored and the issues that growth creates for the business are highlighted. The book concludes by considering how success may be continued as the venture matures and how the role of the entrepreneur changes.

This follows the process of creating a new venture from planning, through initiation and growth to consolidation. It provides a logical framework for ordering the decisions that the entrepreneur must make and makes them accessible. However, the entrepreneur does not face decisions in a simple order. The entrepreneurial venture constantly faces new possibilities and challenges. It may often have to revisit old decisions. Decisions impact on one another. Making one decision leads to a cascade of others. Managing an entrepreneurial venture is not like planning the journey of a space probe where everything can be calculated in advance. It is more like sailing a yacht, where there is a need for constant tacking of the sails. While planning is an important tool for making sure that the venture stays on course, it does not alleviate the need for continuous assessment of the business's situation or adjustments to respond to the possibilities presented.

A book is constrained by the need to present ideas one after the other in a linear progression. Unfortunately, the world of business does not allow decision making to be linear. Having considered the decisions relating to, say, the initiation of the venture, the entrepreneur cannot then forget about them. There may be a need to go back and reconsider them and their implications. Decisions interrelate and interconnect with one another over time. The shape of one decision will have implications for all the others that must be made.

This indicates that the order in which ideas are presented, although a useful one, is not the *only* one possible. Developing and running an entrepreneurial venture is not like following a recipe. It cannot be reduced to a unique sequence of decisions which must be followed. It is more like painting a picture, where selecting colours from a pallet can form an infinite variety of images. Entrepreneurship is a *creative* process.

This book aims to be self-contained. All the ideas are developed from the ground up and no extensive prior knowledge is assumed. The contents aspire to give a thorough grounding in the strategy of entrepreneurial management. Other than information needed to support the active learning exercises (see below), no reading around the text is required. However, entrepreneurship is a fast growing subject. The suggestions for further reading at the end of each chapter aim to give the student who wishes to explore the discipline further a key starting point from which to do so. The list is not intended to be an exhaustive review of the themes developed in the chapter. Rather, the articles are chosen for their practical style and the scope and accessibility of their approach.

The active learning exercises

As well as presenting frameworks for thinking, this book invites you to apply them and draw them into your own active learning cycle. Two projects are suggested as a way of doing this.

1 Analysing a venture as a role-model

The first exercise is an analysis of a practising entrepreneur and the venture they have developed. This will reveal how the frameworks for thinking can be used to make sense of the entrepreneurial process and the decisions that underlie it.

Though you are free to chose any entrepreneur you like, perhaps someone well-known in the public domain or possibly someone less famous whom you know personally, two caveats are advised:

● First, it should be someone who you find inspiring and whose skills you admire. The idea of this exercise is not that you learn the details of the frameworks for thinking, but rather that you gain an understanding of the entrepreneur and a venture to act as a motivating *role model* for you. This does not mean that you must follow their path slavishly, but that you should recognise the decisions that they had to face and understand how they were addressed.

- Second, you must be able to get hold of some information on the particular entrepreneur and their venture. Clearly, information is needed before the analysis can be performed. Such information is not hard to find. The lives and businesses of numerous entrepreneurs are related in biographies. The financial papers regularly report on entrepreneurs and their businesses. Local libraries will have indexes of key articles. Many management text books summarise well-known entrepreneurial ventures in the form of case studies. You will not need a great deal of information, or anything which might be considered commercially sensitive to make good use of this exercise. What matters is the *quality* of analysis performed rather than the *quantity* of information gathered.

2 Developing your own venture

The second exercise is to develop an idea for a business venture of your own. It may be one you have already started or with which you are working closely. If you are not in the position of running your own venture, then developing a plan for a new venture is a very good alternative. This plan may be one you have had in mind for some time, or it may be one that has been suggested to you or that you have come up with specially for the exercise. Do not worry if it is not a particularly well-developed idea at this stage. The point of the exercise is that the business idea should be shaped and refined. It will evolve as the exercise progresses. It should, however, be something you consider to be a good idea, something that has possibility and that you feel will be *worth* developing.

It is advised that both these exercises are undertaken as the book progresses. In this way you will get to apply the frameworks for thinking as they are encountered, and it will allow your ideas to evolve. Remember, these exercises are suggested to give you an opportunity to use the frameworks presented as tools to make sense of your own situation.

A positive approach to active learning can, in time, help to make an entrepreneurial style of decision making second nature. If these activities inspire you to start your own venture then so much the better.

Good Luck!

Philip A. Wickham
September 1997

Part 1 Introductory themes

Entrepreneurship in the modern world

Of all the players who feature in the management of the modern world economy, it is entrepreneurs who most attract our attention. We all have some view of them. We may see entrepreneurs as heroes: as self-starting individuals who take great personal risk in order to bring the benefits of new products to wider world markets. We may express concern at the pace of economic and social change entrepreneurs bring and of the uncertainty they create. We may admire their talents, or we may question the rewards they get for their efforts. Whatever our instinctive reaction to them, we cannot ignore the impact of entrepreneurs.

The modern world is characterised by *change*. Every day we hear of shifts in political orders, developments in economic relationships and new technological advancements. These changes feed off each other and they are global. Developments in information technology allow capital to seek new business investment opportunities ever more efficiently. Success is sought out more quickly; failure punished more ruthlessly. Customers expect continuous improvement in the products and services they consume.

As a result, businesses are having to become more responsive. In order to keep their place in their markets they are having to innovate more quickly. In order to compete, they are having to become more agile. This is not just an issue for profit-making organisations but for all corporate bodies. The boundary between the world of the 'market' and the public domain is being pushed back and blurred.

Consequently, the world is demanding both more entrepreneurs and more *of* entrepreneurs. In the mature economies of the western world they provide economic dynamism. The fast-growing businesses they create are now the main source of new job opportunities. The vibrant economies of the Pacific rim are driven by the successes of thousands of new ventures. It is individual entrepreneurs who must restructure the post-Communist countries of eastern and central Europe and provide them with vibrant market economies. In the developing world entrepreneurs are increasingly responsible for the creation of new wealth and for making its distribution more equitable.

Change presents both opportunities and challenges. The opportunities come in the shape of new possibilities, and the chance for a better future. The challenges lie in managing the uncertainty these possibilities create. By way of a response to this challenge, we must aim to take advantage of the opportunities while controlling and responding to the uncertainties. This response must be reflected in the way we manage our organisations. In short: we must become more *entrepreneurial*. To do this we must understand *entrepreneurship*.

This book aims to provide an insight into entrepreneurship that will be valuable to both practising managers and to students of management (who will be the managers of the future). It is for the manager who wants not only to be more informed about entrepreneurism, but who also wants to be more entrepreneurial. It does this by taking a particular perspective on entrepreneurism. This perspective is easily summarised as follows:

- entrepreneurship is a *style* of management;
- entrepreneurial management aims at pursuing *opportunity* and driving *change*;
- entrepreneurial management is *strategic* management: that is management of the whole organisation; and that, critically:
- entrepreneurism is an approach to management that can be *learnt*.

This book contends that entrepreneurs are just *managers* who make *entrepreneurial decisions*. This book explores these decisions, what they are, what they involve, and the actions necessary to see them through.

Understanding is as much about recognising our misconceptions as it is about gaining knowledge. There are many myths which surround the entrepreneur. If we are to get to grips with entrepreneurship and recognise the potential to be entrepreneurial these myths must be dispelled. For example, this book rejects the notion that the entrepreneur is someone who is 'born' to achieve greatness. It also dismisses the idea that they are driven by psychological forces beyond their control, or that the entrepreneur must have a particular type of personality to be successful. Rather we will regard the entrepreneur simply as a manager who knows how to make entrepreneurial decisions and how to follow them through.

Discussion will not be limited to the issues of owning businesses or starting new ones. These issues may be an important part of entrepreneurship but they are not its entirety. Nor are they an essential component of entrepreneurship: what makes someone an entrepreneur is not their historical or legal relationship to an organisation but the *changes* they create both with it and within it.

In addition to exploring entrepreneurial management, this book also intends to 'demystify' the entrepreneur. This is not an attempt to devalue them or the work they do. In fact, the opposite is intended. It recognises entrepreneurial success as the result of personal application, hard work and learning, not as some innate imperative. What this book does aim to do, above all else, is make entrepreneurship *accessible* by demonstrating that good entrepreneurship is based on management skill, and that the entrepreneurial path can be opened by managers who wish to follow it and to recognise that success follows from personal effort, knowledge and practice, rather than a pre-ordained destiny.

Suggestions for further reading

Bettis, R. A. and **Hitt, M. A** (1995), "The new competitive landscape", *Strategic Management Journal*, Vol. 16, pp. 7–19.

Carroll, G. R. (1994), "Organizations . . . the smaller they get", *California Management Review*, Vol. 37, No. 1, pp. 28–41.

Moore, J. F. (1993), "Predators and pray: A new ecology of competition", *Harvard Business Review*, May-June, pp. 75–86.

The nature of entrepreneurship

CHAPTER OVERVIEW

*This chapter is concerned with developing a picture of what entrepreneurship actually is. It discusses the attempts that have been made to define entrepreneurs and surveys the characteristics that have been associated with them. After concluding that there is no, single, universally agreed definition for the entrepreneur, it reviews three approaches to characterising an entrepreneur: as a **manager** undertaking certain **tasks**; as an **agent** facilitating **economic change** and as an **individual** with a particular **personality**.*

*Schemes for classifying entrepreneurs and the distinction between entrepreneurship and small business management are considered. The chapter concludes by arguing that entrepreneurship is best regarded as a **style of management**.*

1.1 What is entrepreneurship?

> **KEY LEARNING OUTCOME**
> **A understanding of the main approaches to understanding the nature of entrepreneurship. In particular, the distinction between the entrepreneur as a** *performer of managerial tasks*, **as an** *agent of economic change*, **and as a** *personality*.

The word *entrepreneur*, and the concepts derived from it such as *entrepreneurial*, *entrepreneurship* and *entrepreneurial process* are frequently encountered in discussions of the management of new, fast growing, innovative business ventures. These concepts are easily related. Entrepreneurship is what an entrepreneur actually *does*. Entrepreneurial refers to the *approach* they take. The entrepreneurial process is what the entrepreneur *engages* in. A reasonable starting point for any discussion on entrepreneurship might therefore be to put forward a definition of the 'entrepreneur'.

However, offering a definition of the entrepreneur or entrepreneurship presents an immediate problem. This is not that a definition is not available, but rather that there seem to be *too* many definitions. Economic and management literature is full of possible definitions. The problem is there does not seem to be much agreement on what are the *essential* features of an entrepreneur.

In a detailed study of this issue, the American entrepreneurship researcher William Gartner (1990) asked fellow academics and business leaders for their definitions of entrepreneurship. From 44 different definitions obtained, some 90 different attributes of entrepreneurship were identified. The definitions obtained were not just variations on a theme, in fact many shared no common attributes at all!

This indicates that the quest for a universal definition has not moved on much since 1971 when Peter Kilby commented that the entrepreneur had a lot in common with the 'Heffalump', a character in A. A. Milne's *Winnie-the-Pooh*, noting that he is also:

> **a rather large and important animal. He has been hunted by many individuals using various trapping devices, but no one so far has succeeded in capturing him. All who claim to have caught sight of him report that he is enormous, but disagree on his particularities.**

So, although many definitions of the entrepreneur, or entrepreneurship, might be offered, any *one* definition is likely to result in a mismatch with our expectations in some cases. Either it will *exclude* those whom we *know* to be entrepreneurs, or what we *recognise* to be entrepreneurship, or it will *include* people and ventures which we do not *feel* to be properly entrepreneurial. We can illustrate this by examining some of the main features which have been associated with entrepreneurship.

The idea of bearing *risk* is included in many definitions, but this fails to distinguish the entrepreneur from the *investor* who personally accepts the financial risk of a venture. We might insist that an entrepreneur actually *founds* their organisation. Many do, but some well-known entrepreneurs have actually revitalised pre-existing organisations. Some commentators emphasise the importance of maximising *financial returns* to investors. But rewarding investors with a good return, while important, can hardly be said to be the *only* objective entrepreneurs set themselves. Creating value through innovation has also been offered as a defining characteristic. Certainly, this is crucially important to successful entrepreneurship. However, innovation is important to the management of *all* organisations, not just entrepreneurial ventures.

We should not be too disheartened by this failure to pin down a phenomenon as rich and complex as entrepreneurship by a single, universal definition. It is the very variety of entrepreneurship, the endless possibilities that it presents and the way that it provides meaning to approaching *specific* ventures, that makes it so inviting. In any case, being able to *define* something is not the same as *understanding* it. Thus this book does not offer a singular definition of the entrepreneur as a starting point. Rather, the approach will be to develop a broad picture of the entrepreneur, to characterise them and to explore the process they engage in, and then to move on to develop an understanding of how entrepreneurship provides a route to the creation of new wealth.

Entrepreneurship is a *social* and *economic* phenomenon. The entrepreneur is, first and foremost, an individual who lives and functions within society. Entrepreneurs are characterised not by *every* action they take, but by a particular set of actions aimed at the creation of *new wealth*. Entrepreneurship is about *value generation*.

Entrepreneurship is a *particular* approach to wealth-generating activity. Entrepreneurs are characterised by the way they go about creating new value. The recognition of this fact gives us three angles of approach to the entrepreneur in that they might be considered as:

- a **manager** undertaking an activity – i.e. by means of the particular tasks they perform and the way they undertake them;
- an **agent of economic change** – i.e. by the effects they have and the type of changes they create; or as
- an **individual** – i.e. by means of their psychology, personality and personal characteristics.

Each of these three aspects is reflected in the variety of definitions that are offered for the entrepreneur. The function of each of these definitions is not just to characterise the entrepreneur but also to distinguish them from other types of people involved in the generation of wealth (such as investors or 'ordinary' managers).

1.2   The entrepreneur's tasks

> **KEY LEARNING OUTCOME**
> **An understanding of the tasks that are undertaken by, and which characterise the work of, the entrepreneur.**

We recognise entrepreneurs, first and foremost, by what they actually *do* – by the *tasks* they undertake. This aspect provides a starting point for understanding the entrepreneur and the way in which they are different from other types of manager. A number of tasks have been associated with the entrepreneur. Some of the more important are discussed below.

Owning organisations

Most people would be able to give an example of an entrepreneur and would probably claim to be able to recognise an entrepreneur 'if they saw one'. A key element in this common perception is *ownership* of the organisation.

While many entrepreneurs do indeed own their own organisations, using ownership as a defining feature of entrepreneurship can be very restricting. Modern market economies are characterised by a differentiation between the ownership and the running of organisations. Ownership lies with those who invest in the business and own its stock: the *principals*, while the actual running is delegated to professional agents or *managers*. These two roles are quite distinct. Therefore if an entrepreneur actually owns the business then he or she is in fact undertaking two roles at the same time: that of an investor and that of a manager.

We recognise many people as entrepreneurs even if they do not own the venture they are managing. In developed economies, sophisticated markets exist to give investors access to new ventures and most entrepreneurs are active in taking advantage of these to attract investors. For example, when Frederick Smith started the distribution company *Federal Express* he only put in around ten per cent of the initial capital. Institutional investors provided the rest. We do not think less of him as an entrepreneur because he diluted his ownership in this way. In fact, most would regard the ability to present the venture and to attract the support of investors as an important entrepreneurial skill.

It should also be noted that 'ordinary' managers (whatever that means!) are increasingly being given a means of owning part of their companies through share option schemes which are often linked to the company's performance. While this may encourage them to be more entrepreneurial it does not, in itself, make them into entrepreneurs.

Founding new organisations

The idea that the entrepreneur is someone who has established a new business organisation is one which would fit in with most people's notion of an entrepreneur. The entrepreneur is recognised as the person who undertakes the task of bringing together the different elements of the organisation (people, property, productive resources, *etc.*) and giving them a separate legal identity. However, such a basis for defining the entrepreneur is sensitive to what we mean by 'organisation' and what we would consider to constitute to a 'new' organisation.

Many people we recognise as entrepreneurs 'buy into' organisations that have been already founded and then extend them (as Ray Kroc did with *McDonald's*), develop them (as George and Liz Davis did with *Hepworth's*, converting it into *Next*) or absorb them into existing organisations (as Alan Sugar did with *Sinclair Scientific*). Increasingly, management buy-outs of parts of existing organisations are providing a vehicle for ordinary managers to exhibit their entrepreneurial talent.

A more meaningful, though less precise, idea is that the entrepreneur *makes major changes in their organisational world*. Making a major change is a broad notion, but it goes beyond merely founding the organisation, and it differentiates the entrepreneur from managers who manage within existing organisational structures or make only minor or incremental changes to them.

Bringing innovations to market

Innovation is a crucial part of the entrepreneurial process. Peter Drucker proposed that innovation is the central task for the entrepreneur-manager in his seminal book *Innovation and Entrepreneurship* (1995). Entrepreneurs must do something new or there would be no point in them entering a market. However, we must be careful here with the idea of innovation. Innovation, in a business sense, can mean a lot more than just developing a new product or technology. The idea of innovation encompasses any new way of doing something so that value is created. Innovation *can* mean a new product or service, but it can also include a new way of delivering an existing product or service (so that it is cheaper or more convenient for the user, for example), new methods of informing the consumer about a product and promoting it to them, new ways of organising the company, or even new approaches to managing relationships with other organisations. These are all sources of innovation which have been successfully exploited by entrepreneurs.

The entrepreneur's task goes beyond simply *inventing* something new. It also includes bringing that innovation to the marketplace and using it to deliver value to consumers. The innovated product or service must be produced profitably, in addition to being distributed, marketed and defended from the attentions of competitors by a well-run and well-led organisation.

No matter how important innovation might be to the entrepreneurial process, it is not *unique* to it. Most managers are encouraged to be innovative in some way or other. Being successful at developing and launching new products and services is not something which is only witnessed in entrepreneurial organisations. The difference between entrepreneurial innovation and 'ordinary innovation' is, at best, one of degree, not substance.

Identification of market opportunity

An opportunity is a gap in a market where the potential exists to do something better and create value. New opportunities exist all the time, but they do not necessarily present themselves. If they are to be exploited, they must be *actively* sought out. The identification of new opportunities is one of the key tasks of entrepreneurs. They must constantly scan the business landscape watching for the gaps left by existing players (including themselves!) in the marketplace.

As with innovation, no matter how important identifying opportunity is to the entrepreneurial process, it cannot be all that there is to it, nor can it characterise it uniquely. The entrepreneur cannot stop at simply identifying opportunities. Having identified them, the entrepreneur must pursue them with a suitable innovation. An opportunity is simply the 'mould' against which the market tests new ideas. In fact, actually spotting the opportunity may be delegated to specialist market researchers. The real value is created when that opportunity is exploited by something new which fills the market gap.

All organisations are active, to some degree or other, in spotting opportunities. They may call upon specialist managers to do this, or they may encourage everyone in the organisation to be on the look out for new possibilities. Like innovation, entrepreneurial opportunity scanning differs from that of ordinary managers in degree, not substance.

Application of expertise

It has been suggested that entrepreneurs are characterised by the way that they bring some sort of expertise to their jobs. As discussed above, this expertise may be thought to lie in their ability to innovate or spot new opportunities. A slightly more technical notion is that they have a special ability in deciding how to *allocate scarce resources* in situations where *information is limited*. It is their expertise at doing this that makes entrepreneurs valuable to investors.

While investors will certainly look for evidence of an ability to make proper business decisions and judge entrepreneurs on their record in doing so, the idea that the entrepreneur is an 'expert' in this respect raises a question, namely whether the entrepreneur has a skill *as an entrepreneur* rather than just as a particularly skilful and effective manager in their own particular area. Does, for example, Rupert Murdoch, have a knowledge of how to make investment decisions which is *distinct* from his intimate and detailed knowledge of the media industry, backed-up by good management and attributes such as confidence, decisiveness and leadership? Is it meaningful to imagine someone developing a skill in (rather than just knowing the principles of) 'resource allocation decision making' other than it being demonstrated in relation to some specific area of business activity?

It is not clear whether such a disembodied skill exists separate to conventional management skills. In any case, such a skill could not be unique to the entrepreneur. Many managers, most of whom would not be called entrepreneurial, make decisions about resource allocation every day.

Provision of leadership

One special skill that entrepreneurs would seem to contribute to their ventures is leadership. Leadership is increasingly recognised as a critical part of managerial success. Entrepreneurs can rarely drive their innovation to market on their own. They need the support of other people, both from within their organisations and from people outside such as investors, customers and suppliers.

If all these people are to pull in the same direction, to be focused on the task in hand and to be motivated, then they must be supported and directed. This is a task that falls squarely on the shoulders of the entrepreneur. If it is to be performed effectively, then the entrepreneur must show leadership. In fact, performing this task well *is* leadership.

Leadership is an important factor in entrepreneurial success and it is often a skill that is exhibited particularly well by the entrepreneur, but it is a *general* management skill rather than one which is specific to the entrepreneur. That said, an entrepreneurial path may give the manager a particularly rich opportunity to develop and express leadership skills.

The entrepreneur as manager

What can we make of all this? It would seem that the entrepreneur takes on no task that is different to the tasks taken on by ordinary managers at some time or other. We should not be surprised by this. At the end of the day, the entrepreneur is a *manager*. We may wish to draw a distinction between an entrepreneur and an 'ordinary' manager but if we do so it must be in terms of *what* the entrepreneur manages, *how* they manage, their *effectiveness* and the *effect* they have as a manager, not the particular tasks they undertake.

1.3   The role of the entrepreneur

KEY LEARNING OUTCOME
An understanding of the economic effects of entrepreneurial activity.

Entrepreneurs are significant because they have an important effect on world economies. They play a critical role in maintaining and developing the economic order we live under. We have already noted that entrepreneurs create new value. Understanding *how* they do this is of central importance if we are to draw general conclusions about entrepreneurship. Some important economic effects of entrepreneurial activity are listed below.

Combination of economic factors

Economists generally recognise three primary *economic factors*: the *raw materials* nature offers up, the physical and mental *labour* people provide and *capital* (money). All the products (and services) bought and sold in an economy are a mix of these three things. Value is created by combining these three things together in a way which satisfies human needs.

Factors do not combine themselves, however. They have to be brought together by individuals working together and undertaking different tasks. The co-ordination of these tasks takes place within *organisations*. Some economists regard entrepreneurship as a kind of fourth factor which acts on the other three to combine them in productive ways. In this view, *innovation* is simply finding new combinations of economic factors.

Other economists object to this view, arguing that it does not distinguish entrepreneurship sufficiently from any other form of economic activity. While entrepreneurs do affect the combination of productive factors, so does everyone who is active in an economy. It is not clear in this view why entrepreneurship is a *special* form of economic activity.

Providing market efficiency

Economic theory suggests that the most efficient economic system is one in which unimpeded markets determine the price at which goods are bought and sold. Here, *efficient* means that resources are distributed in an *optimal* way, that is the satisfaction that people can gain from them is *maximised*.

An economic system can only reach this state if there is *competition* between different suppliers. Entrepreneurs provide that efficiency. If a supplier is not facing competition then they will tend to demand profits in excess of what the market would allow and so reduce the overall efficiency of the system. Entrepreneurs, so the theory goes, are on the look out for such excess profits. Being willing to accept a lower profit themselves (one nearer the true market rate) they will enter the market and offer the goods at a lower price. By so doing entrepreneurs ensure that markets are efficient and that prices are kept down to their lowest possible level.

Classical economics provides a good starting point for understanding the effects that entrepreneurs have on an economic system. However, business life is generally much more complex than this simple picture gives it credit for. As we will discover, the most successful entrepreneurs are often those that avoid competition (at least *direct* competition) with established suppliers.

Accepting risk

We do not know exactly what the future will bring. This lack of knowledge we call *uncertainty*. No matter how well we plan, there is always the possibility that some chance event will result in outcomes we neither expected or wanted. This is *risk*. Some economists have suggested that the primary function of the entrepreneur is to accept risk on behalf of other people. There is, in this view, a *market* for risk. Risk is something that people, generally, want to avoid. Entrepreneurs provide a service by taking this risk off people's hands.

An example should make this clear. We may all appreciate the benefits a new technology, for example the video recording of television images, can bring. However, there is a risk in developing this new technology. Financial investment in its development is very high. There is also a great deal of uncertainty. Competition between different suppliers' formats is intense. There is no guarantee that the investment will be returned. Yet, we now enjoy the benefits of video technology and we, as consumers, have not, personally, had to face the risks inherent in creating it. In effect, we have delegated that risk to the entrepreneurs who *were* active in developing it. Of course, entrepreneurs expect that in return for taking the risk they will be rewarded. This reward, the profit stream from their ventures, is the *price* that customers have 'agreed' to pay so that they can have the benefits of the product and yet not face the risk of developing it.

The idea that entrepreneurs are risk-takers is one which reflects their popular image. However, we must be very careful to distinguish between *personal* risk and *economic* risk. We may face personal risk by exposing ourselves to dangerous situations, climbing mountains for example, but this is not risk as an economist understands it. To an economist, risk results from making an *investment*. Risk is the possibility that the return from an investment may be *less* than expected. Or, to be exact, might be less than could have been obtained from an alternative investment that was available. As was pointed out in section 1.2, the role of the entrepreneur who manages the venture, and the investor who puts their money into it, is quite distinct.

So, acceptance of risk is something that *investors* do, not *entrepreneurs* as such. However, the popular impression that the entrepreneur is a risk-taker is not completely inappropriate. It recognises that entrepreneurs are good at managing in situations where risk is high; that is, when faced with a situation of high uncertainty they are able to keep their heads, to continue to communicate effectively and to carry on making effective decisions.

Maximising investor's returns

Some commentators have suggested that the primary role of an entrepreneur is one of maximising the returns that shareholders get from their investments. In effect, the suggestion is that they create and run organisations which maximise long-term profits on behalf of the shareholder. In a sense, this is another aspect of the entrepreneur's role in generating overall economic efficiency.

Investors will certainly look around for entrepreneurs who create successful and profitable ventures although the view that entrepreneurs in the real world act simply to maximise shareholders' returns is questionable. Entrepreneurship, like all management activity, takes into account the interests of a wide variety of stakeholder groups, not just those of investors. Nor is it evident that investors demand that a firm maximise their returns whatever the social cost might be. Whereas Lord Hanson openly puts maximising shareholder returns at the top of his agenda, Anita Roddick would argue for a much broader range of concerns for the *Body Shop*.

Processing of market information

Classical economics makes the assumption that all the relevant information about a market is available to and is used by producers and consumers. However, human beings are not perfect information-processors. In practice, markets work without all possible information being made available or being used. One view of the entrepreneur is that they keep an eye out for information that is not being exploited. By taking advantage of this information, they make markets more efficient and are rewarded out of the revenues generated. This information is information about *opportunities*. The idea that entrepreneurs are information-processors is in essence a sophisticated version of the idea that entrepreneurs pursue opportunities and provide competitive efficiency.

In summary, entrepreneurs clearly play an important economic function. It is difficult, though, to reduce this to a single economic process in which the entrepreneur's role is different from that of other economic actors.

1.4   The entrepreneurial personality

> **KEY LEARNING OUTCOME**
> **An understanding of how personal characteristics have been seen to influence entrepreneurial tendencies and performance.**

We are all different, not only in the way we look, but in the way we *act* and the way we *react* to different situations. We talk of people having *personalities*. Personality can be defined as the consistent, and persistent, profile of beliefs, feelings and actions which makes one person distinct from another. Psychologists have long had an interest in personality and have developed a number of conceptual schemes and exploratory devices to investigate it. The personality of the entrepreneur has been an important theme in this research. A number of perspectives on the entrepreneur may be considered under the broad heading of personality.

The 'great person'

An immediate reaction when faced with an entrepreneur, or indeed anyone with influence and social prominence such as a leading statesman, an important scientist or a successful artist is to regard them simply as being special: as a 'great person' who is destined by virtue of their 'nature' to rise above the crowd. Such people are born to be great and will achieve greatness, one way or another. Such a view often underlies the approach biographers take to important people.

Entrepreneurs can certainly be inspiring, and may provide motivating role models. Generally though, the great person view, however passionate, is not particularly useful. For a start it is self-justifying. If an entrepreneur achieves success, it is because they are great; if they fail then they are not. It has no predictive power. It can only tell us who will become an entrepreneur after they have achieved success. Furthermore, it offers no role for the wider world in offering people the chance to achieve success. Most damaging, however, is the way it denies the possibility of entrepreneurial success to those who are not born to be great persons.

Social misfit

Another view which forms a marked contrast to the great person view but which also has a great deal of currency is the idea that entrepreneurs are *social misfits* at heart. In this view someone is an entrepreneur for an essentially negative reason: they are unable to fit into existing social situations. As a result the entrepreneur is driven to create their own situation. It is this that provides the motivation to innovate and build new organisations.

Advocates of this view look towards both anecdotal and psychological evidence for support. Many entrepreneurs achieve success after comparatively unhappy and lacklustre careers working as professional managers. Often they relate their inability to fit into the established firm as a factor in driving them to start their own venture.

Some researchers who have studied the childhood and family backgrounds of entrepreneurs have noted that they are often characterised by privation and hardship which left the person with a lack of self-esteem, a feeling of insecurity and a repressed desire for control. This leads to rebellious and deviant behaviour which limits the person's ability to fit into established organisations. Entrepreneurial activity, it is concluded, is a way of coming to terms with this. It provides not only a means of economic survival but also an activity which enables a reaction against anxiety left by psychological scars.

While the idea of the social misfit may provide insights into the motivations of *some* entrepreneurs, any generalisation of this sort is dangerous. For every entrepreneur whose childhood was unhappy and involved privation, another can be found who was quite comfortable and happy. Many successful entrepreneurs recall being unsatisfied when working within established organisations. However, this is not necessarily because they are misfits in a negative sense. Rather it may be because the organisation did not provide sufficient scope for their abilities and ambitions. This in itself may be demotivating, and therefore managerial performance in an established firm is not necessarily a good indicator of how someone will perform later as an entrepreneur.

Personality type

The conceptual basis for the personality type view of entrepreneurship is that the way people act in a given situation can be categorised into one of a relatively limited number of responses. As a result, individuals can be grouped into a small number of categories based on this response. For example, we may classify people as *extrovert* or *introvert*, *aggressive* or *passive*, *spontaneous* or *reserved*, *internally* or *externally orientated*, *etc*. Each of these types represents a fixed category.

There is a common impression that entrepreneurs tend to be flamboyant extroverts who are spontaneous in their approach and rely on instinct rather than calculation. Certainly, they are often depicted this way in literature and on film. Detailed studies, however, have show that all types of personality perform equally well as entrepreneurs. Personality type does not correlate with entrepreneurial performance and success. For example, introverts are as just likely to be entrepreneurs as are extroverts.

Personality trait

The idea of personality *trait* is different from that of personality *type*. While a person-ality may be *of* a particular type, it *has* a trait. Whereas types are distinct categories traits occur in continuously variable dimensions.

In a very influential study in the early 1960s, David McClelland identified a 'need for achievement' (along with various other characteristics) as the fundamental driving trait in the personality of successful entrepreneurs. Other factors which have also been viewed as important include the need for autonomy, the need to be in control of a situation, a desire to face risk, creativity, a need for independence and the desire to show leadership qualities.

While conceptually very powerful, the trait approach to the entrepreneurial personality raises a number of questions. To what extent are traits innate? Are they fixed features of personality or might they actually be learnt? How does a trait as measured in a personality test relate to behaviour in the real world? Does possession of certain traits lead to entrepreneurship or does pursuing an entrepreneurial career merely provide an opportunity to develop them? Do entrepreneurs simply act out the traits they feel are expected of them?

The idea of traits in the personality of entrepreneurs provides a very important paradigm for the study of entrepreneurial motivation. However, the available evi-dence suggests it is unwise to advocate, or to advise against, an entrepreneurial path for a particular manager based on the perception of traits they might, or might not, possess.

Social development

Both personality type and trait are seen as innate. They are determined by a person's genetic complement (nature) or by early life experiences (nurture) or by some combination of both. (The relative importance of these two things and how they might interact is a highly controversial issue in social theory.) Personality type or trait are also seen as being 'locked into' a person's mental apparatus, and therefore relatively fixed. They can change only slowly, or under special conditions.

The social development view regards personality as a more complex issue. In this view entrepreneurship is an output which results from the interaction of internal psychological and external social factors. The view is that personality develops continuously as a result of social interaction and is *expressed* in a social setting rather than being innate to the individual. The way people behave is not predetermined, but is contingent on their experiences and the possibilities open to them.

In this view, entrepreneurs are not born, they are *made*. While their predisposition may be important it does not have any meaning in isolation from their experiences. A person is not, once and for all, entrepreneurial. He or she may, for example, decide to become an entrepreneur only at one particular stage in his or her life. Equally, he or she may decide to give up being an entrepreneur at another.

A number of factors are seen as significant to the social development of entrepreneurs. In general, they fall into one of three broad categories:

1 *Innate* – factors such as intelligence, creativity, personality, motivation, personal ambition, *etc.*;
2 *Acquired* – learning, training, experience in 'incubator' organisations, mentoring, existence of motivating role models, *etc.*;
3 *Social* – birth order, experiences in family life, socio-economic group and parental occupation, society and culture, economic conditions, *etc.*

The social development model provides a more plausible picture of entrepreneurial behaviour than those that assume entrepreneurial inclination is somehow innate. Entrepreneurship is a social phenomenon. It is not inherent within a person, rather it exists in the interactions *between* people. While entrepreneurs may actively grasp opportunities, they do so within a cultural framework. The social development approach is sophisticated in that it recognises that entrepreneurial behaviour is the result of a large number of factors, some internal to the entrepreneur and, others which are features of the environment within which entrepreneurs express themselves. However, this is also a weakness. While it identifies the factors which might influence entrepreneurship, it cannot say *why* they influence it. While social development models are good at indicating what factors might be involved in entrepreneurial behaviour, they suggest so many factors that their predictive power is very limited.

The limitations of personality models

Personality is a concept of central importance in psychology. It plays a crucial role in aiding our understanding of the social interaction between people and it has both illuminated our understanding of, and enriched our appreciation of, the entrepreneur. However, it is important that we do not let an inappropriate idea of personality distort our view. There is no real evidence to suggest that there is a single 'entrepreneurial personality'. People of all personality types, attitudes and dispositions, not only become entrepreneurs but become *successful* entrepreneurs. A consequence of this is that personality testing does not provide a good indicator of who will, or will not, be a successful entrepreneur.

To be a successful entrepreneur takes many things: ambition, drive, hard work, effort in learning to understand a business and practice as a manger. But it does not demand a particular personality. Experience shows that a reserved introvert who carefully calculates their next move can look forward to as much entrepreneurial success as their more 'theatrical' counterpart. No one with entrepreneurial ambitions should ever dismiss the option of an entrepreneurial career because they do not feel they are the 'right type' of person. To do so reveals more about their misconceptions of entrepreneurship than it does about their potential.

1.5   Classifying entrepreneurs

> **KEY LEARNING OUTCOME**
> **An understanding of how different types of entrepreneur might be distinguished.**

As we have seen, there is no universally accepted definition of an entrepreneur. However, it has been found useful to classify entrepreneurs into different types. Such classification provides a starting point for gaining an insight into how entrepreneurial ventures work and the factors underlying their success. There are a number of potential classification schemes. This section aims to give a flavour of the approaches taken rather than an extensive review of all the schemes. There are two main approaches: either to classify the entrepreneurs *themselves* or to classify their *ventures*.

An early move was to differentiate between *opportunist* entrepreneurs who were interested in maximising their returns from short-term deals, and *craftsmen* who attempted to make a living by privately selling their trade or the products they produced. Craftsmen were less interested in profits as such, but in being able to earn a stable living from their specialist skills. The idea of the 'opportunist' entrepreneur is quite vague, and a later development was to replace it with two more definite types: the *growth-orientated* entrepreneur who pursued opportunities to maximise the potential of their ventures and the *independence-orientated* entrepreneur whose main ambition was to work for themselves. These latter kind of entrepreneurs preferred stability to growth and so were willing to limit the scope of their ventures. A further distinction can be made between craftsmen entrepreneurs whose expertise is based on *traditional skills* and those whose expertise is scientific or *high-technology*.

The American entrepreneurship academic Frederick Webster (1977) considers classification schemes for both the individual entrepreneur and for their ventures. Four types of individual entrepreneur are recognised within his scheme. The *Cantillon* entrepreneur (named after the 18th century French economist Richard Cantillon) brings people, money and materials together to create an entirely new organisation. This is the 'classic' type of entrepreneur who identifies an unexploited opportunity and then innovates in order to pursue it. The *industry maker* goes beyond merely creating a new firm. Their innovation is of such importance that a whole industry is created on the back of it. They do not only develop new products, but also a whole technology to produce them. Examples include Henry Ford and the mass production of motor vehicles, Thomas Edison and domestic electrical products, and Bill Gates with software operating systems. The *administrative entrepreneur* is a manager who operates within an established firm but does so in an entrepreneurial fashion. Usually occupying the chief executive or a senior managerial role they are often called upon to be innovative and to provide dynamism and leadership to the organisation, particularly when it is facing a period of change. An example here is Lee Iacocca's rejuvenation of the Chrysler Motor Company or Jan Carlzon's turnaround of the Scandinavian Airlines System (SAS). Nowadays administrative entrepreneurs are often referred to as *intrapreneurs*. The *small business owner* is an entrepreneur who takes responsibility for owning and running their own venture. The business may be small because it is in an early stage of growth or they may actually wish to limit the size of their business, because they are satisfied that it gives them a reasonably secure income and control over their lives.

Webster classifies entrepreneurial ventures by the ratio of the amount that is expected to be received as a result of the venture's success (the *perceived payoff*) and the number of investors involved (the *principals*). Three types of venture are identified:

(i) *large payoff: many participants* (i.e. a major venture with the risk spread widely over a large number of investors);

(ii) *small payoff: few participants* (i.e. a limited venture with the risk taken on by a few key investors only);

(iii) *large payoff: few participants* (i.e a major venture with the risk taken on by a few key investors).

The remaining possibility, that is a small expected payoff with a large number of investors, is not considered to be a likely scenario.

Wai-Sum Siu (1996) has examined the types of new entrepreneur who operate in China and he gives a fascinating snap-shot of the people behind this fast-growing economy. Basing his assessment on *employment, managerial, financial, technical* and *strategic* criteria he identifies five types of entrepreneur. The *senior citizen* undertakes a venture to keep occupied during his or her retirement. The business is small and based on personal expertise. It is privately funded and has no long-term strategic ambitions. *Workaholics* are also retired but show more ambition for their ventures than do senior citizens. They often possess administrative experience and their businesses are bigger, drawing on a wider range of technical skills. Strategic goals may be explicit and employees may be invited to make a personal investment in the future of the venture. *Swingers* are younger entrepreneurs who aim to make a living from making deals. They may have only limited industrial and technical experience and rely on networks of personal contacts. Their ventures may be moderately large, but they tend not to have long-term strategic goals. The main aim is to maximise short-term profits. Funding is provided through retained earnings, family contributions and personal loans. *Idealists* are also younger entrepreneurs who run moderate-sized ventures. However, their motivation is based less on short-term profit than the sense of achievement and independence that running their own venture gives them. They serve a variety of end-markets and their ventures may be based on high-technology products. Financing is through retained profits, family contributions and private investment. *High-flyers* are motivated in much the same way as idealists. However, their ventures are much larger reflecting success in the marketplace. Again, a variety of products are offered. Corporate goals and strategy tend to be much more explicit than in the idealist's venture, and investment is drawn from a wider variety of sources, including institutional and international agencies.

1.6 Entrepreneurship and small business management: a distinction

> **KEY LEARNING OUTCOME**
> **An appreciation of why the entrepreneurial venture is distinct from the small business.**

Both small business management and entrepreneurship are of critical importance to the performance of the economy. However, it is useful to draw a distinction between them since small businesses and entrepreneurial ventures serve different economic functions. They pursue and create new opportunities differently, they fulfil the ambitions of their founders and managers in different ways, and they present different challenges to economic policy makers. Drawing this distinction is an issue of classification. There are two possible approaches, namely to make a distinction between the characteristics of *entrepreneurs* and *small business managers*, or to make a distinction between *entrepreneurial ventures* and *small businesses*.

The former is problematic. As discussed in Section 1.4, the entrepreneur is not distinguished by a distinct personality type and there is no independent test that can be performed to identify an entrepreneur. The question is consequently a matter of personal opinion. Some people may regard themselves as true entrepreneurs while others may judge themselves to be 'just' small business managers. This can be an emotive issue and it is not clear what benefits are to be gained by placing people into different conceptual bags in this way. Rather than trying to draw a distinction between managers, it is more valuable to draw a distinction relating to what they manage, that is between the small business and the entrepreneurial venture.

There are three characteristics which distinguish the entrepreneurial venture from the small business.

1 Innovation

An entrepreneurial venture is usually based on a significant *innovation*. This might be a technological innovation, for example, a new product or a new way of producing it; it might be an innovation in offering a new service; an innovation in the way something is marketed or distributed; or possibly an innovation in the way the organisation is structured and managed; or in the way relationships are maintained between organisations. The small business, on the other hand, is usually involved in delivering an established product or service. This does not mean that a small business is not doing something new. They may be delivering an innovation to people who would not otherwise have access to it, perhaps at a lower cost or with a higher level of service. However, the small firm's output is likely to be established and produced in an established way. So while a small business may be new to a locality, it is not doing anything essentially new in a *global* sense, whereas an entrepreneurial venture *is* usually based on a *significantly new* way of doing something.

2 Potential for growth

The size of a business is a poor guide as to whether it is entrepreneurial or not. The actual definition of what constitutes a small business is a matter of judgement depending on the industry sector, for example a firm with one hundred employees would be a very small shipbuilder, but a very large firm of solicitors. However, an entrepreneurial venture usually has a great deal more *potential* for growth than does a small business. This results from the fact that it is usually based on a significant innovation. The market potential for that innovation will be more than enough to support a small firm. It may even be more than enough to support a large firm and signal the start of an entire new industry. The small business on the other hand, operates within an established industry and is unique only in terms of its locality. Therefore, it is limited in its growth potential by competitors in adjacent localities. A small business operates *within* a given market; the entrepreneurial venture is in a position to *create* its own market.

A word of caution is necessary here, since having the potential to grow is not the same as having a *right* to grow! If it is to enjoy growth, it is still necessary that the entrepreneurial venture be managed proficiently and that it compete effectively, even if it is creating an entirely new market rather than competing within an existing one.

3 Strategic objectives

Objectives are a common feature of managerial life. They take a variety of forms, for example they may be formal or informal, and they may be directed towards individuals or apply to the venture as a whole. Most businesses have at least some objectives. Even the smallest firm should have sales targets if not more detailed financial objectives. Objectives may be set for the benefit of external investors as well as for consumption by the internal management.

The entrepreneurial venture will usually go beyond the small business in the objectives it sets itself in that it will have *strategic* objectives. Strategic objectives relate to such things as:

- *growth targets* – year on year increases in sales, profits and other financial targets;
- *market development* – activities to actually create and stimulate the growth and shaping of the firm's market (for example, through advertising and promotion);
- *market share* – the proportion of that market the business serves; and
- *market position* – maintaining the firm's position in its market relative to competitors.

These strategic objectives may be quantified in a variety of ways. They may also be supplemented by a formal mission statement for the venture. This is an idea that will be discussed more fully in Chapter 10.

The distinction between a small business and an entrepreneurial venture is not clearcut. Generally we can say that the entrepreneurial venture is distinguished from the small business by its *innovation, growth potential* and *strategic objectives*. However, not all entrepreneurial ventures will necessarily show an obvious innovation, clear growth potential or formally articulated strategic objectives and some small businesses may demonstrate these characteristics. However, in combination they do add up to distinguish the key character of an entrepreneurial venture, that is, a business that makes significant changes to the world (*see* Fig. 1.1).

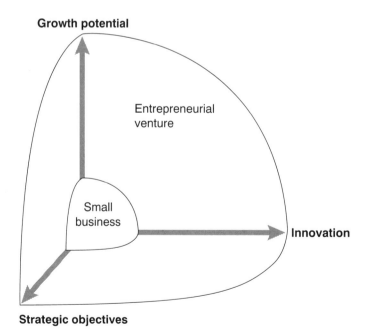

Fig. 1.1 The difference between a small business and an entrepreneurial venture

1.7 Entrepreneurship: a style of management

KEY LEARNING OUTCOME
A recognition that entrepreneurship is management aimed at pursuing opportunity and creating change.

The discussion so far has emphasised what the entrepreneur is *not*, as much as what they *are* because it is important to dispel certain myths about the entrepreneur. In particular, it is important to discount the theories that the entrepreneur is someone with a particular type of personality or that certain people are somehow born to be entrepreneurs. We must also recognise that the entrepreneur does not have a clearcut economic role. However, we must now consider what the entrepreneur actually *is* by developing a *perspective* that will illuminate the way entrepreneurs actually go about their tasks *as* entrepreneurs rather than providing a potentially restrictive *definition* of the entrepreneur.

What we can say with confidence is that an entrepreneur is a *manager*. Specifically, he or she is someone who manages in an *entrepreneurial way*. More often than not they will be managing a specific *entrepreneurial venture*, either a new organisation or an attempt to rejuvenate an existing one. The entrepreneurial venture represents a particular management challenge. The nature of the entrepreneurial venture characterises and defines the management that is needed to successfully drive it forward. Drawing together the themes that have been explored in this chapter it is evident that entrepreneurial management is characterised by three features.

1 A focus on change

Entrepreneurs are managers of *change*. An entrepreneur does not leave the world in the same state as they found it. They bring people, money, ideas and resources together to build new organisations and to change existing ones. Entrepreneurs are not important as much for the *results* of their activities as for the *difference* they make.

Entrepreneurs are different from managers whose main interest is in maintaining the *status quo* by sustaining the established organisation, protecting it and maintaining its market positions. This is not to depreciate a desire for equilibrium as an objective, it can be very important and is an essential ingredient in the effective running of a wide variety of organisations, but it is not about driving change.

2 A focus on opportunity

Entrepreneurs are attuned to opportunity. They constantly seek out the possibility of doing something differently and better. They innovate in order to create new value. Entrepreneurs are more interested in pursing opportunity than they are in *conserving resources*.

This is not to suggest that entrepreneurs are not interested in resources. They are often acutely aware that the resources available to them are limited. Nor does it mean that they are cavalier with them. They may be using their own money and, if not, they will have investors looking over their shoulders to check that they are not wasting funds. What it *does* mean is that entrepreneurs see resources as a means to an end, not as an end in themselves.

Entrepreneurs expose resources to risk but they also make them work by stretching them to their limit in order to offer a good return. This makes them distinct from managers in established businesses who all too often can find themselves more responsible for protecting 'scarce' resources than for using them to pursue the opportunities that are presented to their organisations.

3 Organisation wide management

The entrepreneur manages with an eye to the *entire* organisation, not just some aspect of it. They benchmark themselves against organisational objectives, not just the objectives for some particular department. This is not to say that functional disciplines such as marketing, finance, operations management, *etc.* are unimportant. However, the entrepreneur sees these as functions which play a part in the overall business, rather than as isolated activities.

Entrepreneurial managers as venturers

In short, the entrepreneur is a manager who is willing to *venture*: to create change and to pursue opportunity rather than to just maintain the *status quo* and conserve resources. Of course, the effective entrepreneur does *all* these things when appropriate. There are times when the *status quo* is worth sustaining, and times when it is unwise to expose resources. Part of the skill of the effective entrepreneur is knowing when *not* to venture. However, when the time is right, the entrepreneurial manager *is* willing to step forward.

This is a 'soft' definition. There is no hard and fast distinction between the entrepreneur and other types of manager. This does not make the entrepreneur any less special, nor does it make what entrepreneurs do any less important. What it does do is open up the possibility of entrepreneurship. In being 'just' a style of management it is something that can be learnt. Managers can chose to be entrepreneurial.

A very illuminating characterisation of entrepreneurship is offered by Czarniawska-Joerges and Wolff (1991) who use the language of theatrical performance rather than economics to distinguish between *management* which is:

> **the activity of introducing order by coordinating flows of things and people towards collective action,**

leadership which is:

> **symbolic performance, expressing the hope of control over destiny,**

and *entrepreneurship* which is, quite simply:

> **the making of entire new worlds.**

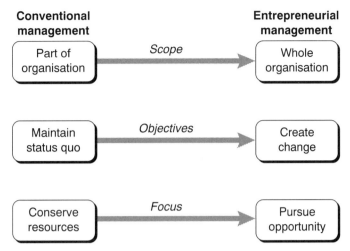

Fig. 1.2 Conventional management and entrepreneurial management: a comparison

In conclusion, we can say that entrepreneurial management is characterised by its *whole organisation scope*, its objective of creating *change* and a focus on *exploiting opportunity*. These characteristics are shown in Fig. 1.2.

Summary of key ideas

- There is no universally agreed definition of entrepreneurship. The wide variety of definitions in the literature emphasise three aspects:
  - the entrepreneur as an *economic agent* generating particular *economic effects*;
  - the entrepreneur as an *individual* of a particular *personality*; and:
  - the entrepreneur as a *manager* undertaking particular *tasks*.

- It is far from clear that there is a particular 'entrepreneurial' personality which predisposes people to business success.

- An entrepreneur is best regarded as a manager who *pursues opportunity* and *drives change* to create *new value*.

- The entrepreneurial venture is distinguished from the small business by virtue of being based on a significant *innovation*, having the potential for *growth*, and having clear *strategic objectives*.

Suggestions for further reading

Barton-Cunningham, J. and **Lischeron, J** (1991) "Defining entrepreneurship", *Journal of Small Business Management*, Jan, pp. 45–61.

Brockhaus, R.H. (1987) "Entrepreneurial folklore" *Journal of Small Business Management*, July, pp. 1–6.

Carland, J.W., **Hoy**, F., **Boulton**, W.R. and **Carland**, J.C. (1984) "Differentiating entrepreneurs from small business owners: a conceptualisation", *Academy of Management Review*, Vol. 9, No. 2, pp. 345–59.

Chell, E. (1985) "The entrepreneurial personality: a few ghosts laid to rest", *International Small Business Journal*, Vol 3, No. 3, pp. 43– 54.

Cromie, S. and O'Donaghue, J. (1992) "Assessing entrepreneurial inclination", *International Small Business Journal*, Vol. 10, No. 2, pp. 66–73.

Czarniawska-Joerges, B. and **Wolff**, R. (1991) "Leaders, managers and entrepreneurs on and off the organisational stage", *Organisation Studies*, Vol. 12, No. 4, pp. 529–46.

Drucker, P.F. (1985) *Innovation and Entrepreneurship*, London: Heinemann.

Dunkelberg, W.C. and **Cooper**, A.C. (1982) "Entrepreneurial typologies: an empirical study", in Vesper, K.H. (ed.), *Frontiers of Entrepreneurial Research*, Wellesley, Mass: Babson College Centre for Entrepreneurial Studies, pp. 1–15.

Gartner, W.B. (1988) "'Who is an entrepreneur' is the wrong question", *American Journal of Small Business*, Spring, pp. 11–32.

Gartner, W.B. (1990) "What are we talking about when we talk about entrepreneurship?", *Journal of Business Venturing*, Vol. 5, pp. 15–28.

Ginsberg, A. and **Buchholtz**, A. (1989) "Are entrepreneurs a breed apart? A look at the evidence", *Journal of General Management*, Vol. 15, No. 2, pp. 32–40.

Guzmán Cuevas, J. (1994) "Towards a taxonomy of entrepreneurial theories", *International Small Business Journal*, Vol. 12, No. 4, pp. 77–88.

Hornaday, R.W. (1992) "Thinking about entrepreneurship: a fuzzy set approach", *Journal of Small Business Management*, Oct, pp. 12–23.

Julien, P.-A. (1989) "The entrepreneur and economic theory", *International Small Business Journal*, Vol. 7, No. 3, pp. 29–38.

Kilby, P. (1971) "Hunting the Heffalump" in *Entrepreneurship and Economic Development*, Kilby, P. (ed.) New York: The Free Press.

McClelland, D. (1961) *The Achieving Society*, Princeton, NJ: Van Nostrand.

Olson, P.D. (1986) "Entrepreneurs: opportunistic decision makers", *Journal of Small Business Management*, July, pp. 29–35.

Olson, P.D. (1987) "Entrepreneurship and management", *Journal of Small Business Management*, July, pp. 7–13.

Peterson, R.A., **Albaum**, G. and **Kozmetsky**, G. (1986) "The public's definition of small business", *Journal of Small Business Management*, July, pp. 63–8.

Petrof, J.V. (1980) "Entrepreneurial profile: a discriminant analysis", *Journal of Small Business Management*, Vol 18, No. 4, pp. 13–17.

Scherer, R.F., **Adams**, J.S. and **Wiebe**, F.A. (1989) "Developing entrepreneurial behaviours: a social learning perspective", *Journal of Organisational Change Management*, Vol. 2, No. 3, pp. 16–27.

Siu, Wai-Sum (1996) "Entrepreneurial typology: the case of owner managers in China", *International Small Business Journal*, Vol. 14, No. 1, pp. 53–64.

Stanworth, J., **Stanworth**, C., **Grainger**, B. and **Blythe**, S. (1989) "Who becomes an entrepreneur?", *International Small Business Journal*, Vol. 8, No. 1, pp.11–22.

Watson, T.J. (1995) "Entrepreneurship and professional management: a fatal distinction", *International Small Business Journal*, Vol. 13, No. 2, pp. 34–46.

Webster, F.A. (1977) "Entrepreneurs and ventures: an attempt at classification and clarification", *Academy of Management Review*, Vol. 2, No. 1, pp. 54–61.

2 The entrepreneurial process

CHAPTER OVERVIEW

*This chapter is concerned with developing a model of the process by which entrepreneurs create new wealth. It suggests that entrepreneurship, in the first instance, is driven by a desire for creating **change** on the part of the entrepreneur. This desire for change leads the entrepreneur to bring together three contingencies, **opportunity**, **resources** and **organisation**, in an innovative and dynamic way.*

The chapter also considers the limits of entrepreneurship and whether it extends beyond the profit-making domain to the management of artistic, social and cultural endeavours.

2.1 Making a difference: entrepreneurship and the drive for change

KEY LEARNING OUTCOME
An understanding of the changes that entrepreneurship makes.

Entrepreneurship is about bringing about change and making a *difference*. The world is not the same after the entrepreneur has finished with it. In a narrower sense, entrepreneurship is about exploiting innovation in order to create value which cannot always be measured in purely financial terms.

The entrepreneur is concerned with identifying the potential for change. The entrepreneur exists in a state of tension between the *actual* and the *possible*, that is

Fig. 2.1 Tension in the entrepreneurial process

between what *is* and what *might be* (*see* Fig. 2.1). This tension is manifest in three dimensions: the *financial*, the *personal* and the *social*.

The financial dimension: the potential to create new value

Entrepreneurship is an economic activity. It is concerned, first and foremost, with building stable, profitable businesses which must survive in a competitive environment. If they are to thrive and prosper they must add value more effectively than their competitors. The new world created by the entrepreneur must be a more valuable one than that which existed previously. The opportunity exploited and the innovation present must create additional value if the venture is to be successful in the long-term since entrepreneurs compete to attract the resources with which they reward their stakeholders.

A point worth noting here is that in creating *new* value, entrepreneurship is not a 'zero sum game'. Even though business is competitive, it is not inevitable that if an entrepreneur wins then someone somewhere else must lose. Entrepreneurship often presents win-win scenarios. The new value the entrepreneur creates can be shared in a variety of ways.

The personal dimension: the potential to achieve personal goals

Entrepreneurs are motivated by a number of factors and although making money may motivate some, it is not the only factor, nor necessarily the most important. A sense of achievement, of having created something, or of 'making an entire new world' is often a much more significant driving factor. The entrepreneurial venture can be an entrepreneur's way of leaving his or her mark on the world, reminding it of his or her presence.

Entrepreneurs may also be motivated by the challenge that the competitive environment presents, namely a chance for them to pit their wits against the wider world. Driving their own ventures also gives entrepreneurs a chance to design their own working environment and instils a sense of control. In order to understand entrepreneurial motivation it is essential to recognise that for many entrepreneurs what matters is not the *destination* of the business they finally build up, but the *journey* – the process of creating the business.

The social dimension: the potential for structural change

Entrepreneurs operate within a wider society. In making an 'entire new world' they must, of course, have an impact on that society. They provide the society with new products and access to new services. They provide fellow citizens with jobs. They help make the economic system competitive. This may be good for the economic system as a whole, but not for the less dynamic and efficient competitors they will drive to the wall.

All of this gives the entrepreneur power to drive changes in the structure of a society. The kind of world that an entrepreneur envisages, perhaps the possibility of a better world, can be an important factor in motivating the entrepreneur. It also means that the entrepreneur must operate with a degree of social responsibility. The kind of world that the entrepreneur would like to see is often a part of their *vision* for their firm and for the future. This vision may be enshrined in the mission that the organisation sets itself.

2.2   The entrepreneurial process: opportunity, organisation and resources

KEY LEARNING OUTCOME
An understanding of the factors in the process of entrepreneurial value creation.

Every entrepreneurial venture is different with its own history. Its successes are the result of it having faced and addressed specific issues in its own way. Nonetheless, it is useful to consider the process of entrepreneurship in a generalised way since this gives us a framework for understanding how entrepreneurship creates new wealth in general terms and for making sense of the detail in particular ventures. It also provides us with a guide for decision making when planning new ventures.

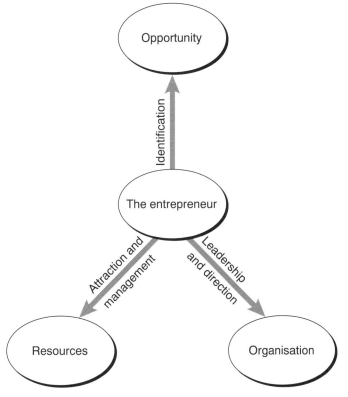

Fig. 2.2 The entrepreneurial process: opportunity, resources and organisation

The approach to the entrepreneurial process that will be described here is based on four interacting *contingencies*. The entrepreneur is responsible for bringing these together to create new value. A contingency is simply something which *must* be present in the process but can make an appearance in an endless variety of ways. The four contingencies in the entrepreneurial process are the *entrepreneur*, a market *opportunity*, a business *organisation* and *resources* to be invested (*see* Fig. 2.2). Each of these will now be explored in some depth.

The entrepreneur

The entrepreneur is the individual who lies at the heart of the entrepreneurial process, that is the manager who drives the whole process forward. Entrepreneurs often act singly but in many instances *entrepreneurial teams* are important. Different members of the team may take on different roles and share responsibilities. They may be from the same family, for example, the Benetton siblings from Northern Italy who revolutionised the manufacture of textiles, or alternatively, they be from an existing management team who have teamed up to initiate their own venture, perhaps through a management buy-out.

Opportunity

An opportunity is the gap left in a market by those who currently serve it. It represents the potential to serve customers better than they are being served at present. The entrepreneur is responsible for scanning the business landscape for unexploited opportunities or possibilities that something important might be done both *differently* to the way it is done at the moment and, critically, done *better* than it is done at the moment. The improved way of doing it is the innovation that the entrepreneur presents to the market. If customers agree with the entrepreneur that it is an improvement on what exists already and if the entrepreneur can supply the innovation effectively and profitably then new value can be created.

Organisation

In order to supply the innovation to the market, the activities of a number of different people must be co-ordinated. This is the function of the organisation that the entrepreneur creates. Organisations can take on a variety of forms depending on a number of factors such as their size, their rate of growth, the industry they operate in, the types of product or service they deliver, the age of the organisation and the culture that it adopts.

Entrepreneurial organisations are characterised by strong, often charismatic, leadership from the entrepreneur. They may have less formal structures and systems than their more bureaucratic, established counterparts. In many respects the entrepreneurial organisation is still learning, but rather than judge this to be a handicap the business turns it into a strength by being receptive to new ideas and responsive to the need for change.

Current thinking on entrepreneurial organisations tends not to draw a hard and fast distinction between those inside the organisation and those who are on the outside. It has been found more productive to think in terms of the organisation in a wider sense as being a *network* of relationships between individuals with the entrepreneur sitting at the centre. This network stretches beyond just the individuals who make up the formal company to include people and organisations outside the venture such as customers, suppliers and investors. The relationships that make up the network are very diverse. Some are defined by contracts, whereas others are defined by open markets; some are formal and some informal; some are based on self-interest, while others are maintained by altruism; some are driven by short-term considerations, and others by long-term interests.

In the network view, the organisation is a fluid thing defined by a *nexus of relationships*. Its boundaries are permeable. The idea of a network provides a powerful insight into how entrepreneurial ventures establish themselves, how they locate themselves competitively, and how they sustain their positions in their markets by adding value to people's lives.

Resources

The final contingency in the entrepreneurial process is resources. This includes the money which is invested in the venture, the people who contribute their efforts, knowledge and skills to it, and *physical assets* such as productive equipment and machinery, buildings and vehicles. Resources also include *intangible assets* such as brand names, company reputation and customer goodwill. All of these features can be subject to *investment*. One of the key functions of the entrepreneur is to attract investment to the venture and to use it to build up a set of assets which allow the venture to supply its innovation competitively and profitably.

The entrepreneur plays a critical role in identifying opportunity, building and leading the organisation, and attracting and managing resources. The three external contingencies quickly develop a momentum of their own and become independent of the entrepreneur at the centre. As the organisation grows, it develops processes and systems and the people within it adopt distinct roles. The entrepreneur must delegate responsibility within the organisation and specialist functions may take over some aspects of the entrepreneur's role. For example, the marketing department may identify opportunities and innovate the firm's offerings to take advantage of them; the finance department may take on the responsibility for attracting investment. In this way, entrepreneurial ventures quickly take on a life of their own. They become quite distinct from the entrepreneur who established them. Consequently, the entrepreneur must constantly address the question of his or her role within the organisation.

2.3 The entrepreneurial process: action and the dynamics of success

KEY LEARNING OUTCOME

A recognition that entrepreneurship is a dynamic process in which success fuels success.

The entrepreneurial process results from the *actions* of the entrepreneur. It can only occur if the entrepreneur acts to develop an innovation and promote it to customers. The entrepreneurial process is *dynamic*. Success comes from the contingencies of the entrepreneur, the opportunity, the organisation and resources coming together and supporting each other. The entrepreneur must constantly focus the organisation onto the opportunity that has been identified. He or she must mould the resources to hand to give the organisation its shape and to ensure that those resources are appropriate for pursuing the particular opportunity. These interactions are the fundamental elements of the entrepreneurial process and together they constitute the foundations of the *strategy* adopted by the venture.

Opportunity–organisation fit

The nature of the opportunity that is being pursued defines the shape that the organisation must adopt. Every organisation built by an entrepreneur is different. Organisations are complex affairs and there are a variety of ways in which they might be described and understood. The essential features are the *assets* of the organisation,

Table 2.1 An outline of organisational *assets*, *structure*, *process* and *culture* for three global entrepreneurial businesses

Organisation	McDonald's	The Body Shop	Microsoft
Opportunity pursued	Desire for fast, convenient, consistent meals	Desire for toiletries produced with a concern for the environment	Desire to process information
Assets	Brand name, outlets, locations, people	Brand name, outlets, locations, people	People, knowledge, patents, brand name
Structure	Series of production/ retail outlets	Series of retail outlets	Project teams based at one location
Process	Production and distribution standardised at outlets. Central financial and marketing.	Production centralised. Distribution through outlets. Promotion largely by store presence.	Product development, production, distribution and marketing centralised.
Culture	Positive attitude, concern for quality, customer focus.	Attitude of concern. Emphasis on wider social responsibility for organisation.	Innovative and creative 'technophilia'. Emphasis on managerial informality.

that is the things which it possesses; its *structure*, namely how it arranges communication links (both formal and informal) within itself; its *processes*: how it *adds value* to its inputs to create its *outputs*; and its *culture*, that is the attitudes, beliefs and outlooks that influence the way people behave within the organisation (*see* Table 2.1).

Assets, structure, process and culture are not separate parts of an organisation. They are merely different perspectives we may adopt in describing it. These four perspectives on the organisation form a unified whole which must be appropriate for the opportunity that the organisation is pursuing. The organisation must be shaped to *fit* the market gap that defines the opportunity.

Resource–organisation configuration

Resources are the things that are used to pursue opportunity. They include *people*, *money* and *productive assets*. In a sense, an organisation is 'just' a collection of resources. The *configuration* of the resources is the way in which a particular mix of resources is brought together to form the organisation's assets, structure, process and (through the attitude of the people who make it up) its culture.

Resource–opportunity focus

The entrepreneur must decide what resources will make up the organisation; for example, its mix of capital, how this will be converted into productive assets and the nature and skills of the people who will make it up are all matters to be decided by the entrepreneur in the first instance. If the organisation is to develop the assets, structure, process and culture that will enable it to fit with its opportunity then the resource mix must be correctly balanced.

Entrepreneurs must be active in attracting resources to their venture such as suitably qualified employees, financial backing in the form of investor's money, the support of

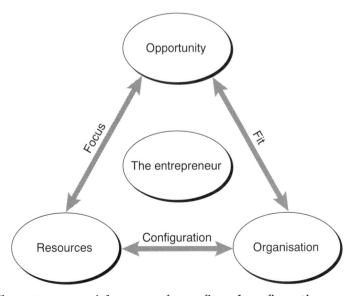

Fig. 2.3 The entrepreneurial process: focus, fit and configuration

customers and suppliers. Even so, they usually find that they do not have access to the same level of resources as established players in a market and because their risks may be higher, they will find the resources to be more expensive. If they are to compete successfully then entrepreneurs must make the resources they can get hold of work much harder perhaps than many established players do. The entrepreneur must be single-minded and *focus* those resources onto the opportunity that has been identified since the performance of the entrepreneurial organisation depends on how well the contingencies of opportunity, organisation and resources are linked together (*see* Fig. 2.3).

Learning organisations

These three aspects of the entrepreneurial process: making the organisation *fit* the opportunity it aims to exploit, *configuring* the resources to shape the organisation and *focusing* the resources in pursuit of the opportunity are not reflected in separate spheres of activity. They merely provide different perspectives on the same underlying management process. However, they do illuminate the essence of the entrepreneur's task and the direction their leadership must take. That leadership must be applied *constantly* since organisations are fluid things and left to themselves they can lose their shape and sense of direction. Furthermore, the entrepreneurial organisation must be a *learning* organisation. That is, it must not only *respond* to opportunities and challenges but must also *reflect* on the outcomes that result from that response and *modify* future responses in the light of experience. The venture cannot afford to acquire assets and set up structures and systems which are incapable of evolving as the organisation develops. Assets and structures must be modified as the organisation grows and changes and, critically, learns from its successes and failures. The entrepreneur must take responsibility for stimulating the firm to change in the light of experience. This learning process is shown in Fig. 2.4.

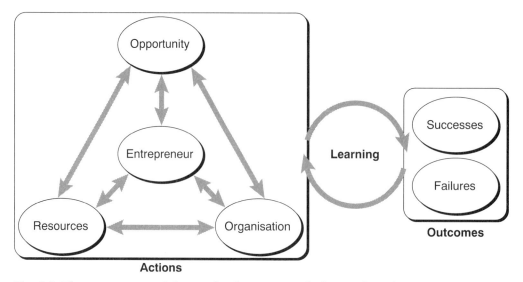

Fig. 2.4 The entrepreneurial organisation constantly learns from its successes and failures

2.4 Beyond profit: entrepreneurship in the social and public domains

KEY LEARNING OUTCOME
An appreciation that an understanding of entrepreneurship can help make non-profit making activities more successful.

Entrepreneurship, as an activity, is intimately associated with the world of business and making profits. However, the picture of entrepreneurship we have developed here has insights that can go beyond purely profit-motivated activity. In particular, we have seen that:

● entrepreneurship is a style of management;
● entrepreneurs are managers who are very effective at pursuing opportunity and creating change;
● entrepreneurship is a social as well as an economic activity; and
● the motivations of the entrepreneur are varied and go beyond a desire to make money; they also involve a desire to create a new and better world.

From this it is clear that we might take a much wider view of 'entrepreneurship' and consider many activities outside the world of business as 'entrepreneurial'. For example, a great cultural, artistic or political endeavour could be entrepreneurial. It is not uncommon to hear talk of 'entrepreneurial' artists or politicians. This is not meant to imply that such people are simply interested in making money out of being artists or politicians (though, of course, many do!), rather it is to imply that such people approach their careers with drive, ambition and a clear vision of what they want to achieve. In order to fulfil their ambitions they are willing to develop and use entrepreneurial skills such as effective communication and leadership.

A hierarchy of entrepreneurial activities functioning in different social areas can be constructed as shown in Fig. 2.5. At the core is what we conventionally understand to be entrepreneurship, namely managing the profit-making venture. At the next level is management of non-profit making organisations such as charities. Above this we might place endeavours in the social and cultural arena such as sporting and artistic ventures. At the top of the hierarchy there are activities aimed at creating wholesale social change

Gain understanding → Political change and leadership / Social and cultural endeavours / Non-profit organisation / Profit-making venture → Contribute understanding

Scope of activity

Fig. 2.5 The hierarchy of entrepreneurship in its wider social context

such as political activity. These levels are not completely separate, of course, and there will be some overlap.

Even though we can recognise entrepreneurship in these wider social arenas it is wise to keep management of the profit-making venture as the central concern for entrepreneurship. If we fail to do so the subject could become so wide as to be in danger of losing its coherence as a field of study. Therefore, this book will concentrate on profit-motivated activities. However, this does mean that insights gained from the management of the profit venture cannot be used to help achieve success in non-profit making ventures, or, conversely, that an understanding of success outside the business sphere cannot be used to illuminate the ways in which entrepreneurship might be improved within that sector.

In a narrow sense, many non-profit activities may still demand a managerial approach. They often involve managing money. Thus the charity still has to attract financial resources to distribute to its clients; sport may involve financial sponsorship; artists must still sell their creations; political parties must attract money from supporters if they are to function. All of these activities can call upon insights from other business areas such as marketing and human resource management. In a broader sense though, entrepreneurship, perhaps more than many other management disciplines, goes beyond the mere management of money. Money is just a means to an end for the entrepreneur, and the end is the creation of a better world. We may offer a description of entrepreneurship at a fundamental level by claiming that it is about:

> **creating and managing vision and of communicating that vision to other people. It is about demonstrating leadership, motivating people and being effective in getting people to accept change.**

This description reflects entrepreneurship as a management skill practised and perfected in a human setting. As such it can play a crucial part in driving any venture forward whether that venture be in the business, social, cultural or political domain.

Summary of key ideas

- The entrepreneurial process is the creation of *new value* through the entrepreneur identifying new *opportunities*, attracting the *resources* needed to pursue those opportunities and building an *organisation* to manage those resources.

- The process is *dynamic* with the entrepreneur and the entrepreneurial organisation learning through *success* and *failure*.

- As a style of management, entrepreneurship has much to offer to, and also much to learn from, the management of projects in the not-for-profit, artistic and political arenas.

Suggestions for further reading

Bouchiki, H. (1993) "A constructivist framework for understanding entrepreneurial performance", *Organisation Studies*, Vol. 14, No. 4, pp. 549–70.

Gartner, W.B. (1985) "A conceptual framework for describing the phenomenon of new venture creation", *Academy of Management Review*, Vol. 10, No. 4, pp. 696–706.

Lessem, R. (1978) "Towards the interstices of management: developing the social entrepreneur", *Management Education and Development*, Vol. 9, pp. 178–88.

Hill, R. (1982) "The entrepreneur: an artist masquerading as a businessman?", *International Management,* Vol. 37, No. 2, pp. 21–6.

3 The individual entrepreneur

CHAPTER OVERVIEW

This chapter is concerned with developing a picture of the entrepreneur as an **individual***. It considers the* **type** *of people who chose an entrepreneurial path, the* **characteristics** *successful entrepreneurs bring to the job and the* **skills** *they use. The chapter concludes by emphasising the importance of understanding the entrepreneur in a social setting and the influences exerted by the culture in which they operate.*

3.1   Who becomes an entrepreneur?

KEY LEARNING OUTCOME
A recognition of the kind of people who take up an entrepreneurial career.

The discussion in Chapter 1 should make it clear that we should be very wary of trying to answer the question 'who becomes an entrepreneur?' by looking for a certain type of personality or trying to identify innate characteristics. In these terms, *anyone* can become an entrepreneur. A more fruitful approach is to look at the broader life experience and events which encourage a person to make a move into entrepreneurship. A number of general life stories or 'biographies' can be identified.

The inventor

The *inventor* is someone who has developed a new innovation and who has decided to make a career out of presenting that innovation to the market. The innovation may be a new product or it may be an idea for a new service. It may be high-tech, or it may be based on a traditional technology.

The inventor often draws on technical experience of a particular industry in order to make his or her invention. However, it may be derived from a technology quite unrelated to the industry they work in. It may be based on technical expertise they have gained as the result of a hobby. Alternatively, the invention may result from a 'grey' research programme carried out unofficially within the inventor's employer organisation or it may be the product of a private 'garden shed' development programme.

It is an unfortunate fact of life that, in general, such 'inventors' have a poor track record in building successful businesses. This is not because their ideas are not good: their innovations are often quite valuable. More often, it is due to the fact that no new product, regardless of how many benefits it might potentially bring to the customer, will manufacture and promote itself. Successful entrepreneurship calls upon a wide range of management skills, not just an ability to innovate. The entrepreneur must establish a market potential for their innovation and lead an organisation which can deliver it profitably. They must sell the product to customers and sell the venture to investors. Inventors can often be so impressed with the technical side of their innovation (often justifiably) that they neglect the other tasks that must be undertaken. An example of an inventor who combined technical insight with consummate business skills is James Dyson who built up not one, but two, highly successful businesses to market innovative new products.

The unfulfilled manager

Life as a professional manager in an established organisation brings many rewards. It offers a stable income, intellectual stimulation, status and a degree of security. For many people, though, this is still not enough. The organisation may not offer them a vehicle for all their ambitions: for example, the desire to make a mark on the world, to leave a lasting achievement, to stretch their existing managerial talents to their limit and to develop new ones. It may simply not let them do things *their* way. Such a manager, confident in their abilities and unsatisfied in their ambitions, may decide to embark on an entrepreneurial career.

The question they face is often 'doing what?' The desire and the ability to perform entrepreneurially means nothing if a suitable opportunity has not been spotted and an innovation to take advantage of it developed. In a sense, the unsatisfied manager faces the opposite problem to the inventor: entrepreneurial ability but nothing to apply it to. If they are to be successful they must put effort into identifying and clarifying a business idea and developing an understanding of its market potential. This can often be resolved by working as part of an entrepreneurial team with an inventor who dreams up the initial idea.

The displaced manager

The increasing pace of technological and economic change means that managers are likely to make an increasing number of career changes during their professional lives. Restructuring trends such as 'downsizing' and 'delayering' means unemployment among professional groups is increasing in many parts of the world. This increases the pressure on managers to work for themselves and one possibility is to undertake an entrepreneurial route. The severance package which may be offered by their organisations (often supplemented with training and support) can sometimes facilitate this possibility.

Many managers approach redundancy positively, seeing it as an opportunity to achieve things they could not within the organisation. In effect, they recognise themselves as unfulfilled managers and feel grateful for the push they have been given. Others, however, may not adopt such a positive approach. They may see the uncertainties looming larger than the possibilities. Making entrepreneurship successful is very difficult, if not impossible, unless it is approached with enthusiasm. If a person does not find the prospect of an entrepreneurial career attractive then it is plainly wrong for them. However, one should not underestimate the power of a few early successes to change attitudes and to alter a manager's perception of possibilities.

The young professional

Increasingly, young, highly educated people, often with formal management qualifications, are skipping the experience of working for an established organisation and moving directly to work on establishing their own ventures. Such entrepreneurs are often met with suspicion. There may be a concern that whatever their 'theoretical' knowledge, they lack experience in the realities of business life. While youthful enthusiasm *may* hide a lack of real acumen, the young entrepreneur should not be dismissed out of hand.

In the mature economies of the western world, young entrepreneurs have been disproportionally important in leading *new* industries, particularly in high-tech areas such as computing, information technology and business services. The fast growing emergent economies of the Pacific Rim and the developing world have populations which are generally much younger in profile than those of the west. Entrepreneurs may *have* to be younger if sufficient entrepreneurial talent is to be available to drive the economy's growth. The post-Communist world of eastern and central Europe is currently undergoing a radical economic and social restructuring. To a great extent it is young people who are taking the lead and making the adaptations necessary to take advantage of the new possibilities these changes are offering.

The excluded

Some people turn to an entrepreneurial career because nothing else is open to them. The dynamism and entrepreneurial vigour of displaced communities and ethnic and religious minorities is well documented. This is not because such people are 'inherently' entrepreneurial, rather it is because, for a variety of social, cultural, political and historical reasons, they have not been invited to join the wider economic community. They do not form part of the established network of individuals and organisations. As a result they may form their own internal networks, trading amongst themselves and, perhaps, with their ancestral countries.

Ethnic entrepreneurship can be very important within a national economy. Small communities often make a contribution to the overall entrepreneurial vigour of a country in a way which is quite disproportionate to their number. Nevertheless, one of the main challenges faced by ethnic entrepreneurs is making the move from running a small business to starting a full-blown entrepreneurial venture. This is because to achieve its growth potential the entrepreneurial venture must spread its network of relationships quite widely in order to achieve its growth potential, and this often involves going beyond the confines of the relatively small community in which it starts. In a sense, this goes against the reason for the business coming into existence in the first place. In making the move, the ethnic entrepreneur may face risks that the non-ethnic entrepreneur does not.

There is growing evidence that after a time, say three or four generations, small business managers from ethnic minorities are increasingly willing to make the move to entrepreneurism. In doing so they add another spur to the wider economy.

3.2 Characteristics of the successful entrepreneur

> **KEY LEARNING OUTCOME**
> **A recognition of the characteristics exhibited by successful entrepreneurs.**

Although there does not seem to be a single 'entrepreneurial type' there is a great deal of consistency in the way in which entrepreneurs approach their task. Some of the characteristics which are exhibited by the successful entrepreneur are discussed below. However, we should be careful to draw a distinction between personality 'characteristics' and the character somebody displays when working. The former are regarded as innate, a permanent part of the make-up of their personality. The latter is just the way they approach a particular set of tasks. This is just as much a product of their commitment, interest and motivation to the tasks in hand, as it is a predisposition.

Hard work

Entrepreneurs put a lot of physical and mental effort into developing their ventures. They often work long and anti-social hours. After all, an entrepreneur is their own most valuable asset. That said, balancing the needs of the venture with other life commitments such as family and friends is one of the great challenges which faces the entrepreneur.

Self-starting

Entrepreneurs do not need to be told what to do. They identify tasks for themselves and then follow them through without looking for encouragement or direction from others.

Setting of personal goals

Entrepreneurs tend to set themselves clear, and demanding, goals. They benchmark their achievements against these personal goals. As a result, entrepreneurs tend to work to internal standards rather than look to others for assessment of their performance.

Resilience

Not every thing goes right all the time. In fact, failure may be experienced more often than success. The entrepreneur must not only pick themselves up after things have gone wrong but learn positively from the experience and use that learning to increase the chances of success the next time around.

Confidence

The entrepreneur must demonstrate that they not only believe in themselves but also in the venture they are pursuing. After all, if they don't, who will?

Receptiveness to new ideas

However, the entrepreneur must not be *overly* confident. They must recognise their own limitations and the possibilities that they have to improve their skills. They must be willing to revise their ideas in the light of new experience. One of the main reasons that banks and venture capitalists give for *not* supporting a business proposal is that the entrepreneur was *too* sure of themselves to be receptive to good advice when it was offered.

Assertiveness

Entrepreneurs are usually clear as to what they want to gain from a situation and are not frightened to express their wishes. Being assertive does not mean being aggressive! Nor does it mean adopting a position and refusing to budge. Assertiveness means a commitment to *outcomes*, not *means*. True assertiveness relies on mutual understanding and is founded on good communication skills.

Information seeking

Entrepreneurs are not, on average, any more intelligent than any other group. They are, however, characterised by *inquisitiveness*. They are never satisfied by the information they have at any one time and constantly seek more. Good entrepreneurs tend to question rather more than they make statements when communicating.

Eager to learn

Good entrepreneurs are always aware that they could do things better. They are aware of both the skills they have and their limitations, and are always receptive to a chance to improve their skills and to develop new ones.

Attuned to opportunity

The good entrepreneur is constantly searching for new opportunities. In effect, this means that he or she is never really satisfied with the way things are any moment in time. The entrepreneur uses this sense of dissatisfaction to make sure he or she never becomes complacent.

Receptive to change

The entrepreneur is always willing to embrace change in a positive fashion, that is to actively embrace the possibilities presented by change rather than resist them.

Commitment to others

Good entrepreneurs are not selfish. They cannot afford to be! They recognise the value that other people bring to their ventures and the importance of motivating those people to make the best effort they can on its behalf. This means showing a commitment to them. Motivation demands an investment in understanding how people think. Leadership is not just about giving people jobs to do; it is also about offering them the support they need in order to do those jobs.

Comfort with power

Entrepreneurs can become very powerful figures. They can have a great impact on the life of other people. Power can be one of the great motivators for the entrepreneur. Effective entrepreneurs are *aware* of the power they possess and recognise it as an asset. They are not afraid to use it and never let themselves be intimidated by it. However, the *true* entrepreneur uses power responsibly, as a means to an end and not as an end in itself.

3.3 Entrepreneurial skills

KEY LEARNING OUTCOME
A recognition of the skills which enhance entrepreneurial performance.

A skill is simply knowledge which is demonstrated by action. It is an ability to perform in a certain way. An entrepreneur is someone who has a good business idea and can turn that idea into reality. To be successful, an entrepreneur must not only identify an opportunity but also understand it in great depth. He or she must be able to spot a gap in the market and recognise what new product or service will fill that gap. He or she must know what features it will have and why they will appeal to the customer. The entrepreneur must also know how to inform the customer about it and how to deliver the new offering. All of this calls for an intimate knowledge of a particular sector of industry. Turning an idea into reality calls upon two sorts of skill. General management skills are required to organise the physical and financial resources needed to run the venture and people management skills are needed to obtain the necessary support from others for the venture to succeed.

Some important general management business skills include:

- *Strategy skills* – An ability to consider the business as a whole, to understand how it fits within its marketplace, how it can organise itself to deliver value to its customers, and the ways in which it does this better than its competitors.
- *Planning skills* – An ability to consider what the future might offer, how it will impact on the business and what needs to be done to prepare for it now.
- *Marketing skills* – An ability to see past the firm's offerings and their features, to be able to see *how* they satisfy the customer's needs and *why* the customer finds them attractive.

- *Financial skills* – An ability to manage money; to be able to keep track of expenditure and to monitor cash-flow, but also an ability to assess investments in terms of their potential and their risks.
- *Project management skills* – An ability to organise projects, to set specific objectives, to set schedules and to ensure that the necessary resources are in the right place at the right time.
- *Time management skills* – An ability to use time productively, to be able to prioritise important jobs and to get things done to schedule.

Businesses are made by people. A business can only be successful if the people who make it up are properly directed and are committed to make an effort on its behalf. An entrepreneurial venture also needs the support of people from outside the organisation such as customers, suppliers and investors. To be effective, an entrepreneur needs to demonstrate a wide variety of skills in the way he or she deals with other people. Some of the more important skills we might include under this heading are:

- *Leadership skills* – An ability to inspire people to work in a specific way and to undertake the tasks that are necessary for the success of the venture. Leadership is about more than merely directing people; it is also about supporting them and helping them to achieve the goals they have been set.
- *Motivation skills* – An ability to enthuse people and get them to give their full commitment to the tasks in hand. Being able to motivate demands an understanding of what drives people and what they expect from their jobs. It should not be forgotten that, for the entrepreneur, an ability to motivate oneself is as important as an ability to motivate others.
- *Delegation skills* – An ability to allocate tasks to different people. Effective delegation involves more than instructing. It demands a full understanding of the skills that people possess, how they use them and how they might be developed to fulfil future needs.
- *Communication skills* – An ability to use spoken and written language to express ideas and inform others. Good communication is about more than just passing information. It is about using language to influence people's actions.
- *Negotiation skills* – An ability to understand what is wanted from a situation, what is motivating others in that situation and recognise the possibilities of maximising the outcomes for all parties. Being a good negotiator is more about being able to identify win-win scenarios and communicate them, than it is about being able to 'bargain hard'.

All of these different people skills are interrelated. Good leadership demands being able to motivate. Effective delegation requires an ability to communicate. The skills needed to deal with people are not innate, they must be learnt. Leadership is as much an acquired skill as is an ability to plan effectively. The ability to motivate and to negotiate can be learnt in the same way as project management techniques.

Entrepreneurial performance results from a combination of *industry knowledge, general management skills, people skills* and *personal motivation* (*see* Fig. 3.1). The successful entrepreneur must not only use these skills but learn to use them and to learn from using them. Entrepreneurs should constantly audit their abilities in these areas, recognise their strengths and shortcomings, and plan how to develop these skills in the future.

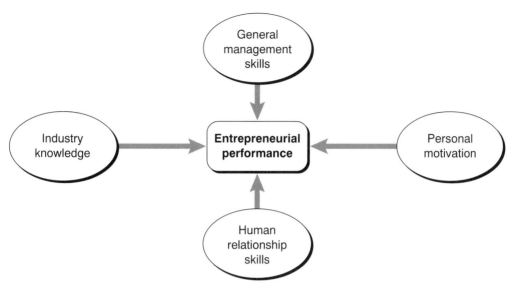

Fig. 3.1 Factors influencing entrepreneurial performance

3.4 Entrepreneurship and culture

KEY LEARNING OUTCOME
A recognition that the behaviour of entrepreneurs is influenced by a wide range of cultural and social factors.

Entrepreneurs are not robots blindly fulfilling an economic function. They cannot pursue opportunities, or strive for economic efficiency without exhibiting some concern for wider issues. Entrepreneurs are human beings operating within societies which define, and are defined by, cultures. Clearly, an American entrepreneur tends to act differently to a Japanese one who, in turn, behaves differently to a Peruvian one. There are not only great differences *between* these cultures which influence the way entrepreneurs work, there is also a wide variety of ways in which *individual* entrepreneurs work *within* these cultures. Culture is expressed in both the value *judgements* an individual makes and the value *system* of their wider community.

The analysis of culture falls properly within the domain of anthropology. The insights gained by anthropologists are of increasing interest to those who study business behaviour and performance. One of the driving forces behind this growth in interest has been the impressive economic growth achieved by countries in various parts of the world. Of particular interest at present are the 'tiger' economies of the Pacific Rim. The contribution that a range of structural, social and cultural factors have made to their success is widely debated.

An analysis of culture is not a straightforward matter since a culture is not something that can be placed under a microscope. It is something we construct in order to explain the world rather than something we experience directly. There is a gulf between those who think that a culture can be examined as an objective reality and those who think it must be interpreted as something that impresses on our experience at a personal level. There is not scope within this book to consider all of these issues. We must be content to note that entrepreneurs are necessarily the product of their cultures and that their cultures mould and influence their actions. What follows is meant to give a flavour of the *factors* which are significant to understanding entrepreneurship in a cultural setting and how they might be approached.

Religious beliefs

Religious belief is a very important factor in shaping a culture. It leads to a view of the world which will influence the individual's approach to entrepreneurship. The sociologist Max Weber famously associated the industrial revolution in western Europe and America with the attitudes engendered by Protestant religious beliefs known as the 'Protestant work ethic'. Modern commentators speculate on the influence of Confucian 'discipline' to the success of Asian economies.

Personal relationships

The type and scope of personal relationships that a culture encourages will be a critical factor in the way entrepreneurial behaviour is expressed. A very important study by the Dutch sociologist of business, Geert Hofstede, analysed human relationships along four dimensions:

(i) *Power distance*: the degree of authority people expect between managers and subordinates, and their willingness to accept that power is not distributed equally.
(ii) *Uncertainty avoidance*: in essence, this is the desire to be in a situation where uncertainty is minimised. Its opposite is a willingness to take risks.
(iii) *Collectivity*: the need to feel that one is part of a group and that one's actions are sanctioned by that wider group. Its opposite is a desire to exhibit individualistic behaviour.
(iv) *Masculinity*: the degree to which the culture emphasises 'masculine' values such as the acquisition of money, prioritising the material over the spiritual, a lack of concern versus a caring attitude, *etc*.

These four factors give a good account of how attitudes towards personal relationships give rise to different styles of entrepreneurial behaviour over a wide range of national cultures.

Attitude towards innovation

Innovation lies at the heart of entrepreneurship, yet to believe in innovation we have to see the world in a certain sort of way. We have to believe in a future which will be *different* to the present. We have to believe that we can act so as to *influence* the world and change it by our actions. Further, if we are to be encouraged to innovate, we must believe that it is appropriate that we are *rewarded* for our efforts in developing innovation.

Many western Europeans will regard these things as 'obvious'. However, they are beliefs which are sensitive to culture. While a western European sees the future as something which brings uncertainties 'towards' them, many cultures, for example, some in west Africa, have a different perspective. They draw a distinction between a 'potential time' which is full of things that *must* happen and a 'no-time' of things which might or might not happen. The potential time is *here and now*, a part of the present whereas no-time is not really a part of time at all. From this perspective, there really is no such thing as the 'future'.

Even if we believe in a future we may not believe that we can influence it. Physical science has often emphasised that the future is *determined*. Marxism is founded on a belief that the world evolves along a pre-destined path. If an innovation occurs, it occurs because it was meant to occur. Hence, it is not the result of personal inventiveness which might *not* have occurred, and if this is so, why then should we reward the innovator? The entrepreneurship scholar Mark Casson has suggested that such a cultural perspective might be significant to the development of entre-preneurship in the post-Communist world.

Networks

A network is the framework of individual and organisational relationships which form the stage upon which entrepreneurial performance is played. It is composed of personal and social contacts as well as economic relationships. A network is shaped by the culture in which it is formed.

The network does not just provide a route for people to sell things to each other. It is a conduit for information. A well developed network is crucial if entrepreneurial behaviour is to express itself. It defines the terrain in which new business opportunities might be identified and assessed, and it provides a means by which contracts are agreed and risk might be evaluated and shared. It offers an escape route for people who do not think their investments are safe. This occurs not only through formal structures such as stock markets but also through informal confidences and relationships. The structure and functioning of such networks is sensitive to a wide range of cultural factors.

It is neither possible nor particularly useful to draw hard and fast rules about managing within a particular culture. However, the idea of culture provides a perspective and might suggest an approach. The entrepreneur must recognise that an individual's response to a particular situation will, to some extent, be shaped by cultural influences. This will affect the way they can be led and motivated. However, the entrepreneur must not forget that individuals are individuals with their own characteristics, and do not necessarily behave with a collective consciousness. Entrepreneurs will also recognise that their own decision making is the product of their cultural experiences. Recognition of these things is becoming increasingly important as the opportunities for entrepreneurial ventures become ever more international. In the global arena, the effective entrepreneur learns to use cultural differences to advantage rather than to be impeded by them.

Entrepreneurs who have built global concerns such as Rupert Murdoch (*News International*) and Rowland 'Tiny' Rowland (*Lonhro*) are renowned for their ability not just to manage people within one culture but to manage across cultures.

Summary of key ideas

- A wide variety of people can become entrepreneurs. Common backgrounds include inventors with new business ideas; managers unfulfilled by working in established organisations; displaced managers; and people excluded from the established economy.

- Whatever their background, successful entrepreneurs are characterised by being hard working and self-starting; setting high personal goals; having resilience and confidence in their abilities; being receptive to new ideas and being assertive in presenting them; being attuned to new opportunities, receptive to change and eager to learn; and being confident with power and demonstrating a commitment to others.

- Effective entrepreneurs use a variety of formal management skills combined with industry knowledge and personal motivation.

- The way entrepreneurs actually manage their ventures is dependent on the culture in which they operate. Good entrepreneurs are sensitive to cultural values.

Suggestions for further reading

Casson, M. (1994) "Enterprise culture and institutional change in eastern Europe", in Buckley, P.J. and Ghauri, P.N. (ed.), *The Economics of Change in East and Central Europe*, London: Academic Press.

Drucker, P.F. (1985) "The discipline of innovation", *Harvard Business Review*, May-June, pp. 67–72.

Hisrich, R.D. and **Brush, C.** (1986) "Characteristics of the minority entrepreneur", *Journal of Small Business Management*, Oct, pp. 1–8

Hofstede, G. (1980) *Culture's Consequences: International Differences in Work-Related Values*, London: Sage Publications.

Hofstede, G. (1980) "Motivation, leadership and organisation: do American theories apply abroad?", *Organisational Dynamics*, Summer, pp. 42–63.

Jones-Evans, D. (1996) "Technical entrepreneurship, strategy and experience", *International Small Business Journal*, Vol. 14, No. 3, pp. 15–39 .

McClelland, D.C. and **Burnham, D.H.** (1976) "Power is the great motivator", *Harvard Business Review*, Mar-Apr, pp. 100–10.

McClelland, D.C. (1987) "Characteristics of successful entrepreneurs", *The Journal of Creative Behaviour*, Vol. 21, No. 3, pp. 219–33.

Morden, T. (1995) "International culture and management", *Management Decision*, Vol. 33, No. 2, pp. 16–21.

Olson, S.F. and **Currie, H.M.** (1992) "Female entrepreneurs: Personal value systems and business strategies in a male dominated industry", *Journal Of Small Business Management,* January, pp. 49–57.

Phizacklea, A. and **Ram, M.** (1995) "Ethnic entrepreneurship in comparative perspective", *International Journal of Entrepreneurial Behaviour and Research*, Vol. 1, No. 1, pp. 48–58.

Sui, Wai-Sum and **Martin, R.G.** (1992) "Successful entrepreneurship in Hong Kong", *Long Range Planning*, Vol. 25, No. 6, pp. 87–93.

Williams, A. (1985) "Stress and the entrepreneurial role", *International Small Business Journal*, Vol. 3, No. 4, pp. 11–25.

4

Making the move to entrepreneurship

CHAPTER OVERVIEW

This chapter is concerned with an exploration of the economic, social and personal factors which encourage an individual to pursue an entrepreneurial career.

4.1   The supply of entrepreneurs

KEY LEARNING OUTCOME
An understanding of the forces which encourage and inhibit entrepreneurship.

If we look at any of the world's economies we will see a certain number of entrepreneurs operating within them. The exact number will depend on how we define entrepreneurship, but their importance to the economy within which they operate will be evident. They will be responsible for providing economic efficiency and bringing new innovations to the market. In mature economies, such as western Europe and North America they are responsible for most new job creation. In the former communist world, the emergence of an entrepreneurial class is a necessary prelude to establishing a market-driven economic order. The question is, what governs the number of entrepreneurs who will emerge at any given time?

If we assume that entrepreneurs are born, or that entrepreneurship is the result of inherent personality characteristics, then the supply of entrepreneurs must be fixed. The number will depend on the number of people who are impelled to pursue an entrepreneurial career. This might reflect deep-rooted cultural factors but it will be largely independent of external influences. On the other hand, if we assume that entrepreneurs are managers who have freely decided to become entrepreneurs, then the number of entrepreneurs at any one time will be sensitive to a variety of external factors.

A simple approach to explaining this uses a model in which there are two pools of labour: a *conventional* labour pool in which people take up paid employment, and an *entrepreneurial* pool in which people are pursuing an entrepreneurial career. Such a model assumes that there is a clear definition of what constitutes entrepreneurship and that it is distinct from 'ordinary' labour. These assumptions, while clearly artificial, do serve to make the model simpler. However, they can be relaxed and more complex models developed to reflect reality more closely. These more complex models still work on the same basic premise. Managers are assumed to make a choice between the two options: a 'conventional' career *versus* an 'entrepreneurial' one (*see* Fig. 4.1). The process of moving from the conventional labour pool to the entrepreneurial pool is known as *start-up*. The reverse process of moving from the entrepreneurial pool back to the conventional labour pool is *fall-out*. The choice will depend on the relative attractiveness of the two options as perceived by the individual manager.

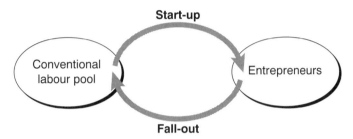

Fig. 4.1 The dynamics of entrepreneurial supply

Two forces are said to work driving the manager from the conventional labour pool to the entrepreneurial: pull factors and push factors. *Pull factors* are those which encourage managers to become entrepreneurs by virtue of the *attractiveness* of the entrepreneurial option. Some important pull factors include:

● the financial rewards of entrepreneurship;
● the freedom to work for oneself;
● the sense of achievement to be gained from running one's own venture;
● the freedom to pursue a personal innovation;
● a desire to gain the social standing achieved by entrepreneurs.

Push factors, on the other hand, are those which encourage entrepreneurship by making the conventional option *less attractive*. Push factors include:

● the limitations of financial rewards from conventional jobs;
● being unemployed in the established economy;
● job insecurity;
● career limitations and setbacks in a conventional job;
● the inability to pursue a personal innovation in a conventional job;
● being a 'misfit' in an established organisation.

The number of entrepreneurs operating at any one time will depend on the strength of the pull and push forces. If they are strong, then a large number of entrepreneurs will emerge. However, the supply of entrepreneurs will still be limited if *inhibitors* are operating. Inhibitors are things which prevent the potential entrepreneur from following an entrepreneurial route, no matter how attractive an option it might appear. Some important inhibitors include an inability to get hold of start-up capital; the high cost of start-up capital; the business environment presents high risks; legal restrictions on business activity; a lack of training for entrepreneurs; a feeling that the role of entrepreneur has a poor image; a lack of suitable human resources and personal inertia. Politicians and economic policy makers increasingly put the elimination of inhibitors to entrepreneurism at the top of their agenda. This is because they recognise the importance of increasing the number of entrepreneurs within the economy to stimulate growth. Figure 4.2 indicates the type of factors operating on managers considering a move to entrepreneurship.

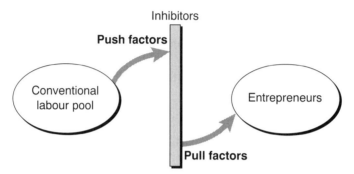

Fig. 4.2 Factors in entrepreneurial supply

4.2   Influences in the move to entrepreneurship

KEY LEARNING OUTCOME
An understanding of the factors involved in making the decision to become an entrepreneur

Whatever the forces acting on the labour market to encourage entrepreneurship the decision to become an entrepreneur is an individual and personal one. We need to understand the factors involved in driving and shaping that decision in order to understand entrepreneurs. We are all active in an economy because we seek the rewards it brings. However, an economy is part of a wider pattern of social life and, although money is important, we seek more than purely financial rewards from the world in which we live. The decision to pursue an entrepreneurial career reflects a choice about the possibility of achieving satisfaction for a variety of economic and social needs.

We might classify the needs of individuals under three broad headings.

(i) *Economic needs*. These include the requirement to earn a particular amount of money and the need for that income to be stable and predictable. The amount desired will reflect the need for economic survival, existing commitments such as the home and family, and the pursuit of personal interests.

(ii) *Social needs.* These represent the desire a person has to be a part of, and to fit into, a wider group and their desire to be recognised and respected within that group. The satisfaction of social needs is reflected in the creation and maintenance of friendships and other social relationships.

(iii) *Developmental needs.* These relate to the desire a person has to achieve personal goals and to grow intellectually or spiritually.

A manager seeking to satisfy these needs is faced with a number of possibilities. There may be a choice between two or more conventional career options as well as the possibility of pursuing an entrepreneurial career. The entrepreneurial career itself may present itself in a number of ways. The manager's decision on which path to take will be based on the potential each option has to satisfy the needs they perceive for themselves (*see* Table 4.1). If the entrepreneurial route is seen to offer the best means of satisfying them then this will be chosen. However, making the move between different options will be sensitive to four factors: *knowledge* of entrepreneurial options open, the *possibility* for achieving them, the *risks* they present and *valence* – the way in which the potential entrepreneur is willing to play off different needs against each other. Figure 4.3 represents a model of the factors involved in making the move to entrepreneurship.

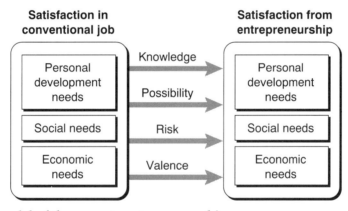

Fig. 4.3 A model of the move to entrepreneurship

Knowledge

The individual must *know* that the entrepreneurial option exists and they must be *aware* of its *potential*. In the case of establishing an entrepreneurial venture, the manager must be aware of a particular business opportunity and have an idea how it might be exploited profitably. After all, the desire to be entrepreneurial must be expressed through the actuality of running a *specific* business venture. It cannot exist in a vacuum.

Possibility

The individual must have the *possibility* of pursuing that option. This means that there must be no legal restrictions on them undertaking the venture (as there was in the former Communist bloc, for example). They must also have access to the necessary resources: start-up funding, human resources and access to the established network. Finally, they must have (or at least feel that they have) the necessary experience and skills in order to make a success of the venture.

Risk

The entrepreneur may have a detailed knowledge of a business opportunity and access to the resources necessary to initiate it. However, the entrepreneur will only make the move if the *risks* are seen as being acceptable. The entrepreneur must be comfortable with the level of risk the venture will entail, and he or she must be sure that the potential rewards are such that it is worth taking the risk. It is useful to distinguish between the *actual* level of risk in the venture, and the level of risk that is *perceived* by the entrepreneur. These may be quite different. Entrepreneurs can often be over-confident and under assess risk. In addition to convincing themselves, entrepreneurs

Table 4.1 A comparison between the potential of entrepreneurial and conventional careers for satisfying economic, social and personal development needs.

	Entrepreneurial career	Conventional career
Economic needs	Can offer the possibility of high financial rewards in the long term.	Financial rewards typically lower, but secure and predictable.
	However, income may be low in early stages and risks are high.	Risks are relatively low.
Social needs	Entrepreneur creates organisational change.	Established organisation usually provides good stage for making social relationships.
	A great deal of freedom to create and control network of social relationships.	However, manager may have only limited scope to control potential of social relationships formed.
	Social status of the entrepreneur usually high.	Social status of manager variable.
Personal development needs	Entrepreneur in control of own destiny.	Good potential to pursue personal development.
	Possibility of creating an 'entire new world'.	However, the direction of personal development may need to be compromised to overall organisational objectives and values.
	Venture may be powerful vehicle for personal development and expression of personal values. However, this is dependent on success of venture.	Career options limited and subject to internal competition.

must convince any investors asked to back the venture that the risks are of an acceptable level.

Valence

The conventional career option and the option to start an entrepreneurial venture do not offer separate opportunities to satisfy economic, social and developmental needs, rather they offer a different *mix* of opportunities. The final factor which will influence the option selected is *valence*, that is the way we are attracted to different options.

Different people are willing to play-off different needs against one other in different ways. While many people 'play safe' and give priority to economic needs, by no means everyone does so. Some people prioritise social needs. Thus they may continue to work in an organisation they enjoy, with people they like, even though the option to move to a higher paid job elsewhere is available to them. The artist starving in a garret or the religious aesthete are pursuing the need for personal development even though it is causing them economic hardship. Similarly, the entrepreneur may be so drawn to the possibilities of personal development offered by the entrepreneurial option, that they will pursue it even though it carries greater economic risks and perhaps, for the foreseeable future, a lower income than a conventional managerial career that is available to them.

Summary of key ideas

- The supply of entrepreneurs is determined by three sets of factors, namely *pull factors* which promote entrepreneurship as a positive option; *push factors* which drive people out of the established economy; and *inhibitors* which prevent the entrepreneurial option being taken up.

- Managers make the move to entrepreneurship after considering the way the option for an entrepreneurial career can satisfy *economic*, *social* and *self-development* needs.

Suggestions for further reading

Dandridge, T.C. and **Dziedziczak, I.** (1992) "New private enterprise in the new Poland: Heritage of the past and challenges for the future", *Journal of Small Business Management*, Apr, pp. 104–9.

El-Namaki, M.S.S. (1988) "Encouraging entrepreneurs in developing countries", *Long Range Planning*, Vol. 21, No. 4, pp. 98–106.

Gallagher, C. and **Miller, P.** (1991) "New fast-growing companies create jobs", *Long Range Planning*, Vol. 24, No. 1, pp. 96–101.

Gilad, B. and **Levine, P.** (1986) "A behavioural model of entrepreneurial supply", *Journal of Small Business Management*, Oct, pp. 45–53.

Kiselev, D. (1990) "New forms of entrepreneurship in the USSR", *Journal of Small Business Management*, July, pp. 76–80.

5 The nature of business opportunity

CHAPTER OVERVIEW

*This chapter presents an examination of the starting point for the entrepreneurial process, that is the **business opportunity**. Entrepreneurs are **motivated** by the pursuit of opportunity. A analogy is developed through which a business opportunity can be pictured as a gap in the landscape created by existing business activities. The different types of **innovation** that can fill that gap and so offer a means of **exploiting** opportunity are considered. It is recognised that exploiting opportunities creates new **wealth** which can be **distributed** to the venture's stakeholders.*

5.1 The landscape of business opportunity

KEY LEARNING OUTCOME
An understanding of what comprises a business opportunity.

All living systems have *needs*. At a minimum, animals need food and oxygen, plants need sunlight and water. Human beings are different to many living organisms in that we are not content simply to survive using the things nature places to hand. We build highly structured societies and within these societies we join together to create *organisations*. Human organisations take on a variety of forms. However, they all exist to co-ordinate *tasks*. This co-ordination allows people to specialise their activities and to collaborate in the production of a wide variety of *goods* (a word taken to mean both physical products and services). Goods have *utility* because they can satisfy human needs. The products produced in the modern world can be used to satisfy a much more sophisticated range of human wants and needs, and to satisfy them more proficiently than can the raw materials to be found in nature.

An organisation is an arrangement of *relationships* in that it exists in the spaces between people. Organisations exist to address human needs. Their effectiveness in doing this is a function of the form adopted by the organisation and the way it works. As the number of people involved increases, so too do the ways of organising them. In fact, the possibilities quickly become astronomical. This leads to a simple conclusion: whatever the organisational arrangement is at the moment, there is probably a *better* way of doing things! Even if, by chance, we did find the optimum arrangement, it would not stay static for long. Technological progress would quickly change the rules.

Ideas from classical economics suggest that the optimal (that is the most productive) organisation is one in which individuals work to maximise their own satisfaction from the goods available and freely exchange those goods between themselves. Such behaviour is said to be *economically rational*. While this provides a very powerful framework for thinking about economic relations it is clearly only an approximation. People gain satisfaction from a variety of things, not all are exchanged through markets (how much does a beautiful sunset, or a personal sense of achievement 'cost'?). Nor is it obviously the case that individuals will maximise their own utility without any consideration towards their fellows. We can, and often do, act from altruistic motives.

Even if we *wanted* to act rationally, we probably could not. We simply do not have access to the information we would need to make decisions on purely rational lines. If all the information *were* available, individuals would still be limited in their ability to process and analyse it. In response to this, some economists talk of *satisficing* behaviour. That is, individuals aim to make the best decision available given a desire to address a wider sphere of concerns than purely economic self-satisfaction and taking into account limitations in knowledge.

An opportunity, then, is the possibility to do things both *differently* and *better* than how they are being done at the moment. In economic terms, *differently* means an innovation has been made. This might take the form of offering a new product or of organising the company in a different way. *Better* means the product offers a utility in terms of an ability to satisfy human needs, that existing products do not. The new organisational form must be more *productive*, i.e. more efficient at using resources, than existing organisational forms. Yet, the decisions as to what is different and whether it is better are not made by economic robots. Both entrepreneurs and the consumers who buy what they offer, are social beings who engage in satisficing behaviour. They must also base their decisions on the knowledge they have to hand, and their ability to use it. Furthermore, they make their decisions while following the rules they have laid down for themselves and the rules of the culture that shapes their lives.

We may think of business opportunity as being rather like a *landscape* representing the possibilities open to us. As we look across the landscape we will see open ground, untouched and full of new potential. We may see areas which are built up, leaving few new opportunities to be exploited. We will see other areas which are built up but where the buildings are old and decrepit, waiting to be pulled down, and something new built in their places. Effective entrepreneurs know the landscape they are operating in. They know where the spaces are and how they fit between the built up areas. They know which buildings can be pulled down and which are best left standing. Critically, they know where to move in and build themselves.

5.2   Innovation and the exploitation of opportunity

KEY LEARNING OUTCOME
An appreciation that innovation is the key to exploiting opportunity.

A business opportunity, therefore, is the *chance* to do something differently and better. An innovation is a *way* of doing something differently and better. Thus an innovation is a *means* of exploiting a business opportunity. Innovation has a definite meaning in economics. All goods (whether physical products or services) are regarded as being made up of three factors: *natural raw materials*, *physical and mental labour* and *capital* (money). An innovation is a new combination of these three things. Entrepreneurs, as innovators, are people who create new combinations of these factors and then present them to the market for assessment by consumers. This is a technical conceptualisation of what innovation is about. It does not give the practising entrepreneur much of a guide to what innovation to make, or how to make it, but it should warn that innovation is a much broader concept than just *inventing* new products. It also involves bringing them to market. Some important areas in which valuable innovations might be made will be discussed below.

New products

One of the most common forms of innovation is the creation of a new product. The new product may exploit an established technology or it may be the outcome of a whole new technology. The new product may offer a radically new way of doing something or it may simply be an improvement on an existing theme. David Packard built a scientific instrumentation and information processing business empire, *Hewlett-Packard*, based on advanced scientific developments. Frank Purdue (founder of the major US food business *Purdue Chickens*) on the other hand, built his business by innovating in an industry whose basic product was centuries, if not millennia old: the farmed chicken. Whatever the basis of innovation, the new product must offer the customer an *advantage* if it is to be successful: a better way of performing a task, or of solving a problem, or a better quality product.

Products are not simply a physical tool for achieving particular ends. They can also have a role to play in satisfying *emotional* needs. *Branding* is an important aspect of this. A brand name reassures the consumer, draws ready-made associations for them and provides a means of making a personal statement. The possibility of innovations being made through branding should not be overlooked. The English entrepreneur, Richard Branson, for example, has been active in using the *Virgin* brand name on a wide variety of product areas following its initial success in the airline business. To date, it has been used to create a point of difference on, among other things, record labels, soft drinks and personal finance products.

New services

A service is an *act* which is offered to undertake a particular task or solve a particular problem. Services are open to the possibility of new ideas and innovation just as much as physical products. For example, the American entrepreneur, Frederick Smith, created the multi-million dollar international business, *Federal Express*, by realising a better way of moving parcels between people.

Like physical products, services can be supported by the effective use of branding. In fact, it is beneficial to stop thinking about 'products' and 'services' as distinct types of business and to recognise that *all* offerings have product and service aspects. This is important because it is possible to innovate by adding a 'customer service' component to a physical product to make it more attractive to the user. Similarly, developments in product technology allow new service concepts to be innovated.

New production techniques

Innovation can be made in the way in which a product is manufactured. Again, this might be by developing an existing technology or by adopting a new technological approach. A new production technique provides a sound basis for success if it can be made to offer the end-user new benefits. It must either allow them to obtain the product at lower cost, or to be offered a product of higher or more consistent quality, or to be given a better service in the supply of the product. An important example here is Rupert Murdoch's drive for change in the way newspapers were produced in the 1980s. Production is not just about technology. Increasingly new production 'philosophies' such as just-in-time supply (JIT) and total quality management (TQM) are providing platforms for profitable innovation.

New operating practices

Services are delivered by operating practices which are, to some extent, routinised. These routines provide a great deal of potential for entrepreneurial innovation. Ray Kroc, the founder of *McDonald's*, for example, noted the advantages to be gained in standardising fast-food preparation. As with innovations in the production of physical products, innovation in service delivery must address customer needs and offer them improved benefits, for example easier access to the service, a higher quality service, a more consistent service, a faster or less time-consuming service, a less disruptive service.

New ways of delivering the product or service to the customer

Customers can only use products and services they can access. Consequently, getting distribution right is an essential element in business success. It is also something which offers a great deal of potential for innovation. This may involve the *route* taken (the path the product takes from the producer to the user), or the *means* of managing its journey.

A common innovation is to take a more direct route, by cutting out distributors or middle men. A number of successful entrepreneurial ventures have been established on the basis of getting goods directly to the customer. This may be an indirect way into high street retailing, for example Richard Thalheimer in the US with *The Sharper Image* catalogue or the *Littlewoods* chain in the UK. Another approach is to focus the distribution chain and specialise in a particular range of goods. This type of 'category busting' focus has allowed Charles Lazarus to build the toy retail outlet *Toys "Я" Us* into a worldwide concern.

New means of informing the customer about the product

People will only use a product or service if they *know* about it. Demand will not exist if the offering is not properly promoted to them. Promotion consists of two parts: a *message*, what is said, and a *means*, the route by which that message is delivered. Both the message and the means present latitude for inventiveness in the way they are approached. Communicating with customers can be expensive and entrepreneurs, especially when their ventures are in an early stage, rarely have the resources to invest in high profile advertising and public relations campaigns. Therefore, they are encouraged to develop new means of promoting their products.

Many entrepreneurs have proved to be particularly skilful at getting 'free' publicity. Anita and Gordon Roddick, for example, have used very little formal advertising for their toiletries retailer the *Body Shop*. However, the approach adopted by the organisation, and its stated corporate values, have made sure that the *Body Shop* has featured prominently in the widespread commentary on corporate responsibility that has regularly appeared in the media. As a result, awareness of their organisation is high and consumer attitudes towards it are positive.

New ways of managing relationships within the organisation

Any organisation has a wide variety of communication channels running through it. The performance of the organisation will depend to a great extent on the effectiveness of its internal communication channels. These communication channels are guided (formally at least) by the organisation's *structure*. The structure of the organisation offers considerable scope for value creating innovations. Of particular note here is the development of the *franchise* as an organisational form. This structure, which combines the advantages of small business ownership with the power of integrated global organisation has been a major factor in the growth of many entrepreneurial ventures, including the *Body Shop* retail chain, the *Holiday Inn* hotel group and the *McDonald's* fast food chain.

New ways of managing relationships between organisations

Organisations sit in a complex web of relationships to each other. The way they communicate and relate to each other is very important. Many entrepreneurial organisations have made innovation in the way in which they work with other organisations (particularly customers) into a key part of their strategy. The business services sector has been particularly active in this respect.

The advertising agency *Saatchi and Saatchi*, founded by the brothers Charles and Maurice in 1970, did not build its success solely on the back of making good advertisements. The brothers also realised that managing the relationship with the client was important. An advertising agency is, in a sense, a supplier of a service like any other, but its 'product' is highly complex, expensive and its potential to generate business for the client is unpredictable. Thus advertising is a high risk activity. The brothers realised that if advertising were to be managed properly, the agency had to become an integral part of the management team within the client organisation and work with them at resolving the issues generated by advertising, as well as helping them to exploit its potential. In effect, they broke down the barrier between their organisation and their customers.

Multiple innovation

An entrepreneurial venture does not have to restrict itself to just one innovation or even one type of innovation. Success can be built on a *combination* of innovations: for example, a new product delivered in a new way with a new message.

5.3   Opportunity and entrepreneurial motivation

> KEY LEARNING OUTCOME
> **An understanding of how the effective entrepreneur is motivated by business opportunity.**

Thus an opportunity is a gap in a market or the possibility of doing something both differently and better; and an innovation presents a means of filling that market gap, that is a way of pursuing the opportunity. Such definitions, while they capture the *nature* of opportunity and innovation from both an economic and a managerial perspective, do little to relate the *way* in which opportunity figures in the working life of the entrepreneur. Opportunity *motivates* entrepreneurs. Therefore, it is the thing that attracts their attention and draws their actions. But good entrepreneurs are not blindly subject to opportunity; they take control of them. It is important to understand how entrepreneurs should relate to business opportunities and allow themselves to be motivated by them.

Entrepreneurs are attuned to opportunity

Entrepreneurs are always on the look-out for opportunities. They scan the business landscape looking for new ways of creating value. As we have seen, this value can take the form of new wealth, a chance to pursue an agenda of personal development or to create social change. Opportunities are the 'raw material' out of which the entrepreneur creates an 'entire new world'. To be motivated by opportunity entails the recognition that the current situation does not represent the best way of doing things; that the *status quo* does not exhaust possibilities. While this may be a spur to move forward, it could also create motivational problems. If we are too conscious of *what might be*, do we not become disillusioned with *what is*? Can the entrepreneur ever get where he or she is going?

There is no simple answer to this question. There are certainly some entrepreneurs who are driven forward because they are not satisfied with the present. However, many, while not losing their motivation for what might be, are still able to enjoy what is. Some gain satisfaction, not from reaching the end-points of their activity, but in the *journey* itself. Others make sure they create space for themselves to take pride in what they have achieved, as well as looking forward to what they might achieve. Entrepreneurs must be aware of their motivation. As well as knowing *what* they want to achieve they must be aware of *why* they want to achieve it and why they will enjoy the *process* of achieving it.

Opportunity must take priority over innovation

It is easy to get excited over a new idea. However, an innovation, no matter how good it is, should be secondary to the market opportunity that it aims to exploit. The best ideas are those which are inspired by a clear need in the marketplace rather than those that result from uninformed invention. Many innovations which have been 'pushed' by new product or service possibilities rather than 'pulled' by unsatisfied customer needs have gone on to be successful. However, without a clear understanding of why customers buy and what they are looking for, this can be a very hit-or-miss process. Mistakes are punished quickly and they can be expensive. Failure is certainly demotivating, but this is not to suggest that new product ideas should necessarily be rejected. It does mean that they provide the inspiration to assess their market potential, not to rush the idea straight into the market.

Identifying real opportunities demands knowledge

One of the misconceptions that many people entertain about entrepreneurs is that they are the 'wanderers' of the business world. The notion that they drift between industries, opportunistically picking-off the best ideas missed by less astute and responsive 'residents' is widely held. This idea can be traced back to the view that the entrepreneur is a 'special' type of person. If they are entrepreneurial by character, then they will be entrepreneurs wherever they find themselves. So, they can move at will between different areas of business taking their ability with them. Such an idea is not only wrong, it is dangerous because it fails to recognise the knowledge and experience that entrepreneurs must have if they are to be successful in the industries within which they operate.

Some important elements of this knowledge include:

- knowledge about the technology behind the product or service supplied;
- knowledge as to how the product or service is produced;

- knowledge of customers' needs and the buying behaviour they adopt;
- knowledge of distributors and distribution channels;
- knowledge of the human skills utilised within the industry;
- knowledge of how the product or service might be promoted to the customer;
- knowledge of competitors: who they are, the way they act and react.

This knowledge is necessary if good business opportunities are to be identified and properly assessed. Acquisition of this knowledge requires exposure to the relevant industry, an active learning attitude and time. Most entrepreneurs are actually very experienced in a particular industry sector and confine their activities within that sector. Many have acquired this experience by working as a manager in an existing organisation. This 'incubation' period can be very important to the development of entrepreneurial talent.

However, industry-specific knowledge does not produce entrepreneurs on its own. It must be supplemented with general business skills and people skills. If an entrepreneur with these skills were to be transplanted between industries, these skills would still be valuable but they would be unlikely to come into their own until the entrepreneur had learnt enough about the new business area to be confident in making good decisions. It is interesting to note that entrepreneurs who do move between industries demonstrate a skill in drawing out and using the expertise that exists within those different industries. Richard Branson, the entrepreneur behind the very diverse *Virgin Group*, for example, is renowned for his ability to work effectively with industry specialists.

5.4 The opportunity to create wealth

KEY LEARNING OUTCOME
An appreciation of the role of wealth creation in the entrepreneurial process.

Entrepreneurs can often become well-known public figures. They are of public interest because they have been *successful*, and this success has often made them quite wealthy. Their success is of interest in its own right, but their wealth may give them a good deal of social (and perhaps political) power. So while entrepreneurship, and the desire to be an entrepreneur, cannot usually be reduced to a simple desire to make money, it must not be forgotten that making money *is* an important element in the entrepreneurial process.

Business success, and the accumulation of wealth this brings, creates a number of possibilities for the entrepreneur and their ventures to dispose of that wealth.

Reinvestment

If the entrepreneur wishes to grow the business they have initiated then it will demand continued investment. Some of this may be provided by external investors but it will also be expected, and may well be financially advantageous, that the business reinvest some of the profits it has generated.

Rewarding stakeholders

The entrepreneurial venture is made up of more than just the entrepreneur. Entrepreneurs exist in a tight network of relationships with a number of other internal and external stakeholders who are asked to give their support to the venture. They may be asked to take risks on its behalf. In return, they will expect to be properly rewarded. Financial success offers the potential for the entrepreneur to reward them, not just financially, but in other ways as well.

Investment in other ventures

If reinvestment within the venture has taken place, and the stakeholders have been rewarded for their contributions, and there are still funds left over then alternative investments might be considered. The entrepreneur may start an entirely new venture (an option which can be particularly tempting to the entrepreneur when their business has matured and they feel that its initial excitement has gone). Another option is that of providing investment support to another entrepreneur. Successful, established entrepreneurs will often act as 'business angels' and offer their knowledge and experience, as well as spare capital, to young ventures.

Personal reward

Some of the value created by the entrepreneur and their venture (though by no means *all* of it) can be taken and used for personal consumption. Funding a comfortable lifestyle is part of this. It may be regarded by the entrepreneur as a just reward for taking risks and putting in the effort the success has demanded. Some entrepreneurs may also be quite keen to put their money into altruistic projects, for example they may sponsor the arts or support social programmes. This may reflect their desire to make a mark on the world outside the business sphere which is part of their desire to leave the world different to the way in which they found it.

Keeping the score

For many entrepreneurs, money is not so important in itself. It is just a way of quantifying what they have achieved; a way of keeping the score on their performance, as it were. The money value of their venture is a measure of how good their insight was, how effective their decision making was, and how well they put their ideas into practice.

As far as the entrepreneur is concerned, money is more usually a *means* rather than an *end* in itself. The fact that we notice the entrepreneurs who are highly rewarded for their efforts should not blind us to the fact that this reward is more often than not the result of a great deal of hard work and it is a reward that is far from inevitable.

5.5 The opportunity to distribute wealth

No entrepreneur works in a vacuum. The venture they create touches the lives of many other people. To drive their venture forward, the entrepreneur calls upon the support of a number of different groups. In return for their support, these groups expect to be rewarded from the success of the venture. People who have a part to play in the entrepreneurial venture generally are called *stakeholders*. The key stakeholder groups are: *employees, investors, suppliers, customers*, the local *community* and *government*.

Employees

Employees are the individuals who contribute physical and mental labour to the business. Its success depends on their efforts on its behalf and therefore upon their motivation. Employees usually have some kind of formal contract and are rewarded by being paid a salary. This is usually agreed in advance and is independent of the performance of the venture, although an element may be performance related. Employees may also be offered the possibility of owning a part of the firm through share schemes.

People do not work just for money. The firm they work for provides them with a stage on which to develop social relationships. It also offers them the possibility of personal development. When someone joins an organisation they are making a personal investment in its future and the organisation is investing in their future. Changing jobs is time-consuming and can be expensive. Someone who decides to work for an entrepreneurial venture is exposing themselves to the risk of that venture, even if they are being payed a fixed salary.

Investors

Investors are the people who provide the entrepreneur with the necessary money to start the venture and keep it running. There are two main sorts of investor. *Stockholders* are people who buy a part of the firm, its *stock*, and so are entitled to a share of any profits it makes. Stockholders are the true owners of the firm. The entrepreneur managing the venture may, or may not, be a major shareholder in it. *Lenders* are people who offer money to the venture on the basis of it being a *loan*. They do not actually own a part of the firm. All investors expect a return from their investment. The actual amount of expected return will depend on the risk the venture is facing and the other investments that are available at the time. The actual return the stockholder receives will vary depending on how the business performs. Lenders, on the other hand, expect a rate of return which is agreed independently of how the business performs before the investment is made. Lenders usually take priority for payment over stockholders whose returns are only paid once the business has met its other financial commitments. Lenders consequently face a lower level of risk. However, they still face the possibility that the venture might become insolvent and not be able to pay back its loans.

Suppliers

Suppliers are the individuals and organisations who provide the business with the materials, productive assets and information it needs to produce its outputs. Suppliers are paid for providing these *inputs*. The business may only make contact with a supplier through spot purchases made in an open market or contact may be more direct and defined by a formal contract, perhaps a long-term supply contract.

Suppliers are in business to sell what they produce and so they have an interest in the performance of their customers. Supplying them may involve an investment in developing a new product or providing back-up support. A new venture may call upon the support of its suppliers, perhaps by asking for special payment terms to ease its cash flow in the early days. Information and advice about end-user markets may be provided. The chance to build a partnership with suppliers should never be overlooked.

Customers

As with suppliers, customers may need to make an investment in using a particular supplier. Changing suppliers may involve *switching costs*. These include the cost of finding a new supplier, taking a risk with goods of unknown quality, and the expenses incurred in changing over to new inputs. If a customer decides to use the products offered by a new venture rather than one with an established track record they may be exposing themselves to some risk. (This is something the entrepreneur needs to take into account when devising a selling strategy.) The entrepreneur's business may sell to its customers on an open market but, as with suppliers, the possibility of building a longer-term partnership should always be considered.

The local community

Businesses have physical locations. The way that they operate may affect the people who live and other businesses which operate nearby. A business has a number of responsibilities to this local community, for example, in not polluting their shared environment. Some of these responsibilities are defined in national or local laws, others are not defined in a legal or formal sense, but are expected on the basis that the firm will act in an *ethical* way.

Corporate responsibility is a political and cultural as well as an economic issue. If the firm is international and operates across borders then the way it behaves in one region may influence the way it is perceived in another. For example, a number of well-known sports shoes manufacturers were criticised recently for paying Indian workers less than half a US dollar for manufacturing shoes that retailed for over $200 in the US. Whatever the fair 'market' price of labour in India, the firm's managers had to react to the damage this criticism did to the brand names they were trying to market in the West.

Government

A major part of a government's responsibility is to ensure that businesses can operate in an environment which has political and economic stability, and in which the rule of law operates so contracts can be both made and enforced. The government may also provide central services such as education and health-care which the workforce draws upon. These services cost money to provide and so the government taxes individuals and businesses. In general governments aim to support entrepreneurial businesses because they have an interest in their success. Entrepreneurs bring economic prosperity, provide social stability and generate tax revenue.

Distribution of rewards

All of the stakeholders shown in Fig. 5.1 expect some reward from the entrepreneurial venture. By working together they can maximise its success. Even so, the new wealth created by the entrepreneur is finite. It can only be shared so far. The entrepreneur must decide how to distribute the wealth among the various stakeholders. To some extent the entrepreneur's hands are tied since the sharing of the profits is, in part, determined by external markets. Legal requirements and binding contracts also play a part in deciding what goes where.

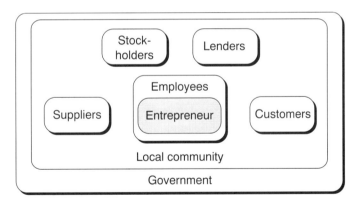

Fig. 5.1 Stakeholders in the entrepreneurial venture

However, the entrepreneur has *some* freedom to decide who gets what. Customers can be rewarded for their loyalty. Higher payments may be used to motivate employees. Profits can be used to support projects in the local community. Distributing the rewards created by the venture is a great responsibility. Using this latitude for rewarding stakeholders creatively is very important to the future success of the venture. If rewards are distributed in a way which is seen as fair and proper they can motivate all involved in the venture. However, a distribution which is seen as illegitimate, is a sure way to cause ill feeling.

Summary of key ideas

● A business opportunity is a *gap* in the market which presents the possibility of *new value* being created.

● Opportunities are pursued with *innovations* – a better way of doing something for a customer.

● Entrepreneurs are attuned to new opportunities and are motivated to pursue them.

● Entrepreneurs not only decide how to create new wealth but also how to distribute it to the venture's *stakeholders*.

Suggestions for further reading

Drucker, P.F. (1985) "The discipline of innovation" *Harvard Business Review*, May-June, pp.67–72.

Donaldson, T. and **Preston, L.E.** (1995) "The stakeholder theory of the corporation: Concepts, evidence and implications", *Academy of Management Review*, Vol. 20, No. 1, pp. 65–91.

Gray, H.L. (1978) "The entrepreneurial innovator", *Management Education and Development*, Vol. 9, pp. 85–92.

Katz, J. (1990) "The creative touch", *Nation's Business*, March, p. 43.

6 Resources in the entrepreneurial venture

CHAPTER OVERVIEW

People, money and operational assets are essential ingredients of the entrepreneurial venture. This chapter explores each of these resource types and the management issues they raise for the entrepreneur. The chapter concludes with a discussion of why investment in such resources leads to risk for the backers of the venture.

6.1 Resources available to the entrepreneur

KEY LEARNING OUTCOME
An understanding of the nature and type of resources that the entrepreneur uses to build the venture.

Resources are the things that a business uses to pursue its ends. They are the inputs that the business converts to create the outputs it delivers to its customers. They are the substance out of which the business is made. In broad terms, there are three sorts of resource that entrepreneurs can call upon to build their ventures. These are:

1 *Financial resources* – Resources which take the form of, or can be readily converted to, cash.
2 *Human resources* – People and the efforts, knowledge, skill and insights they contribute to the success of the venture.
3 *Operating resources* – The facilities which allow people to do their jobs: such as buildings, vehicles, office equipment, machinery and raw materials, etc.

The entrepreneurial venture is built from an innovative combination of financial, operating and human resources (*see* Fig. 6.1). Thus when Frederick Smith founded the US parcel air carrier *Federal Express* he needed to bring together people: a board of directors, pilots, operational staff, *etc.*, together with a fully operational airline which was able to give national coverage. This demanded an investment in the order of $100 million.

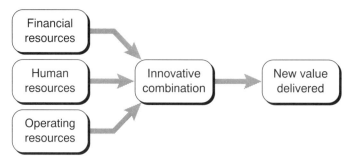

Fig. 6.1 Entrepreneurship and the combination of resources

Regardless of the form they take, all resources have a number of characteristics in common. Resources are *consumed*; they are converted to the products which customers buy and there is competition to get hold of them. A number of businesses, entrepreneurial and otherwise, will be trying to acquire a particular resource; consequently, managers are willing to pay for resources. They have a cost.

The cost of a resource is an indication of how it might be used by a business to create new value. Resources are bought and sold by businesses and their cost is determined by the market created for that resource. Resources with the potential to create a lot of new value will be expensive. This cost is not the same as the value of the resource to a *particular* business since the value of a resource lies in the way a business will use it, how innovative they will be with it and how hard they will make it work for them.

One type of resource can be converted into another. This process normally involves selling a resource thereby converting it to cash, and then using this cash to buy something new. However, in some cases resources may be exchanged directly through 'asset swops'. In places where financial markets are not well developed, such as in parts of the developing world and the former Communist bloc, 'bartering' may be important. Not all markets for resources are equally accessible. Some markets are more developed than others. The ease with which a particular resource can be converted back to ready cash is called its liquidity: *liquid* resources are easily converted back, *illiquid* resources are converted back only with difficulty.

Entrepreneurs must be active in acquiring resources for their ventures. The path through which resources are obtained and exchanged make-up the network in which the business is located. In the long run, the entrepreneur only has access to the same resources as any other business. Competitiveness in the marketplace cannot normally be sustained on the basis of having access to unique resource inputs. If an input is valuable, other businesses will eventually find a way to get hold of it or of something like it. What entrepreneurs must do to be competitive is they must *combine* the resources they have access to in a unique and valuable way. That is to *innovate* with them and then they must make those resources work harder than their competitors do. It is this which ultimately enables the entrepreneur to deliver new value to the customer.

6.2   Financial resources

KEY LEARNING OUTCOME
**An appreciation of the financial resources available for use by the
entrepreneur.**

Financial resources are those which take a monetary form. Cash is the most liquid form
of resource because it can be used readily to buy other resources. The following are all
financial resources which have a role to play in the entrepreneurial venture:

- *Cash in hand* This is money to which the business has immediate access. It may be
  spent at very short notice. Cash in hand may be held either as money, i.e. petty cash,
  or it may be stored in a bank's current account or other direct access account.
- *Overdraft facilities* Such facilities represent an agreement with a bank to withdraw
  more than is actually held in the venture's current account. It is a short-term loan
  which the business can call upon although overdrafts are normally quite expensive
  and so tend to be saved for emergencies.
- *Loans* Loans represent money provided by backers, either institutional or private,
  which the business arranges to pay back in an agreed way over a fixed period of time
  at an agreed rate of interest. The payback expected is usually independent of the
  performance of the business. Loans may be secured against physical assets of the
  business which can be sold off to secure repayment. This reduces the risk of the loan
  to the backer.
- *Outstanding debtors* This represents cash owed to the business by individuals and
  firms which have received goods and services from it. Many debtors will expect a
  period of grace before paying and it may not be easy to call in outstanding debt
  quickly. Outstanding debtors are one of the main reasons why cash flow may be
  negative in the early stages of the venture's life.
- *Investment capital* This is money provided to the business by investors in return for a
  part ownership or share in it. Investors are the true owners of the business. They are
  rewarded from the profits the business generates. The return they receive will be
  dependent on the performance of the business.
- *Investment in other businesses* Many businesses hold investments in other businesses.
  These investments may be in unrelated businesses but they are more often in
  suppliers or customers. If more than half a firm is owned, then it becomes a *subsidiary*
  of the holding firm. Investments can be made through personal or institutional
  agreements, or via publicly traded shares. A firm does not normally exist solely to
  make investments in other firms. Individual and institutional investors are quite
  capable of doing this for themselves. However, strategic investments in customers
  and suppliers may be an important part of the dynamics of the network in which the
  business is located. For this reason such investments tend to represent long-term
  commitments and although they can be sold to generate cash, doing so is not routine.

All financial resources have a cost. This cost takes one of two forms. The *cost of capital*
is the cost encountered when obtaining the money: it is the direct charge faced for

having an overdraft; the interest on loans; the return expected by investors, *etc.* In addition to this direct cost, there is an *opportunity cost*. Opportunity cost is the potential return that is lost by not putting the money to some alternative use. For example, cash in hand and outstanding debts lose the interest that might be gained by putting the money into an interest-yielding account.

Financial resources are the most liquid, and thus the most flexible, resources to which the venture has access. However, they are also the least productive. Cash, of itself, does not create new value. Money is only valuable if it is put to work. This means it must be converted to other, less liquid, resources. The entrepreneur must strike a balance. A decision must be made between how liquid the business is to be, how much flexibility it must have to meet short-term and unexpected financial commitments, and the extent to which the firm's financial resources are to be tied up in productive assets.

Such decisions are critical to the success of the venture. If insufficient investment is made then the business will not be in a position to achieve its full potential. If it becomes too illiquid, it may be knocked off-course by short-term financial problems which, in the long run, the business would be more than able to deal with. Managing the *cash-flow* of the business is central to maintaining this liquidity balance. The financial resources to which an entrepreneur can gain access will depend on how well-developed the economy they are working in is and the type of capital markets available. In the mature economies of western Europe and America, capital is usually provided by explicit and open institutional systems such as banks, venture capital businesses and stock markets. In other parts of the world, provision of financial resources may be through less formal networks. Displaced communities often create financial support networks around the extended family. One of the main challenges to developing entrepreneurism in the former Communist bloc is the setting up of supportive financial institutions.

6.3   Operating resources

> **KEY LEARNING OUTCOME**
> **An appreciation of the operational resources available for use by the entrepreneur.**

Operating resources are those which are actually used by the business to deliver its outputs to the marketplace. Key categories of operating resources include:

- *Premises* – The buildings in which the business operates. This includes offices, production facilities and the outlets through which services are provided.

- *Motor vehicles* – Any vehicles which are used by the organisation to undertake its business such as cars for sales representatives and vans and lorries used to transport goods, make deliveries and provide services.
- *Production machinery* – Machinery which is used to manufacture the products which the business sells.
- *Raw materials* – The inputs that are converted into the products that the business sells.
- *Storage facilities* – Premises and equipment used to store finished goods until they are sold.
- *Office equipment* – Items used in the administration of the business such as office furniture, word processors, information processing and communication equipment.

Operating resources represent the capacity of the business to offer its innovation to the marketplace. They may be owned by the business, or they may be rented as they are needed. Either way, they represent a commitment. Liquid financial resources are readily converted into operating resources, but operating resources are not easily converted back to money. The markets for second-hand business assets are not always well-developed. Even if they are, operating resources depreciate quickly and a loss may be made on selling.

In order to use operating resources effectively it is important that the entrepreneur makes themselves fully conversant with any technical aspects relating to the resources; legal issues and implications relating to their use (including health and safety regulations); suppliers and the supply situation; and the applicable costs (both for outright purchase and for leasing). It is in this area that partnerships with suppliers can be rewarding, especially if the operating resources are technical or require ongoing support in their use.

The commitment to investment in operating resource capacity must be made in the light of expected demand for the business's offerings. If capacity is insufficient, then business that might otherwise have been obtained will be lost. If it is in excess of demand, then unnecessary, and unprofitable, expenditure will be undertaken. It is often difficult to alter operating capacity in the light of short-term fluctuations in demand. This results in *fixed costs*, that is costs which are independent of the amount of outputs the firm offers. Critically, fixed costs must be faced *whatever* the business's sales. Fixed costs can have a debilitating effect on cash-flow. The entrepreneur must make the decision about commitment to operating capacity in the light of an assessment of the sales and operating profits that will be generated by the business's offering, that is on the basis of an accurate *forecast* of demand. Even good demand forecasting cannot remove all uncertainty and therefore the entrepreneur must be active in offsetting as much fixed cost as possible, especially in the early stages of the venture. This may mean renting rather than buying operating resources. It can also mean that some work is delegated to other established firms. In the early stages of the venture, managing cash flow and controlling fixed costs may be more important than short-term profitability. It may be better to subcontract work to other firms rather than to make an irreversible commitment to extra capacity even if this means short-term profits are lost.

6.4   Human resources

KEY LEARNING OUTCOME
An appreciation of the human resources available for use by the entrepreneur.

People are the critical element in the success of a new venture. Financial and operating resources are not unique and they cannot, in themselves, confer an advantage to the business. To do so they must be *used* in a unique and innovative way by the people who make up the venture. The people who take part in the venture offer their labour towards it. This can take a variety of forms:

- *Productive labour* – A direct contribution towards generating the outputs of the business, its physical products or the service it offers.
- *Technical expertise* – A contribution of knowledge specific to the product or service offered by the business. This may be in support of existing products, or associated with the development of new ones.
- *Provision of business services* – A contribution of expertise in general business services, for example in legal affairs or accounting.
- *Functional organisational skills* – The provision of decision-making insights and organising skills in functional areas such as production, operations planning, marketing research and sales management.
- *Communication skills* – Offering skills in communicating with, and gaining the commitment of, external organisations and individuals. This includes marketing and sales directed towards customers, and financial management directed towards investors.
- *Strategic and leadership skills* – The contribution of insight and direction for the business as a whole. This involves generating a vision for the business, converting this into an effective strategy and plan for action, communicating this to the organisation and then leading the business in pursuit of the vision.

The entrepreneur represents the starting point of the entrepreneurial venture. He or she is the business's first, and most valuable, human resource. Entrepreneurs, if they are to be successful, must learn to use themselves as a resource, and use themselves effectively. This means analysing what they are good at, and what they are not so good at, and identifying skill gaps. The extent to which the entrepreneur can afford to specialise their contribution to their venture will depend on the size of the venture and the number of people who are working for it. If it is moderately large and has a specialist workforce then the entrepreneur will be able to concentrate on developing vision and a strategy for the venture and providing leadership to it. If it is quite small then the entrepreneur will have to take on functional and administrative tasks as well. Even so, the entrepreneur must be conscious of how the human resource requirements of the business will develop in the future by deciding what skill profile is right for their business and what type of people will be needed to contribute those skills. But employing people with the right skills is not enough, they must be directed to use those skills. They must also be motivated if they are to make a dedicated and effective contribution to the business. This calls for vision and leadership on the part of the entrepreneur.

Human resources represent a source of fixed costs for the business. The possibility of taking on, and letting go of, people in response to short-term demand fluctuations is limited by contractual obligations, social responsibility and the need to invest in training. Further, motivation can only be built on the back of some sense of security. Hence, making a commitment to human resources involves the same type of decisions as making a commitment to operating resources, namely: what will be needed, to what capacity, over what period, must the resource be in-house or can it be hired when needed? However, people are still people even if they are also resources and such decisions must be made with sensitivity.

6.5 Resources, investment and risk

KEY LEARNING OUTCOME
An understanding of how and why investing in resources creates risk for the entrepreneurial venture.

In one sense, a business is 'just' the financial, operating and human resources that comprise it. Only when these things are combined can the business generate new value and deliver it to customers. Resources have a value and there is competition to get hold of them. A business is *not* being competitive when it converts input resources into outputs of higher value. It is only being competitive if it is creating more value than its *competitors* can do. Thus resources are used to pursue opportunities and exploiting those opportunities creates new value. The profit created by an entrepreneurial venture is the difference between the cost of the resources that make it up and the value it creates. This is the *return* obtained from investing the resources. Though profits are important for survival and growth, the performance of an entrepreneurial venture cannot be reduced to a simple consideration of the profits it generates. Profits must be considered in relation to two other factors: *opportunity cost* and *risk*.

Resources are bought and sold in markets and so they have a price. This price is not the same as the cost of *using* a resource. The true cost incurred when a resource is used is the value of the opportunity *missed* because the resource is consumed and so cannot be used in an alternative way. This is the *opportunity cost*. If the entrepreneur uses the resources they obtain in the most productive way possible then the value created will be higher than that which might have been generated by an alternative investment and so the opportunity cost will be less than the value created. If, on the other hand, the resources are not used in the most productive way possible then some alternative investment could, potentially, give a better return. The opportunity cost will be greater than the value created. Opportunity cost is a fundamental factor in measuring performance. This is because investors are not concerned in the first instance with the *profit* made by a venture but with the *return* they might get if they put their money to an alternative use.

The second factor in considering how well an entrepreneur is using resources is *risk*. We cannot predict the future with absolute accuracy so there is always a degree of uncertainty about what will actually happen. This uncertainty creates risk. No matter what return is anticipated, there is always the possibility that some unforeseen event will lead to that return being lower. Customers may not find the offering as attractive as was expected. Marketing and distribution may prove to be more expensive than was budgeted for. Competitors may be more responsive than was assumed to be the case. Investors make an assessment of the risk that a venture will face. If the risk is high then they will expect to be compensated by a higher rate of return. If they perceive that it is low then they will be happy with a lower return. Consequently there is a pay-off between risk and return. The exact way in which expected return is related to risk is quite complex and is a function of the dynamics of the market for capital. The risk–return relationship for investment in an entrepreneurial venture is shown in Fig. 6.2. In practice, institutional investors will aim to hold a *portfolio*, that is a collection, of investments with different levels of risk and return.

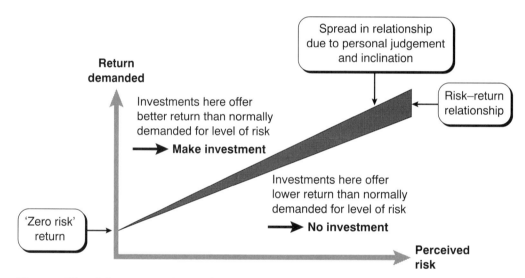

Fig. 6.2 The risk–return relationship for investment in an entrepreneurial venture

Risk occurs because resources must be *committed* to a venture. Once money is converted into operating and human resources it is either too difficult or too expensive, or both, to convert it back. Therefore, once resources have been brought together and shaped to pursue a particular opportunity there is no going back if a better opportunity demanding a different shaping of the resources is identified later. In this way, entrepreneurial innovation demands an irreversible commitment of resources (*see* Fig. 6.3). The opportunity cost must be faced and it is the investor in the venture who must absorb this cost, not the entrepreneur (although obviously the entrepreneur may be an investor as well).

In summary, if an entrepreneur identifies an opportunity that might be exploited through an innovative way of using resources and then asks investors to back a venture

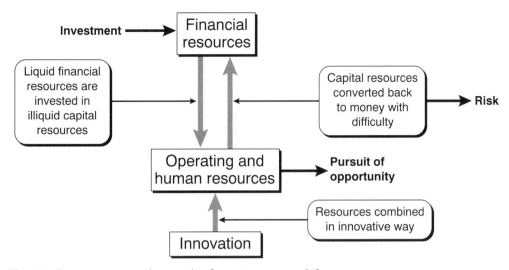

Fig. 6.3 Resource commitment in the entrepreneurial venture

pursuing that opportunity, two fundamental questions will come to the investor's mind. These are: how do the returns anticipated compare to the alternative investments available and what will be the risks? The decision to support the venture or not will depend on the answers to these questions. It should not be forgotten that although, investors are people who put *financial* resources into a venture, individuals who work for a business are also making a *personal* investment in it. They expect to be rewarded for their efforts and to be given an opportunity to develop. They also face opportunity costs in not being able to offer their efforts elsewhere, and face the risk of the venture not being successful. Similarly, non-financial commitments may also be made by customers and suppliers who build a relationship with the venture. In this way risk is spread out through the network in which the venture is located.

Summary of key ideas

- Entrepreneurs must attract resources to their ventures in order to pursue business opportunities.

- The main categories of resources are *financial*, *human* and *operating*.

- Resources are *valuable* and are traded in *markets*.

- The entrepreneur must *compete* with other businesses to get hold of resources by offering a good return from using them.

- Dedicating resources to a particular venture exposes investors to *risk*, namely the possibility that the return gained will be less than expected.

Suggestions for further reading

Peteraf, M.A. (1993) "The cornerstones of competitive advantage: A resource based view", *Strategic Management Journal*, Vol. 14, pp. 179–91.

Wernerfelt, B. (1984) "A resource based view of the firm", *Strategic Management Journal*, Vol. 5, pp. 171–80.

Wernerfelt, B. (1995) "The resource based view of the firm: Ten years after", *Strategic Management Journal*, Vol. 16, pp. 171–4.

7 The entrepreneurial venture and the entrepreneurial organisation

CHAPTER OVERVIEW

The fundamental task of the entrepreneur is to create or to change an organisation. This chapter explores what is meant by 'organisation'. The first section explores the way in which entrepreneurs (and other managers) use metaphors (either consciously or unconsciously) to create a picture of the organisations they manage. The second section looks at how entrepreneurs use organisations to control the resources that make up the venture. The third and fourth sections develop a broader view of organisation and consider the entrepreneur operating within a network of resources. The final section considers how this can provide an insight into developing a practical entrepreneurial strategy.

7.1 The concept of organisation

KEY LEARNING OUTCOME
An appreciation of how different ideas of 'organisation' aids understanding of the entrepreneurial approach to management.

The notion of 'organisation' is fundamental to management thinking. An organisation is what a manager works for and organising it is what they do. The entrepreneur may create a new organisation or develop an existing one. Whichever of these options they choose, they create a new organisational world. Organising resources is the means to the end of creating new value. If entrepreneurship is to be understood then the nature of organisation needs to be appreciated.

There are a number of ways in which we can approach the concept of organisation. We cannot see any organisation directly, all we can actually observe is individuals taking actions. We call upon the idea of organisation to explain why those actions are co-ordinated and directed towards some common goal. If we wish to understand how an organisation actually co-ordinates those actions we must create a picture of it using *metaphors*. Thus, we can think of the organisation both as an *entity*, a thing in its own right, and as a *process*, a way of doing things. The type of metaphor which is used is important because it influences the way in which management challenges are perceived and approached. They underlie the entrepreneur's management style. Gareth Morgan provides an extensive and critical study of how we understand organisation through metaphor in his book *Images of Organisation*.

Some conceptualisations of organisation which are important to understanding entrepreneurship are as follows.

The organisation as a co-ordinator of actions

People do not work in isolation in an organisation. They get together to co-ordinate and share tasks. Differentiating tasks allows a group of people to achieve complex ends that individuals working on their own could not hope to achieve. An organisation is a framework for co-ordinating tasks. It provides direction, routines and regularities for disparate activities. An organisation has goals which are what the people working together in the organisation aim to achieve as a group. The organisation acts to align and direct the actions of individuals towards the achievement of those goals.

Entrepreneurs are powerful figures within their own organisations. Indeed the organisation is the vehicle through which they achieve their ambitions, it extends their scope and allows them to do things that they could not do as an individual. The organisation is the tool entrepreneurs use to create their entire new world. They use their influence and leadership to shape the organisation and direct it towards where they wish to go.

The organisation as an independent agent

An agent is simply something that acts in its own right. Regarding the organisation as an agent means that we give it a character quite separate to that of the people who make it up. The organisation takes actions on its own behalf and has its own distinguishing properties. Thus we can talk about the organisation 'having' a strategy which it uses to pursue 'its' goals. We can talk about the assets 'it' owns and the culture 'it' adopts. This conceptualisation is important from a social and legal perspective. The business organisation is regarded as a legal entity in its own right, quite separate to the identities of its owners and managers. The firm has rights and responsibilities which are distinct from those of its managers. Recognising the organisation as an independent agent is important because it reminds us that the organisations created by entrepreneurs have an existence independent of their creators.

The organisation as a network of contracts

Organisations are made up of people who contribute their labour to the organisation on the basis that they will receive something in return. The organisation is the means people use to pursue their own individual ends. The idea that the organisation is a network of contracts is based on the notion that people work together within a framework of agreements defining the contribution that each individual will make to the organisation as a whole, and what they can expect from the organisation in return. These agreements are referred to as *contracts*.

Organisational contracts take a variety of forms. They may be quite formal and be legally recognised, for example a contract of employment. Frequently, however, a major part of the contract will not be formalised. Many of the commitments and responsibilities that people feel toward their organisation and those they feel it has towards them are unwritten. They are based on ill-defined expectations as to how people should work together and act towards one other. These aspects of the contract may not even be recognised until they are broken by one party. Organisations are built on *trust* and the nature of the contracts that hold the organisation together are a major factor in defining its culture.

The idea of the organisation as a network of contracts is important because it reminds us that individuals do not completely subsume their own interests to those of the organisation, rather the organisation is the means by which they pursue their own goals. They will pursue the organisation's interests only if they align with their own. This concept of the organisation also highlights the fact that the individual's relationship with their organisation goes beyond the written legal contract. It is also defined by trust and unspoken expectations. Individuals will only be motivated to contribute to the organisation if those expectations are met, and their trust is not broken.

The organisation as a collection of resources

Organisations are created from resources including capital (money), people and productive assets such as buildings and machinery. The resource-based view of the firm sees it in terms of the collection of resources that make it up. The organisation is built from resources that can be bought and sold through open markets. What makes a particular firm unique is the *combination* of resources that comprise it. Innovation is simply finding *new* combinations of resources.

Having access to appropriate resources and using them both creatively and efficiently is central to entrepreneurial success. It should not be forgotten that people are the key resource since only they can make capital and productive resources work in new and different ways. The idea of the firm as a collection of resources reminds us that the entrepreneur must be an effective manager of resources which means being a manager of people as much as a manager of assets and processes.

The organisation as a system

A system is a co-ordinated body of things, or elements, arranged in a pattern of permanent, or semi-permanent relationships. The notion that the business organisation is a system develops from the idea that a firm takes resource inputs and attempts to convert them into outputs of higher value. The greater the value that is added, the more productive the system. The elements of the organisational system are the people who make it up and the manner in which they are grouped. The actions people take are defined by the pattern of relationships that exist between them. Permanent relationships and consistent actions lead to regular routines and programmes. The systems view of organisation explains the way organisations develop and evolve by drawing on ideas such as feedback loops and control mechanisms.

The idea that the organisation is a system is valuable because it emphasises the dynamic nature of the organisation. It is what the organisation *does* that matters. It also draws attention to the fact that routines take on a life of their own as the system develops its own momentum. Control mechanisms freeze the organisation's way of doing things. This is valuable. They lock in the organisation's source of competitive advantage. However, in order to remain innovative, the entrepreneurial organisation must avoid inertia which requires a continual assessment of the way it does things and a willingness to challenge existing routines if necessary. Entrepreneurial businesses achieve success by being more flexible and responsive to environmental signals than established firms. New contributions to systems thinking from areas such as chaos theory and non-equilibrium dynamics are providing a valuable new perspective on the way entrepreneurial businesses function and how they succeed.

The organisation as a processor of information

Information is a critical part of business success since information, properly used, leads to knowledge and knowledge can lead to competitive success. The organisation can be thought of as a device for processing information, for example, information on what needs the customer has, what products will satisfy those needs, how they can be prepared and delivered efficiently, how their benefits can be communicated to customers and so on. In this view, the performance of the firm is determined by the quality of the information it has and how well it uses it. Further, by co-ordinating the intelligence of the people who constitute it, the organisation as a whole can exhibit intelligence. It not only uses information, but can constantly learn how to use information better.

Innovation is at the heart of entrepreneurship and innovation must be based on knowledge. The idea of the organisation as an information processor highlights the fact that the success of the entrepreneurial organisation does not just lie in its innovation but in the way it *uses* that innovation and learns to go on using it. The entrepreneurial organisation achieves flexibility and responsiveness through its willingness to learn about its customers and itself.

Overview

These different perspectives on the organisation are not mutually exclusive, indeed to some extent they are complimentary. None of the perspectives gives a complete picture of what the entrepreneurial firm is about, rather each gives a different set of insights into what the firm is, how it performs its tasks, the relation it has to the people who make it up and what the basis of its success might be. If entrepreneurs are to fully understand their business then they must learn to use all of these perspectives to gain a complete view.

7.2   Organisation and the control of resources

KEY LEARNING OUTCOME
An understanding of the way the entrepreneur controls resources in their organisation.

Entrepreneurs use resources to achieve their aims in that they combine resources in a way which is innovative and offers new value to customers. This *is* the pursuit of opportunity. Resources are brought together under the control of an organisation. The power of entrepreneurs to control resources directly is limited because there is only so much that they can do as individuals. Therefore, entrepreneurs must shape the organisation they build and use it to configure the resources to which they have access. As the organisation grows and increases in complexity, tasks must be delegated down the organisational hierarchy. Controlling the resources in the organisation means controlling the actions of the people in the organisation who use them. If entrepreneurs are to be effective in leading and directing their organisation then they must understand how the resources that make it up can be controlled.

Entrepreneurs must make a decision as to what they will control themselves and what control they will pass on to others. The balance of this decision will depend on the size and complexity of the organisation, the type and expertise of the people who make it up, the type of resources with which the organisation is working and the strategy it adopts. This decision must be subject to constant revision as the organisation grows, develops and changes. Even if an entrepreneur has delegated the management of resources to other people within the organisation this does not mean that he or she has given up *all* control over them. A number of control mechanisms are retained (*see* Fig. 7.1).

Directed action

The entrepreneur may retain control by directing that specific tasks are undertaken. The course to be followed will be instructed in detail. The actions are likely to be short-term, or repetitive, with well-defined outcomes. By directing specific actions the entrepreneur is using others to undertake tasks he or she would perform themselves but lack the time to do so.

Routines and procedures

Routines and procedures are used to establish patterns of action to be repeated. No direct control is exercised, but people are expected to follow the course of actions set down. The actions defined by the routine may be specified either in outline or in great detail. The possibility of deviating from the pattern or modifying it will vary depending on the degree of control desired and the need to constrain the outcomes of the actions. When the organisation is too complex to be controlled by directed action, the entrepreneur may concentrate on controlling through procedures.

Organisational strategy

A strategy is a framework for thinking about, and guiding the actions of, individuals within the organisation. The organisation's strategy will be directed towards the achievement of specific goals. It will define the major areas of resource deployment (usually through *budgeting*) and outline the main programmes of activity. The strategy may be imposed by the entrepreneur, or it may be developed through discussion and consensus. People within the organisation might be given a great deal of latitude to develop their own projects of action within the strategy. They will, however, be expected to be guided by the strategy, work towards its goals and operate within its resource constraints. A strategy, even if well-defined, offers a greater scope for interpretation than does a routine.

Organisational culture

The concept of organisational culture is a very important one. A culture is the pattern of beliefs, perspectives and attitudes which shape the actions of the people within the organisation. A culture is unwritten. Its existence may not even be recognised until someone acts outside its norms. Culture is very important in creating motivation and setting attitudes. It can be a critical aspect of competitiveness. For example, a positive attitude towards customer service, constantly seeking innovation or greeting change positively are all determined by culture. Things such as these cannot be enforced through rules and procedures so culture is difficult to manage. It is a state of mind, rather than a resource to be manipulated. However, the entrepreneur can help establish a culture in their organisation by leading by example and being clear and consistent about what is expected from people, what behaviour is acceptable to the organisation and what is not. Tom Peters and Robert Waterman, in their highly influential study of US business, *In Search of Excellence,* identified culture as a critical factor in the success of an organisation.

Communicated vision

A vision is a picture of the better world the entrepreneur wishes to create. The vision is the thing that draws the entrepreneur forward and gives them direction. The entrepreneur can, by sharing that vision, communicate the direction in which the organisation must go. If the people who make up the organisation see the vision and accept what it can offer, then the organisation as a whole will gain a sense of direction. However, a vision only specifies an end, not a means. It indicates where the organisation can go, not the path it must take. A vision leaves open the potential for a wide range of possibilities and courses of action. Different courses must be judged in terms of how effective they will be in leading the organisation towards the vision.

The hierarchy of resource control devices

These means of controlling resources form a hierarchy as shown in Fig. 7.1. As it is ascended the entrepreneur becomes less specific in their direction. Their control becomes less direct and immediate. On the other hand, they give the people who work

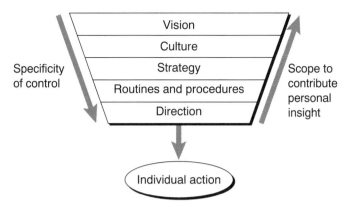

Fig. 7.1 Factors influencing individual action in the entrepreneurial venture

with them more latitude to use their own talent and insights and so make a more substantial contribution to the business. The exact mix of controls used will depend on the size of the organisation, the people who make it up, the tasks in hand and the entrepreneur's personal style. The controls adopted, and the way they are used, will form the basis of the entrepreneur's leadership strategy.

7.3 Markets and hierarchies

KEY LEARNING OUTCOME
An appreciation of the distinction between the market and the hierarchy as forms of organisation.

The business world is full of organisations which offer goods and services to each other and to individual consumers. These goods and services are traded in *markets*. Organisations and markets represent different ways in which individuals can arrange exchanges between themselves.

A market consists of a range of sellers offering their goods to a number of buyers. It is characterised by short-term contracts centred on exchanged products, as shown in Fig. 7.2. Buyers are free to select the seller they wish to buy from. The seller must offer goods at a price dictated by the market. Classical economics assumes that the goods of one supplier are much the same as the goods of any other, although in practice, sellers may be able to differentiate their products from those of competitors. If this differentiation offers advantages to the buyer, then the seller may be able to sustain a price higher than the market norm. In a market, the relationship between the buyer and seller is centred on the product exchanged between them. The seller has no obligation other than to supply the product specified and the buyer has no obligation other than to pay for it. The relationship is short-term with the buyer being free to go to another supplier in the future.

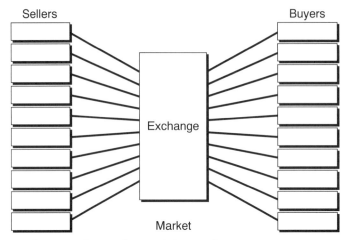

Fig. 7.2 The market as a form of organising exchange

People do not just use markets as a means of organising exchange, they also form organisations such as business firms. Organisations are sometimes referred to as non-market *hierarchies* indicating the way in which the individuals who make them assign responsibilities. In a hierarchy individuals still supply a product, their *labour*, to the organisation. Different parts of the hierarchy will supply products and services to other parts and to the organisation as a whole. The factory may pass on its products to the marketing department for example, or the accounts department may supply financial services. In a hierarchy the relationship between individuals goes beyond the mere product or service they agree to supply. It has a long-term character based on both formal and informal criteria. A hierarchical organisation is based on long-term commitments as depicted in Fig. 7.3.

A hierarchy represents a loss of economic freedom. Within an organisation individuals must use each other's services. They cannot shop around in the market for a better deal. Why then do organisations form? The answer is that markets do not come for free. There is a cost associated with assessing what is available. Gathering

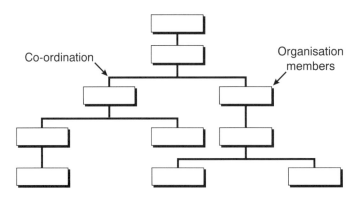

Fig. 7.3 Hierarchical organisation

information may be expensive. If individuals set up long-term contracts then this cost is reduced. Further, if the product is complex and the relationship short-term, the seller may be tempted to cheat and supply less than expected. The buyer may face a cost associated with *monitoring* what the seller supplies. The monitoring cost is reduced if the buyer and seller *trust* one other. Trust is best built in a long-term relationship, and most easily built if the buyer and seller are part of the same organisation.

The 'market' and the 'hierarchy' are pure types lying at the opposite ends of a spectrum of organisational types. Organisations in the real world lie somewhere in between. They have some of the characteristics of a hierarchy with relationships based on long-term agreements and formal contracts, and some of the characteristics of markets in which individuals come and go, offering their labour and services on a competitive basis. This is true not only within organisations, but also between them. Organisations do not just rely on markets, they set up contracts and make long-term commitments to each other. The network provides a more realistic model of how entrepreneurial ventures actually operate than either of the pure types of the market and the hierarchy.

7.4 Networks

KEY LEARNING OUTCOME
An understanding of the concept of the network and its role in the entrepreneurial process.

Individuals use both organisations and markets to facilitate exchanges between themselves. Markets offer a freedom to chose whereas permanent hierarchies emerge when trust is important. Real-life organisations possess some characteristics of both markets and hierarchies. A business organisation has a definite character. It is an agent with legal rights and responsibilities, it has a name. People will know whether they work for it or not. It will have some sort of internal structure.

A business organisation does not exist in isolation. It will be in contact with a whole range of other organisations. Some of these relationships will be established through the market but others may have a longer-term, contractual nature. Businesses set up contracts with suppliers. They may agree to work with a distributor to develop a new market together. An organisation providing investment capital to the venture may be invited to offer advice and support. An entrepreneur may call upon an expert friend to offer advice on marketing. An old business associate may provide an introduction to a new customer. Rather than think about an organisation as closed and sitting in a market, it is better to think of it as being located within a *network* of relationships with other organisations and individuals. In this view the firm does not have a definite boundary. The individuals who make it, and the organisations it comes into contact with, merge into one another. The network is built from relationships which possess both hierarchical and market characteristics. These relationships will be established on the basis of market-led decisions, formal contracts, expectations and trust.

When a new venture is established it must locate itself in a network. This means that it must work to establish a new set of relationships with suppliers, customers, investors and any others who might offer support. The new venture will need to compete with established players. This means that it must break into and modify the network of relationships that *they* have established. A tight network is one in which relationships are established and the parties to them are largely satisfied with these relationships. A loose network is one in which relationships are distant and easily modified. A tight network will be hard to break into, a loose one will be easier. Once a firm is located in a tight network it will find it easier to protect its business from new challengers.

Understanding the nature of the network is important to the success of the entrepreneurial venture. Managing the network will be a crucial part of the strategy for the venture. In particular, the entrepreneur must make decisions in relation to the following questions:

● What is the existing network of relationships into which the new venture must break?
● What is the nature of the relationships that make up the network? Is the network tight or loose? Are the relationships based on formal contracts or on trust?
● How can the new venture actually break into this network of relationships? (Who must be contacted? In what way? What must they be offered?)
● How can the network be used to provide support to the venture?
● What resources (capital, people, productive assets) will the network provide?
● How can risk be shared through the network?
● How can relationships in the network provide a basis for sustaining competitive advantage?

The process of developing answers to these questions will be explored in Part 3 of this book.

In short, a network is a kind of glue which holds a business community together. An entrepreneur initiating a new venture must be active in breaking into a network. Once this has been achieved, the network can be called upon to support them.

7.5 The hollow organisation and the extended organisation

KEY LEARNING OUTCOME
An understanding of how the network may be used to increase the power of the entrepreneurial organisation.

The idea that an organisation is wider than that part of it which is legally defined as the firm provides the entrepreneur with an opportunity. The network offers entrepreneurs the possibility of moving beyond the limits of their own organisation and achieving a great deal more than it would allow them to achieve in isolation. Two types of organisation in particular use the potential of the network.

1. Extended organisations

The extended organisation is one which uses the resources of other organisations in its network to achieve its goals (*see* Fig. 7.4). Access to these resources is gained by building long-term, supportive and mutually beneficial relationships. Particularly important are suppliers who provide the venture with the inputs it needs, associated organisations in the same business who can help manage fluctuations in demand, and distributors who can get the firm's goods or services to its customers. Distributors need not be limited to the functions of storing and transporting goods. They can also be active partners in developing a new market and add their support to achieving and sustaining a strong competitive position. The business may also develop a productive relationship with other businesses who supply the same customers with non-competing products. Here information on customers and their needs can be exchanged and market research costs shared. It may also be possible to share selling and distribution costs.

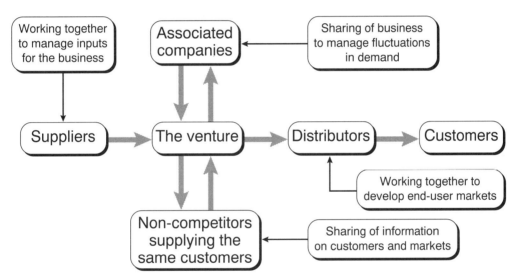

Fig. 7.4 Co-operative relationships in the entrepreneurial network

2. Hollow organisations

The hollow organisation is one which exists not so much to do things itself but to bring other organisations together. In effect it creates value by building a new network or making an existing one more efficient (*see* Fig. 7.5). The formal organisation is kept as small as possible, it may only be a single office, and it sticks to its essential or *core* activities. A common example of a hollow organisation is one which simply 'markets' products. It will buy these products from the company which manufactures them. It will use independent distributors to get the product to customers. It may call upon the services of separate market research and advertising agencies. It may even contract-in its sales team. The hollow organisation does not manufacture, distribute or advertise

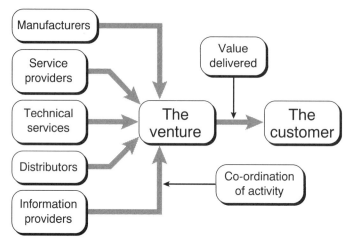

Fig. 7.5 The hollow organisation

goods or services. It simply exists to bring the organisations that perform these functions together. It is rewarded from the value it creates by co-ordinating their activities.

An excellent example of what can be achieved by adopting a hollow organisation strategy is that of *Naxos Records,* a venture founded by the Hong Kong-based, German entrepreneur, Klaus Heymann. This is a business which has established a market leading position in the low cost classical CD market. Yet the core organisation does little itself except co-ordinate the production and marketing of the product. Musicians and orchestras (often from eastern Europe) are commissioned as they are needed. Recording facilities are hired in. Production of the CD and packaging of it are out-sourced (usually in the Far East). Distribution is via independent retailers.

Factors affecting choice of organisation

Both the extended organisation and the hollow organisation are attractive options for the entrepreneur. There are a number of reasons for this:

● they are easy to set up;
● the initial investment needed is small and entry costs are low;
● they allow the entrepreneur to concentrate on their core skills;
● they are flexible and can be easily modified;
● fixed costs are minimised;
● they allow the entrepreneur access to the resources of other organisations;
● growth is relatively easy to manage.

Competition to set up hollow and extended organisations can be quite intense because they are both such attractive options for starting new ventures. If they are to be successful entrepreneurs must be quite sure of the strategy they are adopting. In particular they must be confident about:

- where the business will be located in the value addition chain;
- the value they are adding, i.e. why customers will benefit from what the business has to offer;
- why the product they are offering is different to what is already on offer;
- how they will manage the relationships on which the business will depend;
- how they will sustain those relationships in the face of competitors trying to break the relationships it has established.

These are important ideas which will be developed further in Part 3 of this book.

Summary of key ideas

- The entrepreneur must bring the resources they use together in the form of an *organisation*.

- Organisations are best understood through the use of *metaphors*: the things they are 'like'.

- The *open market* and the closed *hierarchy* are pure forms of organisation.

- The entrepreneurial organisation is best thought of as a *network* of relationships defined through markets and formal hierarchies. The network lies somewhere between the two pure forms.

- Entrepreneurs can create new value by building *hollow* or *extended* organisations which co-ordinate the activities of other organisations.

Suggestions for further reading

Anderson, J.C., Håkansson, H. and **Johanson, J.** (1994) "Dyadic business relationships within a business network context", *Journal of Marketing*, Vol. 58, pp. 1–15.

Anderson, P. (1992) "Analysing distribution channel dynamics: Loose and tight couplings in distribution networks", *European Journal of Marketing*, Vol. 26, No. 2, pp. 47–68.

Birley, S. (1985) "The role of networks in the entrepreneurial process", *Journal of Business Venturing*, Vol 1, pp. 107–17.

Birley, S., Cromie, S. and **Myers, A.** (1991) "Entrepreneurial networks: Their emergence in Ireland and overseas", *International Small Business Journal*, Vol. 9, No. 4, pp. 56–74.

Boisot, M.H. (1986) "Markets and Hierarchies in a cultural perspective", *Organisation Studies*, Vol. 7, No. 2, pp. 135–58.

Falemo, B. (1989) "The firm's external persons: Entrepreneurs or network actors?", *Entrepreneurship and Regional Development*, Vol. 1, No. 2, pp. 167–77.

Jarillo, J.C. (1988) "On strategic networks", *Strategic Management Journal*, Vol 9, pp. 31–41.

Larson, A. (1992) "Network dyads in entrepreneurial settings: A study of the governance of exchange relationships", *Administrative Science Quarterly*, Vol. 37, pp. 76–104.

Larson, A. (1993) "A network model of organisation formation", *Entrepreneurship Theory and Practice*, Vol. 12, No. 2, pp. 5–15.

Morgan, G. (1986) *Images of Organisation*, London: Sage Publications.

Perry, M. (1996) "Network intermediaries and their effectiveness", *International Small Business Journal*, Vol. 14, No. 4, pp. 72–9.

Peters, T. and **Waterman Jr., R.H.**, (1982) *In Search of Excellence*, New York: Harper & Row.

Szarka, J. (1990) "Networking and small firms", *International Small Business Journal*, Vol. 8, No. 2, pp. 10–22.

Tyosvold, D. and **Weicker, D.** (1993) "Co-operative and competitive networking by entrepreneurs: A critical indent study", *Journal of Small Business Management*, Jan, pp. 11–21.

8 The meaning of success

CHAPTER OVERVIEW

Entrepreneurship is about success. This chapter is concerned with defining what success really means and the ways in which it can be measured. Business success is considered not only in financial terms but also in a broader social context. The chapter concludes with an exploration of the converse of success: failure. Failure is not seen as completely negative but rather an experience which is occasionally necessary and which presents an opportunity for the organisation and the entrepreneur to learn.

8.1 Defining success

KEY LEARNING OUTCOME
An understanding of what entrepreneurial success actually means.

Entrepreneurs aim to be successful. It is the possibility of success that drives them on and success is the measure of their achievement. Success is, however, quite a difficult concept to define because it is multi-faceted. Both individuals and organisations enjoy success. It may be measured by hard and fast 'numbers' but also by 'softer', qualitative criteria. Success is something which is both visible in public but is also experienced at a personal level.

Success can be best understood in terms of four interacting aspects:

(i) the performance of the venture;
(ii) the people who have expectations from the venture;
(iii) the nature of those expectations; and:
(iv) actual outcomes relative to expectations.

The performance of the venture is indicated by a variety of quantitative measures. These relate to its financial performance and the presence it creates for itself in the marketplace. The indicators can be absolute and compared to the performance of competitors. Such performance measures relate to the organisation as a whole.

However, an organisation is made up of individual people and success, if it is to be meaningful, must be experienced by those individuals as well as by the organisation. Organisational success is a means to the end of *personal* success. The organisation creates the resources which interested individuals can use to improve their lives. The individuals who have an interest in the performance of the venture are its *stakeholders*. Thus the success of a venture must be considered in relation to the expectations its stakeholders have for it (*see* Fig. 8.1).

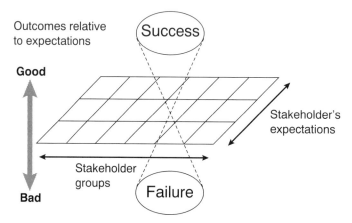

Fig. 8.1 A model of entrepreneurial success

The entrepreneurial venture has six groups of stakeholder, each of which has its own interest and expectations from the venture. The *entrepreneur* (and their dependents) expects the venture to be a vehicle for personal ambitions; *employees* expect reward for their efforts and personal development; *suppliers* expect the venture to be a good customer; *customers* expect the venture to be a good supplier; *investors* expect the venture to generate a return on the investment they have made; and the *local community* expects the venture to make a positive contribution to the quality of local life.

The performance of the venture as an organisation provides the means by which individual stakeholders can use fulfil their own goals. Personal goals are manifest at three levels:

- the *economic* – monetary rewards;
- the *social* – fulfilling relationships with other people; and
- the *self-developmental* – the achievement of personal intellectual and spiritual satisfaction and growth.

Success experienced at a personal level is not absolute. Success is recognised by comparing actual outcomes to prior *expectations*. At a minimum, success is achieved if outcomes meet expectations and success is ensured if expectations are exceeded. If expectations are not met, however, then a sense of failure will ensue.

Different stakeholders will hold different expectations. They will look to the organisation to fulfil different types of goals. The investor may only be interested in the venture offering financial returns whereas the customers and suppliers will want financial rewards, but they may also hope to build rewarding social relationships with people in the organisation. Employees will expect a salary but this will only be their minimum expectation. They will also expect the venture to provide a route for self-development. The venture will be central to the personal development of the entrepreneur.

Success, then, is not a simple thing. The organisation's financial and strategic performance is only part of the picture. Success is achieved if the organisation uses its performance to meet, or better to *exceed*, the financial, social and personal growth expectations of the people who have an interest in it. The success of a venture depends on how its performance helps stakeholders to achieve their individual goals, and the way different people judge the success of the venture will depend on how well these expectations are met (*see* Fig. 8.2).

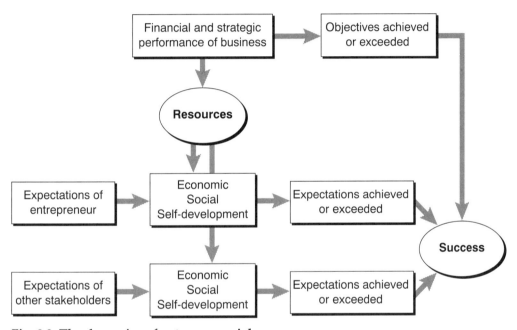

Fig. 8.2 The dynamics of entrepreneurial success

8.2 Success factors for the new venture

KEY LEARNING OUTCOME
An appreciation of some of the main factors involved in the success of a new venture.

A venture is successful if it meets the aspirations of its stakeholders. In order to do this it must survive and prosper in the marketplace. It must attract resources, reward its stakeholders for their contributions and be financially secure. Every venture is different, but a common set of factors lies behind every successful business.

The venture exploits a significant opportunity

The opportunity spotted by the entrepreneur is real and significant. The venture is faced with the possibility of delivering sufficient value to a large enough number of customers to make the business viable.

The opportunity the venture aims to exploit is well-defined

The venture must be clear as to why it exists. It must understand the nature of the opportunity it aims to exploit. This may be codified in the form of a *mission statement*. The danger is not just that the business may fail to find a sufficiently large opportunity for its innovation but also that in pursuing too many opportunities, and opportunities that are not right for the business, the venture will dilute its resources across too many fronts and fail to focus its efforts on creating a sustainable competitive advantage in the areas where it has real potential to be competitive.

The innovation on which the venture is based is valuable

The innovation behind the venture, that is its new way of doing things, must be effective and different from the way existing businesses operate. It must be appropriate to exploit the opportunity identified. Recognising an opportunity, and innovating to exploit it, can only occur if the entrepreneur thoroughly understands the market and the customers who make it up. All new ideas, no matter how good, must be scrutinised in the light of what the market *really* wants.

The entrepreneur brings the right skills to the venture

The entrepreneur possesses the right knowledge and skills to build the venture to exploit the opportunity. These include knowledge of the industry sector they are working in, familiarity with its products and markets, general management skills and people skills such as communication and leadership. The entrepreneur must not only have these skills, but also be active in refining and developing them. The effective entrepreneur learns how to learn.

The business has the right people

Entrepreneurs rarely work alone. They draw other people into their ventures to work with them. The business as a whole must have the right people working for it. Entrepreneurs do not need to employ copies of themselves, rather they need people with skills and knowledge to complement their own. The business will need specialists and technical experts as well as people to actually make the product or deliver the service the business offers. It will need general managers and people able to build relationships outside the firm. The people who make up the organisation will be linked in a suitable framework of communication links and responsibilities, both formal and informal. As the business grows, identifying and recruiting the right people to support its growth is a task of primary importance for the entrepreneur.

The organisation has a learning culture and its people a positive attitude

The new venture is in a weak position compared to established players in the market-place. It is young and relatively inexperienced. It has not had a chance to build up the expertise or relationships that its established counterparts have. It will not have access to their resource levels. The entrepreneurial organisation must turn this on its head and make the disadvantage into an advantage. The entrepreneurial venture must use the fact that it is new to do things in a fresh and innovative way. It must recognise its inexperience as an opportunity to learn a better way of doing things. This can only be achieved if the organisation has a positive culture which seeks ways of developing and which regards change as an opportunity. Adversity must be met as a learning experience. Culture comes down to the attitudes of the people who make up the organisation. They must be motivated to perform on behalf of the venture. The entrepreneur is responsible for establishing a culture in their organisation through leadership and example.

Effective use of the network

Successful entrepreneurs, and the people who work with them, use the network in which the organisation finds itself to good effect. They look toward suppliers and customers, not as competitors for resources, but as partners. They recognise that entrepreneurship is not a zero sum game. If all parties in the network recognise that they can benefit from the success of the venture – and it is down to the entrepreneur to convince them that they can – then the network will make resources and information available to the venture and will be prepared to share some of its risks.

Financial resources are available

The venture can only pursue its opportunity if it has access to the right resources. Financial resources are critical because the business must make essential investments in productive assets, pay its staff and reimburse suppliers. In the early stages, expenditure will be higher than income. The business is very likely to have a negative *cash flow*. The business must have the resources at hand to cover expenditure in this period. Once the business starts to grow it will need to attract new resources to support that growth. Again, cash flow may be negative while this is occurring. The entrepreneur must be an effective resource manager. He or she must attract financial resources from investors and then make them work as hard as possible to progress the venture.

The venture has clear goals and its expectations are understood

A venture can only be successful if it is *seen* to be successful. This means that it must set clear and unambiguous objectives to provide a benchmark against which performance can be measured. Success can only be understood in relation to the expectations that stakeholders have for the venture. These expectations must be explicit. This will be critical in the case of investors, who will be very definite about the return they expect. The business must be sure of exactly what its customers want if it expects them to buy its offerings. Understanding expectations is also important in dealing with employees since it is the starting point for motivating them. The entrepreneur must learn to recognise and manage the expectations of all the venture's stakeholders.

8.3   Measuring success and setting objectives

Ultimately, success is personal. The entrepreneurial venture is a vehicle for personal success. If it is to be an effective vehicle, the venture must be successful as a business. The performance of the venture is subject to a variety of measures including:

- *absolute financial performance* – e.g. sales, profits;
- *financial performance ratios* – e.g. profit margin, return on capital employed;
- *financial liquidity ratios* – e.g. debt cover, interest cover;
- *absolute stock market performance* – e.g. share price, market capitalisation;
- *stock market ratios* – e.g. earnings per share, dividend yield;
- *market presence* – e.g. market share, market position;
- *growth* – e.g. increase in sales, increase in profits;
- *innovation* – e.g. rate of new product introduction; and
- *customer assessment* – e.g. customer service level, customer rating.

These performance indicators are quantitative and are relatively easy to measure. They provide definite goals for the venture to attain. They are *strategic* goals in that they relate to the business as a whole and refer to the position it develops in its external market as well as to purely internal criteria. An entrepreneurial venture is distinguished from a small business by the ambition of its strategic goals.

The specifics of the objectives set for the venture will depend on the type of business it is, the market in which it is operating and the stage of its development. They will be used by management to define objectives, evaluate strategic options and to benchmark performance. Different businesses will set objectives in different ways: they will vary in specificity; they may be for the organisation as a whole or they may define the responsibilities of particular individuals; they may be based on agreement and consensus or they may be 'imposed' on the organisation by the entrepreneur. The way the entrepreneur defines and sets goals, and uses them to motivate and monitor performance is an important aspect of leadership strategy.

The objectives of the firm may not be an entirely internal concern. Financial and market performance measures may form part of the agreement made with investors. They provide manageable and explicit proxies for the success of business and indicate the returns it can hope to generate. They provide a sound and unambiguous basis for monitoring its development. They may also be used in communication with suppliers and customers to indicate the potential of the business and to elicit their support.

8.4   Success and social responsibility

KEY LEARNING OUTCOME
An appreciation of how entrepreneurial success impacts on social responsibility.

An entrepreneurial venture touches the lives of many people. All of its stakeholders have an interest in its success since this success provides the means by which they can fulfil their personal goals. People have expectations about what an entrepreneurial business can achieve and how it should undertake its business. Some of these expectations are formal, others are informal. Some are explicit, others implicit. Some result from binding contracts, others from trust that has been accumulated. Entrepreneurs perform on a social stage and in creating an entire new world they must take responsibility for its ethical content as well as its new value. The moral dimension of their activity cannot be ignored. There are rarely clear-cut answers to moral issues and there are rarely definite methods by which moral issues can be resolved, only frameworks and perspectives for understanding them. The social responsibility ascribed to an organisation, and the people who comprise it, must be determined by precedents, cultural norms and personal judgement. The entrepreneur must be conscious of the nature, and scope of the social responsibility they accept for the organisations they create. Archie Carroll (1979) suggests a multi-dimensional approach to understanding corporate social responsibility. In particular, four dimensions can be identified, as shown in Fig. 8.3.

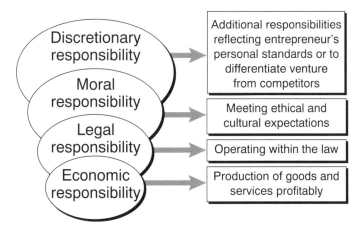

Fig. 8.3 Levels of entrepreneurial responsibility

The first dimension: the *people* to whom the venture has a social responsibility

Potentially, the entrepreneurial venture has a social responsibility towards all those who are affected by its activities, that is its *stakeholder groups*. Stakeholders may be members of distinct groups but they are also individuals. The venture has responsibilities both towards individuals and organisations or groups.

The second dimension: the *levels* of social responsibility accepted

The business may accept a variety of different types of social responsibility. These may be described as *economic*, *legal*, *moral* and *discretionary*.

Economic responsibility

Economic responsibility refers to the basic function of the firm and demands that it produce goods or services and sell them at a profit. This is a minimum level of responsibility. The firm must do this merely to survive within its market. Beyond this basic responsibility, however, the business will recognise a number of other responsibilities.

Legal responsibility

The firm's *legal responsibility* constrains it to operate within the law. The law under which a business operates is defined by the state. Different laws will dictate the way the business operates financially and the way it sets up contracts with other organisations and with individuals. Important examples of laws affecting business are tax and accounting laws and the rules of employment law. A business will be subject to both *criminal* and *civil* law. If the criminal law is broken, the state will act as prosecutor. If a civil law is breached, then it is up to the injured party to bring an action.

Moral responsibilities

A business is a social organisation which operates within a framework of cultural norms. The society within which it exists has ethical standards which it believes must be upheld. These provide rules and norms which create constraints for behaviour. These constitute the firm's *moral responsibilities* and they are difficult to define. They are the unwritten rules about 'what should be done' and 'what should not be done' and they may not be noticed at all until an individual or organisation breaks them. Though a society will not necessarily articulate its ethics and moral standards, they still form an important part of people's expectations and they will react strongly if they are broken.

Discretionary responsibilities

Economic, legal and moral responsibilities comprise the standard constraints operating on the actions of the business. In addition, the entrepreneur may decide to accept *discretionary responsibilities*. Discretionary responsibilities are ones the entrepreneur accepts for their venture even though it is not generally expected that businesses need accept them. They are responsibilities that go above and beyond the norm. Discretionary responsibilities may relate to the way the business will treat its employees, the standards it sets for its products or the way it manages the impact of its activities on the environment. They may reflect beliefs and standards which are held dear by the entrepreneur. They may be used to give the business a point of difference from competitors.

The third dimension: the *issues* which form part of the venture's social responsibility

There are a variety of issues which the entrepreneur can accept as part of the venture's social responsibility. Minimum standards in the treatment of employees, occupational health and safety and product liability will usually be subject to legal regulation. Entrepreneurs frequently take a positive attitude towards wider social issues such as the treatment of the environment, relationships with developing nations and ethnic and sexual discrimination. Occasionally, they may also take a stand on much broader issues relating to social trends such as the growth in 'consumerism'.

The fourth dimension: the venture's *approach* to its social responsibility

The business faces a choice in the way in which it approaches its social responsibilities. It may be *defensive*. This means that the business decides that its social responsibilities are a liability and that they hinder its performance. It may then try to avoid them and to minimise their impact. This may boost short-term profits but it can easily lead to a reaction by stakeholders, especially, but not exclusively, its employees and customers. The business must then put its efforts into defending its actions which can lead to a vicious, and expensive, circle. The more the firm seeks to avoid its responsibilities the stronger can be the reaction by stakeholders so more effort must be put into the defence. This can easily result in a debilitating 'bunker' mentality within the business whereby it feels that its stakeholders are an enemy, rather than partners. Alternatively the business may decide not to go looking for social responsibilities, but will accept them when confronted by them. In this it is *reactive*. The business does not see social responsibilities either as a source of advantage or as a problem, they are just something else that has to be managed. Accepting social responsibility is probably less expensive than defending against it in the long run, but in being reactive the business is allowing itself to be confronted by uncertainties it would otherwise be able to control. Another option is for the business to be *positive* towards its social responsibilities. It can choose to regard them not as liabilities but as opportunities and use them as a source of competitive advantage. Adopting a positive attitude towards social responsibilities brings them under control. They can be made part of the venture's strategy. They can be used to motivate employees and to build a strong relationship with customers and suppliers or they can be used to address the wider concerns of investors and so gain their support. A positive approach to its social responsibilities can be made into a success factor for the entrepreneurial business.

Social responsibilities constrain the actions of a business. They often define what it *cannot* do, rather than what it can. This does not mean they are bad for business. They provide a sound, and shared, set of rules within which the business community can operate. They ensure that the benefits of business activity are distributed in a way which is seen to be fair and equitable. This sustains the motivation of all stakeholders in the venture. Businesses are rarely penalised for meeting their social responsibilities positively. On the other hand, they will be punished if they are seen to evade their responsibilities. This ensures that ventures which set high standards are not penalised by being undercut by those that have lower standards.

Taking on discretionary responsibilities and being proactive with them may be a strategic move. If this meets with the approval of customers and other stakeholders, it can provide a means by which the business can make itself different from competitors and gain an advantage in the marketplace. In recognition of this fact, the entrepreneur may specify the business's social responsibilities in its mission statement. Using discretionary responsibilities to give the business an edge need not conflict with the personal values of the entrepreneur. The entrepreneur can only improve the world with those values if the business is successful. The social responsibilities the venture accepts, and how it defines them, are not merely 'add-ons' to the entrepreneur's vision, they lie at its core. They are the character of the new world the entrepreneur seeks to build.

8.5 Understanding failure

KEY LEARNING OUTCOME
An understanding of what business 'failure' actually means.

Entrepreneurs are always faced with the possibility of failure. No matter how much they believe that their innovation offers new value to customers and regardless of how confident they are that they can build a business to deliver it, they will ultimately be tested by the market. However many success factors they think are present, they may be found wanting in some respects. Uncertainty and risk are always present. Statistics of business failure are widely reported and they are usually quite frightening. Yet 'failure' is not a simple notion. It implies the absence of success and, like success, it can only be understood in relation to people's goals and expectations. Failure happens when expectations are not met. It is a question of degree and means different things to different stakeholders.

From the perspective of the entrepreneur at least eight degrees of 'failure' can be identified based on the performance of the business and way the entrepreneur retains control of it. These are listed in an increasing order of severity below.

1 The business continues to exist as a legal entity under the control of the entrepreneur

(a) The business performs well financially but does not meet the social and self-development needs of the entrepreneur

To most outsiders the business may appear to be a success. It may be performing well financially and making an impact on its market. It may be providing for the economic needs of the entrepreneur and his or her dependents but this does not necessarily mean it is meeting higher needs. The work necessary to keep the business running may be disrupting the entrepreneur's social life. The entrepreneur may have had unrealistic expectations about how the venture would satisfy their self-development needs. If the entrepreneur feels that he or she has failed in this respect it will be demotivating and can have an impact on their personal performance. The entrepreneur may feel that he or she has failed personally despite the financial success of their venture.

(b) The business fails to achieve set strategic objectives

The business may meet the financial targets that have been set for it by the entrepreneur and its investors but even so may fail to meet the strategic targets, such as market share, growth and innovation rate set for it. This may not be of immediate concern if profits are being generated. However, it may warn of challenges ahead and potential problems with the long-term performance of the business. Much will depend on how sensitive to the strategy adopted the performance of the business is and how flexible that strategy is.

(c) The business fails to perform as well as was planned but is financially secure

The venture may not meet the financial objectives set for it by the entrepreneur and investors but still remain financially secure. The objectives may have been quite ambitious setting income targets which were very comfortable in relation to necessary expenditure. Though the business may not be in immediate danger investors may feel disappointed in the returns they will receive. Planned investments may have to be forgone. The entrepreneur may be called upon to address the business's strategy and revise its plans to improve performance in the future.

(d) The business fails to perform as well as was planned, and needs additional financial support

The financial performance of the business may be so weak that income cannot cover necessary expenditure. Cash-flow problems will be encountered and it is likely that the business will not survive without a further injection of cash. This is likely to come from investors but additional support may also be gleaned by agreeing special terms with customers and suppliers. In this instance the entrepreneur is likely to be called upon to address the direction of the business and the way it is being run.

If financial performance falls below a certain level, and the commitments of the business exceed its ability to meet them, then investors and creditors may lose confidence altogether. A change in management may be called for. A number of scenarios are possible.

2 The business continues to exist as an independent entity but the entrepreneur loses control

(a) The business is taken over as a going concern by new management

The business an entrepreneur creates is separate to them in that it has its own legal and organisational identity. It is possible that the business can continue and prosper even if the entrepreneur is no longer involved in its running. The entrepreneur may leave the business for a variety of reasons. Though successful, the entrepreneur may feel that it doesn't offer them sufficient challenges or they may feel that managing it does not fulfil them (as in 1(a) above). They may sell their interest to a new manager or management team and move on to do something else. If this is what the entrepreneur wants to do then it must be counted as a success. The entrepreneur may, however, be called upon to leave the business against their wishes.

If the business is not performing, its backers may decide that their best interests are served by bringing in new management with different ideas and different ways of doing things. Their ability to oust the resident entrepreneur will depend on how much of the business they own, the ability of the investors to liquidate their investment and the contracts they have with the entrepreneur.

(b) The business is taken over with restructuring

As in scenario 2(a), the entrepreneur is called upon to leave. However, rather than run the business much as it was the new management team may feel that performance can only be improved if the business undergoes a fundamental restructuring. This can involve changing its employees and making major acquisitions and divestments of assets.

3 The business does not continue to exist as an independent entity

(a) The business is taken over as a going concern and absorbed into another company

One business may be acquired by another through a takeover. It may retain some of its original character, and a modified legal status, by becoming a subsidiary of the parent. It loses its separate identity and all legal character if it is merged with the parent. In this case its employees move to work for the parent and its assets are combined with the parent's assets. A takeover, or merger, may take place at the behest of the entrepreneur who wishes to sell their interest and move on to something else. It may also be instigated by investors who have lost confidence in the entrepreneur and the venture and wish to cut their loses by liquidating their investment. The entrepreneur may, or may not, retain an involvement by becoming a manager for the new parent.

(b) The business is broken up and its assets disposed of

Takeover and mergers take place if there is a belief that the venture has some potential, even if a completely new management approach is called for. If there is no confidence even in this, then the business may be broken up and its assets sold off as separate items. The proceeds are used to reimburse stakeholders. Creditors and outstanding loans take priority. The investors, i.e. the actual owners of the venture, are only entitled to anything left after all creditors have been paid.

Managing failure

Failure is a fact of business life. It is the possibility of failing that makes success meaningful. Failure is not always a disaster and it does not inevitably mean the end of the venture. Failure is part of the learning process. Minor failures can be positive indicators of how things might be done better. Such failures should not be ignored. They must be addressed before they become the seeds of larger failures. Success and failure exist relative to *expectations*. Failure occurs when expectations are not met. Managing success, and managing failure, have a lot to do with managing people's expectations for the venture, keeping them positive, but at the same time keeping them realistic.

Summary of key ideas

- The success of the entrepreneurial venture must be understood through three dimensions – the *stakeholders* who have an interest in the venture; their *expectations* of the venture; and actual *outcomes* relative to those expectations.

- The most effective entrepreneurs define objectives for success in relation to *all* the venture's stakeholders (not just its investors) and operate with a keen sense of social responsibility.

- Many successful entrepreneurs have demanded that their businesses operate with a higher level of social responsibility than other businesses operating in their sectors.

- 'Failure' has many degrees and is an integral part of venturing. Good entrepreneurs learn from failure.

Suggestions for further reading

Atkinson, A.A., **Waterhouse, J.H.** and **Wells, R.B.** (1997) "A stakeholder approach to strategic performance measurement", *Sloan Management Review*, Spring, pp. 25–37.

Brown, D.M. and **Laverick, S.** (1994) "Measuring corporate performance", *Long Range Planning*, Vol. 27, No. 4, pp. 89–98.

Carroll, A.B. (1979) "A three-dimensional model of corporate performance", *Academy of Management Review*, Vol. 4, No. 4, pp. 497–505.

Dollinger, M.J. (1984) "Measuring effectiveness in entrepreneurial organisations", *International Small Business Journal*, Vol. 3, No. 1, pp. 10–20.

Douma, S. (1991) "Success and failure in new ventures", *Long Range Planning*, Vol. 24, No. 2, pp. 54–60.

Kaplan, R.S. and **Norton, D.P.** (1996), "Linking the balanced scorecard to strategy", *California Management Review*, Vol. 39, No. 1, pp. 53–79.

Osborne, R.L. (1993) "Why entrepreneurs fail: How to avoid the traps", *Management Decision*, Vol. 31, No. 1, pp. 18-21.

Routamaa, V. and **Vesalainen, J.** (1987) "Types of entrepreneur and strategic level goal setting", *International Small Business Journal*, Vol. 5, No. 3, pp. 19–29.

Seglod, E. (1995) "New ventures: The Swedish experience", *Long Range Planning*, Vol. 28, No. 4, pp. 45–53.

Smallbone, D. (1990) "Success and failure in new business start-ups", *International Small Business Journal*, Vol. 8, No. 2, pp. 34–47

Watson, J. and **Everett, J.** (1993) "Defining small business failure", *International Small Business Journal*, Vol. 11, No. 3, pp. 35–48.

Part 2 Choosing a direction

9 Entrepreneurial vision

CHAPTER OVERVIEW

*The presence of a powerful, motivating personal **vision** is one of the defining characteristics of entrepreneurial management. This chapter is concerned with exploring the concept of vision and understanding how it can be used by the entrepreneur to give the venture a sense of direction and purpose. It also addresses how vision can be refined, articulated and communicated to make it into an effective managerial tool.*

9.1   What is entrepreneurial vision?

KEY LEARNING OUTCOME
An appreciation of the power of entrepreneurial vision and of the value it offers for the venture.

Entrepreneurs are managers. They manage more than just an organisation, they manage the creation of a 'new world'. This new world offers the possibility of value being generated and made available to the venture's stakeholders. This value can only be created through change – change in the way things are *done*, change in *organisations* and change in *relationships*. Entrepreneurs rarely stumble on success. It is more usually a reward for directing their actions in an appropriate way towards some opportunity. Effective entrepreneurs know where they are going, and why. They are focused on the achievement of specific goals.

The entrepreneur's vision is a picture of the new world he or she wishes to create. It is a picture into which the entrepreneur fits an understanding of why people will be better off, the source of the new value that will be created, and the relationships that will exist. This picture is a very positive one and the entrepreneur is drawn towards it. He or she is motivated to make their vision into reality. Vision exists in the tension between what *is* and what *might be*. A vision includes an understanding of the rewards that are to be earned by creating the new world and why people will be attracted to them. Vision specifies a *destination* rather than a route to get there. It is created out of possibilities, not certainties.

Entrepreneurial visions have detail. This detail may be extensive, as if the picture were painted with fine brush strokes. Alternatively the detail may be limited and the picture drawn from broad strokes. The details may be in sharp focus and thoroughly defined, or they may be quite vague, calling for further clarification. Whatever the shape of the details, the different parts of the vision will fit together to form a coherent whole. To the entrepreneur the vision pulling the venture forward will have an existence of its own, a unity quite separate from its component parts.

A vision is a 'mental' image in that it is something the entrepreneur carries around in their head. This does not mean it is insubstantial, indeed far from it. It is a very powerful tool for the management of the venture. In particular:

- it provides a sense of direction by being the 'light at the end of the tunnel';
- it helps the entrepreneur to define his or her goals;
- it provides the entrepreneur with a sense of 'warmth' and encouragement when the going gets tough;
- it guides the generation of strategy for the venture;
- it gives the venture a moral content and helps define social responsibilities;
- it can be used to communicate what the entrepreneur wishes to achieve to other people;
- it can be used to attract people to the venture and motivate them to support it; and
- it plays a crucial role in supporting the entrepreneur's communication and leadership strategy.

Vision is an important tool for the entrepreneur. It defines where the entrepreneur wants to go, illuminates why he or she wants to be there and provides signposts for how they might get there. If it is to be an effective tool, vision must be used actively. However, vision must be properly shaped and nurtured. It must be refined and tested. A vision which is unachievable, or which is based on wrong assumptions, or which points in the wrong direction, will easily lead the venture astray. The entrepreneur must learn to challenge vision. It must be defined and shaped so that it is appropriate, viable and achievable, before it can be put to use.

9.2 Developing and shaping vision

KEY LEARNING OUTCOME
An understanding of how entrepreneurial vision can be developed and shaped by the entrepreneur to make it into an effective tool for the management of the venture.

Vision is the starting point for giving shape and direction to the venture. Some sense of vision must exist before strategy development and planning can start. If it is to lead the business in the right direction, vision must be properly examined, refined and evaluated.

Vision develops from the idea that things might be different to, and better than, they are currently. A vision might 'present' itself to the entrepreneur quite suddenly, or alternatively it may emerge slowly, taking shape as the entrepreneur explores an opportunity and recognises its possibilities. No matter how it comes about, vision is something which is constructed personally. It is, first and foremost, a communication with oneself. Communicating with oneself follows similar rules to communicating with anyone else. The objectives behind making the communication should be understood and it must be thought through and properly articulated. If vision is to be used effectively as a force for self-motivation and as a guide to setting goals, developing strategy and attracting support, then the entrepreneur must become aware of his or her vision, isolate it, communicate it to themselves, and refine it.

The vision will be a picture of the new world the entrepreneur seeks to create. It is constructed personally and will vary from entrepreneur to entrepreneur. Whatever form it takes, the entrepreneur must learn to question the vision. At first, the entrepreneur's vision will be ill-defined, with its details out of focus. Questioning it helps bring it into focus. Some important questions to ask are:

- What will be the *source* of the value to be created in the new world?
- Who will be *involved* in this new world (i.e. who are the stakeholders)?
- Why will those involved be *better off* in the new world than they are at present?
- In what way will they *gain* (financially, socially, through personal development)?
- What financial reward will be received *personally* for creating the new world?
- What new *relationships* will need to be developed?
- What is the *nature* of the relationships that will be built in the new world?
- Why will this new world fulfil, or offer the potential to fulfil, personal *self-development* goals?

In short, entrepreneurs must understand *why* their vision offers a picture of a more valuable world and how it will reward them and the other stakeholders involved in the venture. To do this they must understand their personal motivation and the motivations of the stakeholders involved. This questioning must be a *continual* process. Vision must be constantly refined and kept in focus. While it should provide a consistent and constant sense of direction it should be kept flexible. Its shape may change as the entrepreneur's understanding of their personal motivations and the motivations of others evolves. To keep it fresh, entrepreneurs should constantly renegotiate their vision with themselves. Vision should always pull entrepreneurs forward. It should never hold them back.

9.3   Communicating and sharing vision

KEY LEARNING OUTCOME
An appreciation of how entrepreneurial vision can be used to motivate and attract support for the venture.

The entrepreneur's vision gives their venture direction, and motivates them to progress it. Vision is, in the first instance, a personal picture of the new world the entrepreneur seeks to create. If it is to be used to attract other people to the venture this new world must be communicated to them. They must be invited to share in what it can offer. Communication is not just about relating information. It is about eliciting *action* on the part of the receiver. It is not so much about getting people to know things, as about getting them to *do* things. Effective entrepreneurs understand how their vision can be used motivate others as much as it can be used to motivate themselves.

The first stage must be to understand why other people will find the vision attractive. The entrepreneur must identify what the new world will offer stakeholders, both as individuals and as groups. The questions the entrepreneur must ask in relation to the stakeholders are:

- What benefits will they gain if the new world comes into being?
- How will they be able to address their economic, social and self-development needs better in the new world than they can in the existing one?
- Will they be attracted by the moral and discretionary social responsibility entailed in the vision and the specific issues that it addresses?
- What risks will the new world present to them?
- How credible will they find the possibility of achieving the new world?
- How will they view the journey they must take to get to the new world?

Finding the answers to these questions is part of the process the entrepreneur must go through in shaping and refining their vision. The answers will influence the way they communicate it to others. Some important approaches to communicating vision are as follows.

'I have a dream . . .'

In this approach entrepreneurs are explicit about their vision. They describe the better world just as they see it. The vision is presented as a coherent whole. Its parts fit together to create a unified picture. Entrepreneurs expect other people to find it as attractive as they do and to be drawn towards it.

Talking specific goals

Alternatively, entrepreneurs can break down their vision into a series of specific goals, relating, for example, to economic outcomes, to the value that will be gained, to the relationships that will be created, and to the moral content of the new world. Each of these is communicated separately or in particular combinations. The choice of what is communicated will depend on to whom the vision is being communicated, when it is being communicated in what situation and with what intention.

Talking strategy

Here entrepreneurs do not talk so much about *ends* as about *means*. Strategy relates to the approach that the business will take to achieving its goals and the tasks that must be undertaken in order to create the new world. In this entrepreneurs are reliant on the fact that people will be attracted to the journey as well as the destination.

Story-telling

In using this approach entrepreneurs think of their vision as a 'stage' on which the venture is played out. The stakeholders are actors who play parts on that stage. Entrepreneurs give their vision a dynamic form by describing scenarios and telling stories about what might happen. The communication takes shape by relating future events and the roles that people can play in them. Entrepreneurs aim to motivate people by attracting them to their roles within the story.

Why things can be better

The entrepreneur emphasises what is wrong with the world as it *is* rather than what will be better in the new world. The aim is to push people forward using their sense of dissatisfaction, rather than to pull them forward by using the attractions of new possibilities. While it may shake people out of their complacencies, too much emphasis on this approach runs the risk of simply sounding negative and being demotivating, especially if no positive alternative appears to be offered.

What's in it for you

In this approach entrepreneurs focus on the particular benefits that will be gained by the recipient of the communication. The vision is broken down and 'packaged' for the individual. Tailoring the vision in this way is a good way of ensuring the commitment of a particular person. If over-used, however, the recipient may feel that their commitment is being bought. This approach to communication runs the danger of giving the impression that the entrepreneur regards the recipient as being 'mercenary' and purely motivated by personal gain.

Selecting a communication strategy

These approaches to communicating vision are not mutually exclusive. They are individual strands that can be brought together to make up an overall communication strategy for the entrepreneur's vision. By using a diverse approach to communicating this vision the entrepreneur keeps it relevant, avoids being repetitive and keeps the message fresh to recipients. The particular strategy adopted will depend on a number of factors. Some of the more important include:

- the nature of the vision being shared (how complex is it? How much detail does it have?);

- the entrepreneur's leadership style (is it collaborative, democratic, authoritarian?);
- the stakeholders to whom the vision is being communicated (who are they? How many?);
- the nature of the commitment desired from them;
- the stakeholders' particular needs and motivations (economic, social, self-development);
- the stakeholders' relationship to the entrepreneur;
- the situation of the communication (formal or informal, one-to-one, one to many, *etc.*); and
- the medium through which the communication is transmitted (face-to-face, verbal, written, *etc.*).

An ability to articulate the vision and communicate it effectively to different stakeholders in a way that is appropriate to them and in a way that is right for the situation is the basis on which the entrepreneur builds his or her leadership and power.

Summary of key ideas

- Entrepreneurs are managers with a *vision*.

- A vision is a picture of the *new and better world* that the entrepreneur wishes to create.

- Vision can be refined and articulated as a *management tool*.

- Vision can be used as the basis of a powerful *leadership strategy*.

- Visionary leadership demands *communication* of the vision in a way which draws stakeholders towards the venture and *motivates* them to work for its success.

Suggestions for further reading

Campbell, A. and **Yeung, S.** (1991) "Vision, mission and strategic intent", *Long Range Planning*, Vol. 24, No. 4, pp. 145–7.

Filion, L.J. (1991) "Vision and relations: Elements for an entrepreneurial meta-model", *International Small Business Journal*, Vol. 9, No. 1, pp. 15–31.

Gratton, L. (1996) "Implementing a strategic vision – Key factors for success", *Long Range Planning*, Vol. 29, No. 3, pp. 290–303.

Lipton, M. (1996) "Demystifying the development of organisational vision", *Sloan Management Review*, Summer, pp. 83–92.

Shirley, S. (1989) "Corporate strategy and entrepreneurial vision", *Long range Planning*, Vol. 22, No. 6, pp. 107–10.

Stewart, J.M. (1993) "Future state visioning – A powerful leadership process", *Long Range Planning*, Vol. 26, No. 6, pp. 89–98.

Westley, F. and **Mintzberg, H.** (1989) "Visionary leadership and strategic management", *Strategic Management Journal*, Vol. 10, pp. 17–32.

10 The entrepreneurial mission

CHAPTER OVERVIEW

*This chapter is concerned with the development of a **mission** for the entrepreneurial venture. A mission is a formal statement defining the purpose of the venture and what it aims to achieve. A mission is a powerful communication tool which can both guide internal decision making and relate the venture to external supporters. After establishing how a formal mission can actually help the venture, a prescriptive framework for generating, articulating and communicating the venture's mission is developed.*

10.1   Why a well-defined mission can help the venture

KEY LEARNING OUTCOME
An appreciation of the value of a formal mission for the venture.

A mission is a formal statement as to the purpose of the venture. It defines the *nature* of the venture, *what* it aims to achieve and *how* it aims to achieve it. It provides entrepreneurs with a way to codify their vision, to be clear about the difference they will make. Recent surveys indicate that some eighty per cent of all major businesses have a mission or value statement of some kind. Developing a formalised mission can be valuable to the venture for a number of reasons.

It articulates the entrepreneur's vision

Developing a mission offers entrepreneurs a chance to articulate and give form to their vision. This helps them to refine and shape their vision, and it facilitates communication of the vision to the venture's stakeholders.

It encourages analysis of the venture

The process of developing a mission demands that entrepreneurs and those that work with them stand back and think about their venture in some detail. If the mission is to be meaningful, then that analysis must made in a detached way. Entrepreneurs must be able to subject their own vision to impartial scrutiny and consider how realistic and achievable it is. It will challenge them to consider what they wish to achieve, to audit the resources they have to hand, to identify what additional resources they will need, and to evaluate their own strengths and weaknesses. Developing a mission is a piece of communication with oneself. This process is iterative. Entrepreneurs must negotiate the possibilities of creating new worlds with their ambitions and the actuality of what they can achieve.

It defines the scope of the business

An entrepreneurial venture exists to exploit some opportunity. Opportunities are most successfully exploited if resources are dedicated to them and brought to bear in a focused way. This demands that the opportunity be defined in a precise way. The business must know which opportunities lie within its grasp and which it must ignore. Often, success depends not only on the venture taking advantage of a big enough opportunity but also on it not being tempted to spread its efforts too wide. The mission helps to distinguish between those opportunities which 'belong' to the venture and those which do not.

It provides a guide for setting objectives

A mission is usually *qualitative*. It does not dictate specific quantitative outcomes. This is the role of *objectives*. The mission provides a starting point for defining specific objectives, for testing their suitability for the venture and for ordering of their priorities.

It clarifies strategic options

A mission defines what the venture aims to achieve. In this it offers guidance on what paths might be taken. The mission provides a starting point for developing *strategic options*, for evaluating their consistency in delivering objectives and for judging their resource demands.

It facilitates communication about the venture to potential investors

Attracting the support of investors is crucial to the success of the new venture. This is not simply a matter of presenting a series of facts to them, rather it demands that the facts be communicated in a way which makes the possibilities of the venture look convincing. One of their first questions will be *'what is the business about?'*. The mission provides the entrepreneur with a clear, succinct and unambiguous answer to this question. Answering in this way efficiently locates the venture positively in the investors' minds. This facilitates commitment and encourages further inquiry about the opportunity the venture aims to exploit and the rewards it may offer. It also suggests that the entrepreneur has thought about the business in a professional way, that is, it has defined its scope and is focused in its goals.

It draws together disparate internal stakeholder groups

The different stakeholders who make up the business may not agree what the business is about. They may disagree on the goals it should have, how it should go about achieving them and how they will benefit if they are achieved. Organisations are frequently *political* and the mission can be used to provide a common point of reference around which to draw internal stakeholders together. It can guide arbitration when conflicts occur. A broad qualitative mission may be more useful than specific objectives in this respect. Often the very detail of objectives reduces flexibility and can provide a focus for discontent and disagreement.

It provides a constant point of reference during periods of change

The organisation driving the entrepreneurial venture will have the potential to achieve growth. Growth is good because it reflects the success of the business and increases its ability to reward stakeholders. It does, however, present the challenge of managing *change*. As the organisation grows and develops, it will be in a state of flux. It will acquire new assets and develop new relationships. Individuals will come and go. New customers will be found, old ones lost. In these turbulent circumstances, the mission can provide the organisation with a fixed point or a recognisable landmark connecting the organisation's past to its future.

It acts as an aide-mémoire for customers and suppliers

The mission statement can be communicated to the other key stakeholders in the venture, namely its customers and suppliers. It locates the business in the minds of customers and reminds them of what it offers and the commitment being made to them. It also gives the venture a presence in the minds of suppliers, reminding them of the opportunity it presents and of the need for their commitment to that opportunity. This encourages them to give the venture priority and service.

Key features of the mission

The mission provides the entrepreneur with a powerful management tool. However, if it is to be effective and to contribute positively to the performance of the venture, it must be right for the business, it should encapsulate useful information and it must be properly developed and articulated.

10.2 What a mission statement should include

> **KEY LEARNING OUTCOME**
> **An understanding of what information should be included in the mission statement for an entrepreneurial venture.**

A mission statement may define both *what* the business aims to achieve and the *values* it will uphold while going about its business. It relates both what the business does and why its members are proud of what it does. These two parts are often referred to as the *strategic* and the *philosophical* components of the mission statement respectively. For example, the *Body Shop* emphasises corporate values in its mission. It claims to:

Make compassion, care, harmony and trust the foundation stones of business. Fall in love with new ideas.

The fast-growing Scandinavian furniture retailer, *Ikea*, on the other hand, is much more strategic in its approach to defining products, markets and benefits. The company states its 'business idea' in the following terms:

> **We shall offer a wide range of home furnishing, items of good design and function, at prices so low that the majority of people can afford them.**

The strategic component of a mission statement can, potentially, include the following elements:

1 *Product / service scope* – This element specifies exactly what the firm will offer to the world. It stipulates the type or range of products or services that the firm will engage in producing and delivering.

2 *Customer groups served* – This element stipulates which customers and distinct customer groups that will be addressed by the firm.

   Both product / service scope and customer groups need to be specified with three things in mind. First is the *total market* in which the business operates. This is the 'universe' in which the business's offerings are located. Second are the markets that the business *currently* serves since these are the base onto which the business must build its growth. Third are the market sectors, or *niches*, that the business *aspires* to serve. These are where the growth will come from since these niches lie between the current business and the total market. These sectors must stretch the business and make its aspirations demanding, yet they must be realistic given the resources to which the business has access and its capabilities. The sectors must also represent distinct segments of the total market within which the firm's innovation can provide a sustainable competitive advantage.

3 *Benefits offered and customer needs served* – This element specifies the particular needs that the customer groups have and the benefits that the firm's products or services offer to satisfy these needs. Needs (and the benefits that satisfy them) can be defined at a number of levels. Spiritual, social and developmental needs are as important, and often more important than, economic or functional ones.

4 *The innovation on which the business is based and the sources of sustainable competitive advantage* – This element defines the way in which the firm has innovated, how it is using this to exploit the opportunity it faces and how this provides it with a competitive advantage in the market place that can be sustained in the face of pressure from competitors.

5 *The aspirations of the business* – This element defines what the business aims to achieve. It indicates how its success will be measured. It may refer to financial performance, for example to be 'profitable' or to 'offer shareholders an attractive return', or it may refer to market position, for example to be a 'market leader' or to be 'a significant player'. Care should be taken that the aspirations are *realistic*, specify an achievement which is *meaningful* and provide a real *benchmark* for measuring achievements.

In addition to the strategic elements, reference may be made to the discretionary responsibilities taken on by the venture, that is to the *company values* upheld by the business. The philosophical component of the mission statement illuminates the values and moral standards that the organisation will uphold while pursuing its business. This may refer to the way in which the company aims to treat its employees or customers. It may also specify the discretionary social responsibilities that the business will accept. Values may be included in the mission because they reflect the personal principles of the entrepreneur or because the business believes its higher standards will appeal to customers and perhaps investors. These two reasons are not incompatible, indeed positive values are best upheld by a successful business.

Figure 10.1 shows a schematic representation of the elements in a mission statement for the entrepreneurial venture.

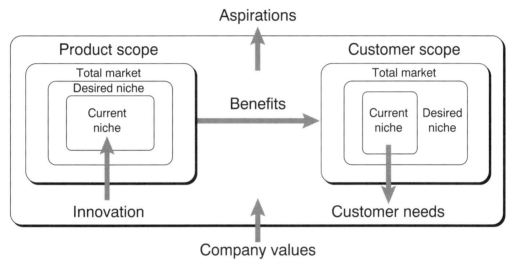

Fig. 10.1 **Components of the entrepreneurial mission statement**

10.3 Developing the mission statement

KEY LEARNING OUTCOME
An appreciation of the practical ways in which a mission can be developed for the venture.

If it is to help the venture, the mission must be right for it and it must be appropriate given the opportunity it aims to exploit and the innovation it intends to utilise. Further, if it is to be more than just so many words, then it must inform and influence people's decision making. A mission must be relevant to those who make up the venture and they must take ownership of it. These conditions will only be met if the mission is developed in the right way. The mission should stretch the business but be consistent with its ambitions, be realistic in terms of the opportunity it faces, and be compatible with its capability to exploit that opportunity. The mission must be developed alongside, and be judged in the light of, a strategic audit for the business. An audit of this nature includes:

● consideration of what the entrepreneur wishes to achieve;
● consideration of what other stakeholders aim to achieve and how the venture might help them;
● an assessment of the opportunity the venture aims to exploit;
● an assessment of market conditions;
● an assessment of the challenges and risks that will be encountered in exploiting that opportunity;
● an assessment of the business's capabilities and its competitive advantages;
● an evaluation of the resources the business has access to, future resource requirements and the resource gap this implies; and
● an assessment of the structure of, and conditions in, the firm's network.

The entrepreneur must also consider how the mission will be generated. Broadly, there are two approaches:

Through consensus

This approach involves getting the whole, or as many parts as possible, of the organisation to contribute towards the development of the mission. The aim is to gather information, create ideas and gain as many insights as possible for generating and evaluating the mission. Allowing people to be involved in creating the mission also gives them a feeling of ownership and so a commitment towards to it. The entrepreneur may go as far as inviting people from outside the formal organisation such as investors, and possibly important suppliers and customers, to make a contribution too. This can be a powerful way of attracting the commitment of these groups and strengthening the network.

Developing the mission in this way may present a logistical challenge, especially if a large number of people are involved. It may be necessary to set up a special forum for the exercise. There is also the question of how the ideas generated will be evaluated and judged and then fed into the final mission. This must be seen to be a rational and fair process, otherwise there is a danger that people may feel their contribution has been ignored or rejected.

By imposition

Alternatively the entrepreneur may feel that consensus is not the best way to generate the mission. He or she may decide that it is better for them to develop the mission him or herself, or in consultation with a small group, and then to impose it on the organisation as a whole. There may be a number of good reasons for this approach. The entrepreneur may see the mission as an articulation of his or her personal vision which may not be negotiable in the way that a consensus-building approach would demand. The entrepreneur may be the only person who has sufficient knowledge about the business and its situation to develop a meaningful mission. If the organisation is growing rapidly, it may be difficult to keep reassessing the mission as new people come in. It might also be inappropriate; after all, the mission is meant to be a constant in a time of flux. New people as they come on board will be asked to accept the mission as it stands (they may, of course, have been attracted by it in the first place!). The entrepreneur may also feel that it suits his or her leadership strategy to impose the mission on the organisation, that is to be seen to give direction and to 'lead from the front'.

Choice of approach

Both these routes for developing a mission have things to offer. The decision as to which is best will depend on the venture, how complex its business is, the way in which it is developing and the leadership style adopted by the entrepreneur. Developing a mission may in fact be one of the key exercises through which the entrepreneur establishes and demonstrates his or her leadership approach to the venture as a whole.

10.4 Articulating the mission statement

> **KEY LEARNING OUTCOME**
> **An understanding of how the mission for the venture might be phrased.**

Once the mission of the venture has been rationalised in terms of the elements in its strategic component and the values the venture wishes to uphold, then it needs to be *articulated* in the form of a definite statement. This statement then *becomes* the mission for the venture. If it is to be a valuable and an effective tool for the management of the venture it must fulfil several conditions. In particular, it must emphasise what is distinct about the venture; it must be informative; it must be clear and unambiguous; it must have impact; and it must be memorable. A balance between each of these requirements must be achieved. One generic format which includes all the elements described in the previous section is as follows:

> The {*company*} aims to use its {*competitive advantage*} to achieve/maintain {*aspirations*} in providing {*product scope*} which offers {*benefits*} to satisfy the {*needs*} of {*customer scope*}. In doing this the company will at all times strive to uphold {*values*}.

The starting point for articulating the mission in this way is to find phrases describing each italicised element. These must be quite short or the mission statement will become too long, therefore it will be immemorable and so will lose impact. Single words are best! Not every element need be included, thus if a particular element is obvious, does not really inform or does not distinguish the business from its sector in general then it may be safely dropped. If in doubt, it is probably better to make the mission statement more, rather than less, succinct.

The business will be faced with numerous opportunities to communicate its mission. It may be posted prominently within the organisation. It may form a starting point for setting objectives. It can be included on promotional material sent to customers. It will feature in the business plan presented to investors. However, not all communication need be so formal. The mission need not always be presented as a formal 'statement', it can easily be slipped informally into conversations. It is, after all, only the answer to the question: 'well, what does your business aim to do?'

Summary of key ideas

- A *mission* is a positive statement which defines what a particular venture is about and what it aims to achieve.

- A well-defined mission helps the venture by encouraging analysis of its situation and capabilities; drawing together its internal stakeholders; and facilitating communication of the venture to external stakeholders.

- The mission statement can include a definition of the venture's market scope, what it aims to do for its stakeholders, its ambitions and its values.

- Entrepreneurs can use development of the venture's mission as part of their leadership strategy.

Suggestions for further reading

Baetz, M.C. and **Bart, C.K.** (1996) "Developing mission statements which work", *Long Range Planning*, Vol. 29, No. 4, pp. 526–33.

Campbell, A. (1989) "Does your organisation need a mission statement?", *Leadership and Organisational Development Journal*, Vol. 10, No. 3, pp. 3–9.

Campbell, A. and Yeung, S. (1991) "Creating a sense of mission", *Long Range Planning*, Vol. 24, No. 4, pp. 10–20.

David, F.R. (1989) "How companies define their mission", *Long Range Planning*, Vol. 22, No. 3, pp. 90–7.

Germain, R. and **Bixby Cooper, M.** (1990) "How a customer mission statement affects company performance", *Industrial Marketing Management*, Vol. 19, pp.47–54.

Klemm, M., Sanderson, S. and **Luffman, G.** (1991) "Mission statements: Selling corporate values to employees", *Long range Planning*, Vol. 24, No. 3, pp. 73–8.

Wickham, P.A. (1997) "Developing a mission for an entrepreneurial venture", *Management Decision*, Vol. 35, No. 5, pp. 373–81.

11 The strategy for the venture

CHAPTER OVERVIEW

Strategy is a central concept in modern management practice. This chapter looks at business strategy from the entrepreneurial perspective. The value of a well-considered and well-defined strategy to the venture is advocated, and the way in which entrepreneurs can control strategy development is considered. The chapter concludes by exploring the strategies entrepreneurs can use to initiate their ventures.

11.1 What is a business strategy?

KEY LEARNING OUTCOME
An understanding of the key elements of the business strategy for the entrepreneurial venture.

The idea that an organisation has a 'strategy' lies at the centre of much management thinking. A strategy can be defined as the actions an organisation takes to pursue its business objectives. Strategy drives *performance* and an effective strategy results in a good performance. An organisation's strategy is multi-faceted. It can be viewed from a number of directions depending on which aspects of its actions are of interest. A basic distinction exists between the *content* of a business's strategy and the strategy *process* that the business adopts to maintain that strategy. The strategy content relates to what the business actually *does* while the strategy process relates to the way the business *decides* what it is going to do. The strategy content has three distinct decision areas: the *products* to be offered, the *markets* to be targeted and the approach taken to *competing*.

The product range

This covers the type and range of products that the firm supplies to its markets (note that the word product here is used in a general sense to include both physical products and services). The decisions the entrepreneur faces here are:

- What type of products should the business offer?
- What should their features be?
- How will they address customer needs? What benefits will they offer?
- What mix of physical and service elements should be offered with the product?
- If the product is are to be successful, in what way(s) must the customer find it more attractive then those of competitors?
- What unit cost is acceptable? (How does this relate to price?)
- How wide should be the product range offered? How many product variants will be necessary?

Market scope

The market scope defines the customer groups and market segments that will be addressed by the firm. Key decisions here include:

- How is the total market to be defined?
- What features (e.g. customer types; customer needs; buying behaviour; location) are important for characterising the market and defining its sectors?
- On what group(s) of customers should the business concentrate?
- In what sectors will these customers be?
- Should the firm concentrate its efforts on a narrow group, or spread its efforts more widely?
- Why will the group(s) selected find the firm's offerings more attractive than those of competitors?
- What will be the geographic location and spread of the customers (e.g. local, regional, national, international)?

Clearly, decisions on product range and market scope are interlinked. The decisions made with respect to one, influence the decisions that must be made for the others. Therefore, it may be better for the entrepreneur to regard themselves as facing a *single* set of decisions about the combined *product–market domain* of the firm.

Competitive approach

Competitive approach refers to the way in which the firm competes within its product–market domain to sustain and develop its business in the face of competitive pressures. This aspect of strategy content reflects the way in which the firm tries to influence the customer to favour their offerings. Important decisions to be made in relation to this approach include:

- How should the product be priced relative to competitors? (Should a discount or premium be offered?)
- What distribution route will be used to get the product to the customer?
- What financial rewards and incentives will be offered to intermediaries and distributors?

- What support (e.g. exclusivity; preferential selling; display) will be expected from distributors?
- How will the customer's buying decision be influenced?
- What message will be sent to consumers about the product?
- How will the message be delivered? (For example, by advertising; by personal selling, or through distributors?)
- Will customers be encouraged to compare the product to the offerings of competitors? (If so, on what basis: price, quality, features, performance?)
- Or will customers be told that the innovation is so great that there is nothing else like it?

Strategy content

The strategy content which the business aspires to achieve must be consistent with the entrepreneur's vision and the mission they have defined for the venture. Decisions about strategy content must be made in light of an understanding of 'external' conditions such as characteristics of the market, the competitive situation and the way in which different sectors can be served, and in light of 'internal' concerns such as the mission and goals of the organisation, the resources it has to hand and its capabilities. The strategy content for the venture is the way in which it competes to sustain and develop its product–market domain (*see* Fig. 11.1).

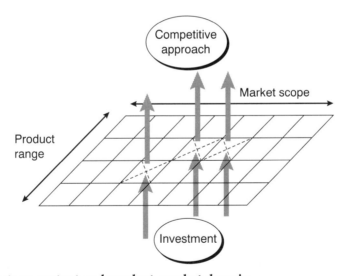

Fig. 11.1 Strategy content and product–market domain

The venture will achieve success if it directs its resources in an appropriate way towards delivering a rewarding and sustainable strategy content. The strategy content dictates the investment of resources that the business must undertake. Investments in financial, operating and human resources will all play a part in supporting the strategy content. Consequently, strategy content decisions must be evaluated in terms of the investments that they entail, the rewards that are likely and the risks involved.

11.2   Strategy process in the entrepreneurial business

KEY LEARNING OUTCOME
An understanding of the ways in which an entrepreneurial business decides on the strategies it will adopt.

The firm's strategy process is the way in which the business makes decisions about the strategy content it wishes to achieve (*see* Fig. 11.2). It is reflected in the way the organisation considers its future, how it selects its goals and the way it decides on how to allocate resources in order to achieve them. Strategy process is embedded in the structures, systems and processes that the organisation adopts, as well as its culture and the leadership style of the entrepreneur running it.

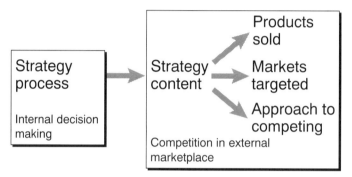

Fig. 11.2 Strategy content and strategy process

The entrepreneurial approach to management is distinct at the level of strategy process, not content. Its not what an entrepreneur *does* (the business they are in) that matters. What makes a manager entrepreneurial is the *way* he or she organises the venture and uses it innovate and to deliver value to the customer in a way that existing players cannot.

At any point in time the venture will have a strategy content, that is, a product range being sold to a distinct group of customers with a particular approach taken to attracting those customers and competing within the marketplace. The strategy content will evolve as the business grows and develops. New products will be introduced, old ones dropped. The competitive approach may alter as the organisation learns and market conditions change. At any moment in time the entrepreneur and other managers in the organisation will have views and expectations about what the business's strategy content should be in the future. This interest may also extend to other stakeholders such as important customers looking for specific new products and influential investors who offer advice on how the business might develop.

The strategy process adopted by the organisation is defined by the way in which decisions about strategy content are taken. As shown in Fig. 11.3, it is reflected in the relationship that exists between the *existing* strategy content, the strategy content

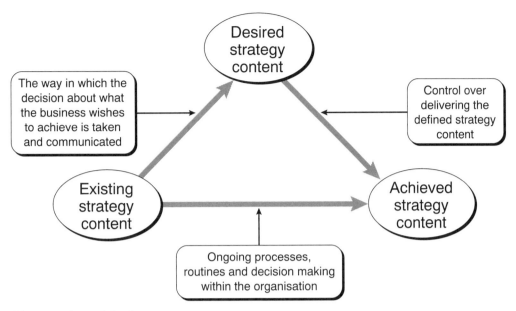

Fig. 11.3 A model of strategy process

desired by the business for the future and the strategy content that is actually *achieved*. The results of these decisions influence the investments made by the venture.

The link between existing strategy content and the strategy content achieved in the future

The strategy content of the business will evolve over time. The way in which the business modifies its range of products, changes its customer base and develops its competitive approach will be the result of a series of ongoing decisions and actions taken by the people who make up the organisation. These decisions will occur even if the organisation does not have an explicit strategy to guide them. They may be incremental and the result of short-term pragmatic considerations or they may be made in response to immediate market opportunities. However, this does not mean that these decisions are not controlled. They will be shaped by a wide variety of organisational and environmental factors including:

- the reporting relationships that define the organisation's structure;
- the mechanisms the organisation adopts to control the allocation of resources;
- the organisation's systems for motivating and rewarding performance;
- the way the organisation manages information and identifies opportunities;
- the organisation's technological competence and any technical developments;
- the organisation's historical performance;
- resource availability within the organisation;
- the organisational culture;
- internal disputes and political infighting within the organisation; and
- the expectations and influence of external stakeholders such as customers and investors.

If these features are allowed to control decision making about the evolution of a business's strategy content without reference to an overriding strategic context then the firm's strategy process may, using the terminology of Henry Mintzberg and James Waters (1985), be said to be *emergent*.

The link between existing strategy content and desired strategy content

An emergent strategy may establish itself for a number of reasons. However, an entrepreneur is unlikely to be satisfied unless the organisation operates with at least some sense of what it might achieve in the future. After all, the entrepreneur is motivated by the difference between what *is* and what *might be*. The future state desired by the entrepreneur can take a variety of forms. It will vary in several particulars, including:

- the types of detail it contains;
- how specific those details are;
- the latitude the entrepreneur will accept in its achievement;
- the time period over which it is to be achieved;
- the way in which it is communicated to other stakeholders; and
- the extent to which it is negotiable with other stakeholders.

There are a number of ways in which the organisation can become aware of the desired strategy content.

The entrepreneur's communication of their vision

The entrepreneur can articulate and communicate their vision to the rest of the organisation. This may be sufficiently powerful and attractive to motivate the whole organisation. A vision may (deliberately) lack detail but it should highlight the desirability of achieving certain strategy contents in preference to others.

The definition of a mission

The organisation's mission will specify the key elements of a strategy content. The amount of detail it provides will depend on how the strategic component in the mission is specified. The mission will, at a minimum, be able to provide a test as to what strategy contents are desirable and acceptable. The mission may be developed by a process of consensus or it may be imposed on the organisation by the entrepreneur.

The setting of objectives

The desired strategy content may be defined explicitly by the setting of specific objectives. These may be financial or strategic in nature. They may refer to the organisation as a whole, or they may relate to a particular project or they may fall within the responsibility of an individual. Objectives may be subject to negotiation and agreed through consensus, or alternatively, they may be imposed by the entrepreneur without opportunity for debate. The approach taken depends upon the entrepreneur's personal style and leadership strategy. Quantified objectives provide a means of bench-marking the achievement of a desired strategy content.

Through informal discussion

The identification of a desired strategy content may not occur by a formal process. It may become evident through ongoing discussions about the business and the opportunities offered by the market. These discussions may involve a variety of people both within, and perhaps from outside, the organisation and they may take place over a period of time.

The link between desired strategy content and achieved strategy content

This link is manifest in the ability of the entrepreneur to actually deliver the strategy content they desire for their organisation. Two things may limit this, first is the potential to achieve that strategy content in the marketplace. If the strategy content is to be delivered it must be both *achievable* given the market conditions and the competitive forces present, and *feasible* in terms of the resources available to make the necessary investments. The second possible limitation, is the control the entrepreneur has over the organisation.

Even though it might be 'their' organisation an entrepreneur is limited in the extent to which he or she can control the actions of the people who make up the organisation. They cannot enforce their will over it completely. Some of the organisation's strategy will always be 'emergent'. The way in which entrepreneurs control the organisation and ensure that it delivers the strategy content they desire is dependent on a large number of factors. Some of the more critical include:

- their personal leadership style;
- the consensus they build for the desired strategy;
- their ownership of resources;
- the way in which they control resources;
- he control mechanisms and procedures they have established;
- their technical expertise;
- their access to information and their ability to control that information within the organisation;
- the way they set objectives;
- the way in which they reward achievement of objectives;
- their creation of, and the way they are legitimatised by, symbolic devices within the organisation;
- their influence over, and control of, organisational politics;
- the relationship they build with external stakeholders; and
- the way they manage *attributions*, that is the way they associate themselves with success and dissociate themselves from failure within the organisation.

The entrepreneur will be motivated by a distinct picture of how the world should be. That is what their vision *is*. Yet they must always match their desire to achieve particular outcomes with their ability to control what the organisation can actually do both internally and in its marketplace. They must also balance their need to control the organisation with giving the people who make up the organisation latitude to make their own decisions and use their insights and intuitions to further its ends.

11.3   Controlling strategy process in the venture

KEY LEARNING OUTCOME
A recognition of the decisions the entrepreneur must make to control the strategy process in their venture.

If the entrepreneur is to maintain control of the organisation and focus it on the opportunities that it seeks to exploit then he or she must control its strategy. This demands control of its strategy *process* as well as its strategy *content*. This means controlling the way the organisation identifies options for its future, the way in which these are communicated and shared, the way in which control is maintained over resource investments aimed at achieving the desired outcomes and the way in which rewards are offered for delivering the outcomes.

The essential decisions that the entrepreneur must make in relation to developing and controlling the strategy process include:

1 Decisions relating to the development of the mission

- By what process will the business mission be developed (through consensus, or by imposition)?
- How will it be articulated?
- To whom will it be communicated?

2 Decisions relating to the development of strategy

- Who in the organisation will be invited to contribute to the development of the desired strategy content?
- How will their ideas be evaluated and judged?
- Where will the information needed to develop the strategy content come from?
- Who in the organisation will collect, store and control that information?
- How will the desired strategy content be communicated to the rest of the organisation?
- How will the strategy content be communicated to external stakeholders?

3 Decisions relating to the control of resources

- What procedure will control how investment decisions are made?
- Who will have responsibility for what level of investment?
- How will new investments be distinguished from routine payments?

- How will budgets be allocated?
- What budgetary control systems will be put in place?
- How will information on budgetary control be stored, manipulated and shared?
- By whom will information on budgetary control be stored, manipulated and shared?

4 Decisions relating to the way objectives will be set, monitored and rewarded

- How will objectives be set?
- Who will be responsible for setting them?
- For whom will objectives be set (the organisation, functions, teams, individuals)?
- What will be the nature of the objectives (financial or strategic?)
- Will objectives be negotiable? If so, in what way and by whom?
- What information will be needed to monitor objectives?
- How will this information be collected and stored? Who will have access to it?
- What will be the rewards for achieving set objectives? What will be the response if they are not achieved?

These decisions will be very influential in giving the organisation its form, structure and systems because they will influence the culture it develops. Consequently they must be subject to constant revision and review as the business grows and develops.

11.4   Why a well-defined strategy can help the venture

> **KEY LEARNING OUTCOME**
> **An appreciation of the value in generating an explicit strategy for the venture.**

Working under an emergent strategy is a far more common feature of managerial life than many textbooks on business planning would have us believe. Developing, assessing and communicating a strategy content represents an *investment*. It takes time, effort and money to achieve a well-defined strategy. Like any investment it must be assessed in terms of the returns it will bring in the way it will improve organisational performance. If this return is not forthcoming then the organisation may well benefit from allowing its strategy to be emergent

There are a variety of conditions under which an organisation's strategy tends to become emergent, for example:

- when its expectations are limited i.e. when the desired strategic content is not very different from the existing one;
- when it is experienced in pursuing its business i.e. when knowledge of how to achieve a particular strategic content is well-established and not subject to extensive discussion;
- when the competitive environment is stable i.e. when environmental shocks do not occur;

- when the competitive structure is stable i.e. when competitors do not tend to infringe on each other's business;
- when the rules of competition are established i.e. when competitor's reactions are predictable;
- when the industry technology is established i.e. new innovations are few and of limited scope;
- when patterns of investment are routinised i.e. managers do not seek guidance at a strategic level when making investment decisions;
- when the organisation's leadership is weak i.e. when power to impose a particular strategy content is limited; and
- when the organisation is political i.e. when agreement on a particular strategy content could not be gained.

These conditions tend to be found in mature, established organisations whose decision making has become routinised and even bureaucratised. They are not the typical conditions to be found in a new, fast-growing venture which is innovating and changing the rules of competition within its marketplace. Thus the entrepreneurial venture would be expected to gain in the following ways from investing in developing a strategy and communicating it to stakeholders.

A strategy encourages the entrepreneur to assess and articulate their vision

A strategy represents the way in which the entrepreneur will achieve their vision. The potential to make a vision into reality will be dependent on the possibility of creating a strategy to deliver it. This possibility will be a function of the *feasibility* of the strategy in the competitive marketplace and of the *viability* of the strategy in terms of the resources available.

A strategy ensures auditing of the organisation and its environment

A strategy is a call to action. If it is to be successful then it must be based on a sound knowledge of the environment in which the organisation finds itself; the conditions within its marketplace, particularly in terms of the competitive pressures it faces; and of its own internal capabilities and competencies. Developing a strategy demands that the organisation's capabilities and competencies are audited.

A strategy illuminates new possibilities and latitudes

A strategy is developed in response to the dictates of the entrepreneur's vision. However, the process is iterative. Strategy development feeds back to vision. It reinforces the vision's strong parts and asks the entrepreneur to readdress its weaknesses. It clarifies the possibilities the venture faces and the latitude the entrepreneur will accept for the achievement of them.

A strategy provides organisational focus

A strategy provides a central theme around which the members of the organisation can focus their activities. It relates the tasks of the individual to the tasks of the organisation as a whole. A strategy is the stream of actions that make up the organisation. As such it is a unifying principle which gives organisational actions meaning and significance in relation to each other.

A strategy guides the structuring of the organisation

A strategy highlights the tasks necessary for the entrepreneur to achieve his or her goals. Some of these tasks will be short-term, others long-term; some will be of a 'general' management nature, others will be specialist; some will be concerned with generating and sustaining external relationships, while others will be concerned with internal technical issues. The nature of the tasks that must be undertaken defines the roles that must be filled within the organisation. This in turn guides the entrepreneur in developing a structure for the organisation.

A strategy acts as a guide to decision making

A strategy provides a framework for making decisions. A decision is a response to proffered possibilities. The strategy helps to highlight and evaluate these possibilities. It indicates how significant a particular decision will be, and the impact its outcomes will have. It illuminates the information that will be needed if the decision is to be made confidently. The strategy then enables the various options to be evaluated and the right course of action to be rationalised.

A strategy provides a starting point for the setting of objectives

By specifying the tasks that need to be undertaken in order to achieve desired outcomes, a strategy provides a starting point for defining quantified measurable objectives for both the organisation as a whole, and for the individuals who make it up.

A strategy acts as a common language for stakeholders

An organisation is characterised by its strategy. The strategy provides the context in which the organisation acts. It is the perspective which enables individuals to make sense of the organisation's actions and their own part in those actions. The organisation's strategy provides a way for its stakeholders to relate to each other: they *interact* through its strategy. Strategy is a common language they can use to talk to each other about the organisation and their relationship to it.

Vision, mission and strategy in the entrepreneurial process

Vision, *mission* and *strategy* are intertwined aspects of a single entrepreneurial perspective (*see* Fig. 11.4). Each of these components represents both a different aspect of the world the entrepreneur seeks to create and the means by which they will create it. Together, they turn the entrepreneur's desire to make a difference in the world into an effective management tool for delivering change. This tool works by reconciling the entrepreneur's vision with actual possibilities and capabilities, by articulating that vision so that it may be communicated to others and by defining the actions necessary to progress the venture.

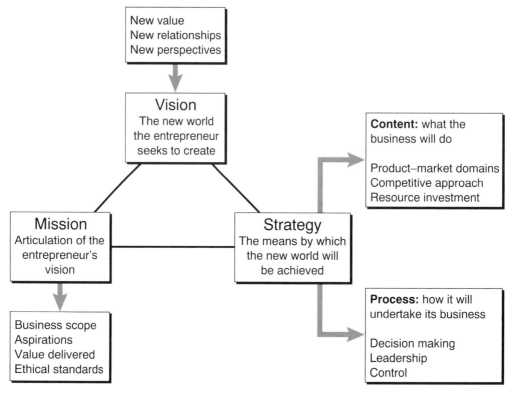

Fig. 11.4 Vision, mission and strategy in the entrepreneurial process

11.5 An overview of entrepreneurial entry strategies

> **KEY LEARNING OUTCOME**
> **A recognition of the strategies adopted by entrepreneurs to establish their ventures.**

A strategy is the pattern of actions that define an organisation. Every entrepreneurial venture is different, and each has its own strategy. However, there are common and recognisable patterns in the way in which businesses compete with one other. These are called *generic strategies*. Entrepreneurial ventures adopt a number of generic strategies in order to establish themselves in the marketplace. These strategies differ in the way in which the venture offers new value to the marketplace and the market they wish to serve (*see* Fig. 11.5).

Product–market domain

The entrepreneur must select the product market domain in which to establish their venture. This defines the scope of the product they wish to offer to what market

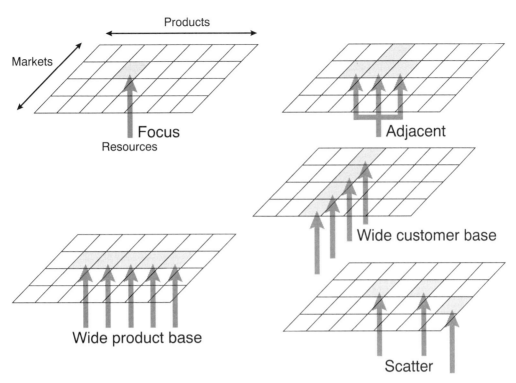

Fig. 11.5 Entrepreneurial entry strategies

segments. The product scope is the range of product categories the firm will provide. Product scope must be understood in terms of the way customers distinguish between different products in the market. Important factors are product features, product quality, patterns of product usage in terms of place, time and quantity, market positioning, and branding and imagery. The market sectors served are the distinct customer groups addressed by the firm.

Customer groups must be classified in terms of the way their needs both coincide and differ. Important factors for consideration here are demographic and sociographic characteristics, psychographic profile, customer location, buying behaviour and usage patterns. Such analysis is a well-established part of marketing thinking. The entrepreneur has five generic entry strategies in relation to product–market domain. These are:

1 *Focused entry* – addressing a single well-defined product–market domain.
2 *Product spread* – offering a wide range of products to a single well-defined market.
3 *Customer spread* – delivering a single or narrow range of products to a wide base of customers.
4 *Broad entry* – offering a wide range of products to a broad customer base. All product–market segments are adjacent in that the characterising features of each segment are continuous or can be related to each other.
5 *Scatter* – a variety of different products are offered to a variety of different customers. The segments are not adjacent.

Competitive approach

Competitive approach refers to the way the venture attracts customers by offering them value that existing competitors do not. Generic strategies in relation to this approach include:

Offering a new product or service

Delivering the customer a new and innovative product or service. This must perform a task for the customer, or solve a problem for them, in a way which is both different to, and better than, existing products.

Offering greater value

Offering the customer a product or service which is comparable to those already in existence but at a lower price, so offering them greater value for money.

Creating new relationships

The entrepreneur exists in a network of relationships built on trust. Trust both reduces costs and adds value. The entrepreneur can be competitive by creating new relationships between providers and users, and by managing existing relationships better.

Being more flexible

Customer's needs are not fixed. Even if they are in the same market segment, different customers will present a slightly different set of needs. Further, a particular customer's needs are subject to constant change. However, at any one point in time a group of customers must satisfy their needs with the limited range of products and services on offer. The entrepreneur can create new value for the customer by being flexible in terms of what they offer. This may involve modifying the products and services they provide to make them specific to the requirements of the customer or developing a means by which the product can be continually modified in response to customers' requirements.

Being more responsive

As customer needs change and evolve, existing products serve those needs less effectively. As a result new opportunities emerge and take shape. The entrepreneur can add value in the marketplace by being attuned to those changes, in terms of recognising the new opportunities as they develop and responding quickly to them by modifying their existing offerings and innovating new ones.

Choice of entry strategy

These two aspects of generic entry strategy, namely product–market domain and the competitive approach, exist in an iterative relationship to each other. The choice of competitive approach will depend on the particular characteristics of a product-market segment. How that presents itself as an opportunity to the business will depend on the resources it has to hand and its capabilities. Exploiting that opportunity will reward the business with further resources to maintain and expand its presence in its product–market domain. The choice of generic entry strategy depends on the resources and capabilities of the organisation (*see* Fig. 11.6).

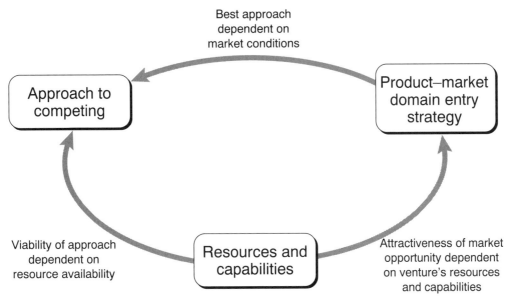

Fig. 11.6 The relationship between strategy, resources and capability

---

Summary of key ideas

- A strategy is the means by which the venture will achieve its aims.

- Strategy *content* defines the products the venture will offer, the customer groups to be targeted and the way in which the venture will compete within its markets.

- Strategy *process* defines the way in which the venture will make *decisions* about the strategy content to adopt.

- A well-defined strategy aids the venture by defining the means by which it will achieve its goals in the marketplace.

- A strategy acts as a guide for decision making and provides a common language for the venture's stakeholders.

Suggestions for further reading

Atkins, M. and **Lowe, J.** (1994) "Stakeholders and the strategy formation process in small and medium enterprises", *International Small Business Journal*, Vol. 12, No. 3, pp. 12–24.

Bowman, C. and **Ambrosini, V.** (1996) "Tracking patterns of realised strategy", *Journal of General Management*, Vol. 21, No. 3, pp. 59–73.

Calori, R. (1985) "Effective strategies in emerging industries", *Long Range Planning*, Vol. 18, No. 3, pp. 55–61.

Grieve Smith, J. and **Fleck, V.** (1987) "Business strategies in small high-technology companies", *Long Range Planning*, Vol. 20, No. 2, pp. 61–8.

Idenburg, P.J. (1993) "Four styles of strategy development", *Long Range Planning*, Vol. 26, No. 6, pp. 132–7.

McDougall, P. and **Robinson, R.B.** (1990) "New venture strategies: An empirical identification of eight 'archetypes' of competitive strategies for entry", *Strategic Management Journal*, Vol. 11, pp. 447–67.

Miller, D. (1992) "The generic strategy trap", *The Journal of Business Strategy*, Jan/Feb, pp. 37–41.

Mintzberg, H. (1973) "Strategy making in three modes", *California Management Review*, Vol. XVI, No. 2, pp. 44–53.

Mintzberg, H. (1978) "Patterns in strategy formation" *Management Science*, Vol. 24, No. 9, pp. 934–48.

Mintzberg, H. (1988) "Generic strategies: Towards a comprehensive framework", *Advances in Strategic Management*, Vol. 5, pp. 1–76.

Mintzberg, H. and **Waters, J.A.** (1985) "Of strategies deliberate and emergent" *Strategic Management Journal*, Vol. 6, pp. 257–72.

Quinn, J.B. (1978) "Strategic change: Logical incrementalism", *Sloan Management Review*, Autumn.

12 The business plan: an entrepreneurial tool

CHAPTER OVERVIEW

A business plan is an essential tool for the entrepreneur. This chapter explores the role of the business plan and the kind of information it should include. It considers the way a business plan can help the venture by guiding analysis, creating a synthesis of new insights, communicating the potential of the venture to interested parties, and promoting management action. The chapter concludes by looking at the ways in which business planning can increase the flexibility and responsiveness of the venture.

12.1 Planning and performance

> **KEY LEARNING OUTCOME**
> **A recognition of the influence of formal planning activity on the performance of the entrepreneurial venture.**

Entrepreneurs, like many other managers, are often called upon to prepare formal, written plans. They may do this of their own accord or it may be at the instigation of external investors such as venture capitalists or banks. The picture of the entrepreneur 'locked away' writing a formal business plan sits ill at ease with the image of them as dynamic individuals actively pursuing their business interests. Many entrepreneurs object to preparing plans because they feel their time would be better spent pushing the venture forward. They claim that they already know what is in the plan and that no-one else will read it!

This objection highlights an important point in that developing a plan demands time, energy and (often) hard cash. It ties up both the entrepreneur and the business's staff. A business plan represents an *investment* in the venture. It must be justified as an investment, that is in terms of the return it offers the business. The relationship between formal planning and business performance has been the subject of numerous statistical studies; however, no clear picture has emerged. The correlation between *formal* planning and performance is weak so it is not possible to say with certainty that formal planning will improve the performance of the business. As a result, there has been something of a reaction against formal planning in recent years, especially in relation to smaller businesses. Henry Mintzberg has offered a profound criticism of at least a narrow approach to planning in his book *The Rise and Fall of Strategic Planning*.

However, the poor statistical correlation should not be taken to mean that performance is unaffected by planning. Statistical studies usually compare 'planning activity' (the definition of this varies between studies) against performance measured in financial or growth terms. Inevitably, these studies must reduce a complex organisational phenomenon to simple variables. Planning is not an easily defined, isolated activity, rather it is an activity embedded in both the wider strategy process of the organisation and the control strategy of the entrepreneur. Financial performance is important but it is not the only measure of achievement which motivates the entrepreneur. The entrepreneur may compromise financial gains in order to achieve less tangible benefits. They may even *plan* to make this compromise. Common sense suggests both that a good plan will lead to an improved performance and equally, that a bad one will lead the business astray. There is also the problem of distinguishing between the existence of a plan and whether that plan is actually *implemented*.

Statistical studies of planning and performance also face the issue of causation; that is, when two things seem to correlate, how can we be sure which is the cause and which the effect? It may be that the variation in performance observed is not so much due to the mere existence of planning but rather to the *quality* of the planning that takes place. It has even been suggested that planning does not lead to performance, but rather that a good performance allows managers the time and money to indulge in planning!

The planning/performance debate reflects the problems to be encountered in teasing out cause and effect relationships in a system as complex and subject to as many variables as an entrepreneurial venture. In short then, it is impossible to give a straight 'yes' or 'no' answer to questions like: 'Should entrepreneurs produce a formal plan?' or 'Should entrepreneurs formalise the way their organisation plans?'. Over-generalisation is unwise. The decision to engage in formal planning, like most other decisions the entrepreneur faces, must be made in the light of what is best for the individual venture, the way it operates and the specific opportunities it faces. Planning, if it is approached in a way which is right for the venture and is aimed at addressing the right issues, would seem to offer a number of benefits. The remainder of this chapter will examine the decision to create a formal plan and explore the ways in which it might benefit the business.

12.2 The role of the business plan

KEY LEARNING OUTCOME
An understanding of how the business plan works as a management tool.

The activity of creating a formal business plan consumes both time and resources. If it is to be undertaken, and undertaken well, there must be an appreciation of the way in which the business plan can actually be made to work as a tool for the business. In principle, there are four mechanisms by which a business plan might aid the performance of the venture.

By working as a tool for analysis

A business plan contains information. Some of this information will be that used as the basis for articulating and refining the entrepreneur's vision, for generating the mission statement and for developing a strategy content and strategy process for the venture. The structure of the business plan provides the entrepreneur with an effective check list of the information they must gather in order be sure the direction for their venture is both achievable and rewarding. Creating the plan guides and disciplines the entrepreneur in gathering this information.

By working as a tool for synthesis

Once data has been gathered and analysed in a formal way then the information generated must be used to provide a direction for the venture. The information must be integrated with, and used to refine, the entrepreneur's vision and used to support the development of a suitable mission and strategy. The planning exercise acts to *synthesise* the entrepreneur's vision with a definite plan of action in a unified way. This synthesis converts the vision into a strategy for the venture, and then into the actions appropriate to pursuing that strategy.

By working as a tool for communication

The business plan provides a vehicle for communicating the potential of the venture, the opportunities it faces and the way it intends to exploit them in a way which is concise, efficient and effective. This may be of value in communicating with both internal and external stakeholders. The plan may draw internal people together and give them a focus for their activities. The business plan is particularly important as a tool for communicating with potential investors, gaining their interest and attracting them to the venture.

By working as a call to action

The business plan is a call to action. It provides a detailed list of the activities that must be undertaken, the tasks that must be performed and the outcomes that must be achieved if the entrepreneur is to convert his or her vision into a new world. The plan may also call upon formal project management techniques such as critical path analysis in order to organise, prioritise and arrange tasks in a way which makes the best use of scarce resources.

The four ways in which the planning exercise contributes to the success drive of the venture do not operate in isolation. They underpin and support each other and the performance of the venture (*see* Fig. 12.1). Together they define not only the plan that should be developed for the venture, but also the way the venture should engage in planning.

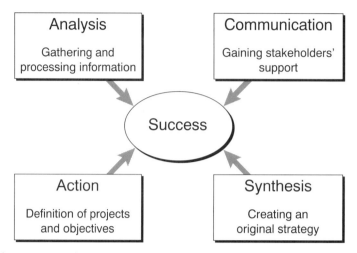

Fig. 12.1 Planning: analysis, communication, synthesis and action

12.3   What a business plan should include

KEY LEARNING OUTCOME
An appreciation of the type of information to be included in a business plan.

There are no hard and fast rules about what a business plan should include since a business plan must be shaped to reflect the needs and requirements of the venture it represents. The entrepreneur and the management team will have their own preferences. The information included will depend on what stage the venture is at: the plan for a new venture may be more exhaustive than the ongoing yearly plan for one which is quite well established. Financial backers may dictate both the format the business plan must take and the information it should include.

The following list indicates the type and scope of information and themes that might be included in a fairly exhaustive business plan.

- *Mission*
  - *The mission for the venture:* the formal mission statement that defines the business.
- *Overview of key objectives*
  - *Financial objectives:* the turnover and profit targets for the period of the plan; the growth desired over the previous period.
  - *Strategic objectives:* achievements in the market and gains to be made in market position.
- *The market environment*
  - *Background to the market:* i.e. how the market is defined; the size of the market; major market sectors and niches; overall growth rate; key trends and develop-

ments in consumer behaviour and buying habits; and technological developments in the product, service delivery and operations.
- *Competitors:* key competitors, their strengths and weaknesses; competitors' strategy and likely reaction to the venture's activity.
- *Competitive conditions:* the basis of competition in the market; the importance of price, product differentiation and branding; the benefits to be gained from positioning.
- *Competitive advantage of the venture:* the important strengths of the venture relative to competitors; sources of competitive advantage.
- *Definition of product offerings:* the products/services that the business will offer to the market.
- *Definition of target markets:* the way in which the market is split up into different sectors; the dimensions of the market important for characterising the sectors; and the market sectors that will be prioritised for targeting by the business.

● *Strategy*
- *Product strategy:* the way in which the product/service will be differentiated from competitors (e.g. features/quality/price); why this will be attractive to customers.
- *Pricing strategy:* how the product/service will be priced relative to competitors (e.g. offer of a premium, discounting); means of establishing price; promotional pricing and price cutting; pricing policy and margins to be offered to intermediaries.
- *Distribution strategy:* the route by which the product/service will be delivered to the customer; intermediaries (wholesalers, distributors, retailers) who will be partners in distribution; strategy for working with distributors; policy for exporting and international marketing if appropriate.
- *Promotional strategy:* approaches to informing the customer (and intermediaries) about the product/service; advertising message, means and medium; sales activity and approach to selling; sales promotions (including price promotions); public relations activity.
- *Networking:* relationship between the organisation and other organisations in the network; use of the network to create and support competitive advantage.

● *Financial forecasts*
- *Income:* revenues from trading activity; structure of the capital provided by investors.
- *Routine expenditure:* expenditure on salaries, raw materials and consumables; payment of interest on debt.
- *Capital expenditure:* major investment in new assets; how these assets will enhance performance.
- *Cash flow:* difference between revenues and expenditure by period; cash flow reflects the liquidity of the business and its ability to fund its activities. If income is more than expenditure then cash flow is positive. If expenditure is more than income then cash flow is negative.

● *Activity*
- *Major projects:* the key projects that will drive the venture forward and deliver the objectives, for example: new product developments, sales drives, launches with distributors and advertising campaigns.

- *People*
  - *Key players in the venture:* the individuals behind the venture; the skills and experience they will contribute to the business; evidence of their achievements; personal profiles and CVs.

The information included in the business plan will depend on how it is intended to use the plan and to whom it will be communicated. The business need not be restricted to a single version of the plan and it may prove advantageous to use different formats for different audiences.

12.4 Business planning: analysis and synthesis

KEY LEARNING OUTCOME
An appreciation of how business planning facilitates analysis of the venture's potential and a synthesis of its strategy.

Effective planning requires information. Information is all around us but it rarely comes for free. Information has a cost: this may be relatively low, a trip to the local library perhaps, or it may be very expensive, commissioning a major piece of market research for example. Even if it has no direct cost, gathering and analysing information takes time. Hence information must be gathered with an eye to how it will be used. The benefits to be gained from having the information must justify its cost.

Information is used to manage uncertainty. Having information means that uncertainty is reduced which in turn reduces the risk of the venture and improves the prospects of its success. Essentially, the entrepreneur is interested in answering the following questions:

What are the customer's fundamental needs in relation to the product category? (What benefits does the product offer? What problems do customers solve with the product?).

How does the market currently serve those needs? (What products are offered? What features do they have?).

In what way(s) does the market fail to serve those needs? (Why are customers left dissatisfied? How often are they left dissatisfied?).

How might customer needs be served better? (How might the product on offer be improved?).

Marketing, as a discipline, offers a number of techniques to develop these answers. In addition, the entrepreneur must know:

How does the better way he or she is advocating add up as a real business opportunity?

What risks are likely to be present in pursuing such an opportunity?

These final two points are of course critical. Developing an answer to these questions and understanding the decisions they involve, will be explored fully through the development of the *Strategic Window* in Part 3 of this book.

Planning certainly supports strategy development but it is not *equivalent* to it. The Canadian management thinker, Henry Mintzberg, observes that planning is about *analysis*; it is about breaking down information to spot opportunities and possibilities. Strategy, on the other hand, is about *synthesis*; it is about bringing the capabilities of the business to bear on the opportunity in a way which is creative and original. Developing answers to the questions listed above is the analysis part of the equation. Reconciling them into a workable, rewarding strategy is the synthesis part. This synthesis must include both the strategy *content* and the *process* to deliver it.

In order to synthesise an original strategy the entrepreneur must decide:

- How will the venture address the needs of the customer (i.e. what is the nature of the opportunity that has been identified)?
- Why will the venture's offerings serve those needs better than those of competitors? (What is the *innovation*? Why is it valuable?)
- How will demand be stimulated? (This involves issues of communication, promotion, distribution.)
- Why can the entrepreneur's business deliver this in a way that competitors cannot? (What will be the *competitive advantage* that the business enjoys? What will it be able to do that its competitors cannot do that is valuable for its customers?)
- What is it about the business that enables them to do this? (What are the *competencies* and *capabilities* of the business?)
- Why will competitors be unable to imitate them? (In what way(s) is the competitive advantage *sustainable*?)

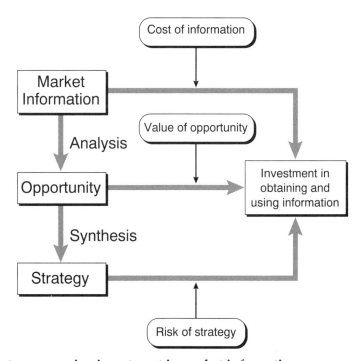

Fig. 12.2 Factors governing investment in market information

Planning helps the business by first demanding an analysis of information about the market, customers and competitors. This information provides a sure basis for decision making. Planning goes on to help the business by synthesis, that is by integrating the information into a strategy. This strategy gives the venture a shape and a direction. It forms the basis for plans and projects which offer definite actions for the people who make up the venture and those who support it to follow. Thus information is valuable because it links the analysis of opportunity with the synthesis of strategy in a planning framework (*see* Fig. 12.2).

12.5 Business planning: action and communication

KEY LEARNING OUTCOME
An appreciation of how the business plan may be used as a communication tool and as a call to action.

Communication is not just about passing on information. It is an attempt to illicit a particular *response* from someone. In business it is not just what we want people to *know* that matters; it is also what we want them to *do*. The ways the business plan functions both as a piece of communication and as a recipe for action are intimately interrelated.

The business plan is a communication that relates in a succinct way a precise and unambiguous account of the venture *and* what it aims to achieve. It defines the decisions the entrepreneur has made in relation to: the opportunity that has been identified; the way the opportunity will be exploited; the value the entrepreneur aims to create as a result of exploiting it; the resources that will be needed in order to progress the venture; the risks those resources will be exposed to; and the projects the entrepreneur will undertake with the resources they receive.

These decisions are communicated with the intention of gaining support for the venture. The entrepreneur will be particularly interested in communicating with and influencing the following groups of people.

Investors

The business plan not only relates the potential of the venture and the rewards it offers to investors but also the risks that it entails. It is also an opportunity for the entrepreneur to convince the investor of the skills they have and make them feel confident that the goods can be delivered. Numerous studies have found that the quality of the business plan and the effectiveness of its communication is a critical factor in gaining investors' interest and support. See, for example, the studies by MacMillan *et al.* (1985 and 1987), Knight (1994) and Mason and Harrison (1996) referenced at the end of this chapter.

Employees

Employees make their own investment in the business by committing themselves to it. The business plan can give them confidence in the future of the venture. It will also specify the key projects that need to be undertaken, so defining individual objectives and the way in which the role the individual plays fits with the goals of the organisation as a whole. Jan Carlzon, the entrepreneur who turned around the failing *Scandinavian Airline Systems (SAS)* in the early 1980s, issued each of the organisation's 20 000 or so employees with a plan which outlined the vision and strategy he had devised. This plan became known as the 'little red book'.

Employee commitment does not just come from letting people in on the plan. Letting them get involved in *creating* it in the first place is also a sure way to gain their support.

Important customers

A customer may face a cost in taking on a new supplier. Moving between suppliers demands the time and attention of managers. In some cases there may need to be a direct investment in new equipment so that the products can be used. If the product is new and innovative, the customer may have to learn to use it, for example, staff may need additional training. The customer may be willing to face these costs if the benefits offered by the new product are high enough. They will resist, however, if they have doubts about the long-term viability of the supplier. Sharing the business plan with them is an effective way of giving them confidence in the entrepreneurial venture and encouraging them to make the necessary commitment. Customers are usually flattered to be asked to become involved with the venture in this way. Therefore, for a new venture, communicating the business plan as well as the product offering, can be an important part of the selling strategy.

Major suppliers

Suppliers may also need to make an investment if they wish to supply the venture. This may take the form of dedicated selling and support activity and may even involve developing bespoke products. Although the venture offers the prospect of new business they will, like the venture's customers, resist making the investment if they harbour doubts about the long term viability of the venture. Again, the business plan may be used to give them the confidence to make an investment of time and resources on behalf of the venture.

In short, the business plan is a communication tool which can be used by the venture to help build the network of relationships which will be critical to its long-term success.

12.6 Strategy, planning and flexibility

KEY LEARNING OUTCOME
An understanding of how planning may be used to make the business responsive, rather than rigid, in the face of opportunity and uncertainty.

Many entrepreneurs are suspicious of formal planning. They may see the written plan as restrictive, and feel that it reduces their room for manoeuvre. They may be concerned that by defining future actions it limits their options. However, these suspicions are ill-founded. If approached in the right way, planning increases, rather than restricts, flexibility. The right sort of strategy can make the business more, not less, responsive.

Focus on ends rather than means

Goals should be given priority over plans. It's what the business aims to achieve that matters. It may be that there is more than one way in which the business can reach its objectives. If so, all of the possibilities should be explored. Not all are likely to be equally attractive and one route may be given priority. However, a knowledge of the alternatives allows for contingency plans to be made and an alternative course can be followed if some routes become blocked.

Challenge assumptions

What are the assumptions on which the plan is based? For example, what assumptions have been made in measuring the size of markets and the venture's rate of growth, in determining how attractive the innovation is to customers and in gauging the strengths of competitors? How sensitive is the plan to these assumptions? What will happen if they are wrong? How can the plan be 'immunised' against poor assumptions by building in contingencies for when they are wrong?

Model scenarios

What are the likely outcomes if the plan is implemented? How certain are these outcomes? In the face of uncertainty what is likely to be the *best* of all possible worlds and what is likely to be the *worst*? What is the *most likely* outcome? Determine what scenarios will result if an *optimistic*, a *pessimistic* and a *realistic* attitude is taken to the outcomes that are expected (particularly in relation to income and expenditure). How will the business fare in the face of each eventuality? How exposed is the business if the pessimistic scenario comes about? Has it (or can it get) the resources to manage the optimistic? Furthermore, have investors been made party to all scenarios, not just the best?

Create strategic flexibility

At the end of the day, a strategy is just a way of doing things. Strategic flexibility is a way of doing things well when faced with uncertainty. It involves actively responding to outcomes and adjusting activity, not just blindly following set plans. Strategic flexibility comes from questioning moves. For example, can the product or service be modified in the light of consumer responses to it (*positive* as well as negative)? If one target market is proving hard to break into, can an alternative one be approached? Can costs be managed in response to demand (for example, how exposed is the business to fixed costs?)? If some relationships in the network prove to be less valuable than expected can new relationships be built quickly?

Leave space to learn

The way in which entrepreneurs and their businesses meet opportunities and respond to challenges is dependent on the way in which they see the world, the knowledge that they have and their range of skills. All these factors must evolve through learning. The entrepreneur must constantly question the business. Are the underlying assumptions still valid? Is this still the best way to do things? Success does not speak for itself and it is important to question why is a particular outcome a success? What was done right? In what way might they have been even *more* successful? What where the failings? How might they be avoided next time? Learning is an active process. The good business plan identifies and highlights those areas where learning can take place. In short, a good strategy should be about flexibility, about enabling the business to take advantage of opportunities as they take shape and to manage the unexpected. It is not about setting a rigid course of action.

Summary of key ideas

- There is no simple correlation between investment in planning and business performance.

- However, a business plan can help the entrepreneurial venture by:
    - ensuring that a full analysis of the situation and the environment has been undertaken;
    - encouraging the synthesis of insights to generate a vision and a strategy;
    - acting as a call to action; and
    - being a medium for communication with both internal and external stakeholders.

- A well-defined business plan will actually increase the venture's flexibility, not impair it.

Suggestions for further reading

Ackelsburg, R. (1985) "Small businesses do plan and it pays off", *Long Range Planning*, Vol. 18, No. 5, pp. 61–7.

Allaire, Y. and **Firsirotu, M.** (1990) "Strategic plans as contracts", *Long Range Planning*, Vol. 23, No. 1, pp. 102–15.

Ames, M.D. (1994) "Rethinking the business plan paradigm: Bridging the gap between plan and plan execution", *Journal of Small Business Strategy*, Vol.5, No. 1, pp.69–76.

Bhide, A. (1994) "How entrepreneurs craft strategy", *Harvard Business Review*, Mar-Apr, pp. 150–61.

Bracker, J.S., **Keats, B.W.** and **Person, J.N.** (1988) "Planning and financial performance among small firms in a growth industry", *Strategic Management Journal*, Vol. 9, pp. 591–603.

Chakravarthy, B.S. and **Lorange, P.** (1991) "Adapting strategic planning to the changing needs of a business", *Journal of Organisational Change Management*, Vol. 4, No. 2, pp. 6–18.

Cooper, A.C. (1981) "Strategic management: New ventures and small business", *Long Range Planning*, Vol. 14, No. 5, pp. 39–45.

Grieve Smith, J. and **Fleck, V.** (1988) "Strategies of new biotechnology firms", *Long Range Planning*, Vol. 21, No. 3, pp. 51–8.

Hamel, G. and **Prahalad, C.K.** (1993) "Strategy as stretch and leverage", *Harvard Business Review*, Mar-Apr, pp. 75–84.

Higgins, J.M. (1996) "Innovate or evaporate: Creative techniques for strategists", *Long Range Planning*, Vol. 29, No. 3, pp. 370–80.

Knight, R.M. (1994) "Criteria used by venture capitalists: A cross cultural analysis", *International Small Business Journal*, Vol. 13, No. 1, pp. 26–37.

Macmillan, I.C., Siegel, R. and **Subba Narashima, P.N.** (1985) "Criteria used by venture capitalists to evaluate new venture proposals", *Journal of Business Venturing*, Vol. 1, pp. 119–28.

Macmillan, I.C., Zeeman, L. and **Subba Narashima, P.N.** (1987) "Effectiveness of criteria used by venture capitalists in the venture screening process", *Journal of Business Venturing*, Vol. 2, pp. 123–38.

McKiernan, P. and **Morris, C.** (1994) "Strategic planning and financial performance in UK SMEs: Does formality matter?", *British Journal of Management*, Vol. 5, Special Issue, pp. S31–41.

Mason, C. and **Harrison, R.** (1996) "Why 'business angels' say no: A case study of opportunities rejected by an informal investor syndicate", *International Small Business Journal*, Vol. 14, No. 2, pp. 35–51.

Mintzberg, H. (1994) *The Rise and Fall of Strategic Planning*, New York: Prentice Hall.

Schwenk, C.R. and **Shrader, C.B.** (1993) "Effects of formal planning on financial performance in small firms: A meta-analysis", *Entrepreneurial Theory and Practice*, Vol. 17, No. 3, pp. 53–64.

Shuman, J.C., Shaw, J.J. and **Sussman, G.** (1985) "Strategic planning in smaller rapid growth companies", *Long Range Planning*, Vol. 18, No. 6, pp. 48–53.

Thurston, P.H. (1983) "Should smaller companies make formal plans?", *Harvard Business Review*, Sept-Oct, pp. 162–88.

Waalewijn, P. and **Segaar, P.** (1993) "Strategic management: The key to profitability in small companies", *Long Range Planning*, Vol. 26, No. 2, pp. 24–30.

Part 3 Initiating the new venture

13 The strategic window: identifying and analysing the gap for the new business

CHAPTER OVERVIEW

Entrepreneurs identify and exploit new opportunities. This chapter considers why there will always be gaps in a market that the entrepreneur can exploit, despite the presence of established businesses. The chapter goes on to develop a picture of opportunity as a strategic 'window' through which the new venture must pass.

13.1 Why existing businesses leave gaps in the market

KEY LEARNING OUTCOME
An understanding of why an established business environment will always leave opportunities for the entrepreneur.

In principle, established businesses are in a strong position relative to entrepreneurial entrants. This is because they have gained experience in their markets through serving customers; they have experience in operating their businesses; they have established themselves into a secure network of relationships with customers and suppliers; they face lower risks and so their cost of capital is usually lower; they may enjoy lower costs by having developed experience curve economies; and they have an established output volume which gives them an economy of scale cost advantage. Despite these advantages, entrepreneurs do compete effectively against established, even entrenched, players. They identify and exploit new opportunities despite the presence of experienced competitors. There is always, it seems, a better way of doing things. There are a variety of reasons why existing businesses leave gaps in the market that the innovative, entrepreneurial venture can exploit.

Established businesses fail to see new opportunities

Opportunities do not present themselves, they have to be actively sought out. A business organisation has not merely a way of *doing* things; it also has a way of *seeing* things. The way in which a business scans the business environment for new opportunities is linked to the systems and processes that make up that organisation. *Organisational inertia*, that is resistance to change in response to changing circumstances, is a well-documented phenomenon. An established organisation can become complacent. It can look back on its early success and take its market for granted. Its opportunity scanning systems can become rigid and bureaucratised or caught up in political infighting. It might adopt a particular perspective or 'dominant logic' which leads it to see the world in a certain way. That perspective may not change as the world changes. As a result it may be less attuned to identifying new opportunities in the market than a hungry new entrant. For example, IBM missed the opportunity for software operating systems that would enable Bill Gates's *Microsoft* to become one of the world's largest companies.

New opportunities are thought to be too small

The value of a new opportunity must be seen as relative to the size of the business which might pursue it. The chance to gain an extra £100 000 of business will mean far more to a business with a turnover of £1 million than for one with a turnover of £100 million. As a result 'small' opportunities may be ignored, or at least not pursued vigorously, by large, established players. The smaller new entrant will, however, find them attractive. They may prove to be just the foot in the door they need!

Technological inertia

Opportunities are pursued by innovation. An innovation is founded on some technological approach. However, a technology is simply a way of doing things. It is a means to address a need. An established organisation may regard its business as based on a particular technology rather than the serving of customer needs. It might prefer to rely on the technological approach 'it's good at'. However, new technological approaches to satisfying needs can develop rapidly. Such technological inertia leaves the field open for new entrants to make technological innovation the basis of their business.

For example, the last mechanical typewriter manufacturer closed recently. The typewriter industry had a great deal of expertise in designing, manufacturing and marketing machines which produced documents. The manufacturers were very good at their business. However, they defined themselves in terms of the mechanical technology used by typewriters. They did not think of themselves as providing customers with a document management service. As a result, they were easy prey for a whole generation of entrepreneurs who moved in with electronic word processing products which provided a much better way to manage documents.

Cultural inertia

Along with its technology, an established business has its own 'way of doing things'. This way of doing things – its culture – influences the way in which it delivers value to its customers. The best way to deliver value to customers will change as the competitive climate evolves. If the business does not change its way of doing things to meet new challenges then it may not be in a position to exploit new opportunities. Newer entrants may take advantage of this by adopting a culture more appropriate to the altered climate.

Thus the Swedish entrepreneur Jan Carlzon turned *Scandinavian Airline Systems (SAS)* into a great aviation success story by changing its culture from one where the needs of aircraft and airports were managed to one where the needs of customers were given priority.

Internal politics

Managers in established organisations often engage in political infighting. This occurs when individuals and groups do not feel their interests and goals are aligned with each other or with the organisation as a whole. Organisations pursue new opportunities in order to achieve their objectives. Being focused on a new opportunity demands a commitment to objectives. If this is not present then, at best, there will be disagreement on the value particular opportunities present. At worst, different factions will work against one other. As a result, opportunities will slip by. This will leave the more focused and less political new entrant free to exploit them.

Anti-trust actions by government

Governments are concerned to ensure that monopolies do not distort the workings of an economy. If a firm is felt to be gaining too much dominance in a market, then the government may be tempted to act against its growth. By definition, this action will work against the dominating players and so will favour the new entrant. Already, questions are being asked by anti-trust agencies in the US about the near monopoly possessed by the software giant *Microsoft* in certain areas of the market.

Government intervention to support the new entrant

In general, governments are acutely aware of the importance, both economic and political, of small and fast-growing new firms in an economy. They are responsible for providing economic efficiency, for bringing new innovations to market and for creating new jobs. As a result governments are tempted to provide support for both the smaller business and the new entrant. This can take the form of tax incentives and more liberal employment laws or it can be more direct and involve cheap loans and credit. Support may also be offered for technical development, education and consulting. Again, this support tips the balance in favour of the new entrant.

A word of warning

The large, established business, despite its inherent advantages, leaves gaps into which the ambitious new entrant can move because they often undervalue new opportunities, are complacent about them and are unresponsive due to internal inertias. While exploiting this, entrepreneurs should never forget that this is a fate that can also await them as their businesses grow!

13.2 The strategic window: a visual metaphor

KEY LEARNING OUTCOME
An appreciation of how the metaphor of the 'strategic window' can be used to give form to the process of identifying and exploiting opportunity.

A metaphor is simply an attempt to understand an idea by drawing parallels with something it can be said to be *like*. One metaphor which is useful for generating a mental image which can guide the identification, analysis and exploitation of opportunity is that of the *strategic window*. The starting point is to imagine a wall. This wall represents the landscape of existing businesses and the value they offer to the customer. Where it is solid, nothing can be seen beyond it; the wall cannot be passed. Here, existing players leave no space for new value to be offered and there is no room for the new entrepreneur. However, there is *always* the possibility of something being done better. Existing players will always leave some gaps, somewhere. At some points in the wall there are *windows*. It is possible to see through these windows to a new world in which more value can be offered. There is the potential to pass through these windows into this new world. This is the gap for which the entrepreneur looks. The window represents an *opportunity*. If that opportunity is identified, and the way in which it can be exploited understood, then it becomes a *strategic window*.

Seeing the window: scanning for new opportunities

This involves scanning the solid wall presented by existing players to find the windows and spot the gaps in what they offer to the market. This process demands an active approach to identifying new opportunities and to innovating in response to them.

Locating the window: positioning the new venture

This involves developing an understanding of where the window is *located*. This demands an understanding both of the *positioning* of the new offering in the marketplace relative to existing products and services and of how the venture can position itself in the marketplace relative to existing players to take best advantage of the opportunity presented.

Measuring the window

This involves evaluating the opportunity and recognising the potential it offers to create new value. In short, it means finding out how much the opportunity might be worth. This demands getting to grips with the market for the innovation, measuring its size, understanding its dynamics and trends, evaluating the impact the innovation might make in it and ascertaining how much customers might be willing to spend on it. Measuring the window also demands that the entrepreneur develop an understanding of the risks the venture might face.

Opening the window: gaining commitment

Having identified, located and measured the window the next stage is to *open* it. Opening the window means turning vision into reality i.e. actually starting the new business. Critical to this stage is the need to get stakeholders to make a commitment to the venture, to attract investors and employees, to develop a new set of relationships and to establish the venture within its network. Once the window is opened, then the entrepreneur can then move through it, metaphorically speaking, by actually starting up the business.

Closing the window: sustaining competitiveness

Once the window has been opened and the entrepreneur has passed through it then the window must be closed again. If it is not, then competitors will follow the entrepreneur through and exploit the opportunity as well. This will reduce the potential of the entrepreneur's business. Closing the window to stop competitors following through means creating a long-term *sustainable competitive advantage* for the business. This provides the basis on which the entrepreneur can build the security and stability of the business and use it to earn long-term rewards.

Each of these stages presents itself to the entrepreneur as a series of *decisions*. Developing the business means addressing those decisions. The following five chapters will explore these decisions in detail.

Summary of key ideas

- A business environment is full of opportunities because existing businesses always leave gaps. There is always the potential to create new value.

- The *strategic window* is a visual metaphor which allows entrepreneurs to make sense of the opportunities they pursue.

- The five stages of the strategic window are: *spotting*, *locating*, *measuring*, *opening*, and *closing*.

Suggestions for further reading

Abel, D.F. (1978) "Strategic windows", *Journal of Marketing*, July, pp. 21–6.

Bettis, R.A. and **Prahalad, C.K.** (1995) "The dominant logic: Retrospective and extension", *Strategic Management Journal*, Vol. 16, pp. 5–14.

Cyert, R.M., Kumar, P. and **Williams, J.R.** (1993) "Information, market imperfections and strategy", *Strategic Management Journal*, Vol. 14, pp. 47–58.

Hannan, M.T. and **Freeman, J.** (1984) "Structural inertia and organisational change", *American Sociological Review*, Vol. 49, pp. 149–64.

Prahalad, C.K. and **Bettis, R.A.** (1986) "The dominant logic: A new linkage between diversity and performance", *Strategic Management Journal*, Vol. 7, pp. 485–501.

Yao, D.A. (1988) "Beyond the reach of the invisible hand: Impediments to economic activity, market failures and profitability", *Strategic Management Journal*, Vol. 9, pp. 59–70.

14 Seeing the window: scanning for opportunity

CHAPTER OVERVIEW

*The first stage in using the strategic window is **identifying** it. This chapter looks at how new opportunities may be spotted, screened and selected.*

14.1 Types of opportunities available

KEY LEARNING OUTCOME
An understanding of the types of opportunity that present themselves to the entrepreneur.

An opportunity is the chance to do something in a way which is both different to, and better than, the way it is done at the moment. It offers the possibility of delivering new value to the customer. In its details, every opportunity is different, but there are some common patterns in the way in which opportunities take shape.

The new product

The new product offers the customer a physical device which provides a new means to satisfy a need or to solve a problem. A new product may be based on existing technology or it might exploit new technological possibilities. It might also represent a chance to add value to an existing product by using an appropriate branding strategy.

The new service

The new service offers the customer an act, or a series of acts, which satisfy a particular need or solve a particular problem. Many new offerings have both 'product' and 'service' dimensions. Robert Worcester, for example, built the enormously successful market research business, *MORI*, founded not so much on the basis that business and politicians wanted a *product* (market information) as on the recognition that they wanted a *service* that would help them make decisions.

New means of production

A new means of producing an existing product is not an opportunity in itself. It will offer an opportunity if it can be used to deliver *additional* value to the customer. This means the product must be produced at lower cost or in a way which allows greater flexibility in the way it is delivered to the customer. For example, Takami Takahashi, the founder of the diversified Japanese multi-national *Minebea*, grew the business from being a small niche player in the ball-bearing market by exploiting its experience in small component manufacturing to offer low-cost products to the electronics, engineering and precision instruments markets.

New distribution route

A new way of getting the product to the customer which means the customer finds it easier, more convenient, or less time consuming to get to the product or service. This may involve the venture developing an innovative way of getting the product to the end-user or a new way of working with intermediaries.

Improved service

An opportunity to enhance the value of a product to the customer by offering an additional service element with it. This service often involves maintaining the product in some way but it can also be based on supporting the customer in using the product or offering them training in its use. Frederick Smith's inspiration for the US parcel service, *Federal Express,* was a recognition of the gap in the market for a business that would be dedicated to providing a high quality parcel delivery service. This gap was left by existing suppliers, chiefly passenger airlines, who offered a parcel service as a side-line to use up excess weight capacity on aircraft but did not consider it to be an important part of their business, and so did not consider the service element to be important to their customers.

Relationship building

Relationships are built on trust, and trust adds value by reducing the cost needed to monitor contracts. Trust can provide a source of competitive advantage. It can be used to build networks which competitors find it hard to break into. A new opportunity presents itself if relationships which will be mutually beneficial to the entrepreneur and the customer can be built. Rowland 'Tiny' Rowland's ability to develop close and trusting relationships with African leaders was an important factor in the success of the *Lonhro* empire. The Saatchi brothers did not merely provide an advertising service, they also concentrated on building relationships with their clients.

Opportunities do not have to be 'pure'. It is often the case that a particular opportunity comprises a mixture of the above elements. A new product may demand an additional support service if customers are to find it attractive. Getting the product to them may demand that relationships are formed. The entrepreneur must take an open mind and a creative approach to the way in which opportunities may be exploited.

14.2 Methods of spotting opportunities

KEY LEARNING OUTCOME
An appreciation of the methods which might be used to identify new opportunities.

It is often assumed that entrepreneurs are graced with some special kind of insight that enables them to see opportunities and the way in which they might be exploited. While creativity is certainly important, the view that entrepreneurs work purely by inspiration undervalues the extent to which they are rewarded for the hard work involved in actively seeking out and evaluating new opportunities. There are a variety of techniques that can be of help in this search. Some are rather rough and ready while others are more formal. Some are so straightforward the entrepreneur may not even realise that he or she is using them. Others are complex and may demand the support of market research experts if they are to be used properly. It is useful to be aware of the ways in which a market may be scanned for new opportunities, and of the techniques available to assist in this process.

Heuristics

The heuristic technique is that most frequently associated with entrepreneurial creativity. It involves *analysis*, that is isolating a particular market or product area and clarifying the concepts which are associated with that area, and then *synthesis*, bringing those concepts back together again in a way which offers a new perspective (*see* Fig. 14.1). This process is *iterative*. Each cycle refines the insight into the opportunity and

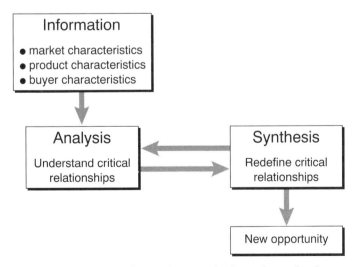

Fig. 14.1 Heuristic discovery: information, analysis and synthesis

159

makes it clearer. This process may be made explicit but more often it is simply the way in which the entrepreneur has learnt (perhaps even *actively* taught him or herself) to develop a decision when faced with opportunities and challenges.

Problem analysis

This approach starts by identifying the needs individuals or organisations have and the problems that they face. These needs and problems may be either explicit or implicit. They may or may not be recognised by the subject. The approach begins by asking the question 'what could be better?'. Having identified a problem the next question is to ask 'how might this be solved?'. An effective, rewarding solution represents the basis of a new opportunity for the entrepreneur.

Customer proposals

An new opportunity may be identified by a customer on the basis of a recognition of their own needs. The customer then offers the opportunity to the entrepreneur. Customer proposals take a variety of forms. At their simplest they are informal suggestions of the 'Wouldn't it be great if...' type. Alternatively, they can take the form of a very detailed and formal brief, for example, if the customer is an organisation and a large expenditure is involved. Some organisations are active in 'reverse marketing' their needs to potential suppliers. Whatever the means used, an effective entrepreneur is *always* keen to solicit ideas from customers.

Creative groups

An entrepreneur does not have to rely on his or her own creativity. The best entrepreneurs are active in facilitating and harnessing the creativity of other people too. A creative group consists of a small number of potential customers or product experts who are encouraged to think about their needs in a particular market area and to consider how those needs might be better served. The customers may be the ultimate consumers of the product or service or they may be industrial buyers.

Creative groups need control and leadership and their comments to be properly analysed if they are to be really informative. Getting people together in the right environment may also present a logistical challenge. Many market research companies offer specialist services in setting up, running and interpreting such creative group sessions.

Market mapping

Market mapping is a formal technique which involves identifying the dimensions defining a product category. These dimensions are based on the features of the product category. The features will differ depending on the type of product, but indicators like price, quality and performance are quite common. The characteristics of *buyers* may also be used to provide a more detailed mapping. A map is created of the market by using the feature-buyer dimensions as *co-ordinates*. Products separate out into distinct groups depending on their location on the map. The map defines the *positioning* of the product. The map may be used to identify gaps in the market and to specify the type of product that might be used to fill them.

A variety of statistical techniques are available for sorting out the information and presenting it in a two dimensional form. Often, though, just an imaginative sketch will do. The map then provides a powerful visual representation of what is in the market, how different offerings are related to each other and, critically, the gaps that are present in it.

Features stretching

Innovation involves offering something new. This means looking for ways in which changes might be made. Features stretching involves identifying the principal features which define a particular product or service and then seeing what happens if they are changed in some way. The trick is to test each feature with a range of suitable adjectives such as: 'bigger', 'stronger', 'faster', 'more often', 'more fun' and so on and see what results from such testing.

Anita Roddick's *Body Shop* provides a good example. Her initial inspiration was to provide good quality toiletries in packs much *smaller* than those offered by other high street retailers. (Environmentalism came later!)

Product blending

As with features stretching, this technique involves identifying the features which define particular products. Instead of just changing individual features, however, new products are created by blending together features from different products or services. This technique is often used in conjunction with features stretching. Both features stretching and features blending make good team exercises and can prove to be quite good fun.

The combined approach

Effective entrepreneurs do not rely on inspiration alone. They actively encourage creativity by thinking methodically about the market areas in which they have expertise. They also encourage other people such as employees, independent technical experts and customers to be creative on their behalf. The techniques listed are not exclusive of each other. They may be used together. Using them in a new and innovative way offers the potential to identify new and unexploited opportunities. For example, Richard Branson, the chief executive of the highly diverse *Virgin Group*, is renowned for his ability to bring out the creative talents in those around him.

14.3 Screening and selecting opportunities

KEY LEARNING OUTCOME
An understanding of the decisions to be taken in selecting opportunities.

Not all opportunities are equally valuable. A business with limited resources cannot pursue every opportunity with which it is faced. It must select those opportunities which are going to be the most rewarding. The key decisions in screening and selecting opportunities relate to the size of the opportunity, the investment necessary to exploit it, the rewards that will be gained and the risks likely to be encountered. Specifically, the entrepreneur's decision should be based on the answers to the following questions:

1 How large is the opportunity?

- How large is the market into which the new innovation is to be placed? (What products will it compete with? What is the total value of their sales?)
- What share of the market is likely to be gained? (How competitive will it be against existing products? What percentage of customers can be reached? What fraction will convert to the innovation?)
- What gross margin (revenue minus costs) is likely? (What price can be obtained? What is the unit cost likely to be?)
- Over what period can the opportunity be exploited? (How long will customers be interested? How long before competitors move in?)

2 What investment will be necessary if it is to be exploited properly?

- What are the immediate capital requirements? (What investments in people, operating assets and communication will be required to start the business?)
- What will be the long-term and ongoing capital requirements? (What future investments will be necessary to continue exploiting the opportunity?)
- Does the business have access to the capital required?
- If the opportunity is as large as expected will the business have sufficient capacity?
- If not, can it be expanded or be (profitably) offset to other organisations?
- What human resources will be needed? Are they available?

3 What is the likely return?

- What profits will be generated?
- Over what period?
- Is this attractive given the investment necessary? (How does return on investment compare to other investment options? What is the opportunity cost?)

4 What are the risks?

- How sound are the assumptions about the size of the opportunity? (How accurate was the data on markets? Have *all* competitor products been considered?)
- What if customers do not find the offering as attractive as expected?
- What if competitors are more responsive than expected? (Have all competitors been considered? How could they react in principle? How might they react in practice?)
- To what extent is success dependent on the support and goodwill of intermediaries and other third parties? (How will this goodwill be gained and maintained?)
- How sensitive will the exploitation be to the marketing strategy (particularly in relation to: pricing, selling points against competitors, customers targeted) that has been adopted?
- Can adjustments be made to the strategy in the light of experience? How expensive will this be?
- Can additional resources be made available if necessary? (Will these be from internal sources or from investors?)
- What will be the effect on cash flow if revenues are lower than expected?
- What will be the effect on cash flow if costs are higher than expected?
- How should investors be prepared for these eventualities?
- How should future revenues be discounted?
- Under what circumstances might investors wish to make an exit? (Will this be planned or in response to a crisis?)
- If so, how will they do it? (By being paid from profit stream or by selling their holding?)

Opportunities only have meaning in relation to each other. The entrepreneur must select opportunities not in absolute terms but after comparing them to each other. A business (like an investor) will find an opportunity attractive only if it represents the *best* option they have to invest for the future. Opportunities must be prioritised. They must compete with each other for the business's valuable resources. What matters is not so much cost but *opportunity* cost, that is not the cost of actually using resources, but the potential returns lost because they were not used elsewhere.

Summary of key ideas

- The first stage in the strategic window is *spotting* it.

- Spotting the window means identifying a new opportunity in terms of the possibility of creating new value.

- There are a variety of methods, both formal and informal, by which entrepreneurs can spot new opportunities.

- Entrepreneurs keep themselves attuned to new opportunities.

Suggestions for further reading

Assael, H. and **Roscoe Jr., M.** (1976) "Approaches to market segmentation analysis", *Journal of Marketing*, Oct, pp. 67–76.

Hague, P. (1985) "The significance of market size", *Industrial Marketing Digest*, Vol. 10, No. 2, pp. 139–46.

Haley, R.I. (1968) "Benefit segmentation: A decision-orientated research tool", *Journal of Marketing*, July, pp. 30–5.

Johnson, R.M. (1971) "Market segmentation: A strategic management tool", *Journal of Marketing Research*, Feb, pp. 13–18.

Mattson, B.E. (1985) "Spotting a market gap for a new product", *Long Range Planning*, Vol. 18, No. 1, pp. 87–93.

15 Locating the window: positioning the new venture

CHAPTER OVERVIEW

*The second stage in using the strategic window is to **locate** it. This means relating the opportunity to the business activity of established firms and understanding it as a gap in what they offer to the market. The idea of **positioning** provides a powerful conceptual framework for doing this.*

15.1 The idea of positioning

KEY LEARNING OUTCOME
An appreciation of how the concept of positioning may be used as a guide to entrepreneurial decision making.

The idea of positioning provides a very powerful tool to aid entrepreneurial decision making. Positioning provides a framework for *locating* the venture in relation to its competitors. Existing suppliers to a market do not serve its customers as completely as they might. They leave gaps in the market which a new venture can attempt to fill so gaining a foothold in that market. Identifying the window of opportunity means spotting where these gaps are. A new venture is, at face value, in a weak position relative to established competitors. Even if the established players had not previously spotted the window of opportunity, a new start-up will signal its presence to them. Their greater resources, established network of relationships and lower costs may put them in a much stronger position to exploit the window.

Positioning the venture means locating it in relation to a market gap such that it can exploit that gap in a profitable way. This involves structuring the business so that it can serve the requirements of a particular market niche *better* than existing competitors. An effective positioning means that the business will be able to develop a *competitive advantage* for serving this niche. This makes the niche *defendable* against competitors. It also enables the new venture to move into the market in a way which avoids direct head-on competition with established players. Head-on competition is usually a difficult game for the new venture to play since the playing field is tipped in favour of the established player. At best, head-on competition will prove to be expensive, and at worst, it will result in failure for the new venture.

Positioning relates to a *location*, and location means occupying a *space*. Understanding positioning, and using it as a decision-making tool demands an appreciation of the characterisation of the competitive space in which the venture operates. In general, a competitive space is characterised by the ways in which competitors seek to distinguish themselves from each other. Two distinct approaches to positioning provide different and complementary insights. *Strategic positioning* looks at the way in which the business's approach to delivering value to its customers is distinct from that of its competitors. Strategic positioning is concerned with the way in which the business *as a whole* distinguishes itself in a valuable way from competitor businesses. *Market positioning*, on the other hand, looks at the way in which the business's offerings to the market are differentiated from those of its competitors. Market positioning is concerned only with the business's products and services. Strategic positioning and market positioning can be used as decision support tools for the entrepreneurial business.

15.2 Strategic positioning

> **KEY LEARNING OUTCOME**
> **An understanding of the decisions which define the venture's strategic positioning.**

Identifying a strategic position is a fundamental element of the strategic planning process. A strategic position is the way the business as a whole is located relative to competitors in the playing field of the market, that is the *competitive space*. Derek Abell, in his book *Defining the Business*, suggests that this competitive space can be defined along four dimensions.

1 Stage in value addition

The goods that are bought by consumers, or which are used by those who provide services to them, are usually highly refined. Yet, ultimately, they are all made from raw materials obtained from the earth. However, there may be a lot of businesses who play a role in the process between the extraction of a raw material and the delivery of the final product.

Consider, for example, a home computer that has been purchased from a distributor. That distributor will have purchased the computer from a hardware manufacturer. The manufacturer will have bought a variety of components such as silicon chips, plastic parts and glass screens from component suppliers. Those component suppliers will have made them from refined raw materials obtained from suppliers of pure silicon, plastics and glass. These suppliers will have refined their products from raw

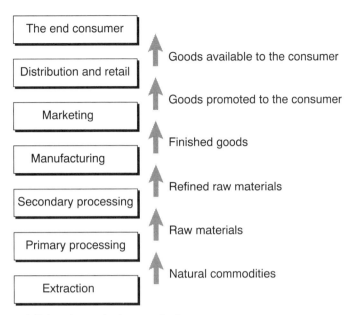

Fig. 15.1 Value addition in an industry chain

commodities obtained from the businesses who collect sand and extract oil from the earth. This process whereby the outputs of one business provide the inputs for the next business along is called the *value addition chain* (*see* Fig. 15.1).

An entrepreneur must decide what stage, or stages, in the value addition process they expect their venture to occupy. This resolves itself into questions about the inputs and the outputs of the business. These questions are:

> **Will the business make a particular input (which might be a physical product or a service) for itself or will it buy it in? :**
>
> **Will the business sell on a particular output to another business for further processing or will it try to add that value itself?**

The decisions made in response to these questions must be based on an appreciation of the competencies of the business, its resources and its competitive advantage relative to both competitors and the businesses adjacent to it in the value addition chain.

2 Customer segments addressed

It is rare that a business can serve the needs of an *entire* market. The strengths of a particular business lie in the way it can appeal to certain groups of customers. When Richard Branson started the *Virgin Airline* he concentrated on business passengers who wanted to cross the Atlantic. Alan Sugar, when he started his consumer electronics business *Amstrad*, was explicit about the fact that he was targeting the 'lorry driver and his family' rather than the hi-fi aficionado. Selecting a well defined customer segment enables the business to focus limited resources, to concentrate its efforts and to defend itself against competitors.

There are a variety of ways in which a customer segment can be defined. Some of the more important include:

Geographic location: where the customer is. Many entrepreneurial ventures start out serving a small local community. As they grow they expand to achieve national and even international scope.

Industry: the industrial sector of organisational buyers. In its early stages an entrepreneurial venture may decide to concentrate on selling its product to a particular industry segment. This option may be attractive because the needs and buying habits of that sector are thoroughly understood by the entrepreneur.

Demographics of buyer: e.g. social class, age, personal attitudes or stage in life cycle. For example, Gerald Ratner revitalised the high street jewellery trade in the UK by targeting his business towards young, low income people.

Buying process: the way the product is bought and the role of influencers and decision makers. Entrepreneurs may concentrate their efforts towards businesses which buy in a certain sort of way. For example, business service firms such as the market research company *MORI* established by Robert Worcester, are adept at negotiating the complex decision-making process that lies behind the buying and use of market research in large organisations.

Psychographics: buyers' attitudes toward the product category. Richard Branson, for example, has moved his *Virgin* brand into personal financial services on the basis that it offers trust in an area where many buyers have suspicions about the existing products on offer.

3 Customer needs addressed

Consumers and businesses have many, and complex, needs and wants. No single business could hope to serve them all. An entrepreneur must decide exactly which of the customer's needs his or her venture will exist to serve. Success depends on gaining customer commitment and the best way to do that is to genuinely serve the needs and to solve the problems they have.

Customers may be aware of their needs or they may not have articulated them to themselves yet, these needs can be explicit or implicit. Different needs are not independent of each other, they often interact and must be prioritised. Satisfying one need may mean that others go unsatisfied. The entrepreneur must learn to understand the needs of their customers, to rationalise them and to distinguish them from each other. The entrepreneur must often articulate the needs of customers on their behalf.

4 Means of addressing needs

Satisfying a need represents an end and there are a number of means by which that end can be achieved. The need to communicate with someone, for example, can be served by a postage stamp, a telephone, the Internet or by going to visit them. Having decided which particular customer needs they will satisfy, the entrepreneur must decide the means, or *technology*, that they will adopt in order to do so. Alan Sugar recognised people's desire to be entertained by listening to music. He provided them with electronic equipment to replay recorded music. He might, conceivably, have served that desire by building concert halls or by providing a service whereby musicians would come and play to people in their homes. For whatever reasons, these were technological alternatives he did not venture into.

The industry building entrepreneur is often the one who has recognised a whole new technological approach for addressing a basic need. Henry Ford recognised that a low cost motor car was a better way of moving from one place to another than horse and cart. Bill Gates recognised that a computer with the right software could transform the way in which a variety of domestic and office information processing tasks would performed. Innovation is not necessarily about creating new technology. It is about understanding how a particular technology can be used to address a need in a new and fruitful way.

These four dimensions as shown in Fig. 15.2 describe the strategic positioning of a venture or its location in competitive space (*see also* Day, 1984, p.21). This is the niche where the new venture sits. It defines who its competitors are and the way in which they are competitors. Of course, merely occupying the niche is not enough. The business must structure itself and adopt operating processes and a culture which allows it to serve that niche effectively.

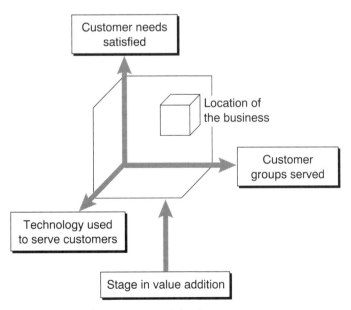

Fig. 15.2 The dimensions of strategic positioning

15.3 Market positioning

KEY LEARNING OUTCOME
An understanding of how the idea of market positioning can be used to differentiate the venture's offerings from those of its competitors.

Strategic positioning describes the way the venture is located in a competitive space. *Market positioning* describes the way its outputs, products and services, are located in the marketplace relative to those of competitors. Success will only be achieved if the new venture offers customers something which is *different* from and more *attractive* than that offered by existing players. This means it must offer them greater value by being more suited to their needs or the same level of benefits at lower cost.

The first stage in market positioning is to develop an understanding of the criteria by which buyers distinguish between the different products on offer to them and the extent to which they consider them to be substitutable. Some general factors in market positioning are:

- *price* – how is the offering priced relative to competitors
- *perceived quality* – is quality seen as high or low (what matters is perceived value for money i.e. quality relative to price);
- *demographic imagery* – up-market *v* down-market, young *v* old; dynamic *v* conservative;
- *performance* – high performance or more limited performance;
- *number and type of features* – e.g. advanced *v* basic; complex *v* simple; hi-tech *v* low-tech.
- *branding imagery* – the associations that the branding elicits;
- *service and support* – additional assistance offered in understanding, using and maintaining the product;
- *attitude towards supplier* – positive or negative associations gained from ethical stance of supplier.

Different buyers will prioritise and weight these factors differently.

One way of thinking about positioning is to consider three aspects of the product or service being offered. A product can be positioned using one or more of the three ways in which its consumer relates to it – *see* Fig. 15.3. At the centre is the *functional core*; that is the features of the product or service which actually deliver its functional benefits. Surrounding this functional core are the aesthetic attractions of the product or service. These include design and branding elements which make the product or service attractive to use. At the outer level are the *emotional benefits*. These are those aspects of the product or service which appeal directly to the consumer's emotional and spiritual needs rather than their purely functional ones. This may be achieved through branding which allows the consumer the chance to say something about themselves by being seen to consume the product.

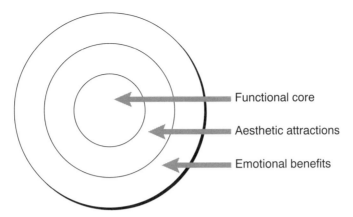

Fig. 15.3 Positioning of the venture's product

The aim of positioning is to reduce the extent to which the customer feels that the product or service is *substitutable* by those of competitors. In effect, this means focusing the offering on the needs of the customer in a unique and effective way. The positioning need not be solely in its functional core. Differentiation can often be achieved very effectively by giving the product or service a unique aspect in its aesthetic attractions and emotional benefits. For example, a £3.99 digital watch may be as good as a *Cartier* watch for telling the time, but the owner of the Cartier would not think it a good swap! The buyer may see their purchase set into a wider social and moral context. The actual 'physical' products offered by the *Body Shop* are easily imitated by other high street retailers, but its customers still feel that the *Body Shop* offers them something more valuable because of its ethical stance. The eponymous chain of jewellers set up by Gerald Ratner revolutionised the UK jewellery retailing sector in the 1980s but did not pretend to be offering products of the highest quality. Nonetheless it was felt to be fun, accessible and unstuffy by its young customers. Charles and Maurice Saatchi of *Saatchi and Saatchi Advertising* reinvented advertising in the 1960s and 70s by positioning themselves as partners in the management process rather than by just supplying advertisements for clients. The *McDonald's* chain of fast food outlets as established by Ray Kroc, are not just places to eat; they are an invitation to share the American Dream.

Positioning is a valuable entrepreneurial tool. It guides the entrepreneur in offering the customer something new and valuable and it avoids the need for head-on competition with established (and more powerful) players. Effective positioning is a critical success factor for the new venture.

Summary of key ideas

- The second stage in the strategic window is *locating it*.

- Locating the window means developing a *position* for the new venture and its offerings to the marketplace.

- *Strategic positioning* relates to the way the venture fits in the marketplace in relation to its stage in the value addition chain; the customer groups it serves; the customer needs it addresses; and the technology it adopts to serve its customers.

- *Market positioning* relates to the way the venture's offerings fit in the marketplace in relation to the offerings of competitors.

Suggestions for further reading

Aaker, D.A. and Shansby, J.G. (1982) "Positioning your product", *Business Horizons*, May-June, pp. 56–62.

Abell, D.F. (1980) *Defining the Business: The Starting Point of Strategic Planning*, Englewood Cliffs, N. J.: Prentice Hall.

Datta, Y. (1996) "Market segmentation: An integrated framework", *Long Range Planning*, Vol. 29, No. 6, pp. 797–811.

Day, G.S. (1984) *Strategic Market Planning*, St Paul's, Minneapolis: West Publishing, p. 21.

Day, G.S., Shocker, A.D. and **Srivastava, R.K.** (1978) "Customer-orientated approaches to identifying product-markets", *Journal of Marketing*, Vol. 43, pp. 8–19.

Garda, R.A. (1981) "Strategic segmentation: How to carve niches for growth in industrial markets", *Management Review*, August, reproduced in Weitz, B.A. and Weley, R. (eds) (1988) *Readings in Strategic Marketing: Analysis, Planning and Implementation*, New York: Dryden Press.

16 Measuring the window: analysing the opportunity

CHAPTER OVERVIEW

*The third stage in using the strategic window is to **measure** it, that is to **quantify** the opportunity and develop an understanding of how much new value might be created. Obtaining information on the opportunity is seen to be an investment in the business, and must be considered as such. Key issues relating to the analysis of opportunity are considered. Methods of market analysis are considered in overview.*

16.1 The need for information

KEY LEARNING OUTCOME
An appreciation of the importance of managing and using market information effectively.

Relevant market information is extremely useful to the entrepreneur. Entrepreneurs are decision makers. They are different to other types of manager because they make the decision to *venture*. Venturing means stepping out into the unknown and information provides a map of how to move forward into this unknown. Information eliminates uncertainty and so reduces *risk*. However, information on its own is not enough, if it is to be valuable, it must be analysed, understood and acted upon.

Information does not come for free, it has a cost. While the entrepreneur will know many things simply as a result of his or her experience within an industry, a lot of additional information may need to be gathered actively. Even if the information has no direct cost (for example information gathered 'free' from a public library) valuable time is used in collecting it. Some information can have a high direct cost, for example, information obtained through formal market research surveys can appear very expensive to the entrepreneur just starting out. However, information represents an *investment* in the business. It is used to increase the performance of the business. The pay-off for that investment needs to be appreciated before the information is gathered.

Information can guide action. However, lack of information should not be an excuse for *inaction*. While it may be sensible to hold back on a move until more information is available and that move can be made with more confidence, there are other times when the entrepreneur must rely on their instincts and 'go for it'. If they wait too long, someone else may make the move first. While information reduces risk, the entrepreneur cannot expect to eliminate *all* risk and sometimes they must make a step into the dark. The entrepreneur must walk a narrow path between making ill-informed and ill-judged decisions, and an inertia caused by the venture becoming more interested in gathering and analysing information than in taking direct action. The founders of organisation systems thinking, F. E. Kast and J. E. Rosenzweig, called these two options 'extinction by instinct' and 'paralysis by analysis'.

Strategic management provides a wide variety of tools and conceptual frameworks to aid decision making. A variety of formal methods is available to guide resource allocation and make competitive moves. While the entrepreneur would be foolish to shun the insights that can be gained through such formal analysis of information they should not be solely dependent on it. Often it is the overall *pattern*, not the *detail* that matters. They must learn to develop their intuition and make judgements based on holistic thinking and their own heuristic approach. The successful entrepreneur learns to see the wood before the trees.

16.2 Analysing the market and identifying key issues

> **KEY LEARNING OUTCOME**
> **An appreciation of the importance of analysing and understanding market conditions.**

If they are to be successful, entrepreneurs must understand the market in which they are operating. This understanding is important because success depends on their ability to serve that market in a way which is better than their competitors.

There are a number of issues about which the entrepreneur must be informed if they are to make effective decisions in relation to their venture. These issues fall into four broad categories. These relate to the existing market conditions and the opportunity they present, the way in which the entrepreneur might innovate and offer something of value to the market, the way in which the entrepreneur can get the venture started and the way in which competitors are likely to respond to the venture. Some specific information requirements are:

- *General market conditions* (customers' needs and requirements; the size of potential markets; market growth rate and trends in its development; the structure of customer groups and segments; and customer and consumer buying behaviour).
- *The attractiveness of the innovation* (customers' satisfactions and dissatisfactions with current offerings; customers' reaction to the entrepreneur's new offering; competitor pricing and customers' pricing expectations; and likely volume of demand).

- *The way the new venture can be initiated and positioned in the marketplace* (resource requirements for start-up; resource requirements for the later development of the venture; the structure of the network into which the venture will be located; sources of investment capital; customers and customer groups to be given priority; and means by which the customer might be informed about the new offering.)
- *The way in which competitors might react to the new venture* (the nature, type, strengths and weaknesses of competitors; strategies adopted by competitors; and likely actions (strategic and tactical) by way of a response).

Information of this nature is available from a variety of sources. Some of it will be knowledge the entrepreneur already holds about his or her industry. Some may be obtained from existing published sources such as market reports and trade publications, such sources are referred to as *secondary* sources. Alternatively, primary research involves a bespoke analysis of a market situation using market research techniques in answer to specific questions.

In many instances the entrepreneur may feel quite informed on these issues. In other instances it may be felt that information is lacking and greater certainty is needed. The entrepreneur must never be complacent. The rule must be always to challenge knowledge and assumptions. When deciding upon the degree of precision required for information, two questions must be asked. First, how sensitive will decision making be to the accuracy of the information used as the basis of those decisions? Second, with respect to this, is the cost of gaining the information worth the return it offers?

16.3 Analysing the opportunity: qualitative methods

KEY LEARNING OUTCOME
An appreciation of the methods by which the 'whys' of the opportunity may be understood.

There are two sorts of question that must be asked if a business opportunity is to be fully appreciated. Both may be answered by appropriate market research and analysis techniques. The first set of questions relate to the nature of the opportunity, its qualities and the approaches that might be taken to exploiting it. These are the 'who?', 'what?' and 'why?' questions. They are best answered using *qualitative* methods. The second set of questions relate to the value of the opportunity and the effort that should be put into exploiting it. These are the 'how much?' and 'how many?' questions. These are best answered using *quantitative* methods.

Qualitative methods might be used to answer questions of the following sort. Who are the customers? How are they defined as a group? How are they differentiated from non-customers? What needs do these customers have in relation to the product category (in terms of functional, social, emotional and developmental needs)? How do they articulate their needs (explicitly or implicitly)? How well do consumers find that current offerings satisfy those needs? In what ways are current offerings unsatisfactory? What are the customer's attitudes towards the product category in general (positive, negative or mixed)? Why do non-customers not use the product category? How might they be attracted to it? If the product is not available, how might other types of product be used as a substitute? How does this define a gap for an innovative offering? How do customers go about buying a product? How are they normally informed about the product category? What is their knowledge of the product category? Who influences their decision when making a purchase? Who influences the consumer when they use the product? How is such influence exercised? How do they greet innovations in the product category? (Positively or with suspicion?)

Many entrepreneurs will feel confident in their ability to answer these questions based purely on their experience in a particular industry sector working with customers and a particular product category. However, if the area is new to them, or they feel the innovation they are offering changes the rules, or they just wish to challenge assumptions then obtaining answers directly from customers and potential users will be a valuable exercise. There are a variety of methods for doing this.

Actively listening to customers

Customers must, ultimately, be the source of all information on a market and the opportunities it presents. After all, it is they who buy the product and reward the entrepreneur. Even an informal conversation with a customer can provide a good deal of information about their concerns, what they find satisfactory, what less so, what might be better, and so on. If this information is picked up on, it can be of enormous value to the acute entrepreneur. Acquiring this information demands *active* listening.

Listening is a communication skill. It does not come naturally. When in conversation, we often use the other person's speaking time as a chance to consider our reply rather than actually listen to what they are saying. It is easy to be distracted, but active listening demands that the conversation be kept on track. The right sort of questions must be asked. The listener should lock onto key phrases and comments and these should be explored if further information might be yielded. Non-verbal communication (facial gestures, body language) should also be noted. What does the conversation reveal about the customer's way of thinking about the product category? Is decision making rational and logical or is it influenced by emotional factors?

Selling situations provide a good opportunity to listen to customers. In fact, it is as important to listen to what they say as it is to present the product to them. Objections to making a purchase should be received positively. After all, if a customer is saying why they will not purchase this time, they are giving a clue as to how they could be persuaded to do so next time.

In-depth interviews

The in-depth interview is really a structured conversation. The objective of the conversation is to gather information and the specific information required is defined in advance. A series of questions to be asked are set out before the interview and these questions are used to prompt the interviewee. The interviewer can introduce additional questions if a particular avenue is opened up and is considered to be worth further exploration.

In-depth interviews are a very effective and flexible way of getting to know the customer and their way of thinking. They are, however, time consuming (for both interviewer and interviewee) and so can prove to be expensive if a large number need to be performed.

Focus groups

A focus group is a gathering of a small group of customers (usually about five to eight) who are questioned about their attitudes and opinions on a particular product category. This not only reveals their thinking as individuals, but also the way they interact with each other when considering the product.

Focus groups can be very revealing and can give substance to vague feelings about gaps in markets. However, they are difficult to run. Controlling them and keeping the discussion on track can be difficult. Interpreting what has been said is also a professional task. Focus groups work best when the right sort of venue is used. Video or sound recording facilities are needed. It can also be difficult to bring even a small group of buyers (especially industrial buyers) together. Consequently focus groups are often most productive when run by trained market researchers.

Usage and awareness studies

A usage and awareness study is based on a written questionnaire which is mailed to users of the product category. The questionnaire aims to explore the users' attitudes and feelings towards the product category, their knowledge of what is on offer, and the way they use products in the category. They provide written answers to the questions or tick prefigured questions and then send their answers back. Such studies can be used to confirm ideas on the types of gap that exist in a market. Usage and awareness studies are an efficient and (relatively) low cost way of gathering the view of a large number of customers. However, return rates can be low. Care must be taken in the way in which they are designed and interpreted, and appropriate statistical methods must be adopted.

Product trials

A very effective way of obtaining customers' opinions on a new product, and how they view it in relation to alternatives, is to let them use it in the way they would be expected to under normal circumstances and then question them about their experience. Product trials work well when the offering is very innovative and the customer needs exposure to the product before they can give an opinion on it. Product trials can be very informative. They can be used as part of the development process for a new product. They are particularly good at identifying what the customer finds attractive about the product and so can be used to refine the selling points of that product.

However, product trials do demand that the product is available to be tested. If the product is not in production then expensive working prototypes may be needed.

16.4 Analysing the opportunity: quantitative methods

KEY LEARNING OUTCOME
An appreciation of the methods which can be used to quantify a market opportunity.

Qualitative methods can be used to give shape to the nature of a market opportunity and the ways in which it might be exploited. However, they say little about how much that opportunity is worth and the entrepreneur needs to know whether an opportunity is worth pursuing and, if so, what amount of investment is sensible. To support this type of decision quantitative methods are needed. The kinds of questions answered by quantitative methods include the following. How large is the market (its volume)? How much is it worth (its value)? How fast is it growing? How large are the key segments in the market? How many customers are there? How much do they buy? How often do they buy? What are the market shares of the competitors supplying the market? What level of investment do competitors make in developing the market and defending their position within it?

In broad terms, three approaches can be used to obtain this information.

1 *User audits*

Questioning of a representative sample of users to learn how much and how often they make purchases in a particular product category and whose products they buy. This may be achieved by mailed questionnaire, telephone interview or face-to-face questioning. By classifying different types of customer, user audits can give inform-ation on the market segments that characterise the market and their relative sizes.

2 *Distributor audits*

Distributor audits involve monitoring how a particular product type moves through a distribution chain. A representative sample of distributors is asked to provide information on how much of a particular item they buy, how frequently they buy it, how much they keep in stock and how much they sell over a particular period.

3 *Manufacturer's output*

The market is assessed by adding together the outputs of all the manufacturers who contribute products to the market.

All three types of audit can be carried out at regular intervals to give an indication of the extent to which, and the ways in which a market is growing.

A reliable quantitative assessment of a market is time consuming and can prove to be expensive. The entrepreneur may undertake the exercise personally but is more likely to call upon the agencies of professional market researchers. Again, the entrepreneur must balance the need for reliable information with the investment he or she feels is proper for obtaining it.

A lot of information on various markets is routinely published by a variety of organisations. This information is quite easily accessed. Although this *secondary* information can be very informative, its value is limited. Only rarely will it examine a market from exactly the perspective that the entrepreneur would wish to see it. This is not least because the entrepreneur should be looking at the market in an innovative way and seeking new relationships between markets.

When examining markets, from either a qualitative or quantitative perspective, a little lateral thinking can be valuable. Insights may be gained not only by asking questions about the market itself, but also by asking questions about *related* markets (*see* Fig. 16.1). The effective entrepreneur also thinks about *end-use* markets (for example, when Lord Hanson bought the London Brick Company he wasn't thinking about the market for bricks but the growing market for new houses), about *supply* markets (for example, Alan Sugar of *Amstrad* was aware not only of the market for domestic hi-fi equipment but developments in the market for electronic components) and about the *co-use* market for products used in association with the product in question (thus Bill Gates of *Microsoft* did not so much concern himself with analysing the market for computer software but with the growth in ownership of computer *hardware* which would need software to operate it).

As always in entrepreneurship, a fresh and innovative approach to asking questions can pay dividends.

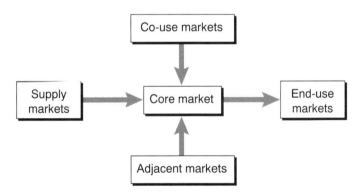

Fig. 16.1 Markets of interest to the entrepreneur

Summary of key ideas

- The third stage in the strategic window is *measuring* it.

- Measuring it means developing an understanding as to the size of the opportunity and what it might be worth.

- A business opportunity is analysed by *qualitative methods* which answer 'what' and 'why' questions and *quantitative methods* which answer 'how much' and 'how many' questions.

- Information can be expensive. Effective entrepreneurs weigh the value of information against the cost of obtaining it. Information is regarded as an *investment* in the business.

Suggestions for further reading

Eisenhardt, K. (1989) "Making fast strategic decisions in high-velocity environments", *Academy of Management Journal*, Vol. 32, pp. 543–76.

Kast, F.E. and **Rosenzweig, J.E.** (1970) *Organization and Management: A Systems Approach*, New York: McGraw-Hill.

Langley, A. (1995) "Between 'paralysis by analysis' and 'extinction by instinct'", *Sloan Management Review*, Spring, pp. 63–76.

Marlow, H. (1994) "Intuition and forecasting – A holistic approach", *Long Range Planning*, Vol. 27, No. 6, pp. 58–68.

17 Opening the window: gaining commitment

CHAPTER OVERVIEW

*The fourth stage in using the strategic window is to **open** it. This means initiating the business and drawing the commitment of stakeholders towards it. This chapter looks at how the venture can enter and establish itself in the business network. In particular the key issues relating to attracting financial and human support are considered.*

17.1 Entering the network

KEY LEARNING OUTCOME
An appreciation of the way in which a new venture redefines the network of relationships that exist within a business community.

Having spotted the window, that is having identified a new opportunity, and having located and measured the window, that is having defined and quantified the opportunity, the entrepreneur must then *open* that window. This means initiating the venture. Initiation demands that a variety of stakeholders be drawn into the venture. The new venture and the entrepreneur driving it must create a new set of relationships with those stakeholders. Yet, in most instances, those stakeholders will already have relationships with a variety of other organisations. In effect, starting a new venture means *redefining* the relationships that stakeholders have with third parties and with one another. The new venture must enter an existing network of relationships and, in doing so, modify that network of relationships. If the venture is to enjoy long-term success it must do this in a way which *increases* the overall value of the network to those who make it up.

The relationships in this network are both competitive and collaborative. The entrepreneur must decide on the way these two dynamics are to be complemented and balanced as the network is redefined. This balancing act must be considered in relation to each and every stakeholder and stakeholder group.

Relationship with investors

Investors seek out opportunities to invest. They look for the best returns on the capital they provide, consistent with a certain level of risk. Because capital, like any resource, is both valuable and limited, investors are selective in the investments they choose to support. Investors are less interested in the cost of an investment than its *opportunity cost*: the money that will be lost if an investment is not made *elsewhere*.

Entrepreneurs must compete for the attentions of investors. If an entrepreneur offers an investor an investment opportunity, then they are limiting the possibility for investment in other ventures by that investor. One entrepreneur's success in attracting investment capital will be another's, perhaps many others', failure. This is harsh. Yet, in the long run, this competition generates an overall increase in value for *all* entrepreneurs in two ways. First, by defining opportunity costs it provides a strong signal as to which opportunities are worth pursuing and which are not. Second, by offering investors a good return, it generates the capital that can be used to make further investments.

Relationship with suppliers

To a supplier, an entrepreneurial venture is a potential new customer. At face value this is good since a new customer offers the prospect of new business. However, the new venture may also complicate life for a supplier. The venture may be competing with an existing customer of the supplier. While the venture may be offering the potential for additional business it may also be simply threatening to replace one set of business arrangements with another. The supplier may not always see the entrepreneurial venture as new business. They can also see the costs of gaining one new (and untried) customer only to face the risks of losing an established one.

If the business is characterised by close and strong relationships between supplier and customer then that relationship may be strained if the supplier is called upon to provide for a customer's competitor. While in many economies a strong legal framework exists to ensure that trading is free and fair and that strong customers do not coerce weaker suppliers, this is not always the case. Even if a strong legal framework exists, informal agreements and expectations can still be influential.

In short, when approaching suppliers the entrepreneur must be conscious not only of the new business they are offering them but also of the way the relationship they are proposing to build will affect the existing relationships the supplier enjoys. New business may not always be as attractive as it first appears!

Relationship with employees

Entrepreneurial ventures can only be progressed if the right human skills are in place. They demand productive labour, technical knowledge, business insight and leadership. Human inputs are traded in markets. Some categories of human skill may be in short supply. If this is the case the entrepreneur may have to compete to get hold of them. This competition takes the form of offering potential employees attractive remuneration packages and prospects for development.

If one entrepreneur employs an individual with a skill which is valuable and in short supply then another cannot employ that individual. More critically perhaps, it is likely that the entrepreneur will attract such a person from an existing business. Most would agree that individuals should have the right to offer their skills and insight to whomsoever they wish. Furthermore, the demand for people with rare talents, reflected by the rewards they are offered, provides an incentive for others to develop those skills.

In practice, however, individuals do not market themselves as commodities within a 'perfect' labour market. They build close relationships with the organisations for which they work. People are motivated by more than just the financial rewards of working. The 'contracts' individuals have with their organisations go beyond the simple terms of the formal written contract of employment. They involve unwritten, often unarticulated, expectations and loyalties on both sides.

As a consequence, while an entrepreneur seeking to attract an employee from a competitor is a proper functioning of the labour market, it can also be seen in negative terms as a kind of illegitimate 'poaching'. This can be traumatic and cause ill-feeling, particularly when the business community is close knit and the employee is felt to be offering not just their general experience, skills and insights but also insider knowledge to a competitor. Some employers use formal contractual devices to restrict the movement of employees in possession of sensitive knowledge to competitors.

While the entrepreneur should never feel ashamed at offering individuals a good reward for the skills and talents they have invested in creating for themselves, the effective entrepreneur must be sensitive to the human dimension of the business they are operating in and its rules when recruiting people. More often than not these rules about what is acceptable and unacceptable in recruitment practice are unwritten.

Relationship with customers

Customers are a key stakeholder group for the entrepreneur. It is their interest in what the venture offers and their willingness to pay for it, that ultimately provides the money which the entrepreneurial venture will use to reward all of its stakeholder groups. The best way to attract the interest of customers is to provide them with goods and services which *genuinely* satisfy their needs, solve their problems and meet their aspirations.

A customer will not usually have a need which is both explicit and unsatisfied. Rarely will the entrepreneur be offering the customer something which they need in addition to everything else they consume. It is much more likely that they will be offering something that will *replace* something else they are using. In short, even an innovative entrepreneurial business will be competing with the potential customer's existing suppliers. Suppliers and their customers do not relate solely through the medium of a market. They also interact at a human level via the business network. In some instances this relationship may be trivial. In many, however, the relationship is far-reaching, deeply established and complex. The relationship may not be sustained by economic self-interest alone but also by friendship and trust.

When a new venture approaches a customer, it is asking not only that the customer buy the offering, but also that they stop buying, or replace the offering provided by another supplier. The success of the selling approach will depend on more than the way the entrepreneur's offering competes against the one they seek to oust. The wider relationship they seek to end and the new one they offer to replace it will also be important. If the entrepreneur is to be successful in marketing and selling his or her products and services to customers they must consider not just the product or service, but also the nature of the individual and organisational relationships that exist between customer and supplier in the marketplace. The entrepreneur must be prepared to create more rewarding relationships. This point will be developed in Section 18.1.

When starting their ventures entrepreneurs are not just offering their product or service into a melée of short-term market exchanges. They are breaking and then reforming a pattern of relationships. Those relationships are governed by rules, some formal, some informal, some based on self-interest, and others governed by altruistic motives. Some are articulated openly, while others are not even recognised – until they are broken. Effective entrepreneurs understand those relationships, and the rules that govern them, so that they can successfully manage their position within the network. This is not to say the entrepreneur should not occasionally break the rules, but they should be aware that they *are* breaking the rules and know *why* they are doing it.

17.2 Gaining financial investment: key issues

KEY LEARNING OUTCOME
A recognition of the main issues associated with attracting financial investment to the new venture.

An entrepreneur will be interested in obtaining a variety of different resources in order to progress his or her venture. However, it is money that is likely to take first place on the list of priorities. This is understandable. Money is the most liquid of resources. It can be used readily to obtain the other things the business needs.

Attracting investment capital is one of the primary functions of the entrepreneur. It is a process that raises a number of critical issues. The entrepreneur must consider these issues carefully and make some fundamental decisions in relation to them. This section will examine the issues in overview and the issues will be expanded upon in Chapter 19.

What level of investment is required?

Broadly, how much money will be needed to start the venture? This will of course depend on the nature of the venture, the opportunity it is pursuing, the stage in its development and the plans the entrepreneur has for the future. Initial investment levels are sensitive to the strategy the business is pursuing, in terms of the initial scope the business must have and the potential this leaves for growth. Some ventures can start on a small scale and build up over time. Anita Roddick started the *Body Shop* with a single outlet and a loan of £4000. The business grew as new outlets were added incrementally over time. On the other hand, when Frederick Smith started the US air freight business, *Federal Express,* he realised that if the business was to work he needed to offer customers a full service from the start. That meant acquiring a fleet of aircraft and a relatively large administrative and support structure. He sought $90 million of start-up financing.

Where is the investment to come from?

While there is an overall 'market for capital', there are a number of sources of investment capital. For example, the entrepreneur's own funds, bank loans, government loans, venture capital, share issues, business angels (experienced manager-investors who offer their expertise to new ventures along with capital), and so on. In other words, the market for capital is a fragmented one. Different capital providers occupy different niches in the market. They are characterised by the way they look for different types of investment opportunity, accept different levels of risk, expect different types of return and assume different levels of involvement in the running of the venture. To be effective in managing the project of attracting funds the entrepreneur must understand these different markets and the way in which they work.

What is the capital structure of the investment to be?

The *capital structure* is simply the mix of different investment sources that are used. In broad terms it refers to the ratio of 'equity' to 'debt' capital, that is the mix of investors who expect a return that will be linked to the performance of the venture to those who expect a fixed return based on an agreed interest rate whatever the performance of the business. In addition, loan capital may be unsecured or secured against some assets of the business.

The capital structure of the venture reflects the way in which the entrepreneur is sharing risk with the investors. Clearly a secured loan exposes the investor to a lower level of risk than an equity share. At the same time, capital which exposes the investor to risk is more expensive than capital which does not. So by adjusting the capital structure entrepreneurs can, in effect, 'sell off' the risks inherent in their venture to different degrees.

How will the investors be approached?

Entrepreneurs and investors need to get in touch with each other before they can work together. Usually, the onus is on the entrepreneur to initiate the contact. That contact must be managed. While investors try to make rational decisions about investment opportunities they are not calculating machines. They are still human beings who are influenced by *how* things are said as well as *what* is said and first impressions are important. The way in which the entrepreneur first approaches the potential investor can have a bearing on the outcome of that contact. In essence, three things must be considered: the *who* of the contact, the *how* of the contact and the *what* of the contact.

First, the entrepreneur must identify suitable sources of investment. That is, *who* to contact. This involves identifying organisations that provide investment capital. However, organisations do not make decisions, *individuals* do and the entrepreneur may find it productive to find out which individual or individuals they should approach within the organisation. They may also consider the decision-making structure within the organisation, i.e. not only who actually takes the investment decisions but who influences them in that decision and the way in which their decisions are policed and judged within the organisation.

Second, the entrepreneur must consider the *how* of the contact. Should it be formal or informal? Does the investor lay down a procedure for making contact? (Most banks and venture capital companies, for example, do.) Does the investor expect a written proposal or a verbal one in the first instance? If it is verbal, do they expect a one-to-one chat or a full blown presentation? If it is a written one, do they lay down a format for the proposal or do they give the entrepreneur latitude in the way they communicate. Many investors will simply reject a proposal out of hand if they are not approached in the right way.

Third, they must consider *what* to tell the investor. At the first contact stage, attracting the investor's attention and encouraging their interest is likely to be as important as giving them information. This will be particularly so if the investor is receiving a large number of approaches. Is it necessary to relate a detailed picture or will a broad outline be more effective? How much room for manoeuvre is there here if the communication has to comply with a set format?

What proposition is to be made to the investors?

The entrepreneur must consider what, exactly, they are offering the investor. Some of the critical dimensions here are:

- the amount of investment required;
- how that particular investment fits with the overall investment profile for the venture;
- the nature of the investment (e.g. loan or equity, secured or unsecured);
- the level of return anticipated;
- the nature (particularly the *liquidity*) of any security being offered;
- the degree of risk to which the capital will be exposed;
- the way 'in', i.e. how the investment will be made (what amount of money at what time); and
- the way 'out', i.e. how the investor will get their return (what amount of money at what time);
- the degree of *control* the investor will be given over (or be expected to contribute to) the way the venture is run.

These things constitute the 'package' that the entrepreneur is offering to the investor. It is on the basis of these factors that investors will make their judgement as to the attractiveness of the investment opportunity. The entrepreneur must never forget that they are *selling* the venture to investors. The entrepreneur must put as much effort into this selling exercise as he or she would do in selling the business's products to customers.

17.3 Gaining human commitment

KEY LEARNING OUTCOME
An appreciation of how the commitment of key people to the venture may be gained.

On its own investment capital can achieve nothing. It must be used by *people* to progress the venture. The money obtained by one entrepreneur is exactly the same as the money obtained by another and, indeed, exactly like that held by established businesses. If an entrepreneurial venture is successful then it must be because its people do something *different* and *better* with the money to which they have access.

While it is conventional in management theory to talk of human beings as a 'resource' it should always be remembered that they are a *special* type of resource. There is more to gaining human commitment than simply bringing people into the business. They must certainly be attracted to the venture in the first instance. Once in, their motivation and dedication must be maintained and constantly developed. The entrepreneur does not just *recruit* to their venture, they must also *lead* it.

The entrepreneur faces a number of decisions in relation to developing the commitment other people have towards the venture.

What human skills are required?

Businesses need a variety of different types of human input. Technical skills, communication skills, functional skills and analytical skills are all critically important to the success of a venture. Different ventures need different mixes of these skills in order to progress. The entrepreneur must decide what profile of skills and experience is right for their venture as it stands now, and what profile will be needed as it grows and develops. In light of the fact that human resources are as likely to be scarce as any other, this may mean prioritising some requirements over others.

Where will those skills be obtained from?

Where are the people with those skills? Are they working for other organisations? If so are they working for competitors or for non-competitors? If they are working for competitors what issues will recruiting them raise?

What will be offered to attract those who have the skills?

In the first instance, this means pay and other aspects of the remuneration package. The entrepreneur must offer a package which is competitive in light of what other employers are offering. But pay is not the entirety of what an organisation offers an employee. Human needs go beyond purely financial concerns. It is critical to ask what the venture offers people as a stage on which to build social relationships. Is it a friendly environment? Will it be fun to work for? Further, what does the venture offer in the way of potential for self-development? How can people progress within it as it expands? What roles will they play? How does the venture represent a theatre for personal growth?

An entrepreneurial venture must compete for people not just with other entrepreneurial ventures but also with established organisations. The venture offers potential employees much the same thing as it presents financial investors, that is risk but with the promise of higher returns. The employee is exposed to the chance of the venture failing. However, there may also be the possibility of much higher rewards in the way of personal development, experience and achievement. Of course, financial investors and employees draw upon quite different mechanisms to manage risk and their exposure to it.

The entrepreneur must be aware of why the option of working for a dynamic, fast-changing, fast-growing organisation might be attractive (and why it might be unattractive) to potential employees.

How will potential employees be contacted?

People must be recruited. There are a variety of means for doing this. In the first instance personal contact and word of mouth can be very productive. If this is not possible then a more formal means of recruiting is called for. This may demand advertising (say, in a specialist press). It may even be felt expedient to delegate the task of attracting people to a specialist recruitment agency.

How will potential employees be evaluated?

Having contacted and attracted the interest of potential employees, then some evaluation and selection procedure must be invoked. Taking on a new employee represents a major commitment for both the business and the employee. Any effort expended in ensuring that the person is right for the organisation, and that the organisation is right for the person, at the recruitment stage, is likely to pay dividends. Mistakes can be expensive and painful for both parties. This is not just a process of ensuring that the person has the right technical skills but also that their attitudes and approach will fit with the organisation's approach, values and culture. However, the entrepreneur should be careful: there is strength in diversity!

If the entrepreneur knows a potential employee well, and has experience of the way in which they work, then the recruitment process may be quite informal (often little more than a job offer over a drink). If they are not acquainted with the person (and the contribution they might make) then at least some sort of interview is required. Some would go further and ask for some sort of *psychometric* or *attitudinal* testing. Of course, these tools exist to aid the entrepreneur is making recruitment decisions. They cannot make them on their own!

Should a skill be in-house or should it be hired when necessary?

Resources are scarce in the entrepreneurial venture. The entrepreneur must make the resources they have work hard. One question they should always ask when faced with the need for a particular human skill is whether it is best to bring that skill in-house, i.e.

to recruit someone to perform the task or it is better to use an external agency to provide it. So should the business employ a financial expert or call on the assistance of a firm of accountants? Should it take on research and development staff or delegate a project to a University?

The 'employ or hire' decision is influenced by a variety of factors. How much of a particular skill input is required? Over what timescale will it be required? Will the business have a long-term need for it? How much control does the entrepreneur need over the person contributing that skill? How much will it cost to employ someone versus hiring them?

It may often appear that the hiring option is the more expensive. However, this expense needs to be considered in the light of the costs of recruitment. There are also risks associated with bringing someone new in to the business. What contribution will they *really* make? How will he or she fit? How will existing employees get along with them? Further, hiring someone tends to add to the business's marginal costs whereas employing them adds to fixed costs. Hiring may be more attractive from a cash-flow point of view. In light of this, in general, employment should only be considered when there is a clear, consistent, long-term need for a particular skill or a particular expertise within the business.

The way the business will gain from the additional level of control that comes from having the skill in-house should also be considered. If the business aims to develop a competitive advantage based on knowledge and an ability to use it to deliver value to the customer then it goes without saying that this knowledge should be held by people who are dedicated to the business.

Leadership and motivation strategy

Commitment is not just given, it must be maintained. In this the entrepreneur must be conscious of their own leadership and motivational strategy and the way they use it to bring out the best in their people. Developing and applying this strategy takes practice. The entrepreneur is the venture's key human resource. The skill they provide comes from being able to manage vision and to use it to lead the organisation.

Summary of key ideas

- The fourth stage in the strategic window is *opening it*.

- Opening the window means gaining the *commitment* of stakeholders and actually starting the venture.

- The key commitments are financial support from *investors*; productive support from *employees* and *network contacts*; agreements to provide inputs by *suppliers*; and agreement to purchase outputs by *customers*.

Suggestions for further reading

Cook, W.M. (1992) "The buddy system", *Entrepreneur*, Nov, p. 52.

Gartner, W.B. (1984) *Problems in business start-up: The relationships among entrepreneurial skills and problem identification for different types of new venture,* Babson, Wellesley Park, Massachusetts: The Centre for Entrepreneurial Studies.

Hall, W.K. (1980) "Survival strategies in a hostile environment", *Harvard Business Review*, July-Aug, pp. 75–85.

Schoch, S. (1984) "Access to capital", *Venture*, June, p. 106.

18 Closing the window: sustaining competitiveness

CHAPTER OVERVIEW

*The final stage in using the strategic window is to **close** it. This means giving the venture some unique and valuable character so that competitors cannot follow through the window and exploit the opportunity it has identified as well. The concept of **competitive advantage** is introduced, what it is, how it can be established and how it can be maintained is considered.*

18.1 Long-term success and sustainable competitive advantage

> **KEY LEARNING OUTCOME**
> An appreciation of how business success is dependent on creating, developing and sustaining competitive advantage in the marketplace.

Having opened the strategic window by gaining financial and human commitment to the venture the entrepreneur must ensure that the long-term potential for success is not eroded by competitors moving in. Entrepreneurs must close the strategic windows to limit the possibility of competitors following them and exploiting the opportunity as well.

The notion of *sustainable competitive advantage* provides a powerful conceptual approach to recognising the ways in which the strategic window can be closed to help guarantee long-term success in the marketplace. It provides an insight into the decisions that must be made in order to keep the business in a position where it can compete effectively. Competitive advantage is a central pillar of strategic thinking which has been developed by Professor Michael Porter in particular.

It is important to distinguish between a *competitive advantage*, which must be understood in terms of what the business offers to the marketplace and the *source* of that competitive advantage which relates to how the business is set up to deliver that offering to the marketplace. Business life is, by definition, competitive. A particular competitive advantage may be imitated, in which case it loses its value. If a business is to enjoy a competitive advantage over the long-term it must be one which competitors find difficult, and in business that means *expensive*, to copy. Consequently, a full understanding of competitive advantage demands decisions at three levels (*see* Fig. 18.1):

1 what will be offered to the marketplace that is unique and valuable – the *competitive advantage*;
2 how that offering will be maintained by the business – the *source* of the competitive advantage; and
3 how that competitive advantage will be protected from imitation by competitors – the way it will be *sustained*.

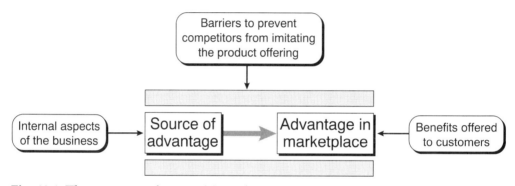

Fig. 18.1 The structure of competitive advantage

Competitive advantage

Competitive advantage is located in what is offered to the marketplace. A competitive advantage is present if the business consistently offers the customer something which is *different* to what competitors are offering, and that difference represents something *valuable* for the customer. In short, a competitive advantage is the reason why customers spend their money with one business rather than another.

The entrepreneur must decide what type of competitive advantage they aim to pursue. Some of the more critical include:

● offering the customer a *lower price*, that is better value for money;
● differentiating the offering through its *features* or *performance*, that is an offering which satisfies needs or solves problems for its customers better than a competitor's product does;
● differentiating the offering through *service*, that is addressing needs or solving problems in a more effective way, or supporting the use of the product more effectively;

- differentiating the offering through *branding*, that is through investment in communicating quality and the business's commitment to the offering;
- differentiating the offering through *brand imagery,* that is by building in associations which address social and self-developmental needs as well as functional needs;
- differentiating through *access* and *distribution*, that is by giving the customer easier, more convenient, less disruptive or less time-consuming access to the offering.

The source of competitive advantage

Being able to *consistently* offer something different and meaningful in the ways described above will only occur if the business is itself different from its competitors in some way. A competitive advantage in the marketplace must be delivered from within the business and be supported by it.

The English academic Professor John Kay has developed a perspective on competitive advantage which sees it as having its source in one of four distinct capabilities:

(i) the *architecture* of the business, that is its internal structure;
(ii) the *reputation* of the business, that is the way key stakeholders view it;
(iii) the way the business *innovates*, that is its ability to come up with new and valuable ideas; and
(iv) the business's *strategic assets*, that is valuable assets to which it has access and its competitors do not.

These four distinctive capabilities are quite general and apply to all businesses. They can be related to four specific sources of competitive advantage for the entrepreneurial venture making its presence felt in the marketplace. These are: *costs, knowledge, relationships* and *structure*.

Cost sources

The business may enjoy an advantage due to lower costs. In economic terms this means that the business will be able to *add value* more efficiently. Cost advantages may be gained from four key areas.

Lower input costs
The business may have access to input factors which are cheaper than those available to competitors. This can include raw materials, energy or labour. Lower input costs can be gained by a number of means. Particularly important are access to unique sources of inputs (say through special contractual arrangements or from geographic location) and achieving buying power over suppliers.

Economies of scale
A business must dilute its fixed costs (which are independent of output) from revenues (which are dependent on output). Hence, *unit* costs tend to fall as output increases. Fixed costs are those which must be borne regardless of the output achieved. These typically include 'head office' costs and often much of the marketing, sales and development activity. A larger output means that these costs are being used

more productively. It may then give a business an overall cost advantage over competitors.

Experience curve economies

Experience curve economies are a consequence of the business learning how to generate its outputs. As a business gains experience in adding value the cost of adding that value is reduced. In short, practice pays! A large number of studies over a variety of different industries has found that a strict mathematical relationship holds between unit cost and output experience. This relationship is exponential. That is, costs fall by a fixed amount every time output is doubled. This means that for a linear output, the cost reductions achieved in a particular time period are seen to fall off as time goes on. This exponential relationship is shown in Fig. 18.2.

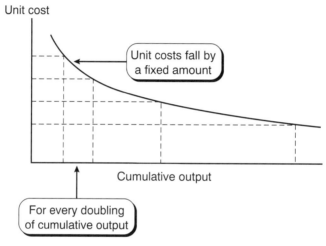

Fig. 18.2 The Experience Curve: costs fall exponentially as experience is gained

Like economies of scale, experience curve economies are related to output. However, the two should not be confused. Whereas economies of scale depend on output in a particular *period*, experience curve economies are a result of *cumulative* output. In general, the firm with the highest cumulative output in a market will be in a position to have developed the lowest unit cost. Most studies of experience curve economies have concentrated on production costs. However, the principle is a general one and applies to any cost of adding value. So experience curve economies may be sought in other parts of the firm's value addition process such as sales, marketing, procurement, *etc*.

Technological innovation

A firm's costs are, technically, the cost of adding a particular amount of value to an input in order to create a saleable output. Costs are related to the technology used by the business to add value. A technological innovation can provide a cost advantage by enabling value to be added more efficiently. In practice a technological innovation can be used to 'reset' the experience curve at a lower level (*see* Fig. 18.3). Such innovation

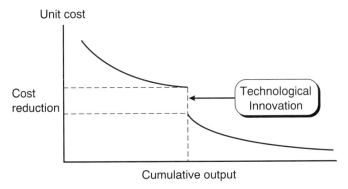

Fig. 18.3 The experience curve and technological innovation

often relates to production technology but in principle it can apply to any value adding activity within the organisation.

Knowledge sources

Knowledge can be valuable. A firm may enjoy a competitive advantage if it knows things that its competitors do not. This knowledge might be in any one of a number of areas.

Product knowledge

A special understanding of the products (or services) that make up the market. Critically, this knowledge must be used to create offerings which are more attractive to buyers. Product knowledge must be used in conjunction with knowledge of the *market*.

Market knowledge

Special insights into the way the market functions. This includes areas such as the needs of the consumer, the way in which customers buy and what can be used to influence them. This knowledge can be used to create effective marketing and selling strategies.

Technical knowledge

A special understanding and competence in making and delivering the offering to the marketplace. This knowledge is not valuable on its own. Rather it must be used to offer the customer something different: a better product, a lower cost product or a better service.

Knowledge does not come for free. It is the result of investment. Product and technical knowledge arise from research and development activities. Market knowledge comes from market research and market analysis. It should be remembered that knowledge is not in itself valuable. It only forms the basis of a competitive advantage if it is used to deliver new value to the customer.

Relationship sources

Relationships are not just a 'nice to have' add-on to business activity, they are fundamental to it. A relationship establishes trust and trust adds value by reducing the need for contracts and monitoring. A business may be able to build a competitive advantage on the basis of the special relationships it enjoys with its stakeholders. Building relationships is essential if the business is to locate itself in a secure, and supportive, network.

Relationship with customers

A firm's relationship with its customers is, of course, a critical dimension of its success. The relationship can be built in a number of ways. Much depends on the nature of the products being sold to the customer and the number of customers the firm has to deal with. A business selling a small number of highly valuable products to a few customers is in a different situation to one selling a large number of relatively low value items to a great number of customers.

Relationships can be personal, that is created through individual contact. Account management and sales activities are important in this respect. The sales–buyer interaction is both a one-to-one contact and a conduit through which value can flow from the business to its customers. If a large number of customers are involved, and personal contact is not possible, then contact may be sustained via the media through advertising and public relations.

Critical to the relationship with customers is *reputation*. A reputation for delivering products which do what they say they will and for delivering them with a high degree of service and for undertaking business in a fair and equitable way is invaluable. Reputation can be hard to build up. It is, however, quite easy to lose.

Relationship with suppliers

Suppliers are best regarded as partners in the development of an end-market. They are integral to the network the business needs to build up around itself. A business can put itself in a stronger position to deliver value to its customers if its suppliers themselves show flexibility and responsiveness. Further, suppliers can be encouraged to innovate on behalf of the business. All of this means that the relationship with suppliers has to go beyond just the concern with negotiating over prices. Though suppliers need to share value with their customers the game need not be zero sum. A customer working with its suppliers can address the end-market better and create more overall value to be shared than one working against its suppliers.

Relationship with investors

Of all stakeholders it is, perhaps, investors who have the most transparent relationship with the entrepreneurial venture. In economic terms their concern is the most one-dimensional: they are concerned to maximise their returns. Investors are, however, still human beings. They engage in communication and relationship building with the entrepreneur. They respond not only to actual returns but also if they feel their interests are being properly addressed by the entrepreneur.

The support of investors can be critical to success. Any venture will have its ups and downs, especially in its early stages. When things are not going too well, the support of investors is invaluable. If they insist on liquidating their investment then, at best, problems will be exacerbated; at worst, the business may not survive. The support of investors can be maintained by developing a strategy to communicate actively with them. This will involve managing the investors' expectations, building their confidence in the venture and avoiding 'surprises' which lead investors to make hasty judgements.

Relationship with employees
Building a motivating and productive relationship with employees is one of the entrepreneur's most important activities. It is the employees who deliver the actions which convert the entrepreneur's vision into reality. The entrepreneurial venture may not enjoy many of the cost, technical and relationship advantages that established players can call upon. All they have is their people, their interest, motivation and drive on behalf of the business. The entrepreneur must draw this out by understanding their employees' motivations and adopting the right leadership strategies.

Structural sources

The final area in which the entrepreneurial business can aspire to develop a basis for competitive advantage is in its structure. Structural advantages arise as a consequence not so much of *what* the business does but the *way* it goes about doing things. This is a function not only of its formal structure, the pre-defined way in which individuals will relate to each other but also in its informal structure, the 'unofficial' web of relationships and communication links which actually define it and its *culture* which governs how those relationships will function and evolve. Since new entrants are unlikely to enjoy cost advantages in the early stages of the business at least, and because relationship advantages take time to build up and knowledge advantages require investment, the entrepreneurial business is likely to be highly dependent on structure-based advantages.

A business can gain a competitive advantage from its structure if that structure allows it to perform better in the marketplace. Such a structural advantage may arise from having the business co-ordinated by a strong leader who keeps the business on track and focuses it on the opportunities at hand. Such leadership ensures that resources are used effectively. The business may also be better at gaining information from the marketplace and using it to make decisions.

This might allow it be more responsive to the needs of customers and so be quicker to offer them new products and services.

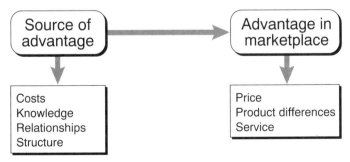

Fig. 18.4 Competitive advantage and its sources

Another structural advantage can arise if the individuals who make it up emphasise *tasks* (what needs doing) rather than *roles* (what they feel their job descriptions say they should do). Such an attitude enables the business to be flexible, to focus on its customers and keep fixed costs to a minimum.

Competitive advantages in the market place can be built on a number of platforms within the organisation (*see* Fig. 18.4). Costs, knowledge, relationships and structures may all be used to offer the customer value in a way that competitors cannot. This makes them sources from which a competitive advantage may be developed in the marketplace. They have the potential to bring success to the venture. However, if this success is to be long-term, the competitive advantages must be maintained in the face of competitive activity. They must be *sustained*.

18.2   How competitive advantage is established

KEY LEARNING OUTCOME
An appreciation of the ways in which competitive advantages may established but can be lost to competitors.

The business world does not stand still. Competitors are aware of each other to varying degrees. They become *acutely* aware if they lose business, or at least are prevented from gaining it, by the activities of a competitor. They may go on to develop an understanding of *why* that business is performing better than they are. A successful business cannot hide its competitive advantage for long. Competitors will then be tempted to imitate and recreate that competitive advantage for themselves. This may be easier said than done. If competitors find a competitive advantage hard to imitate, then the entrepreneurial firm may go on enjoying the rewards that advantage offers. If the advantage is hard to imitate it is said to be *sustainable*.

A reverse perspective is illuminating in this instance. To understand how competitive advantage may be sustained demands an appreciation of how it can be *lost*. Quite simply, a competitive advantage is lost if a competitor *gains* it. In order to offer something that gains an advantage in the marketplace means that a business must create for itself the *source* of that advantage. The framework developed in the previous section applies so competitive advantage is lost to competitors if they achieve lower *costs*; or gain *knowledge* that was exclusive to and valuable to the venture; or build a stronger network of *relationships* than the venture enjoys; or develop *structural* advantages (advantages in the way the business organises itself).

An entrepreneurial venture must constantly strive to prevent competitors gaining advantage in these areas. While the venture actually meets its competitors in the marketplace the basis of competitive advantages provides the points of *strategic contact* between the venture and its competitors. It is these things which give the venture the *power* to compete (*see* Fig. 18.5).

The entrepreneur must be on their guard as to the ways in which competitors might gain the upper hand in terms of competitive advantage. They must consider the

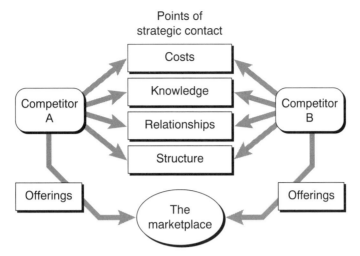

Fig. 18.5 Competitive advantage and competition

possible ways in which competitors might gain the advantage, and be aware of these when they are developing their strategy. A sound strategy must be built on a competitive advantage which can be sustained. Knowing this is part of understanding the nature of the market, the players who make it up and competition within it. The decisions which relate to developing a competitive advantage must be made in relation to the considerations on how *costs*, *knowledge*, *relationships* and *structure* deliver advantages in the marketplace.

Some considerations in relation to cost advantages

Here the chief considerations relate to how cost advantages may be used in the marketplace to achieve volume gains (in other words, how price sensitive the customer is); how competitors can use factor prices to their advantage; and how volume gains are rewarded with further cost reductions (i.e. to what extent volume and cost are linked in a virtuous circle via economies of scale and experience effects). Also important is how established the cost structure of the industry is. In particular, is a technological innovation that changes the cost rules likely to occur, and if so, how quickly will it spread through the sector?

Some important specific questions are:

1 How important is price to the customer?
2 How important is price to intermediaries and distributors?
3 Can volume be gained if price is reduced? (That is, is demand elastic?)

These questions may be answered by the use of appropriate market research techniques.

- Have all the players in the market access to the same inputs?
- Do some players enjoy exclusive access to low cost inputs?
- Are economies of scale important?

- If so, does one player have a significant *period* volume advantage?
- Are experience economies important?
- If so, has one player a *cumulative* volume advantage?
- Do any players have a *technological advantage* that influences costs?
- Is a technological innovation that will alter costs likely in the future?
- If so, how quickly would such a technological innovation spread through the industry?
- How expensive would it be to adopt cost-reducing technological innovations?

These questions may be answered by an analysis of the industry's structure and from knowledge of its technological base. The answers will illuminate the possibility of sustaining a cost-based advantage. In short, it will be sustainable if price is important to the customer and one player can gain a cost advantage from experience or technological sources.

Some considerations in relation to knowledge advantages

Here the considerations relate to how exclusive knowledge may be gained, used and protected by the players in a sector.

Some important specific questions are as follows.

- Is the knowledge the industry uses established or is it in a state of rapid development? (This involves consideration of whether the industry is a high-tech one which spends heavily on product research and development or marketing research.)
- Do the businesses in the industry use a common pool of knowledge or do they rely on their own localised knowledge?
- Is knowledge developed 'in house' or are external organisations used (for example, business service firms such as market research agencies and consultancies and 'non-profit' organisations such as universities) important?
- How important to the industry are knowledge protection devices such as patents, copyrights and registered designs?

Again, these questions can be answered through an appropriate analysis of the industry, its environment and its technology. Clearly, knowledge which is important to delivering customer value, is localised and is protectable offers a more sustainable basis for competitive advantage than knowledge which is accessible to all.

Some considerations in relation to relationship advantages

Relationships are the 'glue' that holds the business network together. If relationships are long-term and secure, then the network can be thought of as 'tight'. If relationships are transitory and easily broken, then the network is 'loose'. A new entrant will find a tight network hard to break into. It may be expensive to break old relationships and establish new ones. On the other hand, once a location in that network has been established the business will find it easy to defend its position. Conversely, a loose network, while being easy to enter, will offer little security from competitors. Some important specific questions are:

- What means are used to establish and maintain relationships with customers? (Personal contact (e.g. sales activity) or contact via the media (e.g. advertising).)
- Are relationships with customers long-term or short-term? (Consider whether purchases are one off or repeat? Is after-sales support important?)
- What *risks* does the buyer face in buying and using the product? (What sort of investment does it entail? What can go wrong when using it?)
- How can a sense of *trust* between the buyer and seller aid the management of those risks?
- How important is the seller's *reputation* to the buyer?
- On what basis can reputation be built? (Consider issues such as product quality, service, ethical standards, behaviour.)

A particularly effective entrepreneurial strategy is to identify a sector in which the network is loose and to create value through 'tightening it up' by offering a higher level of commitment and service. This also locks out competitors and makes the advantage gained sustainable.

Some considerations in relation to structural advantages

As noted in the previous section, structural advantages arise as a consequence not so much of *what* the business does, but the *way* it goes about doing things. A business can gain an advantage over its competitors by having a structure in which roles are more flexible (which can lead to lower costs), by being more focused on the market and so more responsive to signals from customers and competitors and then by using those signals to make faster and better decisions about how to serve the customer. Some important specific questions are:

- What kind of organisational *structures* do businesses in the sector adopt? (Consider, in particular, how important are functional departments, team working, *ad-hoc* structures?)
- How important are *formal* structures? (Consider how the way things *really* happen compares to the way businesses say they *should* happen?)
- What kind of *decision-making processes* are used? (Over what timescale are plans made? Who is involved in decision making? How are particular decisions justified within organisations?)
- How do firms in the sector identify, process and respond to market signals? (Consider whether the market research is formalised? How is pricing policy determined? How is new product development organised?)
- What *cultures* are adopted by businesses in the sector? (Consider customer focus *versus* internal concerns; entrepreneurial *versus* bureaucratic attitudes; the importance of tasks *versus* roles).
- What leadership styles are adopted? (Consider whether they are authoritarian or consensus based? Is power exercised through the control of resources or the communication of vision? Is there a focus on tasks or a focus on people).

Rigid structures provide the entrepreneur with a means of focusing and directing their organisation but they are ambivalent as a source of competitive advantage. It may be better to allow people to use their skills and insights by pushing decision making down the organisation – particularly when it is in a turbulent environment.

Understanding the answers to all of these questions gives the entrepreneur an insight into the way they can establish a competitive advantage in the marketplace in a way which has a secure, and distinctive base within their business. Further, it indicates the potential which a particular competitive advantage has to be *sustainable* in the face of competitive pressure.

18.3   Maintaining competitive advantage

KEY LEARNING OUTCOME
An understanding of the ways in which competitive advantage may be sustained.

Identifying a competitive advantage, that is something the customer finds both different and attractive, and securing that on the basis of some aspect of the business, be it *costs*, *knowledge*, *relationships* or *structure*, in a way which both provides a source for that advantage and differentiates the business from competitors is the *starting point* for long-term success. In order to *ensure* that it happens, the business must make sure that the competitive advantage cannot be imitated, and so the profits it promises cannot be eroded, by competitors. The entrepreneur must decide not only what the competitive advantage of the venture they establish will be but also how it will be *sustained*.

Sustaining cost advantages

The key decision here is how will the business keep its costs lower than competitors? There can only be *one* cost leader in a market. If it is to be based on scale and experience curve economies, cost leadership demands *output volume* leadership. This means gaining and maintaining the highest market share. This can prove to be expensive if the market is price sensitive. Competitors will be willing to compete by cutting their prices. The cost leader will have to use their cost advantage to establish a price below that of competitors' costs. This may mean a low, or even zero, profit margin. A cost leadership strategy may mean a long haul with poor profit levels until competitors have been 'seen off'.

The temptation to increase prices to gain short-term profits must be resisted since this will create a 'price umbrella' under which less efficient competitors can shelter. If the entrepreneur is a later entrant to the market and coming in from behind, then they may need to invest heavily in the short-term to gain a rapid cumulative volume advantage over competitors. Again, this can prove to be expensive in the short run with substantial returns offered only in the long-term. This, of course, introduces a number of risks.

Further, even though experience cost reductions are a function of output volume they do not occur by right. They have to be *managed*. For the cost leader, cost control has to take centre stage, i.e. driving costs down must take priority over all other considerations. This demands that powerful cost control systems be in place. This in turn will influence the leadership and motivation strategies adopted by the entrepreneur and the culture of the organisation they create. Such 'single-minded' organisations are not to everyone's taste, a factor which needs to be considered when recruiting and building the management team.

If the cost leadership is to be established on the basis of a technological innovation then the entrepreneur needs to be sure why they, and they alone, will have access to that technology. It is best to assume that competitors will eventually gain access to the innovation even if it is secured through patents and other intellectual property devices (*see* below). In respect to this it is best to use the innovation as the *starting point* to gain an initial cost advantage which can be built on and sustained using scale and experience effects.

Even if all this is achieved, the entrepreneur must be sensitive to the attentions of anti-trust regulators. A strategy which achieves a large market share on the basis of squeezing competitors out on price may be a just reward for doggedly pursuing efficiency. To outsiders, however, it may seem like an unfair monopoly.

In conclusion there can only be one cost leader in a market. A cost leadership strategy is one which is challenging and, in the short-term at least, expensive, to sustain.

Sustaining knowledge advantages

Knowledge advantages are based on understanding both of the product and the market. These two things operate in tandem with one other. An understanding of what is offered must be tempered with an understanding of why the customer wants it. Generally in business, knowledge soon becomes public. Even if knowledge is 'secure' within the business, the process of launching products and promoting them to the customer sends clear signals to competitors.

Knowledge may be 'protected' by means of patents and other intellectual property devices such as copyrights and registered designs. In principle, these prevent competitors from using the knowledge. They grant the holder a monopoly over the innovation arising from the knowledge. In some industries intellectual property is very important, for example in the biotechnology industry. However, the use of intellectual property devices as a means of securing a competitive advantage should be approached cautiously. Patents and other devices are not granted for every new idea, rather they must reflect a *significant* technological innovation. Even if the new idea is significant, the registration process is time consuming, demands the aid of experts and can be expensive. Registration may also involve the public posting of the invention prior to any patent being granted. In effect this means presenting the patent to challenge by holders of other patents which can tip off competitors. Often not just one, but a number variations of the idea will have to be patented in order to ensure that competitors do not get round the patent by presenting a minor variations to the market.

Furthermore, the patent registration will have to be obtained in a variety of regions if global cover is desired. If comprehensive cover is not obtained then competitors may get round the patent by producing the product in an area where the patent does not hold. Even if global cover is obtained, some countries are lax (because of weak legal structures or even, in some cases, as a matter of policy) in enforcing intellectual property law. If the law enforcement mechanisms will act to protect the patent, it is still down to the patent holder to police their property and challenge infringements. Even if all this is done, there are strict time limits on the protection offered.

These drawbacks do not mean that patents are not valuable, just that they should not be relied upon to provide a source of competitive advantage on their own terms. Rather, they should be used *tactically* to provide an initial advantage which can then be used to develop other advantages based on cost and relationships.

Sustaining relationship advantages

Relationships are valuable because they establish *trust* and trust brings down costs for a variety of reasons. First, it reduces the need for a buyer to be constantly scanning the market for offerings. They simply go to a supplier they know. Second, it eliminates the need to establish detailed contracts between buyer and seller. Third, it eliminates the need for a constant *policing* of those contracts. In this context, we may consider *all* stakeholders to be engaged in contract building with the venture, not just customers, though of course a trusting relationship with the customer is particularly important and has immediate pay-offs.

If trust is built up it can then form the basis for sustaining competitive advantage. Given that cost and knowledge advantages are most easily accrued by the large (and that usually means the established) business, trust can be a potent ingredient in entrepreneurial success, particularly in the early stages of the venture.

Trust can only be built by establishing and developing relationships which exist on a number of levels. At one level is the experience the parties have of each other through personal contact, say as a result of direct selling activities. The salesperson is not just informing the buyer of a firm's outputs; they are acting as an ambassador for the business as a whole. At the next level, is communication through the media using advertising and public relations activity. Product branding and company image are important mediators. At another level is the general *reputation* that a business builds in the mind of the buyer through their wider experience of it. Reputation is established not through absolute outcomes but through outcomes in relation to *expectations*. Quite simply, if expectations are exceeded then a stakeholder will be very satisfied by the outcome; if they are not met then the stakeholder will be disappointed and feel let down.

Thus a strategy for building and maintaining trust must have three interlocking aspects:

1 The management of expectations

The entrepreneur must take charge of what the other party (be they a customer, an investor, a supplier or an employee) expects to come out of the relationship. While entrepreneurs are right to strive to deliver on behalf of the stakeholders in their venture they must avoid 'over' promising as this can easily lead to disappointment, dissatisfaction and a feeling that trust has been broken if what has been promised is not delivered.

2 The management of outcomes

Entrepreneurs must take responsibility for what their venture delivers finally to its stakeholders. They must ensure that these outcomes at least meet, or are better than, what the stakeholder expected. If for any reason they are not (and no-one, not even the most effective entrepreneur, can control all contingencies) then the entrepreneur is faced with the challenge of addressing the stakeholder's disappointment and managing the process of rebuilding trust. The details of how this must be done will vary depending on the stakeholder, the circumstances and the extent of failure that has occurred. The golden rule, however, is that disappointment should *never* be ignored!

3 The management of communication

Expectations and the delivery of outcomes occur on a stage built by communication. Communications between the entrepreneur (and the venture's staff) and stakeholders can take a variety of forms. They can be formal or informal, personal or impersonal, directed to a specific stakeholder or widely broadcast. They may take place via a variety of media. The entrepreneur must be aware of the communication channels that connect, and draw, the venture's stakeholders together, learning how to use them and how to reinvigorate them constantly. He or she must also take control of how those channels are used. In particular, the entrepreneur must take clear responsibility for the promises that are being made on behalf of the venture; not just the promises they make themselves, but also those being made by other people on behalf of the venture.

Sustaining structural advantages

Structural advantages arise when a business, by virtue of the way it organises itself, becomes more attuned to signals from the marketplace, more acute in its decision making and more flexible in responding to the needs of customers. Such responsiveness is a product of the organisation's structure, that is, the network of responsibilities and communication links which give the business its form.

As with relationship advantages, the entrepreneurial business is in a strong position to enjoy structural advantages over larger businesses. Established, older businesses may be hampered by internal structures. These structures may serve an important function but once started they tend to develop a momentum of their own. This can mean that they continue to exist after their usefulness has declined. In the entrepreneurial business, on the other hand, internal structures will be in a state of flux and will be forming in response to market demands.

Decision making within the established firm may also be less acute. Key decision makers may be insulated from the realities of the market, the signals it is sending and the opportunities it is presenting. Decision making may also be distorted by internal 'political' concerns which put internal factional interests ahead of those of the customer and the business as a whole. The entrepreneur, however, should be using the venture's organisation to facilitate and focus decision making, rather than to hinder it. In addition, they are in a position to use strong leadership to draw disparate groups together and co-ordinate their actions.

This demands that entrepreneurs keep themselves in touch with their market and that they do not allow themselves to be 'swamped' by their organisations. Communication systems should be designed with the primary objective of feeding information about the market to decision makers. While information on the internal state of the business is important, this should be used to support market orientated decision making, not be used to compromise it.

Competitive advantage is *dynamic* not static. Once a venture gains a competitive advantage in the marketplace it must use the success this brings to constantly reinvent the advantage. Success offers rewards in excess of market norms. These rewards must be reinvested in the business. This investment should not be aimed at merely reinforcing the existing competitive advantage but at modifying it and, if need be, creating the basis for entirely new ones.

If the venture aims to become a *cost leader* then it must invest in volume leadership and cost control. If it aims to use *exclusive knowledge* then it must invest in developing its understanding of the products and services offered to the market, the way in which they meet the needs of customers and the way in which customers decide to buy. If *relationships* are to be used then investment must take place in developing existing relationships and creating new ones. This means managing expectations, outcomes and communication, and all of these in turn mean investment in the people who communicate to customers on behalf of the business. Maintaining a *structural advantage* demands investment in human and communication systems. The business cannot afford to become stale, that is to let its structures gain a life and a *raison d'être* independent of their function in serving the market. It also demands investment in *change*. Change is not only a structural phenomenon, it also represents development in individual attitudes and organisational culture. The rewards gained from a competitive advantage must be reinvested to maintain, develop and renew the basis of that advantage within the business (*see* Fig. 18.6).

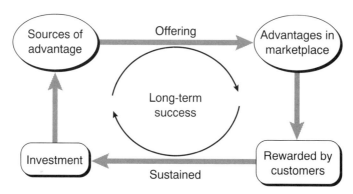

Fig. 18.6 Sustaining competitive advantage

Summary of key ideas

- The fifth, and final, stage of the strategic window is *closing it*.

- Closing the window means creating a *competitive advantage* so that the venture can go on exploiting the opportunity in the face of competitive pressures.

- A competitive advantage is something the business can do that is valuable for the customer which competitors find difficult to match.

- A competitive advantage has a source within the business. The key sources are lower *costs*; *knowledge* of the product and market; stronger *relationships* within the network; and a more flexible and responsive organisational *structure*.

- A competitive advantage must be actively maintained if it is to be *sustainable*.

Suggestions for further reading

Abernathy, W.J. and **Wayne, K.** (1974) "Limits of the learning curve", *Harvard Business Review*, Sept–Oct, pp. 109–19.

Bamberger, I. (1989) "Developing competitive advantage in small and medium-sized firms", *Long Range Planning*, Vol. 22, No. 5, pp. 80–8.

Barnett, W.P., Grieve, H.R. and **Park, D.Y.** (1994) "An evolutionary model of organisational performance", *Strategic Management Journal*, Vol. 15, pp. 11–28.

Brock Smith, J. and **Barclay, D.W.** (1997) "The effects of organisational differences and trust on the effectiveness of selling partnership relationships", *Journal of Marketing*, Vol. 61, pp. 3–21.

Doney, P.M. and **Cannon, J.P.** (1997) "An examination of the nature of trust in buyer–seller relationships", *Journal of Marketing*, Vol. 61, pp. 35 51.

Ghemawat, P. (1985) "Building strategy on the experience curve", *Harvard Business Review*, Mar-Apr, pp. 143–9.

Kay, J. (1993) *Foundations of Corporate Success*, Oxford: Oxford University Press.

Lieberman, M.B. and **Montgommery, D.B.** (1988) "First mover advantages", *Strategic Management Journal*, Vol. 9, pp. 41–58.

Pitt, L.F. and **Jeantrout, B.** (1994) "Management of customer expectations in service firms: A study and checklist", *The Service Industries Journal*, Vol. 14, No. 2, pp. 170–89.

Porter, M. (1980) *Competitive Strategy: Techniques for Analysing Industries and Competitors*, New York: Free Press.

Porter, M. (1985) *Competitive Advantage: Creating and Sustaining Superior Performance*, New York: Free Press.

Russell, M. (1984) "Scales true economies", *Management Today*, May, pp. 82–4.

Snell, R. and **Lau, A.** (1994) "Exploring local competencies salient for expanding small businesses", *Journal of Management Development*, Vol. 13, No. 4, pp. 4–15.

Stevens, H.H. (1976) "Defining corporate strengths and weaknesses", *Sloan Management Review*, Spring, pp. 51–68.

Teas, R.K. (1993) "Expectations, performance evaluation and consumer's perceptions of quality", *Journal of Marketing*, Vol. 57, pp. 18–34.

Tellis, G.J. and **Golder, P.N.** (1996) "First to market, first to fail? Real causes of enduring market leadership", *Sloan Management Review*, Winter, pp. 65–75.

Voss, C. (1992) "Successful innovation and implementation of new processes", *Business Strategy Review*, Spring, pp. 29–44.

Zahra, S.A., **Nash, S.** and **Bickford, D.J.** (1995) "Transforming technological pioneering into competitive advantage", *Academy of Management Executive*, Vol. 9, No. 1, pp. 17–31.

Zeithaml, V., **Berry, V.** and **Parasuraman, A.** (1993) "The nature and determinants of a customer's expectations of a service", *Journal of the Academy of Marketing Science*, Vol. 21, No. 1, pp. 1–12.

19 Gaining financial support: issues and approaches

CHAPTER OVERVIEW

Attracting financial support for the venture is one of the entrepreneur's most important tasks. This chapter considers the supply of investment capital and how backers actually go about selecting investment opportunities. The chapter concludes by advocating that a major factor in successfully attracting investment is the entrepreneur having an understanding of the questions that investors need to ask and preparing answers to them.

19.1 Sources and types of financial investment

KEY LEARNING OUTCOME
A recognition of the different sources of capital available for investment in the entrepreneurial venture.

Investment capital is a valuable commodity. As with any other commodity, markets develop to ensure that supply meets demand. Though 'capital' is itself an undifferentiated commodity (one five dollar bill is exactly like any five dollar bill!) a number of different types of supplier emerge to offer investment capital. These different types of supplier differentiate themselves not in what they supply but in the *way* they supply the capital, the *price* they ask for that capital and the *supplementary services* they offer.

The interaction of supply and demand results in a *price* being set for the capital. This price is the *rate of return* the supplier (the investor) expects from their investment. A number of factors influence the cost of the capital being offered. The critical factors are the *risk* of the investment (that is the probability that the return will be less than that anticipated) and the *opportunity cost* (that is the return that has to be foregone because alternative investments cannot be made). This *risk-rate of return axis* provides one of the key dimensions by which investors differentiate themselves.

Key supplies of capital include the following.

Entrepreneur's own capital

This is money that the entrepreneur owns. It may derive from personal savings, or it may be a 'lump sum' resulting from a capital gain or a redundancy package in which case it might be quite a significant amount. Some successful entrepreneurs liquidate their holdings in their ventures once they mature in order to pursue new business ideas. Clearly, the entrepreneur is free to use this capital as he or she wishes.

Informal investors

An entrepreneur may attract investment support on an informal basis from their family and friends. The expectations of what the returns will be, and when they might be gained, are usually set informally or, at most, semi-formally.

Internal capital networks

Many communities, especially those based around a group of people who are displaced and who are, or at least feel, excluded from the wider economic system, show strong entrepreneurial tendencies. This often enlivens and enriches the economy as a whole. Important examples include a variety of Asian groups in Britain, North Africans in France, Chinese expatriates in South East Asia, and the Lebanese in West Africa. Such groups often encourage investment among themselves. These communities set up *internal capital networks* which direct capital towards new business opportunities within the community. These networks often have an international character. In emerging economies they provide very important conduits for inward investment.

Though often quite informal in a narrow legal sense these networks are guided by a rich set of cultural rules and expectations. Risk, return and the way in which returns are made are often embedded in complex patterns of ownership and control of ventures.

Retained capital

The profits that a venture generates are, potentially, available to be reinvested in its development. However, such profits belong neither to the venture nor to the entrepreneur; rather they are the property of the *investors* who are backing the venture (this group may, of course, include the entrepreneur). Reinvesting the profits might offer a good investment opportunity, but it is an opportunity which the investor will judge like any other on the basis of risk, return and the possibility of taking the profits and seeking alternative investment opportunities.

'Business angels'

Business angels are individuals, or small groups of individuals, who offer up their own capital to new ventures. Business angels are usually people who have been successful in business (perhaps as entrepreneurs themselves) and as a result have some money 'to play with'. Investment structure and return expectations vary, but are usually equity-based and codified in formal agreements. Business angels differ from other types of organisational investor in one important respect. They like to get involved in the ventures they are backing, and in addition to capital backing, they offer their skills, insights and experiences. As a result they usually seek investment opportunities in ventures where their knowledge or business skills are appropriate.

Retail banking

Retail or 'high street' banks usually offer investment capital to new start-ups and expanding small firms. Support is almost inevitably in the form of loan capital and returns are subject to strict agreement. The bank will expect the entrepreneur to make a personal commitment and may seek collateral to reduce the risk of the deal.

Corporate banking

To an extent the corporate banking sector picks up where retail banking stops. Corporate banks are interested in bigger investment opportunities and may settle for longer range returns. Loan capital dominates but some equity may also be offered. Deals may be quite complex and involve conversions between the two forms of investment. Again, a significant commitment by the entrepreneur and asset security may be sought.

Venture capital

Venture capital is a critical source of investment for fast-growing entrepreneurial ventures. Venture capital companies usually seek large investment opportunities which are characterised by the potential for a fast, high rate of return. As such, they tend to take on higher degrees of risk than banks. Venture capital companies will rarely involve themselves with investments of less than half a million dollars and typically seek annual returns in excess of 50 per cent to be harvested over five years or less. Usually the deals are equity-based and they may be complex. However, a clear *exit strategy* which enables the returns to the venture capital investment to be liquidated quickly must be in place.

Public flotation

A public flotation is a means of raising capital by offering shares in the venture to a pool of private investors. These shares can then be bought and sold in an open stock market or *bourse*. There are a variety of stock markets through which capital may be raised. All mature economies have national stock markets of which London, New York and Tokyo are among the most important internationally. There are a number of *emerging* stock markets which trade stock from companies in the developing world and in the post-command economies of central and eastern Europe (that is, the economies that were under Communist control until the late 1980s).

In addition to the stock markets for established companies, there are special stock markets for smaller businesses and for fast-growing ventures. The most important European small-company stock market is the *Alternative Investments Market* (AIM) based in London. This market has some 265 companies listed and a capitalisation of nearly $10 billion. Other European small business markets include the *Nouveau Marché* in Paris, *Easdaq* based in Brussels and the *Neuer Markt* in Frankfurt. It is planned to link all these markets through a network dubbed *EURO.NM*. Small and fast-growing business investment in the US is carried out through a bourse known as *Nasdaq*.

Government

Very few governments nowadays fail to see that they have an interest in encouraging enterprise. New businesses create jobs, bring innovation to the market and provide competitive efficiency. Across the world, however, governments differ in the extent to which and the way in which they engage in intervention to support the creation and survival of new and fast-growing businesses.

Support is usually given to new start-ups when capital for investment is hardest to obtain and when cash-flow can be at its tightest. Generally direct government investment is in decline. However, there are a number of quasi-governmental agencies which can direct grants towards the entrepreneurial start-up. In addition to capital grants, government may offer support in the form of consulting services and training. Examples of this include the *Training and Enterprise Councils* (TECs) in the UK and the *Small Business Administration* (SBA) in the USA. In continental Europe (and increasingly also in central and eastern Europe) local chambers of commerce play an important role in this respect. In addition to overt support, governments often give smaller firms a head start through tax breaks.

Commercial partnerships

An entrepreneurial venture may look towards existing businesses as a source of investment capital. This will usually occur when the established business has a strategic interest in the success of the venture, for example if it is a supplier of a particularly innovative and valuable input. The support demonstrated by IBM for *Microsoft* in its early days is a case in point. Commercial partnerships can also occur when the venture is developing a technology which will be important to the established firm. The wide range of investments by established pharmaceutical companies in biotechnology start-ups in the 1980s provides an example of this.

There is a range of arrangements by which the established firm can impose control over its investment in the entrepreneurial venture. At one extreme is complete ownership, and at the other is a simple agreement to use the venture as a favoured supplier. In between there are a variety of forms of *strategic alliance*.

Choice of capital supply

The types and range of investment capital providers operating in an economy depend on the stage of development of that economy and a variety of other political and cultural factors. The choice of capital supplier by the entrepreneur is a decision which must be made in the light of the nature of the venture, its capital requirements, the stage of its development and the risks it faces.

19.2 How backers select investment opportunities

KEY LEARNING OUTCOME
An appreciation of the process by which investors select investment opportunities.

Investment is a buying and selling process. The entrepreneur is trying to sell the venture as an investment opportunity, and the investor is looking to buy opportunities which offer a good return. As such, a consideration of the marketing-buying behaviour behind investment deals can provide an insight into how that process might be understood and so be managed to be more effective.

Tyebjee and Bruno (1984) have developed a model of the investment process. Though these workers used the model to understand venture capital investment, it is generic in form and so can be used to understand investment in general. The model is outlined in Fig. 19.1.

Fig. 19.1 A model of investment decision making
(Adapted from Tyebjee and Bruno, 1984)

The model identifies five key stages in the investment process. These are as follows:

Stage I: Deal origination

Deal origination is the process by which the entrepreneur and the investor first become aware of each other. This results from a mix of *searching* activity by the investor and *promotional* activity by the entrepreneur. Few venture capitalists actually search for new opportunities. They wait for the entrepreneur, or more often a third party working on behalf of the entrepreneur, to approach them. Similarly, retail and corporate banks place the onus on the entrepreneur to make the first move.

If the business has shares which are available on a bourse then private and institutional investors will be active in seeking out stock which fits their portfolio and offers them an attractive return. Business angels are often informed about investment opportunities through informal networks of business contacts.

Stage II: Deal screening

Many investors specialise in certain types of investment. Deal screening reflects the initial evaluation of the proposal to see if it fits with the investor's profile of activities. Important criteria include the amount of investment being sought, the type of technology on which the venture is based, the industry sector of the venture and the venture's stage of growth.

Stage III: Deal evaluation

If the proposal fits with the investor's portfolio of activities, then a more detailed evaluation of the proposal may be carried out. The objective of this exercise is to compare the returns offered by the venture to the risk that it faces. The key factors to be considered in this evaluation will be the potential for the venture in terms of the innovation it is offering, the conditions in the market it aims to develop and the competitive pressures it will face. If this potential is good then consideration will also be made of the ability of the management team behind the venture to actually deliver it. The investor will also be interested in any security the entrepreneur can offer, say in the form of readily liquidisable assets.

Stage IV: Deal structuring

Deal structuring relates to the decisions that must be made in relation to how the initial investment will be made and how the investor will see that investment bear fruit. The critical issues in relation to the investment stage will be how much the entrepreneur is seeking and over what period that investment is to be made. Critical to the return stage will be the actual return offered, how long the investor must wait before that return is seen and the form it will take. For example, will it be cash or will it be a share in the company? If it is a stake in the company can it be liquidated readily?

Stage V: Post-investment activity

Investors, especially those with a significant interest in the venture, will usually retain a degree of involvement in it. There are two broad areas of post-investment activity: *monitoring* and *control*. Monitoring relates to the procedures which are put in place to enable the investor to evaluate the performance of the business so they can keep track of their investment. Financial reporting by way of a balance sheet and profit and loss account (*see* Section 20.2) provides a legally defined means by which the investor can monitor the business. Important investors may demand more frequent and detailed information, perhaps going beyond purely financial data.

Control mechanisms give the investor an active role in the venture and power to influence the entrepreneur's and the venture's management decision making. One common control mechanism is for the investor to be represented on the firm's management team, perhaps as a director. Business angels often offer this not just as a control mechanism but, because of their experience and insights, as a positive contribution to the management of the venture.

This model highlights some of the key areas of information that are needed by the investor before they can make an effective investment decision. Providing that information and answering the investors' questions must form the basis of the entrepreneur's communication strategy towards the investor. This model can be seen in effect in a study by Mason and Harrison (1996) in which they describe the investment process of one particular group of business angels in great depth.

The group under study was formed by a retired UK businessman after seeing business angels operate in the US. Its members, selected on the basis of experience, compatible personalities and commitment, were attracted by an advertisement in the business opportunities column of the *Financial Times* newspaper. Deals were initiated by a variety of means including newspaper advertisements and by independent business brokers. About half of all deals were initiated by the entrepreneur approaching the group. About one quarter were initiated by the group approaching an entrepreneur and the remaining quarter were the result of introduction by independent agents. All deals were initially offered in the form of a written proposal. Initial screening was undertaken by an individual member of the group. Some 80 per cent of the deals were eliminated at this stage because they did not look financially viable. The remaining 20 per cent were summarised in a standard format and offered to the whole group for comment. If the group felt the deal was worth exploring further (about 10 per cent of all initial proposals) then a project leader was appointed to evaluate the proposal in detail. This was done in conjunction with two other members of the group. This involved background research and a meeting with the investee company. After due consideration, the project team would make a formal presentation and recommendation to the whole group. If, and only if, all members of the group were in favour of the deal, then a formal offer would be made to the investee company. The project team would consider how to structure the deal for entry and exit and would probably offer support in the management of the venture.

19.3 The questions investors need answering

KEY LEARNING OUTCOME
A recognition of the kind of information investors need before they can make an investment decision.

In a narrow economic sense investors are *rational* in that they seek the best possible return from their capital for a given level of risk. However, such rational behaviour is dependent on investors having information from which to make decisions and on their being able to make those decisions efficiently. Neither of these conditions is ever met fully. There is always an *informational asymmetry* between entrepreneur and investor. Clearly, the entrepreneur knows more about his or her venture than does the investor. That is why the investor employs the entrepreneur to run the business! Even if investors have all the information necessary to make an investment decision, they are still human beings who suffer the same cognitive limitations that all human beings face. Though they may be practised in making investment decisions, those decisions are not necessarily optimal in a precise economic sense. Rather, investors, like all human decision makers, exhibit *satisficing* behaviour; that is they make the best decision given the information available, their abilities and the influence of cultural factors. Studies of business angels, for example, have revealed that they rarely use formal methods to determine the return on the investments they make mathematically, rather they seek investments that 'feel right'.

Before an investor will make an investment they will need some information about the venture. Thus the entrepreneur will need to answer a series of questions about it.

Is the venture of the right type?

Many, if not most, investors specialise in certain types of business. Private investors and business angels may confine themselves to industry sectors in which they have knowledge and experience. Some venture capitalists focus on investment opportunities in certain technological areas; for example: biotechnology or information technology. Another important dimension of specialisation is the *stage of development* of the business and the nature of the financing it requires. Of late, venture capitalists have shifted their attention away from new start-ups and have moved to investing in lower-risk management buy-outs (MBOs). Banks will support new start-ups through their retail arms, but will deal with expansion financing through their corporate operations.

The investor will need to be assured that the venture is in the right area and at the right stage for them.

How much investment is required?

Investors will be interested in the amount of financing required. This will be judged in relation to the business the investor is in, their expertise and the costs they face in monitoring and controlling their investments. Retail banks will offer loans from a few hundred to tens of thousands of pounds. Venture capitalists on the other hand, are not interested in investments of less than about £250 000, and are only really interested in investments of several million pounds sterling. A market flotation is usually concerned with raising at least five million pounds.

The key question is, is the investor really the right source given the level of investment needed?

What return is likely?

The return on investment is the likely financial outcome of making a specific investment. The investor will want to know on what basis this has been calculated. Further, they will ask how reasonable it is given the potential for the venture and its management team. The decision to invest will be based on an assessment of the returns in relation to the risks and how the investment opportunity compares to others available. However, it should be noted that even for quite large investments, this comparison may be made on an intuitive rather than an explicit basis. Certain investors specialise in different levels of risk. Venture capitalists seek more risk than retail banks. Specialist high growth bourses usually reflect higher risk investments than mainstream bourses.

What is the growth stage of the venture?

Critically, this question relates to what the investment capital is required for. Is it to start a new business or is it to fund the expansion of an established business? Is the venture at an early stage in its growth requiring capital to fund an aggressive growth strategy or is the business at a mature stage with the capital to be used to fund incremental growth? How does this impact on the risk entailed and return offered? Is this stage of growth right for the investor?

What projects will the capital be used for?

This question relates to how the capital will be used within the venture. Is it to cover cash-flow short falls which result from strong growth or is it to be used for a more specific project, such as development of new products, funding a sales drive or marketing campaign or entering export markets? Again, the question is how does this impact on risk, return and specialism from the point of view of the investor?

What is the potential for the venture?

The investors will want to know what the venture can be expected to achieve in the future. This will depend on two sets of factors. First, on its *market potential*: that is how innovative its offering is, how much value this offers the customer in relation to what is already available and the possibilities and limitations the venture faces in delivering this innovation to the customer. Second it depends on the quality of the entrepreneur and the management team: that is the skills and experience of the venture's key people and their ability to deliver the potential that the venture has. The critical question is will the investor find the venture's potential attractive and if not, why not?

What are the risks for the venture?

To an investor, the risk of the venture is the probability that it will not deliver the return anticipated. Critical to judging this is an understanding of the assumptions that have been made in estimating the likely return. Some critical areas are assumptions about customer demand, the ability of the business to manage its costs, the ability of the venture to get distributors and other key partners on board, and the reaction of competitors.

The investors' judgement of risk will also depend on their ability to exit the investment by liquidating their holding. An investor will ask exactly how liquid the business is and whether or not the investment can be secured against particular liquidisable assets. How do the risks match up with what the investor will expect?

How does the investor get in?

The investor will wish to know exactly how their investment is to be made. Is it to be a lump sum up front or will it take the form of a regular series of cash injections? The entrepreneur must ask whether this is the way the investor normally operates.

How does the investor get out?

The investor will want to know how they will see their return. Will it take the form of cash? If so, will it be a single cash payment at some point in the future, or will it be a series of payments over time? Alternatively, will it take the form of a holding of stock in the firm? If so, how can such a holding be liquidated? Loans are usually paid back in cash form whereas an equity holding will mature as a holding in the firm. Venture capitalists with equity holdings will insist on a clear exit strategy which will enable them to convert their equity to cash, either by selling on a bourse or converting it with the venture.

What post-investment monitoring procedures will be in place?

An investor will want to know the means by which they will be able to keep track of their investment. A business plan will normally be required before an injection of capital is made. The business plan is an excellent way of communicating and of managing the investors' expectations. Regular financial reports will provide key information on the performance of the business and its liquidity (and hence its exposure to risk). The entrepreneur must consider whether the monitoring procedures on offer will be greeted as adequate by the investor?

What control mechanisms will be available?

Monitoring is of little use unless the investor can use the information gained to influence the behaviour of the venture's management. Investors who hold shares can signal their approval or otherwise by buying and selling their stock on the bourse. This buying and selling changes the value of the company. The ultimate sanction is for the value of the business to fall to a level where a takeover can happen and a new set of managers be brought in.

Large investors will usually take a more direct route to control. This may be by lobbying the venture's management or by having a representative permanently on the firm's board. The question that must be asked is how the control mechanisms on offer will influence the investor's decision.

Communication skills

Entrepreneurs and investors meet through a process of communication. Communication is a human process involving not only the passage of information but also an attempt to influence behaviour. Entrepreneurs communicate with investors not just because they wish to tell them about their ventures, but also because they want the investors to support them.

The process of communication between an entrepreneur and an investor is not just a matter of the *what* of the answers but also the *how*. The entrepreneur can exert a positive influence on investors by understanding the questions they are asking, by ensuring that the answers to those questions have been explored, and where appropriate, by having hard evidence to back up the answers given.

Venture capitalists reject the vast majority (over 95 per cent) of proposals made to them. Though banks may back a higher proportion of proposals, rejections still greatly outnumber acceptances. Even if the business idea is sound, an investment of time and energy in making sure that proposals and other communications to backers are sympathetic to their information needs, and are well constructed as pieces of communication, will help the investor make their decision and will reflect positively on the professionalism of the entrepreneur. This will ensure that the venture is in the forefront of the race to obtain capital.

Summary of key ideas

- Financial support is a critical factor in the success of the new venture.

- Suppliers of investment capital are differentiated by the *amount* of capital they will supply, the *risks* they will undertake and the way in which they will expect to see their investment *mature*.

- Investors select investment opportunities by *filtering* them for suitability. This filtering process has formal analysis and informal 'intuitive' aspects.

- The vast majority of investment proposals are rejected.

- Effective entrepreneurs approach investors with an understanding of the *questions* for which they will need answers before they decide to support the venture.

Suggestions for further reading

Camp, S.M. and **Sexton, D.L.** (1992) "Trends in venture capital investment: Implications for high-technology firms", *Journal of Small Business Management*, July, pp. 11–19.

Haar, N.E., Starr, J. and **Macmillan, I.C.** (1988) "Informal risk capital investors: Investment patterns on the east coast of the USA", *Journal of Business Venturing*, Vol. 3, pp. 11–29.

Hall, J. and **Hofer, C.W.** (1993) "Venture capitalists' decision criteria in new venture evaluation" *Journal of Business Venturing*, Vol. 8, pp. 25–42.

Landström, H. (1993) "Informal risk capital in Sweden and some international comparisons", *Journal of Business Venturing*, Vol. 8, pp. 525–40.

Knight, R.M. (1994) "Criteria used by venture capitalists: A cross cultural analysis", *International Small Business Journal*, Vol. 13, No. 1, pp. 26–37.

Macmillan, I.C., Siegel, R. and **Subba Narashima, P.N.** (1985) "Criteria used by venture capitalists to evaluate new venture proposals", *Journal of Business Venturing*, Vol. 1, pp. 119–28.

Macmillan, I.C., Zeeman, L. and **Subba Narashima, P.N.** (1987) "Effectiveness of criteria used by venture capitalists in the venture screening process", *Journal of Business Venturing*, Vol. 2, pp. 123–38.

Maier, II, J.B. and **Walker, D.A.** (1987) "The role of venture capital in financing small business", *Journal of Business Venturing*, Vol. 2, pp. 207–14.

Mason, C. and **Harrison, R.** (1996) "Why 'business angels' say no: A case study of opportunities rejected by an informal investor syndicate", *International Small Business Journal*, Vol. 14, No. 2, pp. 35–51.

Murray, G.C. (1992) "A challenging marketplace for venture capital", *Long Range Planning*, Vol. 25, No. 6, pp. 79–86.

Norton, E. and **Tenenbaum, B.H.** (1992) "Factors affecting the structure of US venture capital deals", *Journal of Small Business Management*, July, pp. 20–9.

Ray, D.M. and **Turpin, D.V.** (1993) "Venture capital in Japan", *International Small Business Journal*, Vol. 11, No. 4, pp. 39–56.

Rea, R.H. (1989) "Factors affecting success and failure of seed capital/start-up negotiations", *Journal of Business Venturing*, Vol. 4, pp. 149–58.

Roberts, E.B. (1991) "High stakes for high-tech entrepreneurs: Understanding venture capital decision making", *Sloan Management Review*, Winter, pp. 9–20

Rock, A. (1987) "Strategy *v* tactics from a venture capitalist", *Harvard Business Review*, Nov-Dec, pp. 63–7.

Sweeting, R.C. (1991) "UK venture capital funds and the funding of new technology-based businesses: Process and relationships", *Journal of Management Studies*, Vol. 28, No. 6, pp. 601–22.

Tyebjee, T.T. and **Bruno, A.V.** (1984) "A model of venture capital investment activity", *Management Science*, Vol. 30, No. 9, pp 1051–66.

Part 4 Managing the growth and development of the venture

20 The dimensions of business growth

CHAPTER OVERVIEW

*The potential for growth is a defining feature of the entrepreneurial venture. This chapter is concerned with an exploration of the process of business growth. A multi-faceted approach is developed and the growth of the entrepreneurial venture is considered from **financial**, **strategic**, **structural** and **organisational** perspectives. The chapter concludes by considering how the growth of the venture creates opportunities for, and impacts on, the lives of its stakeholders.*

20.1 The process of growth

KEY LEARNING OUTCOME
An appreciation of the general dynamics of business growth.

Business growth is critical to entrepreneurial success. The potential for growth is one of the factors which distinguishes the entrepreneurial venture from the small business. Organisational growth, however, means more than just an increase in size. Growth is a dynamic process. It involves development and change within the organisation, and changes in the way in which the organisation interacts with its environment. Though an organisation grows as a coherent whole, organisational growth itself is best understood in a multi-faceted way. It has as many aspects as there are aspects of organisation itself. The case for a multi-perspective approach to understanding organisational growth and change was made very effectively by Henry Mintzberg in his book *The Structuring of Organisations* (1979).

Given the multi-faceted nature of organisation the entrepreneur must constantly view the growth and development of their venture from a number of different perspectives. Four perspectives in particular are important: the *financial*, the *strategic*, the *structural* and the *organisational*.

1 *Financial growth* relates to the development of the business as a commercial entity. It is concerned with increases in *turnover*, the *costs* and *investment* needed to achieve that turnover, and the resulting *profits*. It is also concerned with increases in what the business owns: its *assets*. Related to this is the increase in the *value* of the business, that is, what a potential buyer might be willing to pay for it. Because financial growth measures the additional value that the organisation is creating which is available to be distributed to its stakeholders, it is an important measure of the *success* of the venture.

2 *Strategic growth* relates to the changes that take place in the way in which the organisation interacts with its environment as a coherent, *strategic*, whole. Primarily, this is concerned with the way the business develops its capabilities to exploit a presence in the marketplace. It is the profile of opportunities which the venture exploits and the assets it acquires to create *sustainable competitive advantages*.

3 *Structural growth* relates to the changes that take place in the way the business organises its internal systems, in particular, managerial *roles* and *responsibilities*, reporting *relationships*, *communication* links and resource *control systems*.

4 *Organisational growth* relates to the changes that take place in the organisation's *processes*, *culture* and *attitudes* as it grows and develops. It is also concerned with the changes that must take place in the entrepreneur's role and leadership style as the business moves from being a 'small' to a 'large' firm.

The four types of growth described are not independent of each other. They are just different facets of the same underlying process. At the heart of that process is the allocation of resources to the venture by external markets because it has demonstrated that it can make better use of them, that is create more value from them, than can the alternatives on offer. That better use of resources is a consequence of the entrepreneur's decision making.

The *strategic* perspective must take centre stage. It is this which relates the needs of customers to the ability of the business to serve them. *Financial* growth is a measure of

Fig. 20.1 The dynamics of growth for the entrepreneurial venture

the business's performance in serving the needs of its markets, thus it is a measure of the resources the market has allocated to the firm. The firm must convert those resources into assets. These assets are configured by the structure of the organisation. Additional resources means increasing the *assets* the business holds which in turn demands changes to the *structure* in which they are held.

This structure only provides a framework, however (*see* Fig. 20.1). The decisions which the individuals who make up the organisation make and the actions that they take in relation to the assets it owns are governed by wider dimensions of the organisation such as its culture and attitudes. Strategic growth has a *direction* and that direction results from the vision and leadership the entrepreneur offers.

It must also be added that although growth is a *defining* feature of the entrepreneurial venture, this does not mean that an entrepreneurial business has a *right* to grow. It merely means that, if managed in the right way, it has the *potential* to grow. Growth must be made an objective for the venture and it must be managed. For the entrepreneur, growth is a reward for identifying the right opportunities, understanding how they might be exploited and competing effectively to take advantage of them.

20.2 Financial analysis

> **KEY LEARNING OUTCOME**
> **An understanding of the way in which financial growth is recorded, reported and analysed.**

The financial performance of a firm is important to all its stakeholders. A sound financial position brings security for employees, offers customers the prospect of good service and investment in future offerings, and promises suppliers a demand for their outputs. Investors, of course, have an interest in seeing a good return on their capital. They will take particular note of the financial performance of the businesses they have chosen to back.

Investors and businesses communicate in a number of ways. The degree of personal contact will depend on the type of investors, the amount of investment, and the stage of the business's development. The nature of the economic system in which the business is operating is also important. Investment systems in different parts of the world vary in both their formal and informal aspects. One key difference is in the way the investor seeks to influence the management of the business. If the business seeks investment in an open stock market then two main means are available to effect this. If the stock market is 'liquid' (as it tends to be in Britain and America) then investors can signal their assessment of the firm's performance by buying and selling shares. An increasing share price offers the business security for obtaining further investment. A falling share price can make a business susceptible to takeover. Other economies (typically those in continental Europe) tend towards a greater degree of intervention by investors. Institutional shareholders (such as pension funds and banks) may appoint directors to act on their behalf.

If the business has not yet reached the stage where it is ready to offer investment stock to the stock market and is reliant on private and institutional investment such as banks and venture capital instead, then a high degree of both investor scrutiny and involvement is likely.

Whatever the nature and means of the interaction between business and investor, financial reporting provides a common language by which they can communicate with each other. At the centre of this communication are two documents: the *balance sheet* and the *profit and loss account* (*see* Fig. 20.2). The balance sheet is a summary of *what the business owns*, that is its *assets* and *liabilities*. It represents the state of the business at *a point in time*, specifically the date of the report. The profit and loss account is a report on *what the business has done* over the previous period, that is its trading activity in terms of *sales* (or *turnover*), the *expenditure* involved in achieving those sales and the resulting *profits*. The reporting period is normally one year but can be a shorter interval if investors see the need for more detailed tracking.

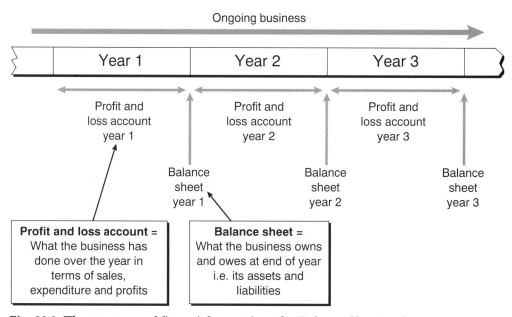

Fig. 20.2 The structure of financial reporting: the Balance Sheet and Profit and Loss Account

The balance sheet

The balance sheet is so called because it is usual to show the assets and liabilities of the firm as being equal (i.e. balancing). The details presented on the balance sheet vary between different countries, however, some of the key lines are as indicated in Table 20.1.

Table 20.1 The Balance Sheet

Assets	Liabilities
Tangible assets The value of all buildings and machinery etc. owned by the firm.	*Short-term creditors.* All creditors (people and organisations to whom the firm owes money) due for payment within one year.
+	+
Intangible assets The valuation of the things 'owned' by the firm, which have no physical form but can, potentially, be bought and sold, e.g. brand names and goodwill.	*Long-term creditors* All creditors due for payment after one year. Important elements include: ● loan repayment due after one year; ● dividends planned for investors (including the entrepreneur's remuneration); ● long-term repayments agreed with suppliers; and ● taxes owed to the government.
+	+
Current assets Cash in hand, stock (including finished goods, work in progress and raw materials), creditor and trade debts owed to the firm.	*Called-up share capital* The permanent capital of the firm in the form of the face value of issued shares.
+	+
Investments Investments held by the firm in other businesses, government stock and other financial instruments.	*Capital reserves* The profits held by the firm. Properly, these are the property of the investors in the firm. Some may be distributed to investors in the form of dividends; others may be retained for future investment.
=	=
Total assets	**Total liabilities**

A number of important relationships can be derived from the balance sheet. Some of the more important are:

1 The fundamental balance sheet identity

Total assets = Total liabilities

2 Net assets are the assets the business will actually have available over the coming year. Net assets represent the sum of assets and working capital. They can also be defined as:

Net assets = Total assets − Liabilities to outsiders

Because of the balance sheet identity, net assets must be equal to the total of shareholders' funds.

3 Net current assets (also known as *working capital*) are those resources which are *liquid*, that is they either already exist in the form of cash, or are expected to be turned into cash within twelve months of the report date. The definition is:

Net current assets = Current assets – Short-term liabilities

4 Capital employed is a measure of the total resources available for use by the firm's management. It is defined as:

Capital employed = (Long-term creditors + Called-up share capital + Capital reserves)

The profit and loss account

The profit and loss account provides a summary of the revenues obtained as a result of trading activity over the period in question. The key lines are shown in Table 20.2.

Table 20.2 The Profit and Loss Account

Income

Turnover from normal trading activities
The income generated as a result of the firm's normal business activities.

Extraordinary income
Additional income which is a result of activities which are not part of the firm's usual profile of business.

Income from investments
Income received as a result of investments owned by the firm in other businesses or other investment instruments.

Outgoing

Cost of sales
The expenditure that was necessary to deliver the sales that were achieved. Important cost elements are:

– raw materials and factors;
– salaries;
– purchase (or rental) of machinery and equipment;
– depreciation charges on machinery and equipment; and
– sales and marketing expenditure.

Interest on debt
Payments to cover interest charges on outstanding debts.

Extraordinary expenditure
Expenditure that has been made but which is not typical of the expenditure the business normally faces. It is a result of special circumstances or a one-off activity. Critically, it is expenditure the business does not expect to face again.

Taxation
Money owed to the government as a result of taxation.

Dividends
Money to be paid to investors as a return on their investment. (This may include some of the entrepreneur's remuneration insofar as the entrepreneur is an investor.)

Profits for a period represent the difference between income and outgoings. A number of different measures of profit level are important:

1 Gross profits

The basic profits generated by the business. This is sometimes referred to as profit before interest payable and tax (PBIT).

Gross profits = Sales – Cost of sales

2 Profit before tax

Profits left after interest on debts has been paid.

Profit before tax (PBT) = Gross profits – Interest

3 Profit after tax

Profits left after any tax owing to the government has been paid.

Profit after tax (PAT) = PBT – Tax

4 Retained profits

Any profit left after tax has been paid is properly the property of the firm's shareholders. Some of it may be distributed to them in the form of dividends. Some may, however, be retained by the firm for future investment. Such profits are called *retained profits*. The retained profit figure on the profit and loss account is equivalent to the *capital reserves* figure on the balance sheet.

Retained profits = PAT – Dividends

Ratio analysis

The performance of the entrepreneurial venture must be measured not only in terms of absolutes – the new value it generates – but also in relative terms, i.e. the new value created given the resources the entrepreneur has to hand. An investor in the venture is interested not so much in 'profits' as in the *returns* the venture will offer for a *given level of investment*.

Ratio analysis can be used to provide a valuable insight into the performance, condition and stability of the venture. As its name suggests, it is based on an evaluation of the ratios between different lines on the Balance Sheet and Profit and Loss Account.

Three types of ratio are important. *Performance ratios* indicate the way the business is performing, that is, the value it is creating from the resources to hand. *Financial status* ratios provide an indication of the financial security of the venture and how exposed a backer's investment is. If the venture has a stock market listing, then *stock market ratios* can be used to compare the performance of an investment in the venture with alternative investment opportunities. Some of these ratios will now be explored in more detail.

Performance ratios

Profit margin

The profit margin of a business is the ratio (expressed as a percentage) of profits to turnover. It is defined as:

$$\text{Profit margin} = \frac{(\text{Profits} \times 100\%)}{\text{Turnover}}$$

The usual profit level for this ratio is profit before tax, but other profit measure levels may also be used.

Return on investment

Return on investment (ROI) is *the* fundamental measure of a venture's performance. Two different ROIs are used. Return on equity (ROE) is the ratio of profit after interest payments have been made but before tax (and normally before extraordinary items too) to shareholders' funds:

$$\text{Return on equity} = \frac{(\text{Profit before tax} \times 100\%)}{(\text{Called up share capital} + \text{Capital reserves})}$$

Return on net assets (RONA) is the ratio of gross profit to net assets:

$$\text{Return on net assets} = \frac{(\text{Gross profit} \times 100\%)}{\text{Net assets}}$$

Although these two measures are related, they offer slightly different perspectives on the performance of the venture. ROE gives *investors* (especially ordinary shareholders) an indication of the profits which are (potentially) available to them in relation to the investment they have made in the venture. RONA gives the *venture's management* an indication of the profits they are generating (which can later be distributed to lenders, investors and taxing authorities) in relation to the assets that they have available to them. In more technical terms, RONA is a performance measure which is *independent* of the capital structure of the firm.

Turnover ratios

In general, turnover ratios are those which look at the number of times some measure of the firm's asset ownership generates some measure of the firm's income. Two are particularly important.

Net asset turnover (NAT) indicates the number of times annual sales are generated by the firm's net assets. It is defined by:

$$\text{Net asset turnover} = \frac{\text{Sales}}{\text{Net assets}}$$

In a similar manner, fixed asset turnover (FAT) indicates the number of times annual sales are generated by fixed assets:

$$\text{Fixed asset turnover} = \frac{\text{Sales}}{\text{Fixed assets}}$$

Financial status ratios

An investor is not only interested in the performance of the firm they have invested in but also in the *risk* that that investment entails. A key element of risk for the entrepreneurial venture is its ability to meet the liabilities it accepts given the revenues it generates. *Financial status ratios* can be used to gain an insight into the business's position with regard to its liabilities. Two sorts of financial status ratio are useful. *Solvency ratios* give an indication of the firm's general financial health and its ability to meet its long-term liabilities. *Liquidity ratios* give an indication of the firm's ability to meet its short-term liabilities where it is called upon to do so in a crisis.

Solvency ratios

The debt ratio represents the capital structure of the firm. It is the ratio of debt (that is money which has been borrowed at a fixed rate of interest) to equity (that is money obtained from investors whose return will depend on the overall performance of the venture). It is defined as:

$$\text{Debt ratio} = \frac{(\textbf{Long-term debt} \times \textbf{100\%})}{\textbf{Capital employed}}$$

where **Capital employed = (Long-term debt + called-up share capital + retained profits)**

A related ratio is titled *gearing*.

$$\text{Gearing} = \frac{(\textbf{Long-term debt} \times \textbf{100\%})}{\textbf{Shareholders' funds}}$$

where **Shareholders' funds = (Called-up share capital + Retained profits)**

Clearly, the debt ratio and gearing provide equivalent information. The debt ratio is more frequently used in the UK whereas gearing tends to be quoted in the US.

Interest cover is a ratio of profits to interest owed to those who lend money to the venture. It gives an indication of a firm's ability to pay interest on its debts. It is given by:

$$\text{Interest cover} = \frac{\textbf{Profit before interest and tax (PBIT)}}{\textbf{Interest on long-term debt}}$$

Liquidity ratios

Liquidity ratios are concerned with *short-term* liabilities. Two ratios are particularly important. The *current ratio* is the ratio of current assets to current liabilities.

$$\text{Current ratio} = \frac{\textbf{Current assets}}{\textbf{Current liabilities}}$$

where **Current liabilities are those short-term creditors who expect payment within one year.**

The *acid test* (or *quick ratio*) is a straight measure of a firm's ability to pay its short-term creditors immediately from its liquid assets. It is defined as:

$$\text{Acid test ratio} = \frac{\text{Liquid assets}}{\text{Current liabilities}}$$

Liquid assets are cash and short-term debtors (and therefore equal to current assets minus stock). An acid test of 1.0 or more indicates that the business is 'safe'. It would, if demanded, be able to pay off its short-term liabilities from the liquid assets it has in hand.

Stock market ratios

If the venture has issued shares and is floated on a stock market, then a number of ratios can be used to evaluate the performance of the business and investments in it. To calculate these ratios, the information given in financial reports must be supplemented with routine reports on share price performance.

Earnings per share

Earnings per share (EPS) are the profits potentially available for each share that has been issued. Profits are measured after interest and taxation but normally before extraordinary items have been paid.

$$\text{Earnings per share} = \frac{\text{Profit after tax}}{\text{Number of shares issued}}$$

Note that if more than one type of share has been issued then the ratio usually refers to ordinary shares.

Price/earnings ratio

The price/earnings ratio (PE ratio) is the ratio of the price at which a share in the business is trading on the stock market to the earnings per share.

$$\text{Price/earnings ratio} = \frac{\text{Market price of share}}{\text{Earnings per share (EPS)}}$$

$$= \frac{\text{Market price of share} \times \text{Number of shares}}{\text{Profit after tax}}$$

The market price per share multiplied by the number of shares represents the market's valuation of the firm as a whole. It is sometimes referred to as the firm's *market capitalisation*.

The PE ratio is an indication of the market's confidence in the business, both in terms of the risk it represents and of its future growth potential. A relatively high price relative to earnings indicates that the market regards the investment as being of relatively low risk or that the value of the investment will increase in the future.

Dividend yield

The dividend yield represents the payment made to investors on each share as a proportion of the market value of the share.

$$\text{Dividend yield} = \frac{\text{Dividend per share}}{\text{Market price of share}}$$

The dividend yield will be dependent both on the total profits generated by the business and on the way in which management offer them back to investors or, alternatively, retain them for future investment. A young, high growth business may have a relatively low dividend yield. However, investors will still value their investment and hang on to it if they feel the venture has the potential to offer high rewards in the future.

Dividend cover

Dividend cover is another measure which indicates the division of available profits by management between passing them to shareholders and retaining them within the business for future investment. Dividend cover represents the number of times the management could, potentially, have paid the actual dividend offered out of the profits that were available to shareholders. It is defined by:

$$\text{Dividend cover} = \frac{\text{Earnings per share}}{\text{Dividend per share}}$$

Clearly, stock market ratios are dependent on share price which is adjusted constantly as new information (both on the business specifically and on the economy in general) reaches the market. The annual financial report is an important factor in providing this information but it is far from its entirety. A share price is just an estimation by an investor of the value of their investment. This valuation responds to the way in which the entrepreneur (and other managers) communicate with, and the message that is sent to, investors.

20.3   Financial growth

> **KEY LEARNING OUTCOME**
> An understanding of how financial analysis provides a context for understanding the financial growth and development of the venture.

The report of the financial situation, that is, the balance sheet and the profit and loss account and the ratios that can be derived from these items provide those interested in the venture (the entrepreneur, other managers, investors and taxing authorities) with a wealth of information which provides a basis on which decisions may be made. However, decisions must be made within a broader context which needs to consider both the firm's performance *relative to its particular business sector* and the overall *trends* in the firm's performance.

There are no absolute measures of performance. The profit margin, return on investment (or any other performance measure) to be expected from a venture will depend on the sector in which the business operates. What matters is not so much the performance of the venture but its performance *relative* to key competitors and to market norms. Similarly, the expected financial status ratios will vary between different industry sectors. The factor which determines how investment capital is distributed between sectors offering different levels of return is, of course, *risk*. The way in which risk is anticipated by investors can be gleaned from a close examination of the stock market ratios of players within a particular sector.

An entrepreneurial venture is not static. It is undergoing constant growth and development. Investors and other decision makers will colour their decisions not just by reference to the indicators for the business at a single point in time but by evaluating the *trends* in its performance. This will be particularly important for investors who are not expecting immediate returns from the venture but who are willing to accept some risk for the promise of higher returns in the future. Investors' decision making (particularly the key decision of whether to hold or exit from their investment) will be influenced by four main factors.

The underlying performance (return on investment) of the venture

Investors will be interested in the performance of the venture not just in absolute terms but relative to their *expectations* of that performance. Their expectations will be a result of their knowledge of the business and the sector it operates in, and of the promises offered by the entrepreneur driving the venture.

The growth in the value of the venture

The *growth* of the venture can be qualified by a number of financial criteria. Growth in *income* (and by implication, *outgoings*), *assets* and *capital* are equally important. Some of the key indicators to follow include changes in turnover; changes in cash profits; changes in tangible assets; changes in total assets; and changes in shareholders' capital. Growth in these measures can be followed both in absolute terms and as a proportion of absolute values. Proportional changes can be indicated as an index or as a percentage. A *growth index* is calculated as:

$$\text{Growth index} = \frac{\text{Value of measure in year}}{\text{Value of measure in year previous year}}$$

Growth as a *percentage* is given by:

$$\text{Growth \%} = \frac{(\text{Value of measure in year} - \text{Value in previous year})}{\text{Value of measure in previous year}} \times 100\%$$

When making a comparison it is often useful to *discount* for general inflation in an economy. This enables the *real* growth of the venture to be measured. To discount for inflation the *nominal* growth calculated for the venture must be divided by the inflation index for the period under consideration.

$$\text{Real growth} = \frac{\text{Nominal growth}}{\text{Inflation index}}$$

Usually, the general retail price index is used but other more specialist inflation measures may be adopted. If inflation is quoted as a percentage it can be converted by the following formula:

$$\text{Inflation index} = \frac{[(\text{Inflation as } \%) + 100]}{100}$$

Growth by the venture is usually received positively. Expansion of the venture drives an increase in the underlying value of a shareholder's investment. Growth also indicates that the venture has a successful formula and so, *in general*, it signals a reduction in risk. Growth does not, however, come for free. It must be *paid for* and a high level of growth may make cash-flow tighter and so lead to less favourable financial status ratios. This may make the venture slightly more risky in the short-term, particularly if there is a crisis and short-term liabilities have to be met.

The trend in the risk of the venture

While growth tends to reduce risk overall, the specific level of risk faced by the business is, to a degree, under the control of the entrepreneur and other managers. An important factor is the debt ratio (gearing) of the venture. Debt, on the whole, is cheaper than equity finance. However, debt must be repaid whatever the performance of the business. Debt repayment must take priority over the repayment of equity or dividends. Therefore a high debt ratio does expose the business (and that means its investors) to more risk.

No generalisation can be made about the optimum level of debt to equity. This is a complex issue and not only are interest rates and industry risk relevant, but taxation effects also have an influence. Comparison to industry norms can provide a rough and ready guide.

Financial status and (if the firm has floated shares) stock market ratios provide an insight into the overall risk status of the venture. In general, as the business grows, matures and stabilises investors will expect risk to be reduced. Having faced risk initially they become ready to enjoy the return they are owed.

The dividends yielded by the venture

At the end of the day, investors will wish to see a capital gain through their investment. This may take the form of them receiving dividend payments on the shares they hold or by selling those shares. These two approaches to liquidating investment differ in timing rather than substance. The buyer of the share does so in the expectation of a future flow of dividends. An independent market values the investment on the basis of the cash-flow it can generate.

Managers in the venture will make a decision about how much of the profits generated is to be passed on to the shareholders and how much is to be retained within the business for future investment. Shareholders will either agree to this split or will not. They will show their approval (or otherwise) either by direct interference in the firm or, if their investment is liquid, by buying or selling their shares thus raising or depressing the share price. In general, while investors may be willing to see managers recycle profits back into a young, fast-growing venture they will at some point expect to see a real cash reward for their investment. As the firm matures, it is likely that investors will expect a greater proportion of profits to be given back to them.

A general scheme for analysing the financial growth of an entrepreneurial venture is indicated in Fig. 20.3.

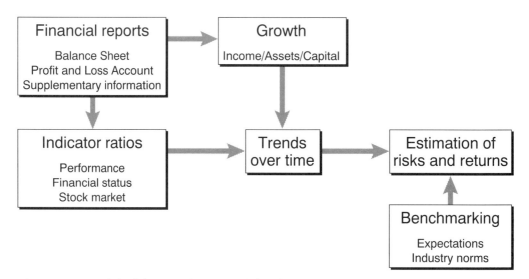

Fig. 20.3 A model of financial appraisal for the entrepreneurial venture

20.4 Strategic growth

KEY LEARNING OUTCOME
An understanding of the ways in which competitive advantage can be developed as the venture grows.

The strategic approach to organisational management regards the organisation as a single *coherent* entity which must be managed in its entirety. It locates the organisation conceptually in an *environment* from which it must draw resources and *add value* to them. The organisation must then distribute the new value created to its stakeholders. The strategic approach also recognises that the organisation is in *competition* with other organisations who also seek to attract and utilise those resources.

From a strategic perspective, the organisation is able to compete for resources by virtue of the *competitive advantages* it develops and maintains. Growth represents the business's success in drawing in resources from its environment. It is a sign that the business has been effective in competing in the marketplace. This suggests that the business has built up a competitive advantage and has managed to sustain it in the face of competitive pressure. However, a competitive advantage is not static. Sustaining an advantage simultaneously develops and enhances it.

All advantages are very sensitive to business growth. In general, expansion of the business can be used to enhance a competitive advantage. This will only occur, however, if the entrepreneur is sensitive to the nature of the competitive advantages that their venture enjoys and strives to actively manage that advantage as the business grows and develops.

Growth and cost advantages

The main source of cost advantages are experience effects. Practice in delivering the outputs leads to a reduction in cost (strictly, the cost of adding a particular amount of value). Costs tend to fall in an exponential way as output increases linearly. Hence, experience cost advantages are (usually) held by the business which has achieved the greatest cumulative output. This can lead to a 'virtuous circle' (*see* Fig. 20.4). Cost leadership means that the customer can be offered a lower price. This increases demand for the firm's outputs relative to those of competitors. This leads to the firm developing a volume output lead over competitors. In turn, this volume advantage leads to enhanced cost leadership and the ability to offer customers and even lower price, *etc.*

Clearly, the entrepreneur can build in cost advantages as the business grows. Such a strategy offers the potential for a consistent and sustainable advantage in the marketplace. It is, however, a strategy which requires certain conditions to be met and it is not without risk. If the strategy is to work the entrepreneur must be sure of a number of features of the market they are developing.

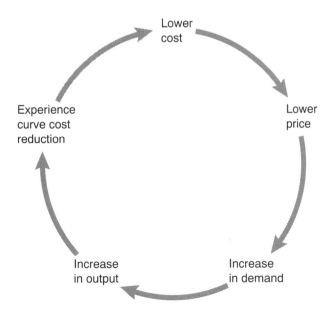

Fig. 20.4 The virtuous circle of cost leadership

Cost advantages have not already been established in the market

If cost advantages have already been established in the market, then the business will risk being a follower rather than a leader. If the venture's costs are not *genuinely* lower than those of the leading competitor then undercutting the leader to subsidise costs and offer the customer a lower price will demand a high level of investment. In some instances such 'undercutting' will be construed as anti-competitive by regulatory bodies. It is, in any case, always expensive.

In order to become a cost leader it is better if the entrepreneur is first into a market. In effect, what this means is that the innovation on which the venture is based is sufficiently different to constitute a 'new' market

Potential volume outputs make entry into the market worthwhile

Experience curve cost reductions only become meaningful when the output volumes are quite high. Consequently a cost leadership strategy is not a realistic option for a small or even a medium-sized business serving a local market. Cost leadership really becomes a serious option for the business which is an industry maker and which aims to deliver its outputs to a wide (which increasingly today means *global*) market. This is not to say that price is not an important factor for smaller businesses or that they should not manage costs, rather that cost as the *mainstay* of competitive advantage is really the prerogative of the large player.

A corollary of this fact is that the entire market must be ready to accept a fairly homogeneous product. If too much specialisation is required at a local level then the extent to which production is repetitive will be lost and hence the possibility of cost reducing experience will also be lost.

Sales of the product they are offering to the market are sensitive to price

Experience cost advantages are gained via volume output. The virtuous circle will only be followed if customers respond to lower prices by buying more of the price leader's offerings. This demands that the products offered are *price sensitive* which means that the firm's products must be *substitutable* with those of competitors. Substitutability implies that the products of different suppliers are pretty much equivalent (from the buyer's perspective) and can replace one another in use. To be substitutable, products must not only be similar in a technical sense but they must not have any switching costs associated with them; that is there should be no additional expense for the customer when moving from one supplier to another.

If switching costs are present *and* the entrepreneur is the first to get customers on board then they may use these costs as the basis of a competitive advantage. Again, this emphasises the importance of innovation in entrepreneurial success.

The experience curve will be steep enough (but not too steep!)

An experience curve has a *gradient*. This is the rate at which increasing output reduces costs, that is the speed at which learning takes place. The experience curve needs to be steep enough for the volume advantages that the pioneering entrepreneur can gain to lead to cost advantages which have a meaningful impact on prices in the marketplace.

If, however, the curve is *too* steep then followers will find it easier to catch up, and any advantage gained initially will be quickly eroded.

Distribution can be maintained.

A price advantage offered to the customer is only useful if the customer can get hold of the product. This implies that distribution can be readily achieved. If independent agencies are involved in the distribution process (e.g. wholesalers or retailers) then there is always the danger that a follower will, in some way or other, interfere with the cost-leader's ability to distribute. In effect, they will look towards distributors as the basis for developing a non-cost competitive advantage. If such a distributor 'lock out' occurs, then the leader will lose volume and any cost advantage can be rapidly lost. Often, such actions are restricted by anti-trust legislation. However, such legislation is difficult to enforce. If the business is multinational, then distributors may be tempted to favour local suppliers. Governments who have seen a 'strategic' advantage in supporting local producers have been known to resist pressure to open their markets by accusing global cost-leaders of 'dumping' (i.e. of selling below cost to establish their presence in a market). Even if such accusations are eventually disproved, volume sales may have been lost already. With a cost leadership strategy, time equals volume which means costs which equals money.

Technological innovation will not reset the experience curve

Experience is gained by repetitive utilisation of a particular operational technology to manufacture or deliver a service. If the technological basis of an industry changes then descent down a new experience curve begins. In cost terms, all bets are off! Innovation, both in the type of product offered to the customer and the means for its delivery, offers both an opportunity and a threat. It may be the means by which the entrepreneur first enters the market and gains an advantage over existing players, but, once they are established, and competitive advantage has been built on a particular technology, they are vulnerable to a new generation of innovators. This means that the entrepreneurial business, even if it is following a cost leadership strategy must still look towards maintaining innovation.

The entrepreneur (and financial backers) have patience!

Cost leadership is not a short-term strategy. The pay-offs are far from immediate. While competing on a price leadership basis, profit margins must be kept slim i.e. just sufficient to cover overhead costs. This is the only way in which the business can be sure that it is reflecting its cost advantage with the most competitive market price. However, it will be tempting to raise prices and to increase short-term profit margins. The entrepreneur may be looking for additional returns to invest in the growth of the business. Investors may be eager to see a positive return on their investment. The business may see a price increase as a viable option. It will be in a market leading position (certainly in volume terms). It may have established a strong relationship with customers. Competitors may have found it hard to gain a foothold in the market. However, the temptation to increase prices must still be resisted!

All these advantages are a *consequence* of keeping prices low. They are the basis on which the business can gain a future reward for maintaining tight profit margins. If the business increases its prices too early then it can create a 'cost umbrella' under which less efficient competitors may shelter. It may be just the gap a competitor needs in order to gain a toe-hold in the market. If a cost leadership strategy is to be effective then the business pursuing it must keep its nerve and keep prices as low as possible for as long as possible. Optimally, prices should be kept to a minimum until market growth has stopped. After this the market will start to lose its attractiveness to new entrants as gaining market share will tend to require the conversion of existing customers rather than drawing new ones into the market. At this point the cost leading business can start to raise prices above costs, to increase profit margins and to harvest its investment.

Figure 20.5 shows how technological innovation and the creation of cost umbrellas both present risks for a cost leadership strategy.

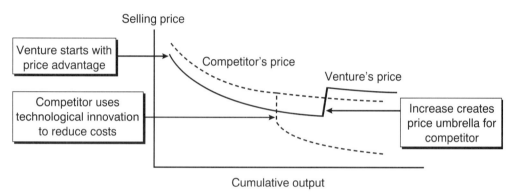

Fig. 20.5 Risks in a cost leadership strategy

Costs are actively managed

Even though costs often follow a mathematical relationship to output volume this does not mean that increasing output *automatically* drives down costs. Increasing output gives the firm's managers the *opportunity* to drive down costs but that is an opportunity they must grasp actively. The management of cost must become the focus of managerial activity. In fact, it must become the key criteria around which decisions are made.

Cost leadership is a strategy which has an impact on, and must be supported by, all of the firm's stakeholders. As noted above, customers must be responsive to price and investors must be willing to play a long game. In addition, suppliers must recognise that they must be competitive in the price at which they offer inputs to the business. Further, employees will become aware (and if not managed properly, *acutely* aware) of the fact that they themselves are 'costs' as well as partners in the creation of the business. There is a danger that this will lead them to see their interests as being counter to that of the business. A focus on managing costs must be single-minded. It must also be implemented with sensitivity.

Growth and knowledge advantages

Knowledge advantages arise from knowing something about the customer, the market or the product offered that competitors do not know, which enables the business to offer something of value to the customer. The development of a knowledge-based advantage is dependent on two factors: the *significance* of the knowledge advantage and the rate at which it will be *eroded*.

How significant is the knowledge advantage?

How *valuable* is what is known? Is the knowledge sufficient in scope and does it have significance to enough customers in order to sustain the growth of the business? If so, what level of growth can it sustain?

How will the knowledge advantage be eroded?

How long will it take competitors to *gain* the knowledge and use it themselves? Can they discover it for themselves or through others? Will the venture's activities *signal* it to them?

Clearly, these two factors work against each other. The more valuable the knowledge, the more that competitors will be encouraged to get hold of it for themselves. Knowledge is difficult to protect. A particular piece of knowledge rarely offers more than a transient advantage. If the business aims not just to survive, but to *grow*, on the back of knowledge advantages, then it must be active in a process of constant discovery about what it is offering the market and why the market buys it.

To do this the business needs to position itself in a market where discovery and innovation are well received and rewarded. This is certainly the case in 'high-tech' markets where technological innovation is the norm. However, the market does not have to be high-tech. More generally, knowledge-based advantages can be gained in any market where customer expectations are in flux and they are likely to respond well to new offerings.

In order to respond to this the entrepreneurial business must ensure that two activities are given priority. First, it requires that resources are put into understanding the market and its customers. In a functional sense this means *market research*. More broadly, it means that the whole organisation must be attuned to new ideas and new initiatives. It particularly demands that the organisation be responsive to the signals sent out by customers about their needs and desires. Second, it requires that the organisation be active in creating, developing and offering new products and services to the customer. Product development activity must be supported by the processes and systems within the organisation. Indeed it must be *prioritised* by them. These systems must be given centre stage as the growth and development of the organisation is managed.

Growth and relationship advantages

Relationships exist between *people*, not just organisations. During its early stages, the business may be 'fronted' directly by the entrepreneur. He or she will be directly responsible for building productive relationships with the venture's stakeholders. Indeed, tying together and securing the threads of the network into which they have entered may be the entrepreneur's key role. Customers, suppliers, employees and investors will be drawn to the venture as a result of the positive relationship they develop with the entrepreneur. The question becomes how can the entrepreneur maintain relationship advantages as the business grows and develops? Further, how can the entrepreneur use such advantages to *drive* growth in the business?

This challenge is acute. In the first instance, the entrepreneur will be located at the centre of the web of relationships and will be in control of them all. As the organisation grows and develops then the web of relationships becomes much more complex. The entrepreneur can no longer represent the organisation to all the parties who have an interest in it. New individuals must develop the organisation's relationships on a specialist basis. For example, salespeople will make representation to customers. Procurement and purchasing specialists must work with suppliers. At some stage it may even be necessary to have finance specialists to manage the venture's relationship with its investors.

To understand how relationship advantages may be maintained and developed as the business grows, it is necessary to have a deep understanding of the ways in which the relationships the business has with its stakeholders are *different* to those of competitor organisations; why that difference is important in offering *value* to those stakeholders; and why competitors find it hard to *imitate* those relationships. In particular the entrepreneur must ask:

Why are the relationships valuable?

What aspect of the relationship creates value for the stakeholder? Does the relationship provide trust which reduces the need for monitoring costs? Does the relationship offer benefits which satisfy social needs? Does the relationship promise the potential to satisfy self-developmental needs? Are these benefits carried as part of the product (say through *branding*) or are they supplementary to it (say through working in *association* with the business)?

What are the expectations of the relationships?

What matters in a relationship is not actual outcomes but outcomes in relation to *expectations*. If expectations are met (or even better, *exceeded*) then satisfaction will occur. If they are not met then disappointment will result. Human relationships are complex. The expectations they generate are multi-faceted. They may be manifest at economic, social and self-developmental levels. Often these interact with each other and the effective entrepreneur must manage relationships at each level.

What practices sustain the relationships?

Relationships are acted out. The parties to the relationship play *roles*. To a greater or lesser extent, relationships are *scripted*. Selling, for example, involves a series of reasonably well-defined steps: first approach, introduction, product presentation, close, *etc.* Internally, employee motivation may be sustained through appraisal and reward procedures. Not all the practices that sustain relationships are explicit. Some may not even be noticed until the practice is broken! Practices, even quite trivial ones, may almost become ritualised. In this, they are one of the building blocks out of which expectations are created. Changing a routine may have an impact on a relationship at a deep level.

By way of an example, consider an entrepreneur whose business is doing quite well. The venture's backers are very happy. Their expectations have been more than met. The entrepreneur provides the backers with a financial report every three months. After a while, this becomes routine. The backers, acknowledging that the business presents them with no concerns, stop examining the report in any detail. After a while the entrepreneur recognises this and decides that the report is 'a waste of time', so the entrepreneur, without informing the backers, stops sending it.

What are the backers to think? Should they be concerned? They contact the entrepreneur who informs them that they should not worry, that the business is still doing well and that the report was stopped because it was not giving them any new information and so the communication 'was not important'. How are the backers to likely to interpret the attitude of the entrepreneur towards them?

What relationship skills are required to maintain them?

Relationships must be managed and this management, like any other form of management, calls upon knowledge and skills. As discussed fully in Section 3.3, the key skill areas that are important for managing the relationships in and around the entrepreneurial venture include *communication* skills, *selling* skills, *negotiating* skills and *motivational* skills.

What behaviour standards are demanded?

Behaviour standards (which are as much about what should *not* be done as what should be) are a critical dimension of relationships. A society will, in general, define the behavioural standards expected for business practice. This is only a minimum guide. The entrepreneur may always look for competitive advantage in accepting discretionary responsibilities that go *beyond* those normally expected for a business in the sector (*see* Section 8.4).

Growth and structural advantages

Structural advantages arise when the business organises itself in a way which gives it more flexibility and responsiveness in the face of competitive pressures. This is often a key area of advantage for the entrepreneurial business. Lacking the cost and possibly the relationship advantages enjoyed by established businesses the entrepreneurial venture must prosper by being more acute to the market's needs and innovating to satisfy them.

The challenge to the entrepreneurial business is to retain this responsiveness and drive for innovation as the business grows and matures. The key to this is understanding the nature of the structural advantages the business has gained and designing the development of the business's structure and organisation so that these are sustained and encouraged to flourish. This important idea will be developed further in Sections 20.5 and 20.6.

20.5   Structural growth

KEY LEARNING OUTCOME
An understanding of the factors which drive the structure of the organisation as it grows.

Every organisation has a unique *structure*. An understanding of this structure is best approached from a broad perspective. It has both static and dynamic aspects. At one level it is the framework of reporting relationships (who is responsible to whom) that describes the organisation. This is how the organisation is often depicted in hierarchical 'organograms'. This formal structure is however just a skeleton. The organisation gains its flesh from the way in which those reporting relationships are played out in terms of the *communications* that take place, the *roles* that must be performed and the *power structures* that define, support and confine those roles. Some of these are formal and explicit, others are informal and implicit but the entrepreneur must learn to manage all of them.

The structure of the organisation, and the way that structure develops as the organisation grows, is both a response to the circumstances in which the organisation finds itself and a reaction to the opportunities with which it is presented. One well-explored approach to understanding how the particular situation of an organisation

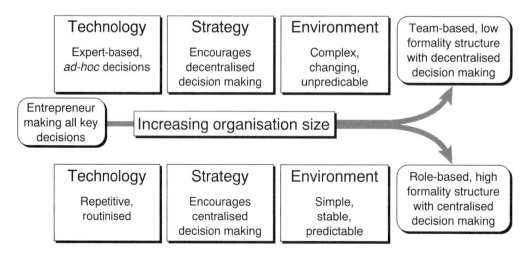

Fig. 20.6 **Factors influencing organisational structure**

defines its structure is provided by *contingency theory*. In essence, contingency theory regards the structure of an organisation as dependent on five 'contingencies', or types of factor. These are: the organisation's *size*, the operational *technology* it uses to create value, the *strategy* it adopts, the *environment* it is in, and the way *power* is utilised within it (*see* Fig. 20.6).

Size

In general, the larger the organisation, the more complex its structure will be. A larger organisation provides more scope for tasks to be differentiated. As more information needs to be passed up to decision makers and more instructions passed back down again, there will be room for more layers of management. Once a certain size is reached, the complexity of the organisation may become so great that it is better to break it up into a series of sub-organisations (functions or departments) each reporting to a common centre.

Operational technology

In broad terms, an organisation's operational technology is simply the way it goes about performing its tasks. Some organisations are involved in repeating a series of relatively straightforward tasks. For example, *McDonald's* restaurants are involved in producing and retailing fast food through a large number of outlets. Others face tasks that are more complex but are still ultimately repetitive. For example, *People Express* must transport air passengers from one place to another. On the other hand, some businesses, particularly 'high-tech' ones, undertake a small number of complex tasks, possibly with very few repetitive elements. An example here might be *Microsoft's* development of software packages.

Contingency theory predicts that organisations which undertake a large number of repetitive tasks will have a more formal structure with well-defined roles and responsibilities then an organisation undertaking less repetitive and predictable tasks which will tend to have a less formal structure. Individuals will tend to define their roles in relation to the demands of a particular project, rather than the expectation of a routine. In this case the organisation may develop expert roles and *ad-hoc* team structures.

Strategy

The strategy adopted by a business is the way it goes about competing for its customers' attention. It is, in essence, what it offers, to whom and the reasons it gives customers to buy. Some organisations, having established their business take up a defensive posture. They understand their products and the reasons why customers buy. They compete by being better at serving 'their' niche than anyone else and they only react to competitors when they move in on 'their' territory.

Other businesses – and entrepreneurs must be in this class – are more aggressive. They aim to grow their business by attacking entrenched competitors. They compete by offering the customer a new innovation which serves a need, or solves a problem, better than existing offerings. Some organisations may combine both these generic strategies: defending established business and using the resources gained to attack in other areas.

More specifically, the organisation's strategy is the way it goes about developing and sustaining competitive advantage, in particular *cost advantages, knowledge advantages, relationship advantages* and *structural advantages.*

There is no simple relationship between strategy and structure. The defining tension is the way in which decision making within the organisation drives the strategy. In short, if decision making can be centralised then a more regular, and formal structure should be expected. If, on the other hand, decision making must be 'pushed down' to lower levels of the organisation then a less formal, more flexible, structure might be expected. Organisations pursuing cost leadership (for example, the Japanese engineering conglomerate, *Minebea*) tend to centralise control in order to ensure that costs are managed. Retail organisations which depend on a strong brand presence (for example, the *Body Shop*) may also enact strong central control in order to ensure that the brand, and the products and services it endorses, are carefully managed.

Businesses based on knowledge advantages, especially where there is a lot of expertise involved, may avoid strong central control systems. Decision making may be localised. Actions may, however, be guided by a strong organisational culture. Team structures may be important as may informal mentoring of less experienced employees by more experienced. Many professional organisations with an entrepreneurial background (for example, *Saatchi and Saatchi Advertising*) have adopted this approach.

The environment

Organisations find themselves in an environment. This environment both offers resources and challenges their availability. Opportunities offer new possibilities whereas threats present the danger that what is enjoyed now may be lost in the future. The environment is defined by a number of factors. In particular: how *complex* it is (that is, how much information must be processed in order to understand it); how *fast* it is developing or changing; and how *predictable* those changes are. As with strategy, the influence of the environment on structure impacts through the way in which decision making is shaped. A known, slow changing, predictable environment encourages centralised decision making. A new or fast changing and unpredictable environment encourages decision making to be passed down to those at the cutting edge of the organisation who are 'in contact' with the environment.

Power, control and organisational politics

The structure of an organisation represents a response to the contingencies of size, technology, strategy and environment. But the extent to which it represents a controlled, deliberate and rational response depends on the extent to which, and the way in which, the entrepreneur can exert control over the organisation as it grows. A powerful central entrepreneur can be a great asset to a business. He or she can provide vision and leadership and keep the organisation focused on the opportunities with which it is presented. In the absence of this, the organisation may lack direction and so lose its momentum. Individuals, and informal coalitions of individuals, can begin to see their interests as being different to those of the organisation as a whole and the organisation can become *politicised*.

On the other hand, if the power the entrepreneur enjoys is misdirected, then the organisation may be led down the wrong path. Entrepreneurial power brings responsibility. It is important that the entrepreneur uses their position and power to create an organisational environment in which individuals are free to express, and act upon, their own analysis and decision-making skills. This is particularly important for the fast growing, innovative business pursuing an aggressive strategy in a changing, unpredictable environment where localised decision making can offer an advantage. Even if the organisation can benefit from a degree of centralisation of decision making the entrepreneur will face practical limitations in the range and number of decisions he or she can make personally. Once the organisation reaches a certain size (and it need not be that large) the entrepreneur is well advised to call upon the skills of a supporting management team. A summary of the influence of contingency factors on structure is provided in Table 20.3.

Table 20.3 A summary of the influence of contingency factors on organisational structure

Contingency	*Influence on organisational development*
Size	Organisational complexity tends to increase with size; development of internal structure occurs. Roles and responsibilities become more specialised.
Technology	Structure driven by nature of organisation's tasks: are they repetitive, *ad-hoc* or based on expert judgement?
	Repetitive tasks tend to favour routinised activities and repeated unit structure with centralised decision making.
	Ad-hoc and expert tasks encourage de-localised decision making, perhaps within a strong 'organisational cultural' framework.
Environment	Well understood, stable and predictable environment favours centralised decision making and formal, routinised structures.
	Poorly understood, unstable and unpredictable environment favours decentralised decision making and empowerment at low levels in the organisational hierarchy.
Strategy	Influence depends on how strategy is sustained through decision making.
	Does strategy adopted demand strong central control or does it favour decentralised decision making?
Power	Can entrepreneur impose strong central control? By what means?

20.6   Organisational growth

KEY LEARNING OUTCOME
An appreciation of how the resource requirements of the organisation can be used as a guide to its design.

The entrepreneur is faced with the task of designing and creating an organisation. Contingency theory provides a valuable insight into the variables that mould the organisation but it does not provide a detailed guide to shaping a particular organisation. A better approach is to consider the resource requirements of the organisation and to design its structure around them.

The 'traditional' path of development for an entrepreneurial venture is sometimes related as follows. At its inception, the business consists of just the entrepreneur and perhaps one or two others. The entrepreneur makes the decisions and undertakes the task of performing the business's activities, perhaps with a little delegation. In its early growth stages, as the business takes on more staff, the entrepreneur is freer to undertake the decision making and delegate more of the actual business generating activity. As growth continues, the entrepreneur may develop a management team to support his or her own decision making. In time, the members of this management team may act as the nucleus for more formal departments or business functions. As this process continues, the entrepreneur's role becomes that of the chief executive and the organisation settles down to maturity.

While this presents a plausible story for the growth of a business it is, at best, retrospective. Models (and there are many) which define the development of an organisation in terms of definite stages should be met with some caution. While they may provide an account of what *has* happened they have little power to predict what *will* happen. Even if particular stages of development do exist, an individual business will move through different stages at different rates and may miss out some stages altogether. Such models are of limited use as a guide to decision making. It is hard to say at a particular time exactly what stage a business has reached or when it can be expected to move on to the next stage.

For the decision maker attempting to design an organisation it is more profitable to ask what governs the structures a particular business should adopt given the (unique) situation with which it is faced. One option is to consider the *resource requirements* of the organisation.

The resource requirement approach

The nature of the resources available to the entrepreneur have been considered in Chapter 6. In essence, the entrepreneurial venture needs only three things: *information* from which an innovation can be developed, *capital* (money) for investment and *people* to make the venture happen. The initial resource requirements of an organisation are shown in Fig. 20.7. In practice, the venture will obtain these things through a variety of routes.

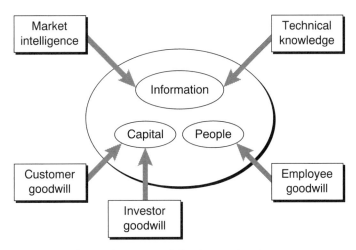

Fig. 20.7 The resource dependency model of organisation

Information

In the first instance, information will be obtained via the entrepreneur's experience within a particular business sector. As the business grows, market intelligence gathering will become increasingly important. As it develops further this may be supplemented by formal market research to provide market information and a research and development programme to provide information on products and technology.

Capital

The entrepreneur may use his or her own money to initiate the business. This may be supplemented by formal and/or informal investment capital. If the business is to be sustained, however, it must attract money from customers. This will, of course, be a result of the business selling its products to them. If this is to occur then the customer's interest and *goodwill* towards the business, and what it offers, is needed. If the business is to grow at a sustainable rate then additional capital may be needed from investors. Again, their interest and goodwill towards the venture is needed.

People

In the early stages of the business the entrepreneur may invite close associates to join in the venture. However, as the business grows more formal procedures for identifying and recruiting personnel and gaining their goodwill will be needed.

The structure adopted by a particular organisation can be thought of as a response to its requirements in relation to these three key resources. Particular functions appear within the organisation in order to manage the acquisition of these resources. The 'conventional' response for the large, mature organisation is to set up *departments* with specific responsibility for the acquisition of particular resources. Thus customer goodwill is captured by marketing and sales; investor goodwill by the finance department; market knowledge by the marketing research function (perhaps integrated into the marketing department); technical knowledge by the research and development function; and so on.

The complete organisation will include two additional functions. The operational system which actually produces the outputs of the business (i.e. production or service provision) is responsible for adding value to the inputs and a strategic control function co-ordinates the operation of the organisation as a whole.

The resource acquisition approach

This is, however, only *one* of a range of possible responses. It represents the limitation of the organisation as it reaches maturity. It also reflects a traditional environment in which different types of resource are independent and quite predictable in the way they may be acquired. It is this feature which allows them to be acquired by 'specialist' managers. The evolution of the entrepreneurial organisation can thus be thought of in terms of it developing internal structures to manage the acquisition of the resources it needs to undertake its business.

In its early stages, the entrepreneur will take a great deal of responsibility for attracting the critical inputs: customer, investor and employee goodwill as well as information. In other words he or she must be the marketing, sales, finance and development specialist rolled into one. The entrepreneur must also maintain strategic control over the business and may be responsible for undertaking operations as well. At this early stage, the entrepreneur's role is a challenging one!

As the business grows then tasks can be differentiated, and the role of the entrepreneur can become more distinct. Usually, he or she will relinquish participation in operational activities and concentrate on managing the business as a whole. As the business grows further, roles can become even more specialised. Individuals can focus

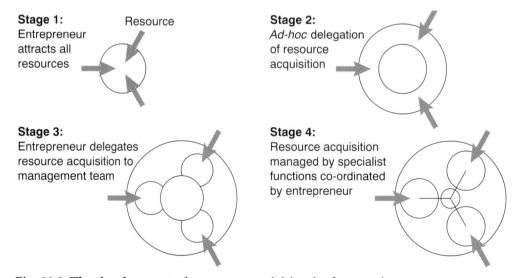

Stage 1: Entrepreneur attracts all resources — Resource

Stage 2: Ad-hoc delegation of resource acquisition

Stage 3: Entrepreneur delegates resource acquisition to management team

Stage 4: Resource acquisition managed by specialist functions co-ordinated by entrepreneur

Fig. 20.8 The development of resource acquisition in the growing venture

their attention on obtaining critical resources. As a result, specific resource acquisition functions can start to emerge. The evolution of input acquiring functions in the development of the entrepreneurial business is shown in Fig. 20.8

This approach can be used as a guide for decision making about the structure the organisation should adopt. The key issues in relation to deciding on structure are:

How large is the organisation?

How many people work for the organisation? How much latitude is there for individuals to take on specialist roles? To what extent is it possible to use outside specialists? (Consider here the points raised in Section 16.3 in particular.

As a rule, tasks, roles and responsibilities should be specialised, if possible.

What are the critical inputs?

All inputs are important. However, the acquisition of some will take priority at any one point and this will alter at different stages of development. The question is what matters *most* at this point in time: information on markets and product technology or investment capital or sales to customers or people? Is the lack of any one of these *in particular* responsible for limiting the venture's potential? To what extent is it possible to dedicate available resources to the acquisition of a particular input? How might this situation change in the near future?

As a rule, attention should be focused on critical inputs – but it is important not to neglect other inputs.

What is the venture's skill profile?

What skills are available in order to be dedicated? How is the venture served for people with selling, marketing, financial negotiating and research skills, *etc.*? How might these be acquired (e.g. through training, new recruitment or external support?)? What does this say about the venture's skill requirements for the future?

As a rule, the venture's skill profile should be built up (but an awareness of fixed costs is important). The entrepreneur must be willing to call on outside help in the short-term if necessary.

What is the nature of the inputs needed?

The nature of inputs the venture needs will differ depending on the environment in which it finds itself. Are they well defined? (If the business is very innovative or if it is in a business environment which is not well developed then they might not be.) Are they easily obtainable? How intense is the competition for them? On what basis does competition take place?

The key issue here is how *specialist* the task of managing the acquisition of a particular input needs to be in order to be successful. As a rule, the possibility of gaining competitive advantage by building in-house specialisation should be considered.

How do different inputs interact?

Different inputs interact with each other. The acquisition of one cannot be considered in isolation since how one input is acquired affects how the others will be. Technical knowledge means little without consideration of what the market wants. The acquisition of investors' capital will be facilitated if the venture has a good knowledge of market conditions. Similarly the goodwill of employees will provide a strong platform on which to build a culture which attracts the goodwill of customers.

This means that one input attracting function must communicate with the others. Those responsible for market research must talk to those responsible for development. The finance department must talk to those responsible for marketing. Inter-function communication is facilitated (or hindered) by organisational structure. If the acquisition of inputs can be considered largely in isolation of each other, then a structure which features dedicated specialist functions co-ordinated centrally (perhaps supplemented by informal inter-functional communication) may be suitable. On the other hand, if detailed co-ordination of input acquisition is necessary, then a matrix or a team structure may be more effective and offer a better route to developing a structural competitive advantage.

20.7 The venture as a theatre for human growth

> **KEY LEARNING OUTCOME**
> **A recognition of the importance of the human dimension in organisational growth.**

Business organisations are not just systems for generating wealth. They are the stages on which human beings live their lives. Individuals use their organisational role to create images of themselves. For many people, what you *do* is who you *are*. In building an organisation, an entrepreneur is not just generating employment opportunities but also creating a theatre in which people will play out the parts which are critical to their personal development. Organisations are the places where people meet and interact. The entrepreneur is not only offering economic rewards, but social and personal development ones as well.

Effective entrepreneurs will recognise this. They will understand that an individual working in the organisation is bringing a number of different expectations operating at different levels with them. Entrepreneurs should be aware of the meaning that the organisation offers to the people who are part of it and, critically, of how that meaning changes as the organisation grows.

The small, informal organisation will offer a different environment to the larger one where roles and relationships are more formal. Of course there is a trade-off. The larger organisation offers more security and the possibility for employees to use and develop specialist skills whereas the smaller one may offer a more flexible and personal environment. The entrepreneur must recognise the balance of benefits from the perspective of the individual employee.

An entrepreneur, like any good manager, recognises that the development of the organisation is also the development of the people within it. Its growth offers them the potential for growth. Developing and communicating vision means writing the story of how the organisation will develop, the roles that particular individuals will play in that development, and what those roles will mean for them.

In practice this means that the entrepreneur must discuss the changes that are taking place within the organisation with individuals, and use those discussions to develop an understanding of what those changes mean for the individuals. Presenting the future possibilities offered by, and removing the fear of, change is the platform on which motivation is built. Such discussions may be quite formal (for example, regular appraisals and objective setting) or informal chats with employees.

Understanding what the prospects and achievement of growth offer and the fears and apprehensions they create for the individual within the organisation is crucial since these are the platform on which the entrepreneur builds his or her leadership strategy.

Summary of key ideas

- The growth of the venture must be approached from a number of perspectives of which the key perspectives are: *financial*: growth in income, expenditure and profits; *strategic*: growth in market presence and competitive advantages; *structural*: growth in organisational form, process and structure; and *organisational*: growth in the organisation's culture and attitudes.

- Effective entrepreneurs recognise that the growth of the venture provides all of its stakeholders with an opportunity for personal growth and development.

Suggestions for further reading

Birley, S. and **Westhead, P.** (1990) "Growth and performance contrasts between 'types' of small firm", *Strategic Management Journal*, Vol. 11, pp. 535–57.

Brocklesby, J. and **Cummings, S.** (1996) "Designing a viable organisational structure", *Long Range Planning*, Vol. 29, No. 1, pp. 49–57.

Gibb, A. and **Davies, L.** (1991) "In pursuit of frameworks for the development of growth models of the small business", *International Small Business Journal*, Vol. 9, No. 1, pp. 15–31.

Greiner, L.E. (1972) "Evolution and revolution as organisations grow", *Harvard Business Review*, July-Aug, pp. 37–46.

Mintzberg, H. (1979) *The Structuring of Organisations: A Synthesis of the Research*, Englewood Cliffs, N.J., Prentice Hall.

Scott, M. and **Bruce, R.** (1987) "Five stages of growth in small business", *Long Range Planning*, Vol. 20, No. 3, pp. 45–52.

van de Ven, A. and **Poole, M.S.** (1995) "Explaining development and change in organisations", *Academy of Management Review*, Vol. 20, No. 3, pp. 510–40.

21 Strategies for expansion

CHAPTER OVERVIEW

*Expanding the business means expanding the amount of trade it undertakes.
Expansion from any base can be achieved in one of four ways, by **increasing core
market share**, by **launching new products**, by **entering new markets** and by
acquiring established businesses. This chapter considers each of these generic
strategies in turn and the decisions the entrepreneur must make in order to deliver
them.*

21.1 Increasing market share

KEY LEARNING OUTCOME
**An understanding of the decisions that need to be made when
considering an expansion strategy based on increasing market share.**

Expansion demands an increase in the volume of the venture's sales. These sales are
made into a market. The impact of this increase in sales volume on the market depends
on the dynamics of the market itself. If the market is enjoying rapid growth then the
business may increase its sales even if its market share is static. On the other hand, if
the market is mature and not increasing in volume, then an increase in sales implies an
increase in market share. Sales growth, then, is a combination of overall market growth,
and increase in the share of that market. As the American business academic, Ansoff
pointed out in his seminal book, *Corporate Strategy,* any expansion strategy must
involve a decision as to whether to base expansion on existing products or to develop
new ones, and whether to rely on established market presence or to enter new markets.

The attractiveness of a market depends on its rate of growth (*see* Fig. 21.1). Studies of
business performance in a number of market areas has suggested that the most
attractive type of market (defined as the one which offers the best return on
investment) is one of moderate growth. This is rationalised as follows. In a low growth
market, increases in business can only be obtained at the expense of competitors. This

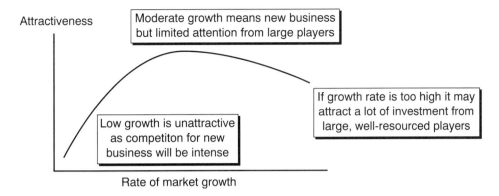

Fig. 21.1 Market attractiveness and rate of growth

makes the fight for market share expensive. Conversely, in a higher growth market the business can be expanded by taking the 'new' business as it becomes available. This reduces competitive pressures. Competitors may not even realise each other's presence. If the growth becomes very high, however, then the market may be seen as so attractive that the attentions of a large number of competitors may be aroused. Big players may invest heavily to gain control of the market. If this happens, then the cost of competing may increase again.

In practice, the simple formula of market growth *versus* share increase needs careful inspection. The dynamics of a market, and the share of a particular business within that market, are dependent on how the market is defined in the first place. A market represents the collection of goods which can be substituted for each other, but a variety of goods can be substituted in different ways. Some goods may make better substitutes than others. The situation is complicated further if the good in question serves a number of different needs.

For example, consider the jewellery that was marketed so successfully by Gerald Ratner in the 1980s. Clearly, the products were in competition with those on offer from other jewellery stores. However, jewellery is often purchased as a gift item and in this they were in competition with a whole host of other products which make interesting gifts such as books, CDS, flowers and so on. Ratner's target market was young people who bought the product to wear when they socialised with one another. With respect to this, the products were in competition with other fashion items that were bought for purposes of socialisation, particularly clothes. In a wider sense still, they were in competition with other areas in which young people could spend money in order to socialise such as meals out, attending concerts and so on. Thus a product sits in a number of markets depending on its pattern of substitution for other goods (*see* Fig. 21.2).

An entrepreneur must recognise that 'the' market in which their business operates is not a single thing at all, but a complex arena of overlapping market sectors. Whether or not a business is growing by increasing its share, or by capitalising on a growth market will depend on which sector of the market is under consideration. The business may, in fact, be doing both of these in different areas of the market.

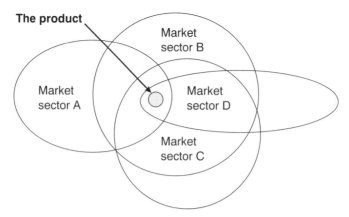

Fig. 21.2 The multi-market location of a product

This framework indicates the considerations the entrepreneur must have in view when developing a market share expansion strategy. These considerations have three parts:

1 *What market sectors are available into which expansion might take place?*

- What product (or products) do the venture's offerings substitute? (What will people stop using if they buy the venture's products?)
- In what ways does substitution take place? (Directly or indirectly?)
- Who supplies the substitute products?
- What benefits does the venture's product offer to the customer in each sector?

2 *What are the attractions of each sector?*

- What is the volume potential within the sector?
- What are the dynamics of market growth in each sector?
- What are the competitive pressures (for example, the strength of competitors, the investment needed to build and sustain market share)?
- How are competitors likely to react to the venture's actions? (Passively or aggressively?)
- As a result, what is the likely return on investment?

3 *What are the venture's competitive advantages in a particular sector?*

- How effectively can the offering be positioned in that sector?
- What are the venture's competitive advantages in each sector in relation to costs, market knowledge, relationships, and structural factors?
- How can competitive advantage be maintained within the sector?

In summary, even though an entrepreneurial venture sells its products into a competitive marketplace, and although increasing the size of the venture means taking competitors' business (and facing their reaction to this), the entrepreneur is free, to a degree at least, to decide which competitors they wish to confront and the way in which they wish to compete. The latitude which the entrepreneur has to do this is dependent on the potential to position the offering in different ways in different market sectors. The decision as to which sector, or indeed sectors, into which expansion will be directed is a feature of how attractive that sector is and the competitive advantages the venture enjoys within it.

21.2   Developing new products

KEY LEARNING OUTCOME
An understanding of the decisions that need to be made when considering a strategy of expansion through new product development.

Most businesses sell more than one product. Many offer hundreds, if not thousands, of lines. When it is initiated, the entrepreneurial venture is likely to have only one, or at most only a few, lines. Thus developing new products must be a critical factor in the venture's plans for expansion. New product development is not just about adding on new lines, though. No business can afford to stand still in a fast-moving marketplace. New products must be developed to replace existing ones and too keep ahead of competitors as the customer's expectations develop.

Product development covers a range of activities from minor modifications of existing products through the development of new variants and models, to the development of entirely new product concepts. Existing product development (EPD) and new product development (NPD) lie at opposite ends of a developmental spectrum.

The details of what existing and new product development mean for a particular business will depend on the nature of the products it is involved with. Clearly, advanced, technology-intensive products will require a different approach to 'simple' products based on established, well-understood technologies. Thus the *Body Shop* is involved constantly in developing new formulations and variants based on the ingredients that Anita Roddick collects on her world travels. The development of *Windows 95* represented a major new product launch for Bill Gates and the *Microsoft* corporation. The satellite broadcasting channel, *BSkyB*, which was set up by Rupert Murdoch's *News International Corporation*, demanded the initiation of a whole new industry. Whatever the nature of the product, its complexity and the resources involved in its launch, the basic 'rules' of effective product development and the decisions that are involved in developing the strategy are similar.

The key is to remember that a product is not a thing in itself but a means to an *end*. The value of a product lies in the benefits it can bring to its users. The product is just a way of delivering an innovation to the market. The entrepreneur must apply the same market-orientated insights to the development of new products as were brought to the innovation on which the business was originally founded.

New product development is not just a technical process. It is something which cuts across every facet of the business. There will be a technical element to the actual creation of the product but product development must be considered in much broader terms than the purely technical. Some of the critical decision areas include the following.

Market positioning

What problems will the product solve? Why will it solve them better than existing products do? How will it be positioned in its marketplace? Against which competitors? How will it be priced relative to competitors?

Branding

Will the product be branded? If so, will it use its own branding or draw on corporate branding? Will it use an existing brand (i.e. a brand extension) or will it represent the establishment of a new brand identity?

Communication

How will the customer get to know about the product? How can it be promoted to them? What communication routes will be used? Will the customer need to be educated about the product? Will endorsement and professional recommendation be a factor in its position? What demands will promotion make on existing sales and promotional resources?

Distribution

How will the customer get hold of the product? Who will be involved in the distribution process? What support will be needed from distributors and other partners to promote the product?

Financial and operational forecasting

What is the anticipated demand for the product? What revenues are expected? Over what period? On what assumptions are these forecasts based? What are the risks if they are wrong?

Technical research and development

What technical challenges does the product present? How does its development fit with the venture's current technical competencies and skills base?

Production and operations

How will the product be manufactured (or the service delivered)? How does its production fit with existing competencies? Is production capacity adequate or must new capacity be established? What are the logistical implications (for example in terms of storage)?

Supply issues

What factors are involved in producing and delivering the new product? Is it based on components which are currently supplied? Does it demand new components from existing suppliers or does it demand that new suppliers be brought on board? If so, how will they be identified and managed?

Resource implications

Does the business currently have the financial resources to fund such a strategy of expansion? Will it create cash-flow problems? Does the business have sufficient human capacity? Are sales resources sufficient to open and serve the new market sectors?

Strategic concerns of product development

Product development demands an investment. That investment must be considered in light of risk, possible alternatives and opportunity costs in the same way as any other investment within the business. This means that the development of new products must be considered strategically. The key questions in this consideration are as follows.

- How does the new product fit with the innovation on which the business was founded? Is it a way of presenting this innovation further or is it a diversification into a new area of innovation?
- How does the new product build on the venture's existing competitive advantages?
- How does the new product contribute to making those competitive advantages sustainable?
- How does the product fit into the venture's existing portfolio of products?
- What will be the resource demands (financial, operational and human) in developing the product?
- Over what period is the product to return the investment made in it? Does it represent a short- or long-term investment?
- What will be the implications of the product for the sales of existing products? (In particular will there be any 'cannibalisation' of existing sales?)

The success of a new product development expansion strategy does not depend solely on the success of the new products themselves. It also depends on the venture's ability to identify and deliver them. An ability to respond to customer demand through the capability of producing new products quickly and effectively is an important way of developing a structural competitive advantage.

21.3 Entering new markets

> KEY LEARNING OUTCOME
> **An understanding of the decisions that need to be made when considering a strategy of expansion through entry into new markets.**

When a new venture is initiated, its market scope is usually quite limited. This is only to be expected since the business's low resource base means that it is well-advised to concentrate on serving defined and narrow sectors where it can gain an initial competitive advantage. Once this has been established, then the option of expanding the business by delivering the product or service on which it is based to a wider audience, quickly becomes attractive.

The routes to expansion through new market entry are varied. To a great extent the options available will depend on the way in which the niche of the business is defined. The main options for new market expansion include the following possibilities.

New geographical areas

In its early stages, a business tends to serve a local geographic area. Therefore, expansion of the business into other geographical areas is an important option. Ultimately this might include expansion into the international arena through exporting, international marketing or even locating offices overseas. In fact, few businesses can now achieve any real size without taking on the international option.

New industry sectors

A new business will usually concentrate on marketing its products to a narrow range of customers. The composition of this customer base will reflect the entrepreneur's knowledge and experience in the application of their innovation. Again, this represents a sound move in terms of creating a defendable niche in the market. It is likely, however, that the innovation will be attractive to buyers with similar needs in other industry sectors. Developing a strategy to market the product to these groups is an important option for expansion.

New groups of consumers

A new product is often targeted at quite a narrow group of consumers. If it is particularly innovative then the nature of buyers will change over time. Initially, take-up will be led by *adopters*, that is consumers who actively seek out new innovations in the product area and greet them positively. *Non-adopters* will hold back until the innovation becomes more familiar. *Resistors* will reject the product out of hand. The product will also have a positioning which will make it more attractive to some groups of consumers (defined in demographic, sociographic or psychographic terms) than others.

Expanding the appeal of the product from the founding target groups to a wider audience demands careful consideration of how the product is communicated, promoted and distributed to different consumer groups. The option is often attractive but when developing the positioning to attract new groups care must be taken to ensure that core groups are not alienated.

The strategic issues which need to be considered in relation to new market entry parallel those that arise in relation to increase of market share and new product development strategies.

Positioning and branding

How does the competitive environment differ between the original sector and the new sectors? Can the positioning that has been developed for the product continue to be utilised as it is expanded into new sectors, or must a new positioning be developed? Can any branding that has been developed continue to be used or must a new branding, or sub-branding, be developed? Can the current pricing strategy continue or must it be changed?

Communication and promotion

What message must be sent to the new sector? How does this compare to the message that is being sent currently? What medium of communication must be used? What promotional tactics might be used in conjunction with the new sector? Can the current sales and selling strategy be used or must a new one be developed?

Distribution

What distribution routes are available to reach the new sectors? Do these demand that new distributors be used? Does this demand that a new *type* of distributor be used?

Resource implications

Does the business currently have the financial resources to fund such an expansion strategy or will it create cash-flow problems? Does the business have sufficient human capacity? Are sales resources sufficient to open and serve the new market sectors?

Product development and expansion into new market sectors

A strategy of expansion by entry into new market sectors can be adopted in conjunction with new product development strategy. Indeed modification of the product to make it more attractive may be an essential element of the strategy of expansion into new markets. A balance must be struck between ensuring that the offering is right for the sector at which it is aimed on the one hand and ensuring that the business does not lose its economies of scale and create logistical complexity by having a large number of low volume lines on the other.

21.4 Acquisitions

> **KEY LEARNING OUTCOME**
> An understanding of the decisions that need to be made when considering a strategy of expansion through acquisition.

Success in the marketplace generates the financial resources which the entrepreneur can use to expand the business further. This money can either come from retained profits or be additional funds offered up by investors. This capital can be used to invest in increasing the market share of existing products, or to develop new products or to enter new market sectors. Such growth comes from 'within' the business and is sometimes referred to as *organic* growth. An alternative to organic growth is to acquire other businesses in their entirety and 'add' them onto the venture. This is referred to as growth by *acquisition*.

There are three sorts of acquisition. These differ in the way in which the integrated firm sits in relatin to the venture in the value addition chain. The first is *vertical integration*. This happens when the venture acquires a firm which is either above or below it in the value addition chain i.e. it acquires a business which is a *customer* or a *supplier*. The acquisition of customers is referred to as *forward integration* and that of a supplier as *backward integration*. The second type of acquisition occurs when the venture integrates a business which is at the same level of value addition as itself, i.e. a business that is, ostensibly at least, a *competitor*. The third type of acquisition occurs in the remaining cases when the integrated business is not a supplier, nor a customer nor competitor. These might be referred to as *lateral* integrations. The various types of integration are shown in Fig. 21.3.

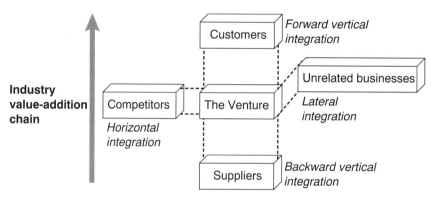

Fig. 21.3 Types of acquisition

Acquisitions are an attractive option for rapid growth because the only limitations on growth rate are the availability of targets and the funds to buy them. For example, Howard Hodgeson built up his funeral directing business from eighteen parlours to well over 500 over a three year period solely by acquisition. Acquisitions do, however, represent a fundamentally different approach to growth than does organic expansion. With organic growth new resources are brought together by the entrepreneur in an innovative combination to create new value. An integrated business, on the other hand, represents resources which are *already combined*.

This means that an acquisition is not valuable in itself unless new value can be created from it. This means that the acquiring venture must do something *different* with the business in order to make the acquisition worthwhile. In short, the entrepreneur must decide how they are going to add value through the acquisition; that is: what they can do, why that is valuable for the business's customers, and why the management of the acquired firm cannot do this on their own.

In strategic terms this means asking how acquisitions can be used to create and develop the venture's competitive advantage. There are four fundamental processes by which acquisitions can help in the development of competitive advantage.

By reducing costs

Does integration reduce overall costs? This may be achieved by eliminating some fixed or overhead costs. Alternatively, it may be gained by achieving some economy of scale in a key functional area. Production and sales are particularly important here. Existing production capacity may be used more efficiently especially if there is some overcapacity. The sales team may find it relatively easy to add new items to the portfolio they are selling. They may also find it possible to serve additional customers in their area. (However, care needs to be taken to ensure that they can still develop a good understanding of the benefits offered by the things they are selling and that they can still give each customer the time they need in order to manage the supplier-buyer relationship.)

By combining and creating knowledge

Does integration increase the value of the knowledge held by the individual organisations? For example, can the acquired firm offer information on products, operational technology or markets that the acquiring entrepreneur can utilise in its own business area? Does the acquirer understand customers in a way which promises to make the selling of the acquired business's products more effective? Can the two organisations learn key skills from each other, for example, in R&D, or in marketing?

By capitalising on relationships

Does integration take advantage of the relationships enjoyed by one party? For example, does it allow the acquirer to use their brand (a relationship with the customer) on a wider range of products? Does the acquired business enjoy a particularly valuable relationship with suppliers or distributors? Does the acquired business have access to new geographical areas or to new customer groups?

Of course, care must always be taken to ensure that the acquisition process itself does not upset established relationships.

By developing organisational structure

Does the integration allow the organisation as a whole to develop structural advantages? For example, does it make the processing of information on the market more effective? Does it make the business more responsive to customer needs? Does it allow the business to react more rapidly in producing new products? Does it enable the business to get its products into new areas or to new customer groups?

It is important to note that these things do not happen just because the organisation becomes larger, but because it changes the *way* it does things, in particular because it differentiates tasks in a more effective manner.

In summary, an acquisition is not a way of adding value in itself. Two businesses added together are not automatically more valuable than two separate businesses. In fact, the reverse is often the case. An acquisition only creates value if it allows the venture to offer the customer something new and useful and allows the new venture to develop its competitive advantage in the marketplace.

Summary of key ideas

- The entrepreneurial venture is characterised by a potential for growth. After initiating the venture, the entrepreneur must develop a strategy to *expand* it.

- The *generic* options for growth are by increasing core market share; by developing new products; by entering new markets; and by acquiring existing businesses.

- The attractiveness of the first three of these options depends on the market characteristics, particularly *growth rate*.

- The attractiveness of the acquisition option depends on the ability of the entrepreneur to genuinely add value to acquired businesses.

Suggestions for further reading

Ansoff, H.I. (1965) *Corporate Strategy*, New York: McGraw-Hill.

Biggadike, R. (1979) "The risky business of expansion", Harvard Business Review, May-June, pp. 103–11.

Bloom, P.N. and **Kotler, P.** (1978) "Strategies for high market-share companies", *Harvard Business Review*, Nov-Dec, pp. 63–72.

Bourantas, D. and **Mandes, Y.** (1987) "Does market share lead to profitability?", *Long Range Planning*, Vol. 20, No. 5, pp. 102–8.

Chaney, P.K., **Devinney, T.M.** and **Winer, R.S.** (1991) "The impact of new product introductions on the market value of firms", *Journal of Business*, Vol. 64, No. 4, pp. 573–610.

Cooper, R.G. (1994) "New products: The factors that drive success", *International Marketing Review*, Vol. 11, No. 1, pp. 60–76.

Hamermesh, R.G., **Anderson, Jr., M.J.** and **Harris, J.E.** (1978) "Strategies for low market share businesses", *Harvard Business Review*, May-June, pp. 95–102.

Newton, J.K. (1981) "Acquisitions: A directional policy matrix approach", *Long Range Planning*, Vol. 14, No. 6, pp. 51–7.

Szymanski, D.M., **Bharadwai, S.G.** and **Varadarajan, P.R.** (1993) "An analysis of the market share–profitability relationship", *Journal of Marketing*, Vol. 57, pp. 1–18.

22 Organisational growth and development

CHAPTER OVERVIEW

This chapter is concerned with developing an understanding of how organisational growth and development present themselves as opportunities and challenges to the decision-making entrepreneur. The first section explores some of the metaphors that decision makers can draw upon to create a picture of organisational growth. Subsequent sections of the chapter deal with setting objectives for growth and then planning for and controlling it.

22.1 Conceptualising growth and organisational change

KEY LEARNING OUTCOME
An understanding of the metaphors used to describe organisational growth.

The idea that organisations and organising are best understood through the use of metaphor was introduced in Section 7.1. The point was made that the way in which management is approached is dependent, to some extent, on the metaphor being used to provide an image of organisation by the entrepreneurial decision maker. As well as influencing the way in which organisation is perceived in a static sense, metaphors also influence the way in which organisational *growth* and *change* are seen to take place. Again, such metaphors provide a base for recognising the challenges the organisation faces and the approaches the entrepreneur might take to meet them.

Andrew van de Ven and Marshall Scott Poole have summarised the most important metaphors of organisational change. These are based on the notions of *life-cycle*, *evolution*, the *dialectic* and *teleology*.

Life-cycle

The notion of life-cycle suggests that the organisation undergoes a pattern of growth and development much like a living organism does. Life consists of a series of different stages: it is born, grows, matures and eventually ages and dies. This pattern is pre-programmed and the changes that take place are both unavoidable and irrevocable. Drawing on the experience of living things this metaphor accounts for the view that youthful entrepreneurial organisations are dynamic whereas older organisations are more sedate and sluggish and that this is a fate that will eventually befall the entrepreneurial venture as it matures itself. The metaphor does not give a definite life-span, however; it does not say *when* this must happen.

This metaphor is limited in that it (falsely) suggests that organisational decline is inevitable. It does, however, serve to warn the entrepreneur against complacency as the venture becomes successful.

Evolution

Evolution is a theoretical scheme which explains changes over time of the morphology of biological populations. It is founded on the concepts of *competition*, *fitness*, *selection* and *survival*. This scheme has been co-opted from biological science to describe changes in populations of business firms.

As a metaphor, evolution reminds the entrepreneur that they are operating in a competitive environment, that they must compete for scarce resources and that the venture must be efficient ('fit') in the tasks it undertakes. While evolution may conjure up an image of untrammelled competition – of a nature 'red in tooth and claw' in the words of the nineteenth century naturalist, Alfred Russell Wallace – a more sophisticated reading reminds us that co-operation within and between species, is also a feature of the natural world. Similarly with the entrepreneurial venture which not only competes, but also grows within a stakeholder network which may be supportive as well as competitive.

The dialectic

The dialectic is a concept which can be traced back to classical Greek philosophy. It has been extensively developed by thinkers such as Marx and Freud. It is based on a notion of progression through conflict and resolution. A system is initially unified but, over time, distinct parts begin to distinguish themselves. These parts recognise that their interests conflict and so they begin to oppose each other. Neither part can actually win the conflict and what eventually emerges is a newly unified system in which both parts have been changed and reintegrated.

As a metaphor of organisational development, the dialectic illuminates conflict and conflict resolution at a number of levels, for example between the entrepreneurial venture and competitor firms, between different stakeholder groups within the venture such as investors and employees, and within stakeholder groups. This latter level would include, for example, political manoeuvring by managerial factions within the business.

The importance of this metaphor for the entrepreneur is not so much its emphasis on the inevitability of conflict as in the idea that value can be created by resolving that conflict. The entrepreneur brings stakeholders (whose interests may differ) together in a way in which all benefit.

Teleology

Teleology suggests a process of change in which a system is progressing toward some future state. This future state both attracts the system or pulls it forward, and defines the shape the system takes as it progresses. More than any other metaphor, teleology introduces the notion of *purpose* to organisational change and growth. The entrepreneur can use his or her vision as the future state which pulls the organisation forward. It can be used to define goals and objectives and it is a critical element in leadership. Visionary leadership is a teleological process.

Chaos

In addition to these four 'traditional' metaphors, a new perspective is becoming increasingly important in providing a context for understanding organisational change. This is based on the notions of *complexity* and *chaos*.

Complexity science has its origins in the physics of turbulent and far-from equilibrium systems. Its insights have escaped from the boundaries of these narrow concerns and they now inform thinking on a wide range of topics including biology, economics and organisation theory. The defining feature of complexity is its rejection of simple lines of causality which characterise traditional systems thinking. In a complex system a small cause may, in time, have a very large and unpredictable effect. The beat of a butterfly's wing eventually causing a hurricane is a dramatic example. Systems theorists modelling the Earth's atmosphere discovered that a slight movement of air in one part of the world (say, from the beat of a butterfly's wing) could cause enough of a disturbance of the global atmospheric system to result in a large effect (such as a hurricane) some time later in a distant part of the world. The atmosphere is a chaotic system. A small cause leads to a large effect that cannot be predicted *ex ante*. Complex systems are not simply disorganised, however. They may show higher levels of form and order as a result of 'emergent' features which do not have a straightforward one-to-one relationship with lower levels of order. This is a perspective which has been developed extensively by Ralph Stacey in his book *Strategic Management and Organisational Dynamics* (1996).

The main question which complexity theory poses to management thinking is, if organisations are chaotic systems, can they be 'managed' at all? The answer usually leads not to a rejection of management but to demands to view it in a more sophisticated light. What is rejected is the idea that management can be reduced to a simple process of moving the venture to a pre-determined end point by a series of controlled steps.

The entrepreneurial venture is inherently unpredictable. By its very nature, it creates a future which is uncertain. Systems emerge to manage this uncertainty, for example the network of stakeholder relationships which define the venture, but they cannot eliminate it completely. The chaos metaphor reminds the entrepreneur that control and direction cannot be 'programmed' into the organisation. Events cannot be foreseen and each contingency must be responded to on its own terms. Entrepreneurial management is a *dynamic* process and it demands a 'hands on' approach. The future of the venture is not pre-determined by its present, rather it is actively shaped by the entrepreneur as new, unseen and often unseeable possibilities emerge.

As with metaphors of static organisation, the entrepreneur must learn to enrich their decision making by recognising the metaphors they are using and by drawing on as wide a variety of metaphors of organisational change as possible. A range of these metaphors are shown in Fig. 22.1 which illustrates the factors influencing organisational change decisions in relation to each metaphor.

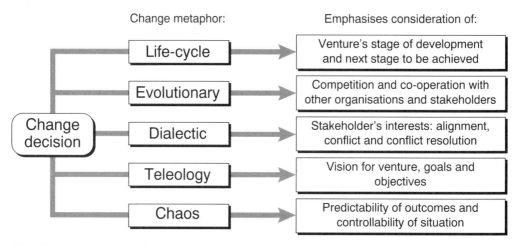

Fig. 22.1 Metaphors of organisational change

22.2 Growth as an objective for the venture

KEY LEARNING OUTCOME
An appreciation of the issues associated with setting growth as an objective for the venture.

The entrepreneurial venture is characterised by its growth potential, but why might an entrepreneur wish to take advantage of that potential and grow their venture? There are a number of answers to this question. It might be the result of a desire to increase personal wealth but this is not usually the main motivation of an entrepreneur. More usually it relates to a sense of achievement. In a sense, the size of the venture is a way of 'keeping the score'. Entrepreneurs are also driven by a desire to make a difference to the world. And in general, the larger the venture they create, the bigger the difference they have made. Driving growth can also relate to the desire for personal control. The bigger the venture the greater the domain over which the entrepreneur can express their power.

For these reasons growth is often an important objective for the venture. However, setting growth targets creates challenges in relation to the venture's strategy and resources and the risk to which it is exposed.

Growth and strategy

Growth has to be achieved. It must be delivered by the achievement of a greater volume of business. Ultimately, it must be driven by increased sales. The venture must have a strategy in place to develop its sales base. As discussed in Chapter 20, such a strategy may be based on exploiting market growth, increasing market share, developing new products or entering new markets.

An expansion strategy must be consistent with the capabilities of the venture, it must draw upon and develop the venture's competitive advantages and be viable given the competitive situation it will have to face. Growth targets must be demanding but they must also be reasonable given the strategic constraints the venture faces.

Growth and resources

Growth is dependent on the venture's ability to attract new resources. The ultimate source of resources is customer money. Investment and loan capital can only be a means to the end of attracting customers.

Capital is not useful in itself. It must be converted into productive assets in terms of people and operating resources. Growth targets must take account of the resources the venture will be able to acquire. Consideration must be made not just of the ability to attract capital from customers, lenders and investors but also the ability of the venture to *use* that capital to bring in the people and specialist assets the venture depends on. If these are in short supply, then any limitations imposed on growth must be taken into account.

Growth and risk

There is a complex relationship between growth and risk. In general, the larger a firm, the less risk it is exposed to. There are two reasons for this. First, size reflects *success*. A large firm is successful which implies that it is good at what it does. Clearly, being effective in the market place is the best way to reduce risk. Second, the larger the firm the more resources it will have. In particular, larger firms tend to have more 'slack' resources. These are resources that are not dedicated to specific projects and can be moved around quickly. The large business can use these resources to buffer themselves from short-term environmental shocks better than can the small firm.

However, growth carries some risk in itself. Growth implies developing new business which means venturing in to the unknown. The degree of risk depends on the way in which the expansion draws upon the venture's capabilities, its knowledge of products and markets and the environment in which it competes. Using resources to fuel growth is an *investment* regardless of whether new investment capital is obtained or profits are reinvested rather than distributed back to shareholders. As an investment, growth must be judged like any other in light of the risks it presents, the returns it offers and the opportunity costs it imposes.

The growth objective for the venture must be set following consideration of these factors. It must define the growth of the venture in terms of increased sales, increased income (including new investment capital) and how these revenues will be converted to assets. Growth targets must be consistent with, and feasible from, a strategy to achieve that growth and they must be acceptable to the venture's stakeholders in terms of the risks this creates.

Not all entrepreneurs set out with high growth objectives in mind. When Anita Roddick established the *Body Shop* in Brighton she only intended to start a small business capable of providing an income for her and her family. However, once the potential of her innovation became evident, growth (particularly through franchising) became a strategic priority for the business.

22.3 Controlling and planning for growth

KEY LEARNING OUTCOME
A recognition of the ways in which growth can be controlled by the entrepreneur.

The fact that growth presents strategic, resource and investment decision-making issues to the entrepreneur means it is a process which must be both planned for, and controlled. Indeed, the objective of growth, once it has been established, should lie at the heart of and drive forward the venture's planning and control process. The idea of controlling growth is critical to entrepreneurial success. It draws together a number of themes which have been developed in this book so far.

The *desirability* of growth must be reflected in the entrepreneur's vision (*see* Chapter 9). This vision must act as a force which co-ordinates and focuses the whole organisation on the tasks it faces. To do this, the vision must not only illuminate the *what* of growth but also the *why*, that is not only what is in it for the organisation but why the stakeholder will gain from it.

The *potential* for growth must be recognised in the venture's mission (*see* Chapter 10). This mission should be reasonable given the venture's capabilities and competitive situation but it should also stretch the organisation to make maximum use of its capabilities and exploit its competitive potential.

The *direction* of growth must be indicated by the venture's strategy (*see* Chapter 11). This should indicate the products the business will offer, the markets it will operate in and the competitive advantages it will develop and exploit in order to serve the customer better than competitors in those markets.

The *management* of growth demands the management of resource flows within the organisation. It means designing the organisation so that appropriate resource acquiring functions are in place to co-ordinate resource acquiring activities effectively. This relates to the ideas developed in Chapter 20.

In summary, the *achievement* of growth is a result of the decision-making processes that go on within the venture. The entrepreneur must control these through their power and leadership strategies. The entrepreneur's need (and desire!) to impose their will on the organisation must always be tempered by the value to be gained from letting individuals use their own insights and initiative. This is a theme to be developed further in Chapter 24.

Summary of key ideas

- Organisational growth, like organisation itself, is best understood through *metaphors* of change.

- Growth is an important objective for the venture. The growth objective must be considered in the light of the venture's *market potential*, its *strategic capabilities*, its *resources* and the *risks* it wishes to undertake.

- Growth must be both planned for, and controlled by, the entrepreneur, both in terms of *rate* and *direction*.

Suggestions for further reading

Bitner, L.N. and **Powell, J.D.** (1987) "Expansion planning for small retail firms", *Journal of Small Business Management*, Apr, pp. 47–54.

Gaddis, P.O. (1997) "Strategy under attack", *Long Range Planning*, Vol. 30, No.1, pp. 38–45.

Hunsdiek, D. (1985) "Financing of start-up and growth of new technology based firms in West Germany", *International Small Business Journal*, Vol. 4, No. 2, pp. 10–24.

McKergow, M. (1996) "Complexity science and management: What's in it for business?", *Long Range Planning*, Vol. 29, No. 5, pp. 721–7.

Oakley, R. (1991) "High-technology small firms: Their potential for rapid industrial growth", *International Small Business Journal*, Vol. 9, No. 4, pp.30–42.

Stacey, R. (1996a) *Strategic Management and Organisational Dynamics* (2nd edn), London: Pitman Publishing.

Stacey, R. (1996b) "Emerging strategies for a chaotic environment", *Long Range Planning*, Vol. 29, No. 2, pp. 182–9.

Tuck, P. and **Hamilton, R.T.** (1993) "Intra-industry size differences in founder controlled firms", *International Small Business Journal*, Vol. 12, No. 1, pp. 12–22.

23 Leadership, power and motivation in the entrepreneurial venture

CHAPTER OVERVIEW

*Managing the human dimension of the venture is critical to entrepreneurial success. This chapter deals with the tools for managing human relationships within the venture: **power**, **leadership** and **motivation** and the way in which they are interconnected.*

23.1 The human dimension: relating leadership, power and motivation

KEY LEARNING OUTCOME
An appreciation of the way in which the concepts of leadership, power and motivation are interrelated.

Entrepreneurs are managers, but they are not just any sort of managers. If we were to seek the one characteristic that distinguishes entrepreneurs from their more conventional colleagues it would most likely be found *not* in their strategic or analytical insights (though these are important) but in the *human dimension*: the way in which they use leadership and power and their ability to motivate those around them. Any discussion of entrepreneurship must, therefore, develop an insight into the ways in which leadership, power and motivation may be used as managerial tools.

An economic perspective suggests that human organisations exist to process resources. The differentiation of labour within them allows that processing to be carried out more efficiently. However, once those resources are processed they must be distributed to the stakeholders who make up the organisation. That distribution is rarely on an 'equal' basis. Further, organisations are not just rational orderings of activities but are also the stages upon which their members act out the roles which define them. Hence any discussion of leadership, power and motivation must be willing to take its cues from a variety of perspectives: *functional* ones which construe the organisation as a deterministic system, *interpretive* ones which explore human experience within organisations and *radical* ones which question the way in which different individuals benefit from organisational life.

In light of this, no one definition can possibly hope to fulfil the complete potential of any of these concepts. However, it is important to give the ideas some kind of conceptual location and basic definitions can be suggested as follows.

Leadership might be defined as the power to *focus* and *direct* the organisation.

Power might be defined as the ability to *influence the course of actions* within the organisation.

Motivation might be defined as the ability to *encourage* an individual to take particular courses of action.

Leadership, power and motivation are distinct concepts but clearly any discussion of one will usually draw in the others since they are different aspects of the overall process of control over the venture. It is useful to regard them as different aspects of the approach the entrepreneur takes to controlling the direction of the venture (*see* Fig. 23.1)

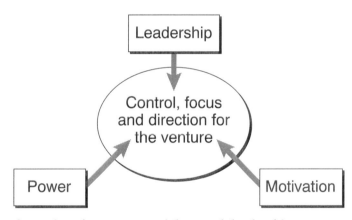

Fig. 23.1 The dynamics of entrepreneurial control: leadership, power and motivation

Leadership, power and motivation come together in the means the entrepreneur choses to shape and drive their venture in the *direction they wish to take it*. They are tools the entrepreneur adopts in order to turn their vision into reality, and as such, they lie at the heart of their project to create an entire new world.

It is important to recognise that entrepreneurial leadership, power and motivation cannot be confined within the formal organisation. They must extend beyond it to draw *all* the venture's stakeholders (its investors, customers and suppliers as well as its employees) together.

23.2 Understanding leadership

KEY LEARNING OUTCOME
An understanding of the factors which underpin entrepreneurial
leadership.

Leadership is one of the most essential ingredients for entrepreneurial success yet it is conceptually elusive. We recognise leadership when we see it but it is very hard to say *what* we are recognising. The way in which the concept has been used, and the framework for understanding it has evolved considerably over the century or so that leadership has been seen as a proper subject for investigation. The challenge is not just to understand leadership but also to provide recommendations on how leadership skills can be developed and used to enhance organisational performance.

Early approaches to leadership looked towards 'great men' to provide examples of how to behave. The main tool was the biography which detailed the life and exploits of appropriate leaders. A development of this approach was to try to distil out the personality traits which made great people 'great' and which underpinned their leadership. Both these approaches still inform a good deal of popular thinking on leadership but they are very limited because they make leadership inherent to an individual. They fail to recognise that leadership involves followers as much as leaders and that leadership takes place in a social setting.

Later modes of thinking, looked towards *influence* (how leaders coax followers) and *behaviour* (what leaders actually *do* rather than who they *are*) in an attempt to minimise these limitations. An important avenue of exploration into leadership amalgamated all these approaches with an integration of behavioural, personality, situation and influence factors. This approach is known as contingency leadership theory.

A number of distinct approaches to leadership emerged in the aftermath of contingency leadership theory. The *transactional* approach emphasised the importance of the pattern of one-to-one relationships or 'dyads' the leader established with the followers. In this perspective the follower was seen to develop the leader as much as the leader developed the follower. The *culture* perspective emphasised that the leader is not solely managing one-to-one interactions or even groups, but is managing the culture of the organisation as a whole: that is the set of expectations and assumptions that define what the organisation should do and should not do and how it should go about its tasks. These expectations and assumptions are often unarticulated and informal. This was the approach advocated by Tom Peters and Robert Waterman in their highly influential book *In Search of Excellence*. The *transformational* approach to understanding leadership develops the notion of the leader using his or her charisma and personal vision to transform individuals into followers. From this perspective, the process of leadership is both collective since the *whole* organisation is involved, and dynamic. Leadership is not so much about being a leader; it is about *leading*.

Thinking about leadership is developing rapidly. In some ways a new post-transformational integration which draws from the whole tradition on leadership

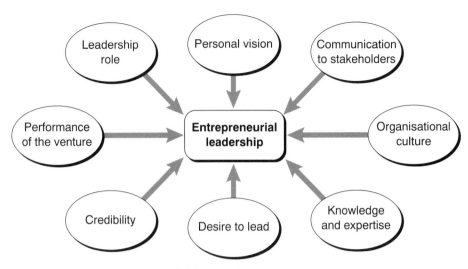

Fig. 23.2 Factors in entrepreneurial leadership

thinking is emerging. By distilling this integration, entrepreneurial leadership can be thought of as having eight key elements (*see* Fig. 23.2).

1 Personal vision

The entrepreneur's vision is the driving force behind leadership. It is vision which transforms a disparate group of stakeholders into the people who will act to move the venture forward. Vision must be rationalised and communicated. As discussed in Chapter 10, it is critical that the entrepreneur turn their vision into a 'narrative' which provides the venture's stakeholders with roles and responsibilities and defines the rewards they will get for participating in the venture.

2 Communication with stakeholders

The entrepreneur must relate their vision to stakeholders through a variety of communication channels and forums, for example, one-to-one talks, meetings, formal presentations, sales pitches, business plans, *etc*. Such communication is not simply a passing of information, it is a *call to action*. What matters to the entrepreneurial leader is not so much what people know as a result of a particular communication but what they will *do* in response to it. The content of communication is not confined to what is said. *How* things are said is just as important. In face-to-face communication non-verbal aspects such as body language can have a great influence on how things are interpreted. Leadership is built on effective communication and the style of communication can be as important as content.

3 Organisational culture

An organisation's culture is the web of rules which define how it goes about its tasks. These rules are often unspoken. Culture is, in a sense, 'the way things are done round here'. The culture defines what is allowed, and what is not allowed, for both internal and external relationships. An organisation's culture is created along with the organisation itself. It is the entrepreneurial leader's role to shape that culture by setting standards and defining values for the organisation. It also becomes manifest through the objectives the entrepreneur sets for the venture and the rewards and sanctions used to manage outcomes and expectations for both individuals and groups. The relationship between leadership and culture is reciprocal. Leadership creates the organisation's culture and, in return, the organisation's culture creates a space to be filled by a leader.

4 Knowledge and expertise

Entrepreneurs are experts. This expertise may be in some specialist technology (for example, Bill Gates' knowledge of computing) or in the particulars of an industry sector (for example, Rupert Murdoch's extensive knowledge of the newspaper business). In addition to this specialist knowledge there is the general sense of an entrepreneur being an 'expert' decision maker. Expertise provides a basis for leadership in that it offers authority for decision making.

5 Credibility

Credibility is critical for leadership. If credibility can be built up, then leadership (that is attracting followers) becomes easier. Conversely, if an entrepreneur loses credibility, then leadership is likely to be made more problematic if not lost altogether. Leadership offers the possibility of shaping the venture and directing it in a particular way. Leadership will only be accepted by followers if they are confident in the ability of the entrepreneur to take the venture in a direction that will benefit them.

6 Performance of the venture

Credibility comes, in the main, from being seen to make decisions which lead to successful outcomes. This is often an issue of association rather than causation. Decisions, not least those made at the higher levels of the organisation, usually lead to a cascade of further decisions. Causal chains can be hard to trace, especially when a good deal of latitude for decision making is allowed to subordinates. Further, success itself cannot be reduced simply to financial performance, it needs to be considered in the light of all the stakeholders' expectations (*see* Chapter 8).

If credibility comes from being associated with success, it is not *necessarily* true that credibility is automatically lost as a result of the occasional failure. Failure might have occurred for the 'right' reasons (a risky option was taken and it didn't pay off even though it was well thought out, the course was well managed and all parties involved were prepared for the possibility of failure). An ability to learn quickly and effectively from failure can, in fact, be a way to build credibility. One sure way to lose credibility, however, is to attempt to distance oneself from failure and to shirk responsibility when it is clear where responsibility lies!

7 Leadership role

The entrepreneur will usually be the most senior manager in the venture. They will be expected to take on a leadership role merely by virtue of being an entrepreneur.

Entrepreneurship itself comes, as it were, with the option of taking the position of leader.

However, care must be taken here. Though being an entrepreneur presents the *possibility* of being a leader, it does not offer it as a matter of *right*. Setting up the venture provides authority, not power (a distinction to be developed in Section 23.3). While people involved with the venture will look towards the entrepreneur for leadership, that is, they will set themselves up as followers, the entrepreneur must actively fulfil their expectations by exhibiting leadership behaviour. The entrepreneur must constantly use his or her position to reiterate the leader-follower relationship.

8 Desire to lead

The thing which ultimately underpins leadership is the desire to lead. No-one can be an effective leader unless they *really* want to take on the role of leader. Effective entrepreneurs recognise this in themselves. They accept positively the need they have to express their desire for power. The freedom to lead and use power is one of the great motivators driving many, if not all, entrepreneurs.

23.3 The basis of power and using power

> KEY LEARNING OUTCOME
> An appreciation of the nature and role of power within the entrepreneurial venture.

As with leadership, power is a concept which appears to be central to successful management which has resisted being reduced to a simple conceptual formula. To many people the term has a negative connotation. Power means power 'over' people. It suggests coercion and is something which must be curtailed.

However, if we define power as an ability to influence the course of actions within the organisation it becomes a necessary feature of organisational life. Power is a feature of situations in which resources are limited and outcomes are uncertain. Under these conditions actions *must* be influenced or the organisation would not be an organisation! In this respect power is an inevitability and, like the organisation itself, it can be made to work for good as well as ill. Certainly, entrepreneurs must recognise the basis for power within their organisation and learn to use it both positively and effectively. This is an approach taken by Jeffrey Pfeffer in his important study, *Power in Organizations*.

Power must be distinguished from *authority*. Authority presents a *right* to influence the course of actions due to the position the holder of that authority has within the organisation. This right is not the same as *ability*. The way in which authority translates into actual power depends on how the people who make up the organisation regard the holder's standing and the position they occupy. While one group may recognise the position, others may not do so. The entrepreneur may be given a high degree of ostensible authority by the social system in which they operate. The venture may 'belong' to them and be seen as the property of the individual entrepreneur. They will probably be seen as the chief executive, that is, the most senior decision maker. However, this in itself is no guarantee that they will actually have power over their venture. As with leadership, the entrepreneur's position *potentiates* power rather than provides it.

An important line of analysis sees power manifest itself as the control of different aspects of the venture. The relationship is reciprocal. Power gives access to control, and control provides a basis for power. Dimensions of control which are important for the development of the entrepreneur's power base are *resources*, *people*, *information*, *uncertainty*, *systems*, *symbols* and *vision*.

Control of resources

The fast-growing entrepreneurial venture is characterised by a constant influx of new resources. The decision as to how those resources will be used is one which must be addressed constantly. The entrepreneur, if not actually making those decisions, will normally be in a position to influence them greatly and to sanction those they oppose.

Control of people

The phrase 'control' of people sounds ominous and has authoritarian overtones. However, in the context of the entrepreneurial venture, the notion corresponds more to positive qualities of leadership (offering people a direction forward) and motivation (encouraging and supporting them in taking that direction) than it does to the negative aspects of coercion.

Control of information

Information informs decision making and makes it more effective. It has a critical role to play in establishing power structures. The entrepreneur is in a special position in relation to the information on which the venture is founded. In the early stages of the venture, he or she may actually be responsible for bringing in information on products, customers and finance. Later they will have control over what information is regarded as important and should be invested in. At every stage of development, it is the entrepreneur who has the unique position of viewing the venture from a strategic perspective.

Control of uncertainty

All stakeholders experience some uncertainties in relation to the entrepreneurial venture. Employees will be concerned about their remuneration and job security. Customers are often concerned about continuity of supply. Suppliers have an interest in the success of their customers, and investors are eager to ensure that their investments are sound ones. Managing this uncertainty provides a basis for power and the entrepreneur is in a unique position when it comes to managing this uncertainty. After all, it is the entrepreneur who will deliver the venture and ensure its success. As was discussed in Section 8.1 the process of managing success is as much about controlling *expectations* as it is about delivering outcomes.

Control of systems

Once the organisation grows beyond a certain size it becomes impossible for the founding entrepreneur to make all resource allocation decisions. At this point a number of systems emerge to control the process of resource allocation. These take the form of routines, procedures and operating practices. As the organisation grows the entrepreneur can, and indeed must, develop their power base by shifting their attention from controlling resource allocation itself, to controlling the systems which guide resource allocation.

Control over symbols

Symbols are very important in organisational life. Symbols may be overt, like company names, logos or brand names, or they can be more covert, like the arrangement of office space. They may take the form of stories or 'myths'. A good example is the way the *Disney Corporation* has co-opted the story of its founding father, Walt Disney, as a defining force for the organisation. The entrepreneur can access power within the organisation by learning to use, and claiming the right to use, the venture's symbolic forms in the right way. This can be an important factor in managerial succession for the entrepreneurial venture (*see* Section 25.4).

Control of vision

Vision, when properly used, is a powerful driving force for the entrepreneurial venture. However, there can only be one vision which dominates within the venture. There is no room for an alternative. Two or more visions offering different directions within the same organisation will inevitably come into conflict. An important, perhaps *the* most important, element in the power base of the entrepreneur is the ability to compose, articulate and control the elements of *the* vision that shapes and drives the venture as a whole.

Power brings responsibility. The right to exercise power brings with it the need to direct it in an appropriate way. Many entrepreneurs are seen to be motivated by power, but effective entrepreneurs are motivated not by power as an end in itself, but by using power as a tool to deliver the venture in a way which offers success to all of its stakeholders. This is not only a positive use of power, it is, in the long run, the only way in which power can be sustained.

23.4 Self-motivation and motivating others

KEY LEARNING OUTCOME
An insight into how entrepreneurs may motivate themselves and those around them.

People work best when they are motivated to do so. The entrepreneur cannot *demand* effort from someone; they must *support* the individual and encourage them to offer their efforts.

Self-motivation

The first person whose motivation the entrepreneur must address is his or her own! It is difficult, if not impossible, to motivate others if one's own motivation is lacking. This can be a challenge. The entrepreneurial course offers great rewards but it also demands resilience. The knocks are frequent and often hard. Failure, as well as success, must be managed with a positive response. Some important elements to address in terms of self-motivation are as follows.

Why am I doing this?

Good entrepreneurs know why they have chosen to be entrepreneurs. They constantly remind themselves why they have chosen the entrepreneurial path. The model developed in Section 4.2 gives an insight into this process. The attractions of entrepreneurship can be understood in the way that the course fulfils economic, social and self-developmental needs better than alternative routes open to the entrepreneur. Self-motivation must be built on an understanding that the option taken is one which is desirable.

Learning from mistakes

Like any other manager, entrepreneurs make mistakes from time to time. Sales may not be made or investment propositions may be rejected. Personal interactions may be mismanaged. Entrepreneurs are, however, very sensitive to the mistakes they make. This is not just because the consequences of the mistakes are greater than those made by other managers (although they may be) but because entrepreneurs present themselves as experts in managing their venture and its associated uncertainty. Errors of judgement cut to the heart of this role. They can be a great blow to the entrepreneur's confidence.

Of course, mistakes are an inevitable part of any managerial career, not just the entrepreneurial one. Effective entrepreneurs try to avoid mistakes by thought and preparation before entering situations, but when mistakes do occur they are met positively. The good entrepreneur does not try to deny the mistake or pass off responsibility to others. Rather, mistakes are regarded as an opportunity to learn. This means that ego must be detached from the incident and a cold analytical eye brought in to view the situation to identify a way of avoiding a similar mistake in the future.

Enjoying the rewards

All too often the entrepreneur can become so involved in running the venture that they forget to enjoy its rewards. At one level, this could mean spending the money that has been made. However, this consumption can only be a narrow part of the rewards of entrepreneurship. Money is rarely a major motivating force for the entrepreneur and, in any case, significant financial rewards may only be accrued a long way down the line. The main rewards lie in the job itself: the challenges it presents, the opportunity to develop and use new skills, the power to make changes, the satisfaction of leadership, and so on.

Learning to recognise these rewards and to savour them is a major factor in developing and sustaining self-motivation.

Motivation of others

Once self-motivation has been achieved the entrepreneur is in a strong position to start motivating others. Motivation is a behavioural phenomenon. Individuals are motivated (or demotivated) by the way people act towards them. This behaviour is an integral part of leadership. It is sensitive to personality and situation. As such, motivating behaviour is a complex process although some common patterns of motivating behaviour can be identified. Figure 23.3 shows a framework for managing individual motivation. Its key elements are:

Understanding personal drives

Before someone can be motivated, it is important to recognise what they want to gain from the situation they are in. Management occurs in a social setting and the needs which individuals bring to a situation are a complex mix of financial, social and developmental needs. The effective entrepreneur lays the groundwork for motivating the people in the venture to undertake specific tasks by involving them in the vision that has been created for the venture. This is achieved by communicating the role they will play in this vision and what they will get out of it.

Setting goals

People are not just motivated in an abstract sense. They are motivated to *do something,* i.e. motivation must lead somewhere. The entrepreneur is responsible for setting the goals that must be achieved. The degree to which these are specific objectives and the

Fig. 23.3 A framework for individual motivation

formality they take will be dependent on the situation, the entrepreneur's personal style and the cultural setting.

Whatever their form, individuals must recognise their goals and be able to locate them in relation to the goals of the organisation as a whole. Such goals should stretch the individual but also be realistic. They should demand effort but must be achievable given the personal and organisational resources the individual commands.

Offering support

Setting objectives is just the first step in motivating people. If people are to deliver, they require support. This can take the form of ongoing encouragement, advice, the provision of resources and influencing behind the scenes. The support offered should be commensurate with the level of the task and the demands on the person undertaking it. Effective motivation means giving people room to use their skills and insights but never letting them think that they are out on their own.

Using rewards

Rewards take a wide variety of forms. In character, rewards are the means that satisfy an individual's economic, social or developmental needs. In scope, the term 'reward' covers everything from a simple nod of approval from the entrepreneur to a complex deal offering a share in the financial performance of the venture. Whatever the nature of the reward an entrepreneur who knows how to motivate understands how best to use it.

First, rewards must be *appropriate* for the task undertaken. They must match the individual's expectations of what the reward should be. Second, their magnitude must be right: too small and they can lead to cynicism; too large and they can engender suspicion. Third, rewards must be used on the proper *occasions*. Rewards which are given too freely (and this includes simple things like comments of approval) become devalued. Fourth, they must be seen to be *equitable*. If the reward structure for different individuals and groups is seen to be unfair then jealousy and conflicts can result.

A positive approach to sanctioning

The entrepreneur must occasionally resort to sanctioning individuals who fail to perform in an appropriate way. The way this necessary task is handled is important, not just for maintaining the motivation of the individual, but for the signals it sends to the organisation as a whole. In general, a positive approach to sanctioning is to be advocated. The objective of the sanctioning must be seen to be one of helping the individual to deliver at the proper level, not just as a punishment. It should not (primarily) be about what was done wrong in the past, but about how performance can be improved in the future. This should also encourage a forum which allows the issues to be discussed while personality and ego are put to one side. Indeed, it can provide an opportunity for the entrepreneur to show his or her goodwill. All in all, sanctioning, so far as possible, should be seen as a positive experience.

Summary of key ideas

- *Leadership, power* and *motivation* are interrelated and interdependent tools which the entrepreneur can use to control the venture and give it direction.

- Leadership is the power to *focus* and *direct* the organisation. Entrepreneurial leadership is based on the communication of *vision*.

- Power is the ability to influence the *course of actions* within the organisation. Power is based on the control of *resources* and the *symbolic* dimensions of the organisation, particularly the vision which drives it.

- Motivation is the ability to *encourage* an individual to take a particular course of action. Motivation is based upon an understanding of drives and the ability to reward effort.

Suggestions for further reading

Boyce, M.E. (1996) "Organisational story and storytelling: A critical review", *Journal of Organisational Change Management*, Vol. 9, No. 5, pp. 5–26.

Cropanzano, R., James, K. and **Citera, M.** (1992) "A goal hierarchy model of personality, motivation and leadership", *Research in Organisational Behavior*, Vol. 15, pp. 267–322.

Hamilton, R. (1987) "Motivations and aspirations of business founders", *International Small Business Journal*, Vol. 6, No. 1, pp. 70–8.

Hofstede, G. (1980) "Motivation, leadership and organisation: Do American theories apply abroad?", *Organisational Dynamics*, Summer, pp. 42–63.

Kuratko, D.F., Hornsby, J.S. and **Naffziger, D.W.** (1997) "An examination of owner's goals in sustaining entrepreneurship", *Journal of Small Business Management*, Jan, pp. 24–33.

Peters, T. and **Waterman, Jr., R.H.** (1982) *In Search of Excellence*, New York: Harper & Row.

Pfeffer, J. (1981) *Power in Organizations*, Cambridge, Massachusetts: Ballinger.

Van Seters, D.A. (1990) "The evolution of leadership theory", *Journal of Organisational Change Management*, Vol. 3, No. 3, pp. 29–45.

Tait, R. (1996) "The attributes of leadership", *Leadership and Organisational Development Journal*, Vol. 17, No. 1, pp. 27–31.

Taylor, B., Gilinsky, A., Hilmi, A., Hahn, D. and **Grab, U.** (1990) "Strategy and leadership in growth companies", *Long Range Planning*, Vol. 23, No. 3, pp. 66–75.

Zaleznik, A. (1977) "Leaders and managers: Are they different?", *Harvard Business Review*, May-June, pp 67–78.

24 Consolidating the venture

CHAPTER OVERVIEW

The entrepreneurial venture is characterised by growth, but at some stage growth slows and the venture becomes a mature organisation. This chapter is concerned with describing the process of consolidation, how the rules of success change and how some of the entrepreneurial vigour of the venture might be retained through intrapreneurship.

24.1 What consolidation means

KEY LEARNING OUTCOME
A recognition that maturity is accompanied by significant changes in the way the venture functions at a financial, strategic, structural and organisational level.

No business can grow forever. There must come a point at which its expansion slows. In the same way the entrepreneurial venture must *mature*. However, maturity is associated with more than a simple cessation of growth. As discussed in Chapter 20, the growth of a business is a complex and multi-faceted phenomenon. It has financial, strategic, structural and organisational dimensions. As the venture matures the slowing of growth is associated with a number of changes in each of these aspects of the organisation. Together these changes are referred to as *consolidation*.

At the *financial* level, consolidation means that turnover (and profits) begin to plateau out. Turnover should still increase, at a rate not less than the overall expansion of the economy in which the business operates (which would imply a contraction in real terms), and it is not unreasonable to set growth objectives above this. But, dramatic increases in turnover are not to be expected (unless, perhaps they are achieved through acquisitions). Growth in the assets supporting turnover will also slow to a similar level. New assets will tend to be a replacement for the depreciation of existing assets.

Consolidation means that *investment* in the growth of the business can be reduced. So it is at this point that financial backers will be looking for their returns. Shareholders will expect to receive a greater share of the profits and to see their dividends increase. Venture capitalists will look to exit and liquidate their investment.

Strategically, consolidation means that the venture has successfully defined its position in the market. The place it occupies in the industry value addition chain, the customer groups it serves and the technology it uses to serve will be *largely* established – only largely because there is always room for development of the strategic position through organic developments and acquisition. The business's attention will shift from aggressive strategies aimed at encroaching into competitors' territory to more defensive postures aimed at preventing competitors (including new entrepreneurial ones!) from taking business away.

In *structural* terms, consolidation means that the internal configuration of the business develops some permanence. During the growth phase organisational structures and the roles and responsibilities they define will tend to shift, merge and fragment as the business's complexity increases. Consolidation allows the venture to give key roles and responsibilities a longer-term definition. These roles and responsibilities will tend to be defined around the resource needs of the organisation with structures emerging to manage the acquisition of key inputs.

Alongside structural consolidation there will also be *organisational* consolidation. Growth means that the organisation's systems, procedures and operating practices must be in a state of constant flux. Maturity allows these systems to settle down into more permanent patterns of activity. Out of the complex interaction between the entrepreneur, the venture's stakeholders and the wider social world, the organisation's culture will take a final shape.

The prospects and rewards the business offers its employees will also change as it consolidates. Risks will be lowered and job security may be higher. The positions within the organisation will be better defined and career pathways will become more predictable. Change will be at a slower pace. On the other hand, some may miss the challenge that comes from managing rapid growth, including the day-to-day changes this brings and the excitement of not knowing, exactly, what the future might bring.

24.2 Building success into consolidation

KEY LEARNING OUTCOME
An appreciation of how the rules of success change as the venture matures.

The rules of success change as the entrepreneurial venture consolidates. The business becomes less concerned with making rapid strides forward and more concerned with progressing in a measured and sure-footed way. Success is measured not so much by what might be achieved tomorrow but by what is being achieved today. This is not to say that the mature business can afford to forget about the future. Far from it. All businesses must plan for an uncertain tomorrow and invest accordingly. It is to suggest, however, that the balance of interest shifts from the possibility of long-term returns towards the reality of short-term rewards.

In Section 8.1 the success of the venture was defined in terms of the *stakeholders* with an interest in it, their *needs* and their *expectations* of what it will offer them. This framework provides an insight into how the terms of success change as the venture consolidates.

For investors, the main shift in their expectations is in relation to the risks and returns offered by the venture. After initiation, and while it is growing strongly, the entrepreneurial venture is offering the prospect of high returns for the investor at some point in the future. Returns cannot be offered immediately because any profits generated will need to be ploughed back into the business. In any case, profits are often low during growth. This is certainly the case if a cost leadership strategy is being pursued (as described in Section 18.3. The future is uncertain: profits promised in the future carry a higher risk than those on offer today. The plan for the venture must be based on assumptions. Risk enters the equation because there must be some doubt about the validity of those assumptions.

Investors accept risk if the future returns, properly discounted, are attractive enough. There will come a point, however, when they will want to see those returns. Many investors hold a *portfolio* of investments. This portfolio mixes investments which are currently net generators of money (and are therefore low risk) with those demanding money on the basis of future return (high risk). The entrepreneurial venture starts as a high-risk absorber of capital. If it is to remain in the investor's portfolio long-term it must eventually move to be a lower-risk generator of capital (*see* Fig. 24.1).

From the perspective of the investor, the success of the venture stops being measured in terms of the way it is growing its sales and assets and establishing its position in its marketplace to the short-term return it is generating on the (investor's) capital it is using. The key measures of performance become the *profit margin* and *return on capital employed*.

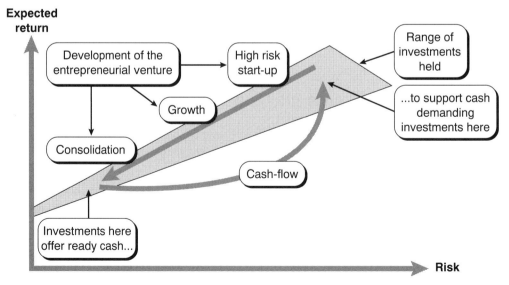

Fig. 24.1 The changing position of the entrepreneurial venture in the investor's portfolio

Stakeholders other than investors also share in the risks taken on by the entrepreneurial venture. Employees who make a contribution to the venture in its early stages are called upon to make a special effort. The demands will be high. Roles and responsibilities may be poorly defined. Job security will be low. The immediate financial rewards may be less than can be obtained elsewhere. In return for this commitment employees will, in general, expect an increase in remuneration, a well-defined role and an improvement in job security as the venture consolidates.

While the financial and security rewards of the entrepreneurial venture may be more limited than those offered by the established business, working with a fast-growing and dynamic organisation brings its own rewards at the social and personal development level. Some may perceive a loss in the way the organisation can satisfy these needs, as it consolidates. To such people, the venture's consolidation may signal an end to the sense of personal success it promises. They may feel it is time to move on to new entrepreneurial pastures.

Suppliers and customers may also have offered a commitment to the venture in its early stages. The turnover of the business will have been quite low. Many suppliers may nonetheless, have made a commitment to supplying it with a high level of customer service even though it may have cost more in real terms than they got back. Customers may have taken on the business as a supplier even though switching costs had to be faced and continuity of supply was not assured. Such suppliers and customers will see the venture as successful if it returns this early commitment by operating within the business network as a fair, effective and rewarding customer/supplier itself.

24.3 Encouraging intrapreneurism

KEY LEARNING OUTCOME
An appreciation of the potential and limits to intrapreneurship in the consolidating organisation.

In recognising the power of the entrepreneurial organisation, it is important not to be too dismissive of what the established 'non-entrepreneurial' organisation has to offer its stakeholders. After all, an established business is only established because it has enjoyed success. The entrepreneurial organisation and the established organisation both have advantages. The entrepreneurial shows an acceptance of (even a need for) change and an ability to exploit new opportunity. The established demonstrates an ability to consolidate around success, manage risk and control resource flows.

A combination of the two, that is an organisation which recognised the basis of its success and was able to manage it to reduce risk and yet at the same time was flexible to the shifting needs of its stakeholders, remained attuned to new market opportunities and responsive to the need for change, would suggest itself as an ideal type of business. The *intrapreneur* provides a means of achieving the established-entrepreneurial synthesis. The intrapreneur is a role defined by Gifford Pinchot in his book, *Intrapreneuring*. In essence, the intrapreneur is an entrepreneur who works within the confines of an established organisation. The intrapreneur's role would parallel that of the entrepreneur. In particular they would be responsible for developing and communicating organisational vision; identifying new opportunities for the organisation; generating innovative strategic options; creating and offering an organisation-wide perspective; facilitating and encouraging change within the organisation; challenging existing ways of doing things; and breaking down bureaucratic inertia. This role has also been described as that of a 'change master' (Kanter, 1985).

Intrapreneurism offers an exciting option for the consolidating entrepreneurial venture. It promises a way to build on success while retaining the original dynamism of the venture. It suggests a way to reduce risk while still pursuing fleeting opportunities. However, any organisational form which promises such high rewards must also present some challenges. There are limitations to intrapreneurship.

Entrepreneur's comfort

Allowing a role for the intrapreneur to develop demands that the entrepreneur actually create space for the intrapreneur to operate. That means letting go of some degree of control. The entrepreneur, having brought the organisation to where it is by exerting control, may not feel comfortable with this. In effect, allowing the intrapreneur to operate means that the entrepreneur must share a part of his or her own role at a core rather than a peripheral level.

Decision-making control

Entrepreneurs exist to challenge orthodoxies. They seek a better way of doing things. They must be dissatisfied with the *status quo*. This same dissatisfaction must also motivate the intrapreneur. Unlike the entrepreneur, however, the intrapreneur must operate within some sort of organisational decision-making control. If they were not, then they wouldn't actually be working for the organisation at all! The question here is to what extent the intrapreneur can be allowed to challenge existing decision-making procedures and to what extent they must be bound by them. A balance must be created between allowing the intrapreneur freedom to make their own moves and the need to keep the business on a constant strategic path.

Internal politics

The intrapreneur must question the existing order and drive change within the organisation. For many individuals and groups within the organisation such change will present a challenge. As a result the intrapreneur is likely to meet resistance, both active and passive, to the ideas they bring along. An ability to predict and understand that resistance, and developing the leadership skills necessary to overcome it, presents a considerable challenge to the manager. Intrapreneurs are a rare breed. Tom Peters has suggested that intrapreneurs must be able to 'thrive on chaos'.

Rewards for the intrapreneur

This point really results from the latter. The intrapreneur, if he or she is to be effective, must bring along the same type, and level, of skills that entrepreneurs themselves offer.

The question is, can the organisation *really* offer the intrapreneur the rewards (economic, social and developmental) they might come to expect in return for using them? In short, if someone is an effective intrapreneur how long will it be before the temptation of full-blown entrepreneurship is felt and he or she moves off to start a venture of his or her own?

Clearly intrapreneurship presents itself as a spectrum which, as a style of management, acts to connect 'conventional' management with entrepreneurial management. It offers a way to bring the advantages of both types of management together. In this it is a compromise. The entrepreneur can only facilitate intrapreneurship within the business by recognising the nature of this compromise and making decisions in relation to it. The central question relates to how much latitude the venture's strategy gives individuals to make their own decisions. The question is not just strategic. An entrepreneur must decide to what extent he or she will be willing to accept dissent from the intrapreneur. Will it be received as a challenge? How does active dissent fit with the leadership strategy the entrepreneur has nurtured?

Entrepreneurs must also ask how the reward structure they have set up encourages and discourages individual decision making. What does the individual get in return for venturing on behalf of the business? What sanctions come into force if things go wrong? The entrepreneur must remember that such rewards and sanctions are not always formal and explicit. Further, the entrepreneur must recognise the level of resistance that agents driving change meet from the organisation and accept responsibility in helping the intrapreneur to overcome this. No less than any other member of the organisation, the intrapreneur needs support, encouragement and leadership.

Summary of key ideas

- As the venture matures, its rate of growth slows. This process is known as *consolidation*.

- Consolidation involves changes to the *financial*, *strategic*, *structural* and *organisational* dynamics of the venture.

- Consolidation offers the venture a chance to create a defendable competitive position in the marketplace. This offers the promise of rewarding the commitment stakeholders have shown towards the venture.

- *Intrapreneursim* is a form of management which, potentially, offers the venture a way of combining the flexibility and responsiveness of the entrepreneurial with the market power and reduced risk of the established organisation.

Suggestions for further reading

Kanter, R.M. (1985) *The Change Masters*, London: Unwin Hyman.

Osborne, R.L. (1991) "The dark side of the entrepreneur", *Long Range Planning*, Vol 24, No. 3, pp. 26–31.

Osborne, R.L. (1992) "Building an innovative organisation", *Long Range Planning*, Vol. 25, No. 6, pp. 56–62.

Peters, T. (1989) *Thriving on Chaos*, London: Macmillan.

Pinchot, III, G. (1985) *Intrapreneuring*, New York: Harper & Row.

Stopford, J.M. (1994) "Creating corporate entrepreneurship", *Strategic Management Journal*, Vol. 15, pp. 521–36.

Vrakking, W.J. (1990) "The innovative organization", *Long Range Planning*, Vol. 23, No. 2, pp. 94–102.

Weseley Morse, C. (1986) "The delusion of intrapreneurship", *Long Range Planning*, Vol. 19, No. 6, pp. 92–5.

The changing role of the entrepreneur in the consolidated organisation

CHAPTER OVERVIEW

This chapter is concerned with an exploration of the way in which the entrepreneur's role changes as the organisation's rate of growth slows and it consolidates its position in the marketplace. The role of the entrepreneur is compared and contrasted to that of the Chief Executive. It is considered why, despite its many strengths, entrepreneurial control may not always be right for the mature venture. The chapter concludes with a consideration of the responsibility of the entrepreneur in planning for passing on control to others after they have departed the organisation.

25.1 The entrepreneur *versus* the Chief Executive

KEY LEARNING OUTCOME
An appreciation of the differences between the roles of the entrepreneur and the Chief Executive Officer.

The vast majority of organisations offer a role for a single, most senior manager. This position has a number of titles. In for-profit businesses it is often the *managing director* or *president*. Generically, the role is referred to as the *Chief Executive Officer* (CEO). while all organisations have a Chief Executive Officer of some description, not all are led by someone we would recognise as an entrepreneur.

So while the entrepreneur *may* be a chief executive officer, the Chief Executive Officer is not *necessarily* an entrepreneur. Clearly, both roles present considerable management challenges. Both demand vision, an ability to develop strategic insights and provide leadership. That said, the two roles are distinct in a number of ways.

Internal co-ordination *versus* external promotion

The resource-based view of the organisation presented in Section 20.6 emphasises the role managers have in bringing in the resources that are critical to the success of the venture: capital, information, people and the goodwill of customers. The entrepreneur, especially when the venture is at an early stage and has limited management resources, will take on the responsibility for bringing in nearly all of these things. They will be the venture's salesperson, its finance expert, its recruitment specialist and so on.

The Chief Executive of even a moderately large organisation will not have direct responsibility for doing these things. He or she may not even have responsibility for *delegating* them, at least directly. What they will have responsibility for is setting up *management structures* within the organisation which will enable these tasks to be co-ordinated and carried out in a way that is effective and is responsive to the overall strategic direction chosen by the business. They may also recognise a need to manage the organisation's *culture*. The Chief Executive is not, primarily, responsible for acquiring resources so much as making sure that those which are acquired are used in the best possible way.

In these terms, the entrepreneur provides a bridge between the small business manager and the chief executive of a large firm. In growing the venture, the entrapreneur transforms the role of acquiring resources into that of creating and maintaining structures to manage resources. The role changes from one of *external* promotion (that is, managing the venture in its wider *network*) to one of *internal* co-ordination.

Managing continuity *versus* driving change

As related in Section 2.1 entrepreneurs are interested in driving change. So are chief executives. In a fast-changing world organisations must change if they are to survive and prosper. The management of change is now properly recognised as one of the key responsibilities of senior management, whatever sector their organisation is operating in. Entrepreneurs and chief executives are both interested in changing their organisations in response to the opportunities presented to them.

However, there is a difference in the *degree* of change entrepreneurs wish to see and that which chief executives would normally wish to occur. Entrepreneurs are interested in *radical* change. The entrepreneur's vision is created out of a tension between 'what is' and 'what might be'. For that vision to be powerful, the difference between what is and what might be achieved must be great. Chief executives, on the other hand, are more likely to be interested in *incremental* change. This is understandable. After all, their organisations have proved their success, at least historically. They must be doing something right! Incremental change can build on that success: strengths are managed in, while weaknesses are managed out. Radical change threatens to throw away the strengths as well as address the weaknesses.

Management by 'right' *versus* management by appointment

The third feature that distinguishes entrepreneurs from chief executives is the basis on which they obtain authority to manage the business and the influence this has on the power base they develop. As noted in Section 23.3, *authority* and *power* are quite different things. Power is an ability to influence the course of actions within the organisation. Authority merely offers the potential to influence the organisation by virtue of a position within it. Authority is an *invitation* to power, not power itself.

Chief executives obtain their authority to run the business by virtue of appointment to the position. They may arrive at this position as a result of internal promotion or by being recruited into the organisation. The appointment process is governed by established organisational procedures. The views not only of internal managers but also of important investors may be sought. Once in this position, the power of the chief executive arises from the way they control resources and systems and the leadership they offer.

Entrepreneurs also gain authority from the position they occupy, their management of resources and systems, and the leadership they give to the organisation. However, an entrepreneur has an additional source of authority providing not only authority to run the business, but also a *right* to run it. While the chief executive is employed by the organisation, the organisation is perceived as 'belonging to' the entrepreneur. This perceived right can be derived from the entrepreneur's ownership of the business. However, owning the organisation they lead is not a necessary characteristic of the entrepreneur. The business is actually owned by those who invest in it. More important is the entrepreneur's historical relationship to founding the organisation and their association with *building* it up.

This difference is important not only for the way the entrepreneur actually manages the organisation but also for the way in which they are exposed as a result of its performance. While we would expect a chief executive to be ousted if the organisation

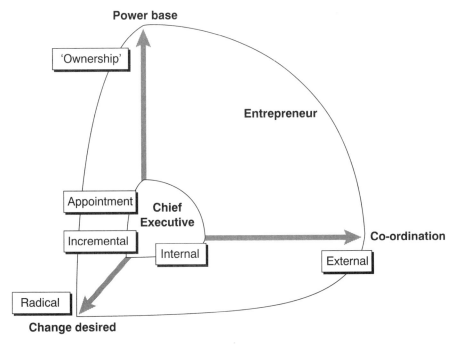

Fig. 25.1 The difference between an entrepreneur and a chief executive

he or she manages fails to perform, we can still be surprised when an entrepreneur who is seen to have created the organisation is greeted with the same fate.

Of course these three criteria do not create hard and fast categories. We are dealing with fuzzy concepts in the same way as we were when we discussed the distinction between the small business and the entrepreneurial venture in Section 1.6. Whom we regard as an entrepreneur and whom we see as 'merely' a chief executive is a matter of judgement based on a consideration of the balance between all three criteria.

As with the distinction between the small business manager and the entrepreneur, we should not rush to make a judgement as to who is, or is not, an entrepreneur. We should not look towards the individual to assess whether they are an entrepreneur or not, rather we should look at what and how they manage in terms of the balance between internal and external co-ordination, the change they seek to create and the way authority is ascribed to them, i.e. the basis of their power (*see* Fig. 25.1).

25.2 The dangers of entrepreneurial control in the mature organisation

KEY LEARNING OUTCOME
An appreciation of some of the limitations of an entrepreneurial style of management in the mature venture.

Entrepreneurial management has a lot to offer. The entrepreneur's vision offers the potential for leadership. That vision and leadership can be used to give the venture direction. It provides an impetus for the changes that are necessary if a venture is to survive and prosper in a rapidly changing world. However, as a *style* of management, entrepreneurship is merely one style among many, and while entrepreneurship is a very powerful style of management it, like any other style, has its limitations.

Entrepreneurial management is concerned with the *whole* organisation. In the early stages of the venture this allows the entrepreneur to manage the organisation in an integrated way. The entrepreneur can put balanced emphasis on attracting all the resources the organisation requires: money, people, customers, and knowledge. Unfortunately, this may lead the entrepreneur to underestimate the value of the management of particular functions. They may be quite dismissive of the need for a dedicated approach to marketing or finance or human resource management as the venture grows and matures. This can lead the entrepreneur to underestimate the contribution that specialists can make to the venture. Having made a success of the venture themselves they can become suspicious of the need for 'experts'. As a result, the entrepreneur may find it difficult to give specialist managers sufficient room to make the decisions they need to make.

Further, entrepreneurial management is concerned with driving change. This is a key and positive aspect of the entrepreneur's approach. It is only from change that new value can be created. However, it is often the case that the entrepreneur exhibits a greater desire for change than do other stakeholders. The entrepreneur may still be seeking new ways to push the venture forward while investors and employees seek consolidation and stability. As a result there may be a conflict over the type of investments undertaken by the mature venture. A number of high-profile run-ins occurred between highly successful entrepreneurs and institutional investors at the end of the 1980s in both America and the UK as the financial climate became more difficult. For example, both Anita and Gordon Roddick, founders of the *Body Shop* and Alan Sugar, founder of Amstrad, became involved in expensive share buy-backs to increase control of their enterprises.

This touches on a wider issue. All organisations develop an *inertia* or resistance to change. Entrepreneurs and the organisations they create are not immune to this. While the entrepreneurial organisation is founded on an innovation there is no guarantee that it will be innovative in its innovation! Often, the innovation sets a pattern of strategic activity which the venture attempts to repeat in another sector. The initial success may not always translate to other sectors. Alan Sugar and his *Amstrad* venture were phenomenally successful with a formula which presented uncomplicated, easy-to-use and low cost hi-fi systems to the general public. However, the same formula was not repeated so successfully with business computers, a sector where the customer buying criteria were quite different.

All in all, an entrepreneurial style of management has a great and valuable role to play in the mature organisation. However, it is essential that entrepreneurs recognise that the way they involve themselves with and apply their talents to the mature organisation differs from the way they did when the organisation was in a fast-growing state.

25.3 The role of the founding entrepreneur in the mature organisation

> **KEY LEARNING OUTCOME**
> **An appreciation of the types of role the entrepreneur can undertake in the mature organisation.**

The role of the entrepreneur must change as the venture develops. Growth offers founding entrepreneurs the same opportunity as it offers every other member of the organisation: the chance to develop and specialise the role they play within the organisation. Some of the more important types of specialisation are listed below (*see also* Fig. 25.2).

Chief executive

The most obvious role for the entrepreneur to play is that of chief executive. In this the entrepreneur has a clearly defined position at the head of the organisation. He or she retains the power to make and influence key decisions about the way the business

Fig. 25.2 The roles of the entrepreneur in the mature organisation

should be conducted. The chief executive role is, of course, one which the entrepreneur can drift into by virtue of always being at the head of the business. However, the points made in the previous section about the differences between the way the entrepreneur leads the growing business and the chief executive manages the mature business must be considered here.

Visionary leader

As discussed in Section 7.2 the entrepreneur has a variety of means at his or her disposal when it comes to influencing the direction the organisation takes and the way it manages its resources. Entrepreneurs do not have to direct every decision personally. They can use indirect means of communicating vision, directing strategy and controlling the organisation's culture. This means that the entrepreneur can specialise the role they play along the leadership dimension. By taking on the role of a visionary leader, the entrepreneur avoids making decisions personally. Rather they create an environment which brings out the best in the organisation's people by motivating them and giving them an overall sense of direction. This is the kind of role played by the *Virgin* chief, Richard Branson, who while providing leadership to his organisation leaves most of the decision making to his professional managers.

Manager of business development

Entrepreneurs sometimes find it difficult to let go of the entrepreneurial approach they have developed. They do not find the chief executive role a comfortable one. Yet they can still recognise the need for a consolidatory approach to the management of the mature venture. They may resolve this dilemma by concentrating on the development of new business, a task which is well suited to an entrepreneurial style. The entrepreneur then delegates management of the established business to another manager. If the business is made up of a number of independent business units then this arrangement can be made explicit. The entrepreneur can leave the running of the business units to their managers and can concentrate on making new acquisitions for example. On the other hand, if the business is a single coherent organisation then the arrangement may be more implicit and be based on internal delegation.

An example here might be Rupert Murdoch with his *News International* and *BSkyB* business ventures. While taking a very active interest in the established business, Murdoch is most active at the cutting edge of his growing empire.

Technical specialist

Sometimes the entrepreneur may decide to give up the chief executive position altogether and take on what, at face value, appears to be a subordinate role within the organisation. In this role they will specialise in some way, perhaps in managing product development or marketing. Though uncommon, this sometimes occurs in high-technology organisations which have been founded by technical experts. An example of this is Martin Woods, a physicist, who while based at the Cavendish Laboratories founded the successful *Oxford Instruments Company*, a major manufacturer of components for hospital scanners. Once the venture had passed the stage where product innovation was the most important thing, and marketing and financial management became of greater importance, Dr Woods passed on the day-to-day running of the company to marketing and finance professionals and moved back to the laboratory as the company's research and development director.

Promoter of the venture

The entrepreneurial venture must continue to attract the support of external stakeholders, not least customers and financial backers. The entrepreneur may take on the role of figure head and work at promoting the organisation to these stakeholders. An important example of this kind of approach is that of Anita and Gordon Roddick and the *Body Shop* organisation. The conventional chief executive role is largely played by Gordon while Anita Roddick represents the organisation in the media, promotes it to existing and new franchise holders and seeks out new ingredient suppliers in the developing world.

Entrepreneur in an alternative venture

Entrepreneurs can, of course, decide that the consolidated organisation has little to offer them. They may decide to liquidate their holding and use the resources to start another venture. This is precisely what Howard Hodgeson of *Hodgeson Holdings* and James Dyson of *Dyson Appliances* have done.

25.4 Succession in the entrepreneurial business

KEY LEARNING OUTCOME

A recognition of the importance of managing leadership succession when the entrepreneur leaves the venture.

The average life of a business is probably about the same as the working life of a manager. However, this average can be misleading. It includes a lot of businesses which only last a few years. The successful entrepreneurial venture should be expected to last a lot longer than the career span of the founding entrepreneur. This longevity raises the issue of *succession*.

Succession creates a number of issues for the venture. Even though the business has an existence independent of the entrepreneur, the entrepreneur is more than an 'optional extra'. He or she is an integral part of the organisation. The loss of the entrepreneur represents the loss of one of its key resources. The entrepreneur must be replaced. How the entrepreneur is to be replaced, by whom, when, and in what way, represent critical decision areas for the business.

The need for continuity ...

All organisations need some continuity. The entrepreneur, especially if they are a motivating leader, offers a reference point about which the organisation can cohere. After the entrepreneur has gone that coherence may be lost. As a result the business risks losing focus and direction.

... and for change

On the other hand, all organisations must recognise the need for change in response to a rapidly changing environment. Founding entrepreneurs, while they may be effective managers of subsequent change, may also impart an inertia to the business which makes some changes difficult. Bringing a new leader presents an opportunity which, if used properly, offers the chance to effect necessary and beneficial changes in the way the business is run.

Choosing a successor

Change at the top is a contingency which may be planned for. The entrepreneur may not like to think in terms of ending their relationship with the venture but they owe it to all the other stakeholders to consider the possibility and prepare for it. A major part of this is identifying a successor. It is important here for the entrepreneur to recognise the opportunity for change. The business will have moved a long way from its foundation. The characteristics the entrepreneur originally brought to the venture may not be the same ones it needs from a chief executive now. In choosing a successor, the entrepreneur must look for someone who is right for the business, not someone who is a copy of themselves.

The entrepreneur should also look for advice in choosing a successor. The opinions of other managers and key outsiders (particularly investors) may be valuable and influential. A successor may be sought within the business or they may be brought from outside. There are a number of key questions that must be asked about any candidate for succession.

- Do they have the necessary technical knowledge of the business sector?
- Do they have the right business skills?
- Do they have the ability to manage and develop the relationships the entrepreneur has established?
- Do they have an ability to lead the business?
- How will the leadership style offered compare with that of the outgoing entrepreneur?
- Do they have the ability to take on the entrepreneur's vision and continue to communicate it?
- Do they have the ability to provide a sense of continuity?
- Yet are they also capable of offering a new perspective?
- Will they be acceptable to all the stakeholders in the venture?

Mentoring

The entrepreneur may be replaced as the head of the business. However, this is only a transfer of title. Being made the new chief executive only offers a promise of *authority*, that is the potential to create change, not *power* which is an ability to create change. (Consider the points made in Section 23.3). Exercising power demands not only a position but also influence over the organisation's resources. This means not just tangible resources, but also the intangibles of generating vision and control of the symbolic dimensions of organisational life.

Mentoring may offer a means by which these things may be transferred. The entrepreneur selects a successor well ahead of the time when succession actually need take place and the successor is then trained to take over. This process involves the transfer of knowledge, education and support and a passing on of power. The successor is made *visible* as a successor. The organisation is made to recognise the successor as its future leader. The entrepreneur educates his or her successor not only in the details of the business, but also in terms of how it may be led and controlled. The actual transfer of power may be gradual with the successor given responsibility for distinct aspects of the business over time.

Remember the business

Choosing a successor is not easy. It demands that the entrepreneur admit to being mortal. It may also be tempting for the entrepreneur to favour a relative as successor. While the offspring of entrepreneurs often show great business acumen and leadership ability, there is no reason why they *must* do so. Entrepreneurship is learnt, not inherited! Keeping a business within the family may be appropriate (especially if it is privately owned). However, the entrepreneur has a responsibility to *all* the organisation's stakeholders. The entrepreneur should always remember the business and select a successor who is able to manage it as effectively as they themselves could.

Succession is an important issue and it is one which good entrepreneurs address openly, rationally and honestly. Successful entrepreneurs build entire new worlds. There is no reason why that new world should not continue after they have left it. The businesses they leave are testaments to the differences they have made.

Good luck in making the difference you want to!

Summary of key ideas

- The roles of the entrepreneur and the chief executive are subtly different, although they overlap in many ways. The entrepreneur is more interested in creating change, and may be more willing to take risks than the role of chief executive properly calls for. This can expose the mature venture to unnecessary risk.

- Consolidation gives entrepreneurs an opportunity to specialise their roles within their organisations.

- Effective entrepreneurs manage the process of *succession* (the handing over of power within the venture) when it is time for them to move on.

Suggestions for further reading

Gabarro, J.J. (1985) "When a new manager takes charge", *Harvard Business Review*, May-June, pp. 110–23.

Pearson, G.J. (1989) "Promoting entrepreneurship in large companies", *Long Range Planning*, Vol. 22, No. 3, pp. 87–97.

Slatter, S., **Ransley, R.** and **Woods, E.** (1988) "USM chief executives: Do they fit the entrepreneurial stereotype?", *International Small Business Journal*, Vol. 6. No. 3, pp. 10–23.

Wills, G. (1992) "Enabling managerial growth and ownership succession", *Management Decision*, Vol. 30, No. 1, pp. 10–26.

Appendix – selected case material*

Case study	Theme of article
A man of audacity: a profile of Robert Holmes à Court, *Financial Times*, 8 May 1985, Western Australia Special V	The individual entrepreneur (Chapter 3)
Easing into independence, *Financial Times*, 14 May 1985	Making the move into entrepreneurship (Chapter 4)
Rise and rise of Telesis, *Financial Times*, 12 May 1985	The nature of business opportunity (Chapter 5)
Venturing in and out of a 'golden triangle' *and* Rationale of a partnership, *Financial Times*, 11 August 1987 Collapse in Micro Focus profits brings over 50% fall in shares, *Financial Times*, 17 May 1989	Resources in the entrepreneurial venture (Chapter 6)
A dream they never sold, *Financial Times*, 9 June 1986	The meaning of success (Chapter 8)
Men with a mission, *Financial Times*, 10 May 1993	Entrepreneurial mission (Chapter 13)
Glen Dimplex: rising to market adversity *and* Melding pieces of an industry, *Financial Times*, 20 June 1986	The strategic window (Chapter 13)
Word spreads of a profitable niche, *Financial Times*, 10 December 1987	Locating the strategic window (Chapter 15)
James Meade puts his shirt on mail order, *Financial Times*, 7 May 1985	Opening the strategic window (Chapter 17)
No reflection of Nordic altruism *and* SAS aims to beat objections with 'iron-clad' case, *Financial Times*, 9 December 1987	Sustaining competitive advantage (Chapter 18)
The painful and costly process of growing bigger, *Financial Times*, 20 May 1985	The dimensions of business growth (Chapter 20)
Why Sony has to find a solution to the complexity of world markets, *Financial Times*, 4 December 1987	Strategies for expansion (Chapter 21)
Finding growth in a contracting market, *Financial Times*, 23 June 1986	Leadership, power and motivation in the growing organisation (Chapter 23)
Now Conran's magic misses its first trick, *Financial Times*, 12 June 1986	Sustaining success (Chapter 24)
The family spirit, *Weekend Financial Times*, 18 May 1985	Succession in the entrepreneurial business (Chapter 25)

*Note that these articles have been drawn principally from the mid to late 1980s when there was a considerable volume of contemporary media comment on entrepreneurship.

All articles published by permission of the *Financial Times*, © The Financial Times Ltd., 1985–93.

A man of audacity

Profile: Robert Holmes à Court

8 May 1985

LAUGHTER echoed around the panelled walls of the City brokers' dining room, when it was suggested that an unknown Australian businessman would win control of a British media group.

Mr Robert Holmes à Court's assault on Associated Communications Corporation nevertheless came off.

Today, he runs a world-wide group of companies from a modest Perth office. They have annual sales of at least A$500m, have consistently improved profits for many years, and the extent of his audacity is still to be tested.

He is not the typical Okker pirate who is the stuff of Fleet Street mythology.

His inevitable grey suit, quiet manner and infinite courtesy belie his reputation for ruthlessness, for the unexpected attack.

His current attention is directed at confirming a strong bridgehead in the U.S. mineral group, Asarco, mainly because of its holding in the Australian company, M.I.M. Holdings

Mr Holmes à Court enjoys the struggle, and the American taste for litigation is entirely to his taste (there have already been a series of court hearings over the Asarco holding).

It is only one area where expansion is considered. He still has long-term ambitions to have a major influence on Australia's biggest company, BHP, in which he has a major holding (that is, considering its wide spread of shares).

His interests range from the media operations of ACC, including films and TV, to a newspaper and TV group in Australia, earth-moving, oil, gas and minerals and many other smaller operations.

Yet he is best known for his many and spectacular takeover bids, some of which have succeeded, but others have "failed", leaving him big profits by quitting the substantial holdings he has built up. He is sensitive to the claim that the bids are made only for this latter purposes – all begin as a serious attempt to gain control, he says.

As a young man who began to build his empire with a small textile mill (which he still owns) in a West Australian country town, he quickly showed a brilliance in financial analysis which is the key to recent successes; the ability to see basic strengths in a company shunned by the markets, (ACC was a prime example).

His legal training offered no clue to his financial skills which, he says, take no esoteric shape – it is all just hard work, using conventional financial principles.

And work he does, 18 hours a day, with the ability to concentrate single-mindedly on a problem. Small-talk plays no part in his conversation, though he has a surprising sense of humour, and a relish for financial gossip.

He enjoys telling stories against himself. An example: soon after he acquired control of ACC, he attended a Hollywood party, still in a grey business suit, bizarre in that setting. A local producer who knew Mr Holmes à Court, noted his singular appearance as an outsider and said to him "You look like ET."

At home, with a charming Perth-born wife and three children, he is rarely off the phone. But he does have some diversions, those one would expect with his wealth –

thorough-bred studs (reputedly worth A$15m), and a fine art collection (he employs his own curator).

Last year he was in London when one of his horses won Australia's richest and most famous race, the Melbourne cup.

His wife Janet woke him with the news, which he took with great calmness.

For even his associates, Robert Holmes à Court remains an enigma, never showing any more than the most proper level of emotion, never revealing a vice or foible. However, they are united in their awe of his powers of logic, his ability to think laterally, and come up with an expected solution to a problem.

Yet his daring is matched, he claims, by great caution – "I never take a step unless I know there is an alternative available to me if I need it."

He regards most of Australia's more rakish businessmen with distaste, and in fact also remains largely aloof from the local establishment.

A piquant touch is provided by the contrast between his patrician manner (his forebears were the Heytesburys, and one of his studs, and his family company have the name) and his insistence that he is a true Australian. He resents any suggestion of a remaining association with Zimbabwe, where he was a child, or South Africa, where he had his early education.

The single-minded, hardworking enigma may be Australian, but his ambitions are wider.

There is less laughter now when he begins one of his international incursions.

Easing into independence

14 May 1985

Transfer of technologies from the laboratory bench to the market place has become an important issue worldwide as industrial observers recognise the economic value of small science-based companies.

Such transfers, however, can often be difficult because banks are unwilling to back them until they are well on the way to commercial success. One way to get round that problem is through what is known as the "soft company" model, whereby a researcher employed by an existing business, or an academic, develops a project in his spare time, until he is ready for independence.

Scores of small U.S. technology groups, like SRI International, a consultancy firm, or Teknowledge in artificial intelligence, have grown up along these lines, but this pattern has only recently become established on any scale in the UK. Such entrepreneurs – the founders of the two U.S. groups both came from Stanford University – generally start by doing occasional work tailored to specific customers' requirements, operating from their own homes or university premises, before striking out into wider markets to become "hard" companies.

In the UK, Cambridge has come to provide a fertile breeding ground for "soft" companies because of its special blend of good technical ideas which flow from the university, a flexible attitude on the part of university authorities, and a network of small subcontractors able to service the needs of researchers on the business trail. A group of about 300 small high technology companies formed in the region over the past five years, provides a classic example of the soft company model. Founded by Dr Philip Gaffney, a geophysics graduate employed as a research fellow by Churchill College, it has turned over £70 000 in the past 10 months without having to tap any external sources of finance.

During his time as a student, Gaffney hit upon image analysers as a promising technology that could be exploited commercially. Image analysing equipment allows pictures from a television camera to be converted into digital codes and interpreted by a computer.

A host of applications for the equipment has emerged in recent years. In industry, image analysers can be hooked up to robots so that the machines "see" objects in front of them and so know, for instance, which way to pick up an object. They can be used in hospitals and drugs laboratories, in the automated analysis of particles like blood cells or chromosomes, and in food factories, where the equipment can save human labour by inspecting products such as chocolates for defects.

There are also uses in security – keeping track of intruders through analysis of television scans – and in printing, where image analysers can keep a continual check on quality.

Although many big electronics companies sell such devices, Gaffney realised there could be a niche for a small enterprise selling customised products to university research laboratories, which needed the hardware for specific but limited applications.

Together with Jane Aldridge, another Cambridge graduate (who has a full-time job with another company in the town) he set up Seescan and rented a small office in the back streets of Cambridge 18 months ago.

Gaffney would have found it much harder to get off the ground had it not been for the liberal attitude taken by his college authorities. While still working on his PhD, he designed and built his first analyser, selling it for £5 000 to Cambridge University's engineering department. He kept his costs to a minimum by using his college's laboratory facilities to construct and demonstrate his product.

For a while, Gaffney wrestled with selling different types of systems which were largely built to different clients' special requirements. He sold about 20 systems, at prices varying between £680 and £10 000 to customers like hospitals and research departments of universities. All the equipment was built by hand by Gaffney and his one employee, Katherine Taylor, former technician at Cambridge's Addenbrookes Hospital.

Last summer, Seescan's transformation from a "soft" to a "hard" venture began. It was becoming impractical to go on building equipment by hand, given the growing volume of orders. Gaffney realised he had to start putting production on a more formal basis.

As the small electronic equipment companies in Cambridge have grown, an array of even smaller subcontractors in areas such as printed-circuit board assembly and metal working has arisen to do much of the production work for these enterprises. Gaffney was fortunate in being able to tap the resources of these organisations, rather than face the costly and disruptive process of setting up his own production lines.

Seescan is now taking orders for two different types of analyser, a £3 500 device for applications such as factory robotics and a more sophisticated version, selling for about £19 000, that will process colour images. Gaffney is finding that companies, not just university researchers, are now interested in his products.

Ferranti, Plessey, the UK Atomic Energy Authority and the Central Electricity Generating Board are among the organisations that have expressed interest in the higher priced devices. Instrument suppliers are considering them for incorporation into existing products.

Having sold products worth £70 000, over the past ten months, Gaffney now has an order book worth £110 000. That should keep his small company busy until the end of the summer. Turnover for the first full year is a projected £200 000.

The company has been entirely funded by Gaffney and Aldridge, the co-founder, who between them have put £20 000 into the venture. Seescan has just taken on a third employee, Ed Fordham, another Cambridge graduate, and three more employees, all products of the university, should start in the summer, two of them on a temporary basis.

The evolution of the company is, of course, far from complete. Gaffney may find that he needs to gain extra sources of finance to fund his growth and to take on staff with specialist skills in areas like marketing. Those problems are in the future; for the moment, the important thing is that the hardening process has started.

Rise and rise of Telesis

12 May 1985

MORE IS likely to heard in the UK soon of Telesis, the Chelmsford, Massachusetts-based engineering design automation (EDA) company which has just set up a subsidiary in Windsor.

EDA, an extension of computer-aided design (CAD), is the description being applied in the electronics industry to all the on-screen work of deriving electrical schematics, laying out circuits, generating artwork for manufacturing processes and feeding instructions to production tools.

Telesis, which is barely three years old, raised its turnover to $30m last year and claims to have 40 per cent of the US market for printed circuit board (PCB) design systems that use stand-alone workstations.

Worldwide, it claims 25 per cent. So far it has steered clear of semiconductor chip design, where companies like Daisy, Valid and Mentor are battling it out. In board design in Europe, Racal Redac is the main competitor for Telesis, although several of the CAD majors offer systems.

The company was started by a group of CAD experts from Computervision who wanted to develop standalone systems for printed circuit board (PCB) design at a time when CV was mainly committed to the idea of a large computer shared by several workstations.

The Telesis approach is to supply software for particular purposes on appropriate standalone workstations that can be linked together over a local area network.

Thus, at the early stages of design the IBM personal computer offers sufficient power for engineers to create schematics of their circuits and to derive pin and net lists (the detailed listing of interconnected points in the circuit).

At prices from £15 000, Telesis believes such software/workstation packages can be put on the majority of design engineers' desks cost-effectively.

An important benefit is that the machine can be used for other jobs like report writing using word processing and for other engineering software.

Having established the basic design of his circuit, the engineer can download the information to the Telesis EDA 300 colour screen design workstation where processing-intensive tasks like placement of the components on the board and the physical routing of interconnections are carried out. In a typical network, several PCs might work in conjunction with one design workstation.

Where needed, a standalone analytical processor, the EDA 500 can be connected to the net to provide more power.

The board design software is "re-entrant" – which means that the designer can intervene at any point in the automatic processes carried by the computer.

There are no sizing restraints – grid size, conductor line widths and line spacings are all user-selectable in increments of 0.001 inch.

Choosing from a stored component library, the designer can use the placement software to arrange the components on the screen – repetitive re-arrangement is quick and easy with assistance from automatic placement algorithms and with the ability to move whole groups of components from one place to another.

There are a number of other aids. For example, all the shortest distance diagonal connection lines are automatically displayed, converging lines immediately indicating poor placement.

In addition, channel density across the board is shown in histogram form at the bottom of the screen, allowing areas of congestion to be identified quickly.

Routing of the conductors in up to 14 separate signal layers is automatic and levels of completion exceed 95 per cent. The remainder are dealt with manually.

At the same time, up to 16 design rules (spacings, widths, "no go" areas and so on) are automatically obeyed.

On completion, the connections finally established are automatically compared with the original schematic, eliminating manual checking.

Other software allows for the relatively straightforward two-dimensional mechanical design of the board.

Telesis has tackled the whole design process by keeping all the accumulated information in a relational database. This enables outputs to be provided for artwork plotting, bill of materials, assembly drawings, fabrication drawings and NC drilling tapes.

Recently the company announced a program that will carry out a thermal analysis of the board on the PC work-station at any stage of the design – the first such package to be marketed, it claims.

Many board failures are thermally-based and can now be discovered before manufacturing starts. To date, thermal tests of completed boards have usually been necessary.

Telesis has just landed two (unnamed) customers in the UK and Mr Patrick Regester, UK manager, expects to win business worth £2m in the first year.

Venturing in and out of a 'golden triangle'

11 August 1987

EUROPE'S only venture capital company operating on a transnational basis has made a promising start, according to Vladimir Mollof, its managing director. Less than two years after it was set up, the Geneva office of Baring Brothers Hambrecht and Quist (BBHQ) has already invested over £9m in 14 young, growing enterprises in eight countries.

Intended originally to serve the "golden triangle" between Frankfurt, Florence and Toulouse, the office has placed capital in four French, three Swiss, three Italian and one West German businesses. Outside the triangle single investments have been made in Spain, Scandinavia and the US.

Participation is just being negotiated in a fourth Swiss company, Comco of Lausanne, which through a smart card provides users of portable computers with two-way links to databases, electronic mail services and company hosts during trips abroad.

If two investments, in Switzerland and France, made by BBHQ before it branched out from London, are added, the Geneva office now manages 16 placements totalling more than $10m.

Mollof claims two singularities for BBHQ. It is the only private company advising venture capital investment funds which operates on a European scale (others work on a national basis) and its staff are managers, not bankers, accountants or lawyers. It is thus geared to offer business-oriented management advice with its investments.

BBHQ was formed in 1984 at the initiative of Baring Brothers, the London merchant bank, with Richard Onians as its chief executive. Its other partners are Hambrecht and Quist, one of the big US venture capital groups, and Orient Capital, a Japanese venture capital fund.

Currently able to call on $50m from its funds, by the end of June BBHQ had invested more than £26m in 45 concerns, almost two-thirds of them in Britain. In 17 cases start-up capital was provided for the formation of a business or the market launch of a product or service.

The diversity characterising the investments from the Geneva office is not only geographical. They vary from machine-tool manufacturers through makers of biotechnical equipment, healthcare, leisure, and communications to a small batch of financial services companies.

Five received start-up money, five businesses heading into profit required expansion capital to finance growth and four not yet profitable were given early stage injections to finance working capital needs.

Investments have ranged in size from just over £100 000 to nearly $2m. No limit is placed on the amount but it is always a minority holding. Three main criteria are applied:
● The business must have capable, well above average management;
● Its market segment must be of adequate size, show unusually high growth and offer the opportunity for international expansion;
● It should provide a product or service that has a competitive edge in added value.

Selection is fairly rigorous. Mollof estimates that the Geneva office will examine close to 300 proposals this year, about half of which come through direct applications or were identified by the Geneva office itself.

In Mollof's view BBHQ's European strategy is already working out. He believes that he sees more deals than if activity had been concentrated on one country. Companies looking for international expansion turn to the Geneva office, attracted by the international management expertise it can offer.

So far both the smallest and the biggest investments have gone to financial services concerns, the smallest into a venture capital management company in Spain and the largest to Arca, a merchant bank in Milan.

Three investments made earlier this year by BBHQ's Geneva office added to its industrial portfolio. ITS is a Swiss company building computerised health assessment centres. Metravib Instruments, a French company, makes vibration monitoring instruments for leak detection and materials analysis. Stama of West Germany is a family-owned machine tool manufacturer, mainly for the automotive industry.

It is too early to judge the profitability of BBHQ's European investments. None has yet been converted into stock exchange listings but Mollof envisages three or four next year and a whole series in 1989. According to Onians, BBHQ is looking for a return on investment "in excess of 25 per cent".

Rationale of a partnership

11 August 1987

HENRI NIJDAM is very lucid in explaining why he turned to BBHQ's Geneva office when looking for capital to expand his young, trade-publishing venture in France.

BBHQ has just taken a 5 per cent stake in Marketing Finance, his holding company, which went to the Paris unlisted bourse in May. The aim is for Groupe Strategies, its main subsidiary, to gain a listing on the Paris secondary market in 1989.

After a career in marketing with Colgate-Palmolive, the US household products group, and as European marketing director for Britain's United Biscuits, Nijdam, in 1984, bought for FFr 26m Strategies, the first trade publication in France to cover advertising, marketing and the media.

By 1986 the weekly had almost trebled turnover to FFr 91.5m (£9.2m) and started two regional editions. Nijdam also invested FFr 16.4m in starting Creation, a monthly advertising and design journal, and Marketing Mix, a magazine covering product and market sectors, market studies, distribution and communications. A further FFr 3.3m was spent on equipment.

Heavy indebtedness – and a three-week journalists' strike – left its mark on the 1986 accounts which showed a consolidated pre-tax loss of FFr 9m. Financial charges amounted to FFr 5m.

Following a capital restructuring which left Nijdam with 60 per cent of the holding company, Groupe Strategies expects to turn in net consolidated earnings of FFr 6m this year and of FFr 11m in 1988, when sales are scheduled to reach FFr 115m. The journal is now the market leader in France.

As well as its three main publications, the group issues a daily bulletin of French and foreign news items about advertising and marketing and publishes an agency directory, a dossier of advertising campaigns and a guide to marketing professionals. All this is complemented by an information service to advertising agencies.

France, Nijdam estimates, is 12 to 15 years behind the US and Britain in marketing and communications. There has been strong growth since the French government launched its privatisation campaign but Nijdam believes the potential for further expansion is big.

However, he needed to consolidate, reduce his borrowing costs and find new capital for expansion. He runs through the possibilities to explain why he ended up with BBHQ.

French publishing is a "paranoiac business", Nijdam believes, so it would be too dangerous to take private partners. French banks are "too political' and in any case it would not be healthy under French banking practices to use the same bank for short-term and long-term finance.

Taking a larger publishing group into partnership was an alternative but Nijdam judged this would better suit a business approaching the top of its growth curve and looking for synergy effects.

The stock market would have provided the best answer, but Strategies had not reached sufficient size. The line of argument led Nijdam to look for a source of risk capital, but here he made a distinction.

He was wary of taking capital from a "financially minded" venture company looking for quick returns and aiming to maximise added value. Such partners, he feared, would "either drop you or try to take control".

Trade publishing, Nijdam argued, called for a longer term approach and a more "business-oriented" venture capital partner. When his auditor told him about BBHQ Geneva, Nijdam felt he had found what he was looking for.

BBHQ's "Anglo-Saxon" management approach is easier to work with than the more "impassioned" management style of French venture capitalists "who feel forced to pretend that they know business inside out", Nijdam claims.

Having missed two earlier opportunities to buy up companies abroad, Nijdam also appreciates BBHQ's special interest in young businesses wanting to expand outside their own borders.

Collapse in Micro Focus profits brings over 50% fall in shares

17 May 1989

MICRO FOCUS, one of the stock market's favourite high-technology companies, surprised the City with news of a collapse in profits which led to a fall of more than 50 per cent to £45m in the group's stock market capitalisation.

The computer software company made just £721 000 pre-tax in 60 weeks to the end of January, against £2.8m in the previous 53 weeks. The stock market, which had expected profits above £4m, brought the shares to 325p, a fall of 420p.

Micro Focus, which is not paying a divi-dend, blamed its troubles on difficult trading conditions in the micro computer industry, particularly in the US.

Mr Tom Hartnett, the company's general manager in the US, has resigned.

Mr Brian Reynolds, group chairman, said: "The industry climate has changed … We have become more exposed to the risk of our customers experiencing trading problems."

Micro Focus was a pioneer in the development of COBOL, a computer language used by most business machines. Its most recent product – VS Cobol Workbench –

launched earlier this year, takes it into the market for supplying large mainframe computers for the first time.

Mr Reynolds said: "We believe the market potential of VS Cobol Workbench is many times that of earlier Micro Focus products."

The company sees subsidiaries of major US computer companies as its main competitors, both in the US and in its other main markets in the UK, continental Europe and Japan.

Other UK-based companies, notably Acorn Computer and ACT, have been forced to pull back from ventures in the US, but Micro Focus sees this as a vital market. Mr Reynolds said: "It is bigger than the rest. We have to be there."

The company has made an £833 000 provision for doubtful debts. It has also become "more conservative" in its accounting policy, deferring some of its US revenues to allow for delays in customer payments and bigger risks of defaults.

As a result, total gross revenues of £21.4m have been cut by £6m to £15.4m

net, which was still 75 per cent higher than 1983's £8.8m.

However, operating and development costs also rose strongly, from £5.7m to £13.2m, as the company expanded, increasing staff from 126 to 291.

Mr Reynolds said he expected to see the benefits of this expansion in 1985. "The group is well positioned to continue its market leadership into the current year."

Micro Focus, which has been one of the City's most favoured stocks since it joined

the USM in 1983, moved to the main market last year.

The company was largely blamed for the 9.8 fall in the FT Ordinary share index yesterday when the news led to a sell-off of high technology and electronic stocks.

The announcement seems bound to increase investors caution over computer-related companies. Earliest indications of an industry shakeout were seen in the US last year.

A dream they never sold

9 June 1986

AS RECENTLY as five years ago, Britain had a golden opportunity to lay the ground for a world-class industry in the fast-growing area of computerised design and manufacturing.

Having developed highly regarded products in computer-aided design and manufacturing (CAD/CAM), which is used both to design new products and program the tools to make them, British companies failed to organise effectively and to make inroads in selling in the US, which accounts for roughly half the world market in this technology.

As a result, in the past five years, four youthful British companies in CAD, all of them with promising products but short on marketing skills, have been purchased by much bigger US groups.

It was "like a marathon runner who sits down 10 minutes before the end," says Mr Charles Foundyller, president of Daratech, a Massachusetts consultancy.

Today, UK-owned companies are also-rans in the $5bn-a-year CAD/CAM business, which is growing at about 25 per cent a year and in which US enterprises account for some 70 per cent of sales. It is a particularly dispiriting example of Britain failing to turn good technical ideas into a commanding commercial position.

More than this, the tale illustrates the general problems in the UK of building up significant businesses based on the activities of small, technology-oriented companies. Such developments are widely thought to be crucial to Britain's future.

The CAD/CAM story starts in the early 1960s, Aerospace and car companies,

including Lockheed, Boeing and General Motors in the US, and Dassault in France, were among the early pioneers.

In Britain there were four early strands of activity. In 1968 Ferranti, which had built up expertise by using CAD, to design radar parts, started a division to sell CAD systems. Today the company is a minor player in the industry.

Also in 1968, ex-Plessey engineers set up Dorset-based Quest Automation, which sold CAD systems for electronics design. Quest made good progress for a while, but three years ago sold its CAD operations to Marconi after hitting financial problems.

A more fruitful activity began in 1965 when Racal, the UK electronics group, set up Racal Research (later Racal-Redac) to develop CAD expertise for printed circuit boards.

In charge of the Tewkesbury-based company was Mr Eric Wolfendale, who had worked on the technology while at Mullard's Southampton laboratories in the 1950s. Racal-Redac has built up to sales of £40m annually, four-fifths exported, and is the country's leading CAD/CAM supplier.

The UK's fourth, and most important, set of CAD developments was centred on Cambridge. In 1965 the university's computer laboratory started a CAD group, headed by Dr Charles Lang, a mathematician who had become interested in the technology during a spell at the Massachusetts Institute of Technology.

Cambridge University has been one of Britain's leading centres in computing skills since the Second World War. To ensure that more of these ideas permeated into industry,

the Wilson Government established the CAD Centre, a state-funded laboratory. It opened in 1969 on the outskirts of Cambridge.

The plan worked, up to point. More UK companies became acquainted with CAD/CAM ideas. But no large company was set up to sell the technology to industry.

Instead, a dozen or so small concerns, led by people either leaving the CAD Centre or the university's computer laboratory, were born.

All found it difficult to build up a commanding position in the industry, which, by the end of the 1970s, was already dominated by big US names such as Computervision, IBM, Calma, Applicon and Intergraph. In 1979, world sales of CAD/CAM were worth only about $300m, roughly a 16th of the total today, but, even then, US companies accounted for some 90 per cent of the market.

One of the few British companies which seemed to have the technical skills to dent this dominance was Shape Data, which four academics from Cambridge University, including Dr Lang, started in 1974. The four set up in business almost by accident, largely because their grants ran out.

None the less, Shape Data attracted worldwide attention by developing Romulus, a highly thought-of software product for visualising engineering items in three dimensions. Annual sales, however, took off slowly and by 1981 had only reached £500 000.

The company made no secret about preferring research to marketing. It ran itself as a form of co-operative, not appointing a managing director until 1983.

One man who thought he could beef up the business was Mr Wolfendale of Racal-Redac. Early in 1981, he told the ex-academics he would like to take them over.

After months of agonising, Dr Lang and his colleagues turned him down. So keen was Mr Wolfendale on the acquisition that next morning he turned up on the door step of Shape Data to make a last-ditch bid. Dr Lang nearly ran into Mr Wolfendale on his bicycle.

"We felt their dreams didn't coincide with ours," says Dr Lang. "We thought they might switch us round to other directions and make us conform."

Even now, Mr Wolfendale, who left Racal in 1982 and runs a research company in Cheltenham, is rueful.

Had the marriage between the academically-inclined Cambridge company and the more hard-nosed, market-oriented Racal subsidiary been consummated, an important precedent would have been set for combining UK forces in what was then the still fledgling business of CAD/CAM.

The big US companies did not take long to show their interest in the UK minnows. Later in 1981, Dr Lang and his colleagues sold their company for $2.5m to Evans and Sutherland of Salt Lake City, a computer-simulation company which had previously distributed Romulus in the US.

According to Dr Alan Grayer, one of Shape Data's founders, the group had no regrets about turning down Racal-Redac's advances. This is even though the chosen marriage did not turn out a success. Dr Grayer, Dr Lang and a third founder, Dr Ian Braid left Shape Data last year to form their own consultancy, Three Space. The fourth original partner, Peter Veenman, remains in charge of the company, now 90-strong, which retains its name but is fully integrated into the US operation.

Compeda, set up by the UK Government in 1977 to market products from the CAD Centre was also to fall prey to a big US concern. A subsidiary of the National Research Development Corporation (a government organisation now part of the British Technology Group), it encountered financial problems and was snapped up for about £1m in 1982 by Prime Computer.

The most spectacular rise of any British CAD company was that of Cambridge Interactive Systems (CIS), set up in 1977 by four ex-managers at the CAD Centre. After dabbling in computer graphics for TV commercials, the Cambridge company started in 1979 a inspired relationship with Hunting Engineering, the Ampthill-based defence contractor.

Out of a chance inquiry from Hunting for new CAD software that would be an advance on anything the US giants could offer came a set of computer programs called Medusa. "It was a humdinger of a product," enthuses Mr Norman Williams, CAD manager at Hunting.

Medusa was not only a hit with the Ampthill concern. In independent tests performed as recently as 1982, it outperformed comparable products from much bigger US companies such as Applicon, Intergraph and Calma.

CIS's annual sales started to quadruple each year, reaching £10m by 1983. This posed unexpected difficulties for the founders.

All were, in the words of Mr Tom Sancha, until last year the company's chairman, "programmers who had struck lucky. We could barely manage ourselves, let alone a growing company."

An effervescent character who studied computing at Cambridge University and lasted nine weeks in his first job with IBM because he disliked the regimentation, Mr Sancha recalls the early period at CIS: "Until Medusa, we had three idyllic years. We were a bunch of friends having lots of people drooling over us and saying how wonderful we were. Then we had a phenomenal success on our hands and life became a problem."

In 1980 CIS decided against setting up a separate subsidiary in the US to sell Medusa, instead concluding a hasty distribution agreement with Prime. Two years later, when the Cambridge company had fallen out with Prime, Mr Sancha and his colleagues attracted the attention of Computervision of the US.

The Massachusetts concern, which started in 1969 and dominated the early years of the CAD/CAM industry, operated in a different world from the Cambridge group. In 1981, it accounted for a full 30 per cent of the world market for CAD/CAM, with revenues that year of $271m of which $32m was profit.

Computervision's directors flew to England on Concorde, took the CIS partners out to dinner and made them an offer they could hardly refuse: cash and shares worth $35m, enough to make them rich beyond their wildest dreams. By early 1983 CIS had become a US subsidiary.

The fourth UK concern to fall into the hands of a big US company was Applied Research of Cambridge, started in 1969 by a group of Cambridge University architects to develop design software for construction and mapping. By last year it had grown to about 100 staff and annual sales of £9m. Last summer, McDonnell Douglas bought it for $12m, having distributed the UK enterprise's products in the US since 1981.

How did it all go wrong? Certainly not through shortage of ideas about rationalising the UK industry.

Before the Computervision takeover, Rediffusion and GFC Industrial Products had considered bids for CIS. And at Racal-Redac the indefatigable Mr Wolfendale had on several occasions tried to cement a relationship with the CAD Centre by acting as the laboratory's marketing outlet.

Software Sciences (later owned by BOC and today, a subsidiary of Thorn EMI) and Cambridge Consultants put in formal offers for the CAD Centre after the Government invited privatisation bids in 1976. The laboratory finally moved into the private sector seven years later. It is now run by an ICL-headed consortium and expects to turn in a profit for the first time this year on sales of about £8m.

As for the Government, it was only in 1982 that the Industry Department tried unsuccessfully to promote the merger of Racal-Redac, Ferranti, Quest and Compeda (the latter before becoming part of Prime Computer).

Two factors stand out from the story. No one – except perhaps Mr Wolfendale, whose efforts came to nothing – was able to convey with sufficient authority the economic logic for putting the smaller concerns together.

As Mr David Thomson, ex-chairman of Compeda who is now in the venture-capital industry, puts it: "The CAD companies were run by clever, individualistic people who didn't like losing their freedom. Life in Cambridge running these companies was quite agreeable. Who wanted to be involved in all the hassles of mergers?"

Second, apart from Racal-Redac (which set up its own US subsidiary early on) the UK CAD companies largely ducked out of the challenge of selling in the US. Instead, they preferred to sell via distributors over which they had no control (and which in two cases eventually bought them).

To sell in the US, says Mr Foundyller of Daratech, the consultants, "you have to expend energy. You have to kick some asses and take names." On this occasion, the UK had a weak kick and suffered extreme myopia in weighing up the opportunities.

Men with a mission

10 May 1993

On every desk at Dun & Bradstreet is inscribed a corporate prayer. "As the men and women who are The Dun & Bradstreet Corporation, we are a team – One Company, united through shared values" it begins, inciting the 56 000 employees to "strive relentlessly" and to "work to be the best".

In the 2 000 heel bars of the Minit Corporation around the world is a framed statement declaring that the company's mind is "positive, optimistic and determined". In the pockets of every Motorola worker is a laminated card bearing that company's mantra.

Corporate values have come out of the closet. In the last few years most big US organisations have felt the need to make a public statement about what they believe in, what they are about and where they are going.

The trend has now crossed the Atlantic. According to a report by Digital Corporation, some 80 per cent of British companies have put their values into words.

There is no standard form to these pronouncements. Some are just a line or two, others run to a small volume. Some take the shape of "mission" or "vision" statements, setting strategic goals for the business as a whole, while others lay down standards of behaviour of the people inside the organisation. But all are trying to capture the essence of the company: to find something that will tie a diverse group of people and interests to a single goal or set of values.

It is no surprise that these statements have recently caught on. As the old hierarchies within companies have toppled, employees have had to take more decisions for themselves. "If you flatten an organisation, people have nothing else to turn to when they make judgments," says John Humble, the management consultant who prepared the report for Digital. At the same time shareholders have increasingly demanded clear statements from companies justifying their existence.

The most common form of mission statement involves a description – usually spelt out in the annual report – of the company's aims. This can range from the banal to the baroque, and may include a statement of its values.

At one extreme is "Ikea's Business Idea", which simply states as its guiding principle: "We shall offer a wide range of home furnishing, items of good design and function, at prices so low, that the majority of people can afford to buy them." At the other extreme is the Body Shop which proclaims in giant type on the back of its annual report: "Make compassion, care, harmony and trust the foundation stones of business. Fall in love with new ideas."

Other companies state goals that reach beyond their actual business: J Sainsbury rather grandly talks not just of selling groceries but of "contributing to the public good and to the quality of life in the community".

When it comes to listing their values, the same ones appear again and again: most companies cite the need to care for people, customers, quality, competitiveness, innovation, the community and the environment. Yet not all statements are so fashion conscious, nor so bland. The Yorkshire conglomerate BBA unashamedly announces: "The Victorian work ethic is not an antique", and "grit and gumption are preferable to inertia and intellect".

But how worthwhile are these statements? Some seem so obvious as to be barely worth saying, while others are hard to say while keeping a straight face. Academic evidence from the US suggests that companies with a strong mission tend to have outperformed their competitors, but then those companies seem to be better managed generally. The mere existence of a statement of corporate values or of a mission appears to have little, if any, effect on a company's performance. The Digital survey shows that more than 60 per cent of value statements are not strictly adhered to by managers, let alone by the rest of the workforce.

This is an alarming finding, as a statement which is not being followed properly can be a liability. "If you bang on about a mission that is not believed, you are devaluing management," says Mike Jeans of consultants KPMG.

So how can companies make their statements work better? Philip Mellor from Dun & Bradstreet says the company's value statement is part of a broad programme of cultural change. To make the values stick, everyone is trained for five days every year and employees are rewarded on how well they live up to the values.

The Minit Corporation claims that its statement has been a success partly because it consulted 300 managers in 27 countries before the final draft was drawn up.

However, not everyone agrees that companies should have value statements at all. According to Andrew Campbell of Ashridge Strategic Management Centre, statements are really only helpful in companies that already live by them. They are an *aide memoire*, but not of much use in motivating people or in helping them change their behaviour.

A case in point is Marks and Spencer, which has grown a strong sense of corporate value without any formal statement. "We do not hand out principles like the 10 Commandments and say thou shalt abide by them," says a company spokesman.

Campbell argues that companies should initially limit themselves to the flattest statements of what they do, and perhaps what it wants to be. "But the 'I believe' stuff is very dangerous. If you write it, you'd better believe it," he warns.

No doubt BBA really does believe its philosophy of hard grind; whether all those companies that declare a belief in their people or in the environment live up to their words is another matter.

Glen Dimplex: rising to market adversity

20 June 1986

MARTIN NAUGHTON does not believe in flagpoles or doormen. Nor does he have much time for electronic calculators.

His aversions bear witness to his dislike and mistrust of all forms of corporate titivation. His attachment to the careworn slide rule which graces his desk is more a testament to his training as a hands-on mechanical engineer than any evidence of his slipping behind the times.

In their way these foibles have each contributed to the development of his private company, Glen Dimplex, based at Dunleer, in Co Louth, in the Irish Republic, into one of Europe's leading independent electrical appliance companies.

Starting with a modest £120 000 bankroll of mortgages, government support and bank loans, Naughton set up Glen Electric in Newry, Co Down, in 1973. The unpromising Northern Ireland location apart, he could not have chosen a worse time to start. The first energy shock was breaking and those prophets who noted his modest venture forecast disaster. A company established at that time solely to manufacture domestic electric oil-filled radiators in direct competition with Dimplex, which had the market to itself, was not expected to prosper.

The workforce had increased from 24 to 200 and sales had risen almost 30-fold to £2m by 1977 when Naughton made his first major advance. He paid cash to take Dimplex – which had crumpled in the recession – off the receiver's hands.

A raft of acquisitions followed, including the Dunleer works of AET, his now-defunct former employers Brunner, a leading name in French heating, Belling heating, FCF – a design and development subsidiary of GKN and Chilton, best known for shaver sockets.

Last year Burco Dean Appliances and the Blanella electric blanket business were absorbed, along with Morphy Richards, one of the best known small appliance brands in the UK. Sales this year are expected to be well over £100m from a huge range of products which includes toasters, fan heaters, catering equipment, cooker hobs, towel rails, fuel effect fires and an iron built to a 1936 design. A fifth of turnover comes from exports to 30 countries. All but 5 per cent of the company's products and components are made in-house.

Picking his way through the industry over the years, Naughton has developed a strong feel for the source of its difficulties and an insight which has played a large part in developing his management style.

● The electrical appliances business, he maintains, has been carved up, not by Far Eastern makers, but by high-cost producers in Europe. Naughton prides himself on his workmanlike, low-cost factories. "All 10 production centres are profitable in themselves," he says. Each individual product must also show a profit. "If not, we attack from an engineering base, cutting production costs. If this does not work we put prices up and leave it to the market and the consumer. If necessary we let the market kill it."

● UK manufacturers have fallen behind in product design, he says. Naughton hired a top designer at the outset – even before he had an accountant on the payroll. He now has about 100 design and R&D staff in the group and wants more, paying constant attention to even the most workaday of his products. His storage heaters, for example, were 24 inches wide 10 years ago. Now they stand 6 inches from the wall. Naughton himself was responsible for a sleek new convector heater which is £2 cheaper to produce than its older equivalent.

● Competitive pressures have stifled capital investment, Naughton claims. His philosophy has always been to spend on production.

This principle was most recently applied when the company was preparing its first new products for the Morphy Richards name. Naughton ordered his engineers to make no compromises. "Even if none of the old components could be used it did not matter … we go from scratch if necessary" he says. This leaves no slack for fripperies. "We don't have doormen or flagpoles outside."

● Remote, top-heavy, centralised management has also contributed to the decline of the industry. Naughton strives to run his group as a collection of small businesses, aiming to keep the workforce at each factory down to about 250–300, to allow local managers to keep in close contact with the workforce. The headquarters management team numbers five, including a secretary.

He and his deputy, Lochlann Quinn, consider they allow individual company managers a generous amount of room in which to operate. Once a month they "walk the land" attending each operating company's board meeting. Beyond that there are no formal committees or other meetings apart from contacts between the three-man main board and a once-a-year session when all senior management lock themselves away from the telephone, usually abroad, to draft a three-year strategy.

"We never pull the ownership strokes," promises Quinn. "The managing directors have enormous power. Our only demand is that they inform us of major decisions … and they must not surprise us."

Each company drafts its own annual budget for approval at headquarters. Over-ambition appears to be the main problem among operating company managers, and occasionally it has to be reined in.

Once complete, the budget is "absolutely sacrosanct". Then it is up to individual managers. "They have a very strong incentives scheme based on the bottom-line profit of their operation and control of working capital. A large part of their income depends on their controlling both," says Naughton, although money is not everything. "We also offer excitement and freedom to manage."

They are acutely aware of the responsibilities which go with the freedom, and some of their experiences have left a sour taste. Quinn is particularly bitter about walking into certain ailing businesses which still maintained "fat" overheads at head office. There, he recalls, the management policy appeared to be: "You can shaft the factory, but you can't shaft your mates."

At no stage has Naughton revealed what he paid for his acquisitions, but he is clearly a cautious man, not given to profligacy.

The subject of company finance takes on a fresh dimension when investment, overheads and acquisition cash come ultimately out of the executives' own pockets.

"Every Monday when we come in we know the cash basis of the company," says Quinn, who was hijacked in the early days from his job as head of the audit department at Arthur Andersen's Dublin office. "We keep up a three-month rolling forecast with the fourth month on a weekly basis. We always know if there are any little shocks up ahead of us."

The company also keeps in close contact with its Irish and City bankers, meeting them twice a year with formal presentations. "This is vital for our policy of responding quickly to acquisitions or calls for investment," Quinn declares. "They know as much about the business as we do. Some say they know too much."

As a private "cash-in-the-bank" company with no long-term debit, Glen Dimplex has a refreshingly straightforward approach to acquisitions. "One of the first questions asked is: 'Do I prefer to have £5m in that company or in my bank account?' Writing a cheque concentrates the mind," says Quinn.

Concentrating the mind is now clearly a vital element in management strategy. The empire has grown rapidly. It specialises in difficult niche markets which are often saturated if not declining, and, with the development of Morphy, it is moving off its base in heating into fashion-sensitive consumer products, such as kettles, which are increasingly the domain of large multinational groups like Philips and Allegheny International. Demands on its three-man main board and cheque-book are increasing.

However, more acquisitions seem irresistible. Even though the group is little known outside its sector, it is now one of the first stops for the troupes of merchant banking hawkers seeking buyers for private companies and unwanted appliance subsidiaries of quoted groups.

Naughton and Quinn still relish the thrill of doing a deal. "I feel a bit itchy now," Naughton admits. "I think we need to look at the next step." Already discussing joint ventures in heating elements in West Germany, Spain and Italy, he says: "I'm drawn like a pin to a magnet to Europe and the US.

"We have been opportunistic in the past. Now we are more strategic ... but that doesn't mean to say that if the opportunity presents itself we won't be off like a streak of lightning."

Next time, the opportunity will have to be a sure payer, he insists. "I will not make any acquisition which could do fundamental damage to the group." Buying Dimplex was the last and only time in his life, he promises himself, when he put all his chips on the table.

The group also has to allow for its grand ambitions for Morphy Richards. Plans to build on its base as UK market leader for toasters and irons are already well advanced. "Turnover at Dimplex increased from £8m to £60m in eight years. We want to do the same again," Naughton says.

The process started with a change of management. After a spell at the Morphy tiller "to learn the language," he recently handed over to a former chief executive of Creda, the TI Group appliances subsidiary.

Fruits of the second stage – getting the products right – reach the shops next month, following a swift £1m development, design and tooling programme in which Naughton the engineer and chief toaster-tester was again personally deeply involved.

The follow-up is a costly three-year plan to extend the range to make the most of the famous name. "Morphy Richards is the most under-traded brand in the market. It is a household name ... not just in the kitchen,"

Naughton says, hinting at wider ambitions. He plans £2m capital investment for the Yorkshire company this year and is counting on possibly spending at that rate for three years.

The pressure seems to be considerable. The group's portfolio contains some sleepier brands like Burco Dean, which could also benefit from a re-launch. Naughton is tempted to extend his interests in consumer electronics – at present limited to radios.

Another company might choose to prune down the cumbersome range, but Glen Dimplex's solid record of making its products work makes this a difficult option for Naughton and Quinn to accept at present.

And all the while they are diverted by new opportunities and offers of other companies for sale. Although they resolutely stick to their "small business" philosophy, it has been greatly modified over the years. The group has expanded far beyond Naughton's initial aim of limiting the company to £1m turnover a year in a single specialist market.

Acquisition and diversification have already taken the company through three or four different cultures. Quinn says. "I would hesitate to say now that I know how to run a £500m company," Naughton admits, looking ahead with apparent if uncharacteristic trepidation, and perhaps giving a hint of his next target.

Melding pieces of an industry

20 June 1986

"THERE is more fluidity in the electrical appliances business than I have ever seen. And we have not seen the end of it," says Michael Montague, chairman of Valor.

Like Martin Naughton, he has been busily picking up the pieces of the industry and melding them into a coherent whole under his company banner. Like Glen Dimplex, Valor has its base in heating appliances. It, too, is branching steadily outwards in a logical progression which, Montague says, will make it a major force in household appliances of all types.

Valor's former strength in paraffin heaters helped it as it developed in the gas market, making heaters, fires, then cookers. Moving on into electrical heating, it launched its first electric cooker earlier this year.

Acquisitions and developments include the Heatrae Sadia water heating business, Heatrod elements, catering equipment and commercial refrigeration. More recently, having gained experience with electrical products, it has begun to follow a path parallel to that of Glen Dimplex.

A flurry of acquisitions in the past two years has brought it Dreamland electric blankets and small appliance companies like

Monogram, Breville, best known for sandwich toasters, and Magimix, a leading name in food processors.

From their different starting points, the two companies have become the most energetic in the British market. Their paths began to merge in the 1970s when Glen outbid Valor for Dimplex.

Their rivalry apart, both companies have developed similar business tactics.

● Both are hungry for good brand names which they can develop at home and overseas. Naughton, declaring himself "in love" with Morphy Richards sees no limit to the possibilities for the names. He has, for example, installed a Teflon, non-stick coating plant, which gives some hint of his intentions.

Apart from talks with European element makers, he has also won a huge contract to make certain appliances for an internationally famous company.

Montague's Dreamland company makes electric blankets for Philips, and the group is also forging links with equally well-known names in West Germany and Japan.

● Both concentrate closely on their core businesses, another factor which helps them, as specialists, to develop joint-venture contacts with other companies.

● Both have ambitions overseas. Morphy Richards, which is well known all over the Commonwealth, already has a firm base. Valor has happened on a strong market in the US. "Gas companies there have got gas coming out of their ears and are rushing around selling appliances like mad," says Montague.

● And both shrug off the threat from multinational competition like Allegheny International of the US – known best for its Rowenta and Sunbeam brands, and Black & Decker, which recently launched a range of small appliances on the back of its position as European market leader in power tools.

Allegheny's recent results suggest it may have over-reached itself. "Its financial situation is such that someone is going to take it over, rather than the opposite," says Montague. Indeed, Allegheny, together with joint parent, Rothmans Deutschland, has just sold Rowenta to Chicago Pacific of the US, which owns the Hoover brand.

He also believes B&D has an uphill task persuading women, who buy most small appliances, to transfer their allegiance from the brands they know.

Word spreads of a profitable niche

10 December 1987

THE MARKET for electronic publishing equipment – the word processors, workstations, laser printers, image scanners and software that give users control over creation and reproduction of documents – is one of the fastest growing computer businesses.

Propelled primarily by big business customers, projected sales will soar to $4bn by 1990 in the US alone. Banks, brokerages, accounting firms, industrial companies and even government agencies are tapping into the convenience and savings that can accrue once initial investment costs are recouped.

But not everybody is in a position to make investments of this scale or even less. Costs range from a few thousand pounds for personal computer-based equipment to several millions for the sorts of multiple-workstation, software-intensive, top-of-the-market machines needed for 30 000-or-so-page technical manuals.

In one recent deal, Boeing Co. spent $1.5m on Interleaf Inc. software to upgrade its electronic publishing systems needed during development of the manned space station which the National Aeronautics and Space Administration plans to put in orbit in the mid-1990s. Boeing won the contract to provide the laboratory and habitation modules.

But not only is such equipment costly, invariably, specially-trained people are needed to operate it. The investment, even for low-end systems, can be a burden many companies do not wish to saddle themselves with.

In that burden, Gordon Sadler and his competitors spotted a market niche: following a trend in the US, they would buy the equipment themselves and set up electronic publishing bureau services for companies unwilling or unable to acquire their own systems.

Offering £700 000 worth of advanced equipment, Sadler's two-year-old Newcastle upon Tyne venture, called Corporate Publishing Services (CPS), has grown from nothing to a company with half a million pounds in turnover this year. It has only recently become profitable, says Sadler, who has just sold CPS, which he still runs, to Ferguson Industrial Holdings, the UK printing, packaging and publishing group.

Simon Beales of competitor Infograph points to one customer, a tractor manufacturer wanting to print parts catalogues: "It did not want to do it itself," he says. "To set up the equipment we've got would cost over £1m. The company said it made tractors and did not want to go into the publishing business."

Sadler says his market research shows that £1.2bn worth of work is now available in the UK.

Such a market is naturally attracting numerous competitors, all offering different types and levels of services. The several dozen contract printing agencies serving the City of London, for instance, are able to expand their range of services by adding electronic publishing software, says Oswy Hornby, managing director of Interleaf UK, a subsidiary of the US software company, which opened in Britain in June.

Interleaf sells its system software directly as well as through others, including Kodak which markets a package comprising Interleaf software, Sun Microsystems hardware and its own top-end laser printer. This package is called Kodak Ektaprint Electronic Publishing System, or KEEPS. Xerox and Xyvision, of the US, market competing arrangements of proprietary equipment.

At the other end of the market are so-called desktop publishing systems that can typeset and reproduce text and graphics. Such personal computer-based systems allow copy shops to provide a bureau-type service in the lower end of the market.

Software from Aldus, called PageMaker, has helped popularise this equipment. Now Interleaf has developed its more advanced typesetting software to run on Apple Macintosh II computers, heightening competition by bringing more publishing capability into lower-cost equipment. The company will not confirm industry speculation that it will launch, within the year, a product with similar capability for the ubiquitous IBM-compatible personal computer market.

Sadler, Beales and their half dozen or so competitors, are getting into a new high-end, full-service niche, also appearing in the US with companies such as Xanthus in Texas and Techset in Minnesota. Beales got into the business gradually from a conventional photocopying and lithographic printing service for corporate clients which he set up nine years ago.

"We thought initially electronic publishing would be a separate business," he says. "It took a very long time for it to take off." (One of the problems was that manufacturers failed to set common standards, making it troublesome for machines of different makes to communicate without translation "filters".) But gradually, he explains, "demand for electronic publishing began generating more business for our traditional reprographics and we merged the two companies."

Infograph takes copy in any form, and turns out either limited runs of up to 3000 copies using laser printers, or camera-ready copy for photo-offset reproduction in large volume.

Not all companies, however, want to depend on outsiders to handle their printing

work. Thomas Toon, print manager at ICI Pharmaceuticals, says that purchase of electronic publishing equipment is under consideration for the "simpler types of materials for our own use." He says this will be set up in-house "in order to have greater control" over the amount of time the work takes.

Others see big cost savings in keeping the job in-house. Harry George, vice-president of Interleaf, in Cambridge, Massachusetts, tells the story of the North Carolina General Assembly. He says the Assembly has calculated it is saving $40 000 a year in typesetting costs with $70 000 worth of electronic publishing equipment.

Minutes from daily legislative sessions are tapped into word processors on the floor of the chamber and sent electronically into Interleaf machines, where they are formatted and typeset into camera-ready hard copy. This is handed straight away to contract printers, cutting the total turnaround time from six weeks to one day, according to George.

Electronic typesetting eliminates the time-consuming and repetitive drudgery of the cut-and-paste method of page composition. Not only is type formatted, but graphics can be scanned in electronically, then edited or moved around in the same way as text.

The US General Services Administration has estimated that the conventional means of producing a page with text and graphics costs between $25 and $40 per page, against between $1 and $5 if the same work is done electronically.

"That's more than we estimate," says George of Interleaf. "But it's this kind of rapid payback that's driving market growth."

Interleaf has been shipping its products for three and a half years. "Most of the demand has been from companies wanting to do technical documents. They can get a payback in less than a year, some in under three months," claims George. However, at Imedia Graphics, a new London electronic publishing bureau, managing director Ivor Jacobs says he thinks it will take a bit longer: about two years to recoup the £120 000 spent on KEEPS equipment he is installing for his business.

Most of the demand for electronic publishing equipment is still coming from corporate customers, says Tim Allen at Xyvision in Wakefield, Massachusetts. He says he cannot estimate the share of sales that goes to electronic publishing bureau companies.

But to Sadler, the market is just now opening up. "People are becoming more information-oriented," he says. "Computers were supposed to bring about the paperless office, but the opposite has happened."

James Meade puts his shirt on mail order

7 May 1985

A RABBIT WARREN-like office underneath a railway arch in Brixton might seem an unusual base from which to tackle head on the top quality shirt-makers of London's Jermyn Street.

Yet it is from those surroundings that 35-year-old James Meade, a former major in the Coldstream Guards, sold £300 000 worth of high class made-to-measure shirts in the year to last October and plans to sell another £500 000 worth in the current 12 months.

James Meade Shirts' mail order business is a striking example of how to undercut profitably the leading players in an upmarket industry by selling products of an almost equal quality through apparently downmarket channels.

On the face of it the formula looks simple. Meade reasoned that the Jermyn Street tailors' rates and rents were so high as a proportion of their total costs that they would be unable to cut prices to meet mail order competition from a supplier located in one of London's cheapest areas.

Meade's shirts – the made-to-measure bits only include the collars and sleeves – start at £23.50, which he maintains represents almost a 100 per cent gross margin over his contracted-out production costs. By contrast, a ready made shirt at Turnbull & Asser in Jermyn Street starts at £40, while T&A's fully tailored garments – which take about 15 individual measurements into account – start at £60. Donald Amore, T&A's general manager, does not divulge his gross margins, but indicates that they are a long way short of 100 per cent.

Meade has successfully found a niche halfway between fully tailor-made and mass-produced shirts. He has been assisted by overcapacity in the textiles industry, which has helped him to keep sub-contractors' bills to a minimum. The penalties, however, have been uncertainties about the survival of those suppliers, the high cost of building up a mail order list (Meade's most important asset), and the £80 000-worth of stock that Meade needs to finance continuously to ensure the smooth running of deliveries.

To put that into perspective, however, Meade demands that his customers pay cash with their orders, while his suppliers' credit terms are up to 90 days for repayment.

But why mail order shirts? Meade left his administrative job in the Army six years ago with a yearning for self-employment, but he was unsure exactly what. A year at the London Business School convinced him that mail order was one business – apart from building – that he could enter at low cost.

Shirts were easy to store and to post, and there seemed to be a gap at the top end of the market. "To go and compete with Marks and Spencer wasn't a starter. There was no competitive advantage, and the volumes required would have been enormous," says the dapper Meade.

But the four clearing banks he approached – including his own Coutts – were less convinced, and refused Meade's application for an unsecured loan because of his lack of business experience. "Credibility was my biggest hurdle," he recalls.

Ironically, a member of the Money-Coutts family is now one of Meade's 10 000 customers. Eventually 3i, the small firms financing institution, came forward with a £25 000 mixture of government-guaranteed debt and equity in return for 5 per cent of the business, which Meade matched with £20 000 of his own.

Starting work from his Fulham home, and using his brother-in-law's empty house for storage, Meade moved in late 1982 to a starter unit in the Great Eastern Workspace in Brixton's Coldharbour Lane, which had been brought to his notice by a lecturer at the business school.

For 3i, it was clearly a marginal proposition. The UK mail-order industry has seen its share of total retail sales decline since 1978 from 6 per cent to 3.4 per cent, according to stockbrokers Capel-Cure Myers, even if direct-mail-order groups like James Meade have fared better than agencies, which sell a wide range of other people's products through catalogues.

It was the high cost of advertising – up to £35 per customer, reckons Meade – which forced the business into a disappointing loss in its first six months to October 1982, having projected a profit for the period. "Of course, once you have built up the mailing list, you are in a very strong position," says Meade, who now has a copy of his brochure in 30 000 homes. "My greatest competition

will come from anybody who can build up such a list. The only way that somebody like T&A could compete with me would be to sell their shops," he claims.

The next blow came when the company's sole sub-contractor, the former Altrincham-based textile manufacturer William Pickles, went into receivership, luckily just a month after delivering a £12 000 order.

It was not hard to find other sub-contractors short of work in such a depressed industry, but the Pickles collapse highlighted a widespread problem for any small company attempting to spread its sub-contracting risk among a number of groups.

Meade now has four suppliers in Scotland, Northern Ireland, Manchester and Southend, but in the early stages of his business volumes were so low that he could not have sustained more than one even if he had wanted to. "You need to offer them a certain amount of scale to make it worthwhile," explains Meade.

The mailing list, built up through a series of minutely monitored advertising campaigns in the national press and upmarket glossies like Harpers & Queen and Country Life, soon began to pay for itself. By last year, revenues began to overtake advertising costs and Meade moved into the black for the first time. It was uneconomic to expand into more starter units in Coldharbour Lane, so the company moved last July to underneath the arches of the nearby railway.

Others in the same business have been less lucky. Meade's main competitor, the Devizes-based Seel Staley (selling under the Shirtmakers' Guild brand name) went into voluntary liquidation in February, citing heavy advertising costs as a reason. Seel Staley's failure presented Meade with another credibility problem; that of persuading customers that he would not go the same way.

Meade, however, believes that his sector of the shirt market is a long way from being fully exploited. He quotes US research, which suggests that 40 per cent of people do not accord with standard shirt sizes, and points out that he has only just begun to explore the women's market. Moreover, he feels that his existing range of 24 designs in 28 sizes could be considerably enlarged at low cost.

No reflection of Nordic altruism

SAS prepares attempt to overturn CAA decision on BCal

9 December 1987

HELGE LINDBERG does not like to be interrupted. When he gets into full flow about the development of Scandinavian Airlines System, listeners' efforts to break in are swept away with the wave of a cigarette.

In several meetings over recent weeks, however, the Civil Aviation Authority got its message across to the Scandinavian airline's deputy president and former chief operating officer with a single word: "No."

The CAA rejected its rescue plans for British Caledonian as insufficient to guarantee that the British airline would remain UK-controlled and thus keep its route licences. UK ministers, moreover, gave barely veiled hints that they were opposed to any SAS role in BCal.

Undeterred, Mr Lindberg, a Norwegian who has spent most of the past three months in London (his birthplace) working on the BCal deal, is preparing to have a final go.

The airline's dogged approach does not, however, reflect a mission of Nordic altruism to save Caledonian cousins from an unwelcome takeover.

The Scandinavian airline desperately wants to find a partner with a complementary route network, a good image with business passengers, and the same business philosophy so that it can provide daily worldwide services for its home market of only 17m people.

SAS does not want to become only a regional feeder into a future "gang of four or five" European long-haul carriers. It wants a more central European hub – the goal of its now-inaccurate talks with the Belgian carrier Sabena – and more routes to the Middle and Far East. It especially wants to plug into BCal's network in Africa, to which SAS does not fly.

It already has an agreement with the Varig of Brazil and Argentinas Aerolinas to connect SAS flights with onward destinations in South America. SAS passengers also feed into the Thai International's Far Eastern routes in Bangkok. Passengers coming into Europe, of course, feed into SAS's network.

SAS thinks Gatwick has great potential and says it would be eager to move the air-craft overhaul work (currently done by Swissair in Zurich) to Gatwick where BCal staff have the expertise to overhaul DC10s.

The success of SAS lies mainly with its rather flashy (by Scandinavian standards at least) president and chief executive, Mr Jan Carlzon. He joined SAS in 1980 after climbing the ladder to the top at Vingresor, Sweden's largest tour operator, followed by three years as head of Linjeflyg, the Swedish domestic airline, which he restored to profitability.

When he came to SAS, the airline was "floundering," according to analysts, with poor control over costs and a high degree of overstaffing.

Mr Carlzon styled SAS as "the businessman's airline" – introducing a super-club service in Europe for all full-fare economy passengers and placing reduced emphasis on the less lucrative discount and tourist markets – and said that customers, rather than the aircraft, would be the company's major assets.

SAS began to fly frequent, non-stop services, often in smaller aircraft, and cut back on unprofitable routes. It invested in comfortable airport lounges, and check-in facilities at designated hotels.

Staff were trained at what were soon nicknamed the "charm schools", planes were spruced up, and punctuality improved. By giving responsibility for problem-solving to employees on the front line, he rapidly turned SAS from loss into profit.

If the past looks rosy, the future does not look quite so good, because of a stagnating market and the trials of deregulation, although Mr Carlzon believes that "every crisis is a big opportunity."

SAS has already taken steps in building up a joint computerised reservation and distribution system called Amadeus, with Air France, Iberia, Lufthansa and Air Inter. The system is a rival to the Galileo system launched by British Airways, KLM, Swissair, and United Airlines. BCal is likely to shift from Galileo to Amadeus if the SAS deal goes through.

Meanwhile, SAS's relationship with the Danish, Swedish and Norwegian governments which indirectly hold 50 per cent of the consortium has become ambiguous, according to one London analyst, who says: "SAS bears the burden of being a state airline and derives none of the benefits."

The governments rarely lobby on the airline's behalf. SAS, for example, wants unrestricted landing rights in the US, where it is limited to only four destinations.

It has little to lose in its campaign for an "open skies" policy which would allow any national carrier to fly where it wants. Many US destinations are attractive for SAS, only Stockholm, Oslo and Copenhagen are of interest to US carriers.

Strategically, SAS is moving in the same direction as Swissair, where more and more of the group business is non-airline. This is a sound strategy, according to analysts, who believe that perhaps one third of group profits could soon come from the other businesses – the hotel, catering, and tour operations.

It contrasts, however, with BCal's disposal of almost everything except the airline over the past two years.

Apart from winning employee and union support by saying that the minimum 1 500 UK redundancies predicted by BA would not happen under its own plan, SAS has kept a discreet and politically necessary silence about what changes may be necessary at BCal.

The official line is that SAS will have one non-executive director on the BCal group board, and the UK airline otherwise will be free to manage itself.

However, outsiders, including City analysts, doubt whether BCal's problems can all be ascribed to the lack of connecting routes into Gatwick and unfortunate ill-timing in the swap of its long-haul routes with BA.

It is probably inevitable that a new broom will sweep through BCal before long. If the CAA finally allows SAS to take a stake, it will have done the Scandinavians a favour by ensuring that there is a large British shareholder to share the responsibility.

SAS aims to beat objections with 'iron-clad' case

9 December 1987

SAS has requested a meeting with the Civil Aviation Authority this morning to discuss its proposed rescue of British Caledonian but has not yet submitted a revised package for the CAA to study.

SAS was trying last night to put together an "iron-clad" case, to answer all the objections raised by the CAA at the last meeting on Friday when the agency said that BCal would lose its designation as a UK airline

and its route licences under the proposals then on the table.

The Scandinavian airline is now understood to have sorted out the financial side of its proposal, including finding a UK shareholder to balance the size of its own equity stake.

The delay is believed to involve non-financial aspects of the package – relating to management influence over BCal – rather

than financial control. The CAA yesterday underlined its scrutiny of the "totality" of an airline's structure in determining whether control rested in the UK.

BCal directors must formally reply by this evening to the full bid from British Airways. They will not be allowed to change their recommendation before next Wednesday, the day on which BA intends to close its cash terms.

The painful and costly process of growing bigger

20 May 1985

THE first wave of new biotechnology companies, spawned by the break-throughs in the science of molecular biology in the mid-1970s, are no longer precocious infants but fast approaching their adolescence. Their all-consuming problem is how to keep growing at an exponential rate.

Their fate will be a topic of debate and much rumour at Biotech-85 in Geneva this week, the first of three international conferences by the same organisers, with others to follow in Washington DC and Singapore in the autumn.

The bio-entrepreneurs who founded such companies as Genentech, Cetus, Genex, Biogen and Celltech – and several hundred more – raised venture capital against the promise that they could harness novel scientific methods such as genetic engineering and cell fusion to make much-sought drugs such as interferon, or infallible tests for hepatitis and many other diseases.

Some bio-entrepreneurs surprised even themselves with the speed with which they picked up the new techniques, and cloned substances they had targetted.

They demonstrated convincingly how techniques that were hot off the academic laboratory bench could be transferred with little delay into a commercial setting. They opened the way to bio-synthesis of chemicals far too complex to synthesise by conventional methods at present.

Dr Sydney Brenner, director of Britain's

most fertile source of ideas in this field, the Laboratory of Molecular Biology in Cambridge, says he sees the new biotechnology firms filling a gap in the academic canvas, while universities set about creating more commercially orientated departments of genetic technology to facilitate technology transfer to industry.

In Britain, this gap is slowly filling despite shortages of cash.

Universities like Bath, Leicester and Warwick are building a capability in biotechnology with substantial industrial support from ICI to John Brown Engineering. But some of the bio-entrepreneurs have ambitions that go far beyond any idea of being merely a stop-gap while the academics adjust to industry's latest requirements. They talk boldly of growing into big industries, particularly in health care.

Their optimism is rooted in the idea that new biotechnologies still being developed will permit the scientist to cut through the costly tedium and delay in discovering new drugs. Instead of screening thousands of possibilities for one that might solve a medical problem – which can take a drug company 10 years – their goal is to specify the protein exactly at the outset, then set out to make it by biotechnology.

They cannot do this 'protein engineering' yet. But they believe they can move much faster than the big drug houses, which have so much of their research effort committed to the traditional pattern of research.

Their problem is how to persuade their financial patrons to be very patient while they – and the universities behind them – perfect their techniques.

Mostly they raised venture capital on the basis that they would be engineering new products for an investment of a few million dollars and within about five years. Now the payoff date looks more like the 1990s and the investment needed could be many tens, even hundreds, of millions of dollars.

This is because, even if the new scientific techniques successfully short-circuit the research phase, there is no way the companies will be able to bypass the very lengthy development phase to prove the safety and efficacy of the product.

The dilemma of the adolescent biotechnology firm which has grown from a few wide-eyed enthusiasts to a few hundred employees is how to present this problem to its patrons. "It's quite staggering how many people want small companies to remain small," says Mr Wensley Haydon-Baillie, chairman of Porton International, one of the latest British biotechnology ventures.

The dilemma has already been resolved in many cases by selling out to bigger companies seeking a ready-made pocket of experience in biotechnology.

Bethesda Research Laboratories near Washington DC, one of the first, which in 1981 declared its intention of becoming 'the

315

IBM of biotechnology,' is now part of a bigger company, Gibco, and renamed Life Technologies.

Agrigenetics, launched in 1975, is now part of Lubrizol, a USA oil additives group. Genex, another US pioneer, has been cutting staff and is said to be ripe for takeover.

Rumours are rife that Biogen based in Geneva and Boston, Massachusetts could be another. Its running costs rose by 49 per cent last year, to nearly $44 m, mostly for research and development.

Biogen's loss of Dr Walter Gilbert, its founder and recruiter of its top scientific talent, who retired abruptly as chairman late last year has helped to feed these rumours.

Dr Gilbert never disguises the fact that he modelled Biogen on Genentech, the Californian start-up founded in 1975. Genentech raised US venture capital to back an idea supported by Herbert Boyer, one of the co-inventors of genetic engineering. Biogen sought to repeat it with capital raised outside the US but has consistently raised less than it wanted.

Genentech is the outstanding success story among the new biotechnology firms, with an unparalleled record of scientific innovation. Its conquests range from genetically engineered 'living' substances such as interferons (as cancer treatments), insulin and Factor VIII (the blood clotting factor that most haemophiliacs lack) to bovine and porcine growth hormones, expected to make a dramatic impact on the productivity of beef, dairy and pig farming. It was the first to declare plans to take on the big drug houses.

From the outset many big companies have been among the patrons of the new biotechnology ventures, while more slowly developing their in-house resources. Socal and Shell supported Cetus. Schering-Plough backed Biogen.

Eli Lilly and Hoffman-La Roche were among Genentech's first clients for contract research.

Genentech's spending grew from $31.9 m in 1982 to $45.5 m in 1983, to $66.8 m last year. But in 1984 its total revenue – up by 48 per cent – came out $2.7 m ahead of the expense of a payroll almost double that of Biogen. It has sufficiently impressed big business to negotiate three joint ventures involving four major US groups – Hewlett-Packard, Baxter Travenol (a healthcare company), Corning Glass and AE Staley (an agribusiness group).

Celltech, the leading British biotechnology start-up, still less than five years old, has copied the Genentech pattern. It has negotiated joint ventures with Boots and Air Products, in each case for a substantial downpayment for its special skills.

Like Genentech and Biogen, Celltech has one over-riding ambition – 'to be a darned big company in ten years' time,' as Mr Gerard Fairtlough, its chief executive sees it. The initial backers in 1980 were four City institutions, British and Commonwealth Shipping, Midland Bank, The Pru and ICFC, which put up 56 per cent of the cash being sought. This substantial injection of private cash was enough to persuade Sir Keith Joseph, then Secretary of State for Industry, to find the other 44 per cent.

ICFC has since got cold feet over the timescales – and the Government, as a matter of principle, has reduced its stake to 15 per cent. In has come Biotechnology Investments, NM Rothschild's dedicated trust whose chairman, Lord Rothschild, has stated that it seeks investments with a payoff time of up to seven years.

'We always go into these investments on the complete understanding that we are going to have to put in more money,' says Mr David Leathers, fund manager of Biotechnology Investments. Another of its executives has what he calls the 'pi-rule' – you end up putting in 3.14 times your original investment.

Biotechnology Investments owns 11.1 per cent of Celltech, Mr Fairtlough believes that, even though "most people who joined Celltech were thought to be crazy," the company has already proved that you don't need to be in California to start a highly competitive biotechnology company. He forecasts revenues of about $5 m this year, mainly from sales to the US.

Although it could require $100 m to make Celltech 'a darned big company' at a time when other biotechnology start-ups are disappearing, its executives believe that Britain is ripe for several more Celltechs,

each exploiting a particular facet of British research – the strongest in this sector outside the US according to science advisers to the British Government.

Finance should not be the problem, the City says, particularly now that Celltech has cleaved a path. But each would need to transfer its technology as efficiently from academia as Celltech has done in medical research. This is not easy. The eagerness to co-operate shown by Medical Research Council scientists is not yet apparent in other promising sectors.

Ironically, each start-up, as it grew, would probably need to enter into joint ventures with big business in order to preserve its identify as an independent biotechnology company.

Mr Haydon-Baillie has no doubt about the dangers of a 'little England' approach to biotechnology. For him, it is inescapably a totally worldwide technology.

Porton International, although launched only last year, is an infant only in name. The name, registered last year, is a reminder that the laboratory was once a world-famous centre of germ warfare research. Mr Haydon-Baillie has been assembling his company for eight years, from constituents which have been in biotechnology for as long as 40 years. As he sees it, the company fulfils three fundamental requirements. It is market-led, it is fully international, and it has "command over, rather than access to, its prime technology." Like Biotechnology Investments, it has assembled a portfolio of investments, but in this case it wholly owns most of them.

Like Genentech and Celltech, Porton also sees the future in terms of joint ventures with established companies. But so diversified is the biotechnology company that Mr Haydon-Baillie has created that he forecasts that it will negotiate about 40 joint ventures worldwide within the next five years.

LEADING RESEARCH COMPANIES

Company	Country	Objective
Amgen	US	Diagnostics
Biogen	US/Europe	Healthcare/Diagnostics
Celltech	UK	Healthcare/Diagnostics
Centocor	US	Diagnostics
DNA Plant Technology	US	Crop enhancement
Genentech	US	Healthcare
Genetics Institute	US	Healthcare
Genetic Systems	US	Diagnostics
Genex	US	Speciality chemicals
Hybritech	US	Diagnostics
Immunex	US	Healthcare
Molecular Genetics	US	Healthcare

Why Sony has yet to find a solution to the complexity of world markets

4 December 1987

NO COMPANY is more closely associated with Japanese industry's relentless international expansion than Sony. With 70 per cent of its $8bn total sales last year outside Japan, its name is synonymous worldwide with consumer electronics.

Yet, according to Ken Iwaki, Sony's head of corporate planning: "That does not necessarily mean we are an international company." True, Sony has done more than most to bridge the cultural divide between managers of different nationalities. Iwaki says that since it set up regular quarterly meetings in 1975 between its top Japanese and American executives (conducted in English), each side has learned from the other. For instance, Sony in Japan now uses internal budgeting and planning methods imported from the US.

It is also committed to increasing sharply overseas production, which is due to rise to 35–40 per cent of total sales by 1990, from 20 per cent last year. However, the company admits it is still groping for a satisfactory answer to managing the complexity of global markets riven by currency instability and trade protection.

In Western Europe, where the company has six plants, local management is keen to lay down deeper roots, partly in response to political pressure on trade from the European Community. "It's not sensible to keep everything in Tokyo," says Jack Schmuckli, Swiss-born president of Sony Europe. "We have to move everything here, from engineering to strategic marketing and components."

The company recently set up an engineering centre in Stuttgart, West Germany, which Schmuckli hopes will eventually develop new products from scratch. He sees this as a key step to sourcing more components in the EC, because "engineers usually design around parts they know, and if they're sitting in Tokyo, they may not know what's available in Europe."

However, satisfying demands for more local design autonomy in Europe must be reconciled with company-wide pressures to cut costs by standardising components worldwide. Sony hopes to do this by linking all its designers to an electronic network which enables them to work together on a single computer database.

Iwaki worries that the standardisation drive may handicap innovation and creativity in a company renowned for giving engineers free rein. "It's a difficult balance. We're not sure yet if we can achieve it."

Choosing locations for the company's major plant investments is another area of contention. "We only need two small picture tube plants, one of them in Japan," says Schmuckli. "From a pure cost standpoint, it would be much cheaper to have the other in South East Asia. But if you look at the "total picture, it has to be in Europe. It's economics versus politics."

Iwaki accepts the logic of the argument, pointing out that "once we produce in one regional market, we get the right to import as well as to export."

However, he adds, with more than a hint of yearning for a simpler world: "Globalising production is a positive development, but the key reasons for it are negative. From a cost point of view, it would be most economic to concentrate production in one plant and have Japan as factory for the world. But other countries would never accept it."

Finding growth in a contracting market

23 June 1986

BREAD, so conventional wisdom has it, is a mature industry in Britain. Year after year of price warfare has eaten away at margins: the supermarkets are compounding the problems of a saturated marketplace by usurping the role of the High Street baker with their in-store bakeries: and all it takes is a long, hot summer to wipe out the profits from the rest of the year.

The food giants seem to agree. Throughout the early 1980s Associated British Foods, Ranks Hovis McDougall and United Biscuits – which transformed the bread industry in the 1960s and 1970s by gobbling up local bakers' shops and turning then into chains of national bakeries – have slowly, but surely, beaten a retreat from bread retailing.

Yet over the same period Greggs has grown from a baker's shop in Newcastle into the country's largest independent bakery with a stock market listing and a chain of over 300 shops across the country.

The catalyst for Greggs' growth has been the introduction of a highly flexible man-

agement style, which includes considerable autonomy for local managers, and the encouragement of employees to contribute to the company's development through concepts like quality circles. This has helped Greggs to be responsive both to its workforce and to market trends.

In the last year or so this flexibility has enabled the company to make the most of changes in public taste towards high fibre diets and healthier eating by diversifying away from white bread (where price competition is severe) towards more profitable products like crusty, granary and wholemeal loaves.

"The retail bakery business is very complex, and increasingly competitive, thanks to the development of in-store bakeries, a relatively small part of the food giants' operations," says David Stoddart, a retail analyst at stockbrokers Capel Cure Myers.

"So the food giants are withdrawing from the retail sector. ABF has sold off some of its shops, RHM seems to have called a halt to

developing its Lite Bite chain and United Biscuits has effectively pulled out by turning the Crawford group in the North East from bakeries into cafeterias."

So how has Greggs succeeded at a time and in an industry in which so many others have failed?

"They have succeeded because they are a very, well managed company," says Stoddart. "Marks and Spencer is the classic example of a company that has outperformed its competitors by looking after its people. Greggs isn't far behind.

"The quality of industrial relations is excellent. The management has paid attention to all the little things, to providing communal canteens for managers and workers, to ensuring that everyone is on first-name terms. In personnel management they are years ahead of their competitors."

Greggs' commitment to personnel management is a product of the company's structure. As the company diversified away from Tyneside in the 1960s each new regional operation was devised as an autonomous division.

Although Greggs makes the most of economies of scale by supplying its shops from central bakeries – whereas the food giants have tended to supply their retail bakeries from single, centralised production units – Greggs has established regional bakeries, each with the capacity to supply up to 100 shops within a 50 or 60 mile radius.

The management of each regional division therefore exerts complete control over not only the retail units within the region, but the production process too.

"There are certain constraints on local management, but we have kept them to a minimum," says Ian Gregg, the chairman. "We have always believed in giving our people as much responsibility as possible. So in terms of what is manufactured, how the retail chain expands, production targets and the marketing policy, they have complete freedom."

Structural autonomy is augmented by a complex series of employee incentive schemes. All employees, from board directors to sales assistants, participate in profit sharing and in bonus schemes. The company has also encouraged staff to buy shares, through option and savings related schemes. Employees already hold 4 per cent of Greggs' shares, with an additional 6 per cent under option.

Greggs also encourages its staff to share in decision making. Two years ago the policy of regular briefings was formalised by the introduction of the Japanese concept of quality circles to three of the bakeries.

Within the quality circles, specially trained members of staff generate discussion on every aspect of the company's activities in an attempt to stimulate suggestions on ways of increasing productivity, improving product quality, cutting costs and making the working environment more pleasant.

"Given that each of our divisions operates independently it is essential that staff are committed to the company and feel motivated," says Gregg. "We have done everything we can to ensure that they identify with the business. But this is a very important area and one at which we just have to keep trying harder."

Although each Greggs division benefits from the cost advantage of large scale manufacturing, each shop is presented to the consumer as if it were a traditional, local bakery. The majority of the shops' products – around 60 per cent – is sourced from the central bakery, but each shop has its own oven and the rest of its stock is baked on the premises.

"We try very hard to encourage people to look upon our shops as their own local bakery," says Gregg. "The sign above each shop even reads 'Greggs Bakery,' singular.

"Of course as the company has expanded this has become increasingly difficult. We now present ourselves to the City as a substantial, national company, yet we want our customers perceiving us as a quaint, traditional bakery. It is a dilemma."

Nonetheless functioning as a large operation goes beyond impressing the institutions. Fluctuations in the cost of raw materials and the growth of supermarket in-store bakeries has made price competitiveness more important than ever before.

Perhaps, perversely, in-store bakeries could offer an avenue for growth. Greggs already supplies Sainsbury in the West Midlands and the Co-op in Yorkshire and, in the long term, should the in-store bakeries erode its market share, Greggs could act as a supplier.

In the meantime it is concentrating on retailing as a source of growth. Greggs will continue to expand its established divisions. Some 14 new shops are planned for the current financial year.

"So far we have adopted a very single-minded approach to our business," says Gregg. "From time to time we have looked at moving into other areas of retailing, but never seriously. It always seemed to me that the amount of effort required to secure growth in a new field would be so much greater than the effort needed to improve our performance in the field we know so well.

"Eventually we will expand outside baking. But in the meantime we still have 50 per cent of the country to expand into as Greggs the Baker."

IAN GREGG did not set out to be a baker. He began his career as a solicitor but took over the family business, the baker's shop in Newcastle, on his father's death in 1964.

Throughout the 1960s Greggs expanded by opening new shops in and around Newcastle. At the end of the decade it moved further afield, into Glasgow, Leeds and Manchester.

By the mid-1980s Greggs sported four regional divisions and some 260 shops. Ian Gregg drafted in Michael Darrington, from United Biscuits, to take his place as managing director, leaving him free to concentrate on his role as chairman and to prepare the company for a stock market flotation.

Greggs sailed onto the market in April 1984 with an issue that was 97 times oversubscribed. The flotation gave it paper to play with, and a cash pool, part of which was ploughed into the acquisition of Braggs, a West Midlands bakery the following autumn, and part into the purchase of the Merret and Parker chain of bakers' shops in Wales a year ago.

Earlier this month Greggs reported a 38 per cent growth in pre-tax profit to £2.65m in 1985. The share price has risen from its striking price of 165p to hover around 240p and the company, which now has a market capitalisation of £25m, is scouting about for acquisition opportunities.

Now Conran's magic misses its first trick

12 June 1986

"DOES anyone think we can fail?" was the injudicious quote from Sir Terence Conran in the autumn of 1983 on the launch of Now, a new fashion chain aimed at the post-Mothercare generation of British teenagers.

Such is the magic touch associated with Sir Terence, now chairman of the Storehouse group of major retailers, that few at that time thought that failure was a word in his vocabulary.

But last week he was forced to admit that Now has been a flop – the first time that Sir Terence's flair appears to have deserted him since the first Habitat store was opened in Fulham Road, London, in the swinging 1960s.

The 28 loss-making Now stores are shortly to be phased out, although Sir Terence has plans to open a new chain aimed at the fashion-conscious teens and twenties market – perhaps the most volatile and fickle consumer market of them all.

"This sector is usually for those retailers with a death-wish," suggests John Richards, a stores analyst with stockbrokers Wood Mackenzie.

"But we can draw some encouragement that Conran has had the courage to drop Now before it became too much of a profits drain," he adds. "It's put him back in the land of the mortals and shown everyone that he's not infallible."

What happened to Now also calls into question the whole retail concept of narrow market segmentation pioneered by the Next fashion chain and since adopted by many others. It is a lesson that may assume increasing importance as consumer markets change and develop in the late 1980s.

The Now concept emerged in October of 1983 but had been in question for at least 18 months before that. Mothercare, which Sir Terence's Habitat chain had taken over in late 1981, had been under pressure from customers to extend its range upwards from age 10 to 16. (Its original concept of everything for the mother-to-be and her child up to age five had been extended to age 10 in 1975).

Test-marketing by Mothercare of two sizes larger than its normal child sizes had shown that there was a demand not for high teenage fashions but for reasonably priced, good quality clothes with style.

It was the sort of market that Marks and Spencer might reasonably expect to exploit; it tried, in 1979, with its Miss Michelle range of teenage fashions but had to pull the range out of its test stores within weeks because sales fell far short of expectations.

Undismayed by Michelle's fate and fresh from his experience at the Hepworth group where he had a hand in creating the Next women's wear chain, Sir Terence and his colleagues came up with the concept of a separate chain of fashion stores selling to the 10 to 16 age group.

Their belief was that a strong design identity would enable Mothercare to succeed in carving out a niche for itself in a market where other major clothing retailers feared to tread because of the volatility of customer tastes.

"The early results from the experiment were very encouraging," recalls Sir Terence, "and so we decided to press ahead with the next stage of expansion from five to 28 stores."

The original concept had five Now stores positioned either in or next to Mothercare but the expansion took some stores into High Street fashion locations where they were in competition with the boutiques and other multiples. Eventually there were 10 Now shops next to Mothercare sites, and 18 located elsewhere.

But this is where the problems started. Divorced from the Mothercare environment, the Now stores in fashion locations attracted an older range of customers in their late teens and twenties. Not surprisingly they were frustrated to find sizes only ranging up to age 16.

The response was to increase the sizes to accommodate this new demand – a move, which Sir Terence now admits, "tended to confuse people since we had started as such a tightly targeted operation."

The move into fashion locations also created financial problems for Mothercare. The 28-chain operation was too small to achieve the benefits of bulk buying with the consequence that "our margins were too small to cope with the high rents, costs and competitive pricing in such locations."

But Now had an added problem. While demand was booming in the fashion-located Now stores, sales were falling off in the outsets sited next to Mothercare shops. "Kids appeared to want to turn their backs on Mothercare when buying clothes," recalls Sir Terence.

"It was, perhaps, trying to reconcile the impossible," suggests Wood Mackenzie's Richards. "Teenage customers tend to have their own very firm views about the clothes they wanted – but it was often their parents who were paying." The "mini-Next" look of the Now stores may have appealed to parents but not necessarily to their children. Not surprisingly, the children usually won.

Now, however, might have survived these problems had not Sir Terence turned his attention to merging with British Home Stores in a deal struck late last year. The merger led to a comprehensive review of all retailing activities – encompassing Habitat and Mothercare in the UK and abroad and also the Richards womens wear chain, Heals furniture shops, SavaCentre discount stores and Conran's, the US furnishing stores.

This review not only turned up problems in BHS (which decided last week to pull out of food retailing) but also led to Now's future being questioned. "We had to decide whether to go on with an operation where we knew we had made mistakes or whether to learn from our errors and start again from scratch," says Sir Terence.

The decision was made to start again. Sir Terence, however, is being rather coy about the new venture – likely to get under way in the autumn – since it depends on a link-up with a major international clothing company exclusively selling fashion clothes in the new chain.

The new operation is likely to trade under the company's name but be owned and run by Storehouse executives. Initially the 18 Now stores located in fashion sites will be converted to the new name, with a further half dozen on the immediate horizon, and eventual plans – if the concept works – of a chain of 150 stores.

But will Sir Terence make it work second time round? In a highly fragmented market, he believes that there is room for a fashion chain aimed at a younger and more design-conscious market than that sought by Next and his own re-vitalised Richards womenswear stores which are aimed at the working woman in her late 20s and 30s.

However, Sir Terence now feels that close targeting of this younger age group is wrong. The new stores will appeal from age 16 but will still go up to the early 30s, he says. It is a market which Benetton, the Italian-owned franchise chain, has captured with a vengeance. "We must accept the reality of this market-place in that we are going to appeal to a much broader range of customers than before," says Sir Terence. "Of course there will be a core of customers that we will be aiming at, but there will be significant numbers on the fringe."

But seasoned Conran-watchers are less sure about the wisdom of trying again in such a fickle market. "There are too many others – such as Etam and Top Shop apart from the boutiques – who are trying to do the same thing," points out Katherine Wynne, an analyst with stockbrokers Capel-Cure Myers.

"The general economic climate is still unfavourable to the teens and twenties market," suggests Richard Hyman, retail market analyst with the Verdict research group. "The profit margins are such that you have to work very much harder to do well in this market than any other."

Sir Terence appears unlikely to be swayed by such doubters. But he has already been gratified by the "dozens of letters" he has received from Now customers imploring him not to close the chain down and is considering keeping the Now name as shops-within-shops in re-vamped BHS stores.

The family spirit

18 May 1985

An everyday story of Cointreau folk: Dallas, Dynasty and Bleak House are tame thrills compared with the battle for control of the Remy Martin empire

THERE is a favourite saying in the Charentes, the *département* centred round Cognac: "*Il se fait gendre.*" Translated literally, this means: "He turned himself into a son-in-law." A better translation would be the old Hollywood expression: "The son-in-law also rises." The present battle for control of two firms of cognac producers – Remy Martin, the third biggest in the world, and Frapin, once the most famous – is the story of three sons-in-law; the late André Renaud and his sons-in-law, André Heriard-Dubreuil and Max Cointreau.

Renaud was the most remarkable of the three. Although from a relatively humble background, he earned a doctorate in law at the Sorbonne. Back home he married a girl 15 years younger than himself – Marie Frapin, daughter of the biggest grower in the Grande Champagne, the finest of the seven *crus* into which the Cognac area is divided.

At the time, M Frapin's cognacs were considered by the British aristocracy as the finest on the market (Berry Bros and Rudd, one of London's oldest merchants, still buys its cognacs from the firm). But Renaud was after bigger game. In the years after World War I he bought control of an old but virtually dormant firm, Remy Martin.

In the 15 years before World War II he shaped the strategy that was to bring such success after 1945: for example, he took advantage of the Chinese love of cognac and, at the same time, sold exclusively cognacs from the champagnes. Remy Martin concentrated on those entitled to the label "Fine Champagne," implying a mixture of brandies from the Grande Champagne and the slightly less desirable Petite Champagne area, but containing at least 50 per cent of Grande Champagne. This policy came naturally to someone with access to Frapin's incomparable stocks; and Renaud took advantage of the worldwide distribution network already built up by the Cointreau family liquer empire, then headed by a friend: they had joint distribution arrangements in countries as far apart as the U.S. and Switzerland.

Nevertheless, even in 1939 Frapin was a bigger company than Remy Martin. Renaud remained a grower at heart: he is remem-bered by the locals as a redoubtable wheeler-and-dealer in the peasant tradition and, within the family, as a patriarch, lunching promptly at noon every day after a morning spent in the vineyards.

He and Marie had three children: a son, Pierre, killed in a riding accident while still in his teens, and two daughters, Anne-Marie and Genevieve. During World War II, new company law forced Renaud to spread the ownership of his shares in Remy Martin. Some went to Anne-Marie, who was at the time the only one of the two children old enough to legally own any; this was to provide her with the potential of controlling the company when the remaining shares were divided on the death of her parents.

Anne-Marie married a man almost as remarkable as her father, André Heriard-Dubreuil. His family were merchants and growers, but, like his father-in-law, he aspired to a higher education and passed the appalling stiff exams required to enter the Ecole Polytechnique, the school which has trained most of France's governing elite since Napoleonic times. During the war he returned to Cognac to work with his father-in-law. His sister-in-law, Genevieve, a notably gentle character, then married Max Cointreau, the grandson of Renaud's old friend.

After Renaud died in 1965, aged 82, Heriard Dubreuil naturally took over and everyone assumed the old man had blessed the legal accident that, through Anne-Marie's holding – the shares she got during the war and those she inherited on her father's death – gave the Heriard-Dubreuils 51 per cent of Remy Martin … and turned Genevieve into a minority shareholder.

Heriard-Dubreuil pursued his father-in-law's policy with increased success and Remy Martin's VSOP became the standard-bearer for luxury cognacs the world over: for more than a decade the firm's sales grew at 30 per cent a year. Whereas before the war VSOP cognac accounted for a mere 5 per cent of total sales, it now accounts for nearly a third of the hundred million bottles of cognac sold in the world.

Inevitably, the rise of one family firm overshadowed the other. Frapin's name virtually disappeared from the consumer market; it diminished into a mere supplier and by the mid-1970s two-thirds of its sales were of bulk cognacs to Remy Martin. The Frapins did not object.

Under Heriard-Dubreuil – a ruddy, robust, commanding figure – Remy Martin has always gone its own way. Its headquarters are more utilitarian than those of other cognac companies, and, unlike them, it does not go out of its way to welcome visitors to its stills and warehouses. The families remained nominally united until 1973 when Max Cointreau presented himself as a candidate in the local elections in Segonzac, the sleepy little town at the heart of the Grande Champagne which is the home of only one cognac firm – Frapin, which is still housed in rustic simplicity round a charming, rose-strewn courtyard. He was opposed by Roger Plassard, chief buyer for Remy Martin and thus a powerful figure in deciding the economic prospects of many of the town's electors. Nevertheless, Cointreau won.

During the 1970s Albert Frapin died, soon followed by his wife – beloved "Tantine" to both sides of the family. Naturally, their half-share in Frapin was divided equally between Anne-Marie Heriard-Dubreuil and Genevieve Cointreau. But matters came to a head after the death of Madame Renaud in November 1978, aged 85. Remy Martin promptly stopped buying any cognacs from Frapin, partly because it was naturally reluctant to add to its stocks as sales of cognac were showing the first sign of a downturn after 30 years of almost continuous growth. But, even so, it is strange that it cut off relations so abruptly. The reason for the abruptness soon emerged – just before her death, Mme Renaud had signed a final will ensuring that her younger daughter, Genevieve, would control Frapin, as her elder, Anne-Marie, controlled Remy Martin.

Her death set off an avalanche of law suits. These are amazingly convoluted but boil down to two essential elements. First, the Heriard-Dubreuils are claiming that the final will is invalid. They say Mme Renaud did not know what she was doing when she signed; and that she was badly advised by the family's notary, M Guerin (who has since died).

The case has often degenerated into farce: the Cointreaus' handwriting experts have testified that, although crippled by rheumatism and thus unable to sign her name properly, Mme Renaud could read even the small print with the help of a magnifying glass. The Heriard-Dubreuils have produced equally expert evidence that her hand had been "held and guided." The Cointreaus retorted that she wanted Genevieve to have control of Frapin as compensation to balance Anne-Marie's controlling stake in Remy Martin, and that she had said as much in earlier wills.

In return, the Cointreaus have enjoyed some success with their claim that, in relation to Remy Martin, they have been denied the considerable rights to which minority shareholders are entitled under French law because of the alleged refusal of the Heriard-Dubreuils to provide adequate information about the company: at one stage, Genevieve was forced to go to the Remy Martin offices accompanied by a court official to try to see relevant documents. The courts have also agreed with the Cointreaus that the sudden withdrawal of Remy Martin orders materially damaged Frapin's business. (The firm cases, now involve not only the two couples but also their children. Remy Martin now is run by Marc and Francois Heriard-Dubreuil although their father is still a dominant figure.)

Outside the courts, the Cointreaus have succeeded in blocking any increase in Remy Martin's now-inadequate share capital. This amounts to a mere FFr 35m, totally inadequate for a firm with a total turnover of FFR 1.7bn in 1983 – bigger even than Cointreau.The Cointreaus have professed themselves willing to agree to an increase in the equity capital, but only on conditions the Heriard-Dubreuils could never be expected to approve – including an involvement in management, renewed purchases from Frapin, a halt to legal proceedings and a restructuring to ensure that the Cointreaus did not have to pay wealth tax on their shares in the firm. The Heriard-Dubreuils have reacted by getting Remy Martin itself to claim that the Cointreaus, in refusing to agree to an increase in the firm's capital, are abusing the rights of the majority – a doc-

trine, unlike minority rights, not enshrined in French legislation.

Remy Martin has been hit less badly than its rivals by the slump in sales in the home market, because 95 per cent of its sales were exports: but, even so, it has been forced to increase its stocks. Increased financial charges have reduced profits. Yet the problems have not prevented major and expensive changes in Remy Martin's strategy. Even before open war broke out it had introduced a cheaper VS brand, competing for the first time with the standard brands that account for 60 per cent of the sale of other firms.The move was triggered by the requirements of the British market, which has increasingly turned to the even cheaper grape brandies in recent years, but Remy's VS is now also sold in the United States. Nevertheless, it accounts for a mere 15 per cent of the firm's sales and it has been counterbalanced by increased sales of the firm's range of luxury cognacs.

Remy has also almost completed divorce proceedings in its various distribution relationships with Cointreau (the only remaining joint arrangement is in Switzerland).

Even more expensive has been the firm's deliberate move away from cognac, for Heriard-Dubreuil believes this is a mature business that ought to liberate sufficient cash flow to encourage diversification through investment in other firms selling up-market alcoholic drinks. In the past decade, he has turned his theory into practice. Until 1974, Remy Martin was wholly dependant on cognac: that year, it bought control of Krug, which occupies the uncontested pole position in the champagne quality stakes. In the 1970s, too, it set up joint ventures to make wine in Australia and brandy in California and, more recently, another one in China producing Dynasty wine. In the past couple of years his firm has bought control of the venerable Bordeaux wine merchants, De Luze. Earlier this year Remy Martin acquired Vins Nicolas, the loss-making chain of Parisian wine shops that still holds the finest stock of old French wines in the world. (In Heriard-Dubreuil's view, this stock more than counterbalanced the firm's trading losses.)

Outsiders have worried at the financial burden imposed by these sweeping changes, since financial charges amounted at one time to 18 per cent of the firm's sales. But Heriard-Dubreuil is unworried. Logically, he feels, such costs are part of the industrial

expenses involved in making cognac, a product which depends on ageing as part of its production costs just as much as the "*part des Anges*" – the annual 4 per cent loss through evaporation.

In the French tradition, the family war has been kept out of the public eye. Outside the courts, the only open sign of the battle has been political. In the 1981 elections Cointreau was opposed by Gerald Montassier (at the time, son-in-law of Valery Giscard'Estaing), who was – like Roger Plassard in 1973 – strongly supported by the Heriard-Dubreuils. Montassier lost, partly because of local resentment against an outsider, partly because of the general anti-Giscardian mood. For the 1985 elections, Cointreau went on the offensive. A month beforehand, he published a book, *La Crise de Cognac*. In it he proposes solutions – in themselves perfectly sensible – to the problems faced by cognac and also subtly contrives to suggest that he, not Heriard-Dubreuil, was the true spiritual heir of their joint father-in-law. Nevertheless, this time Cointreau lost, a victim of the general swing against the Left.

The Cointreaus, however, are far from popular. Their challenge to the objectivity of the local commercial court – which resulted in primary jurisdiction for proceedings being moved from Cognac to Bordeaux – was taken very badly by local merchants. The court, a well-respected local body, naturally includes many of their executives, all of whom scrupulously ruled themselves ineligible in any of the cases. Nevertheless, claimed the Cointreaus' lawyer, they were both judges and parties to the argument. Heriard-Dubreuil, meanwhile, professes to be totally unconcerned by the legal battles. "They're not what keeps us awake at nights," he says. "If only they [the Cointreau family] would leave us in control of Remy Martin, we would leave them in charge of Frapin."

His statement marks the end of only one episode of the series which is fascinating the Charente – for the Cointreaus may have an ace up their sleeve. The Remy Martin share register for the years between 1957 and 1961 – which could contain details of relevant transfers – has been mislaid and the Cointreaus are taking advantage of this piece of carelessness to cast doubt on the ownership and control of the money.

Compared with these heavyweight French contenders, the Ewings of Dallas are just amateurs in the family feud business.

Index